LEARNING SOCIAL LITERACY

LEARNING SOCIAL LITERACY

Joyce E. Bellous

Jean M. Clinton

TALL PINE PRESS
Edmonton, Alberta

Tall Pine Press
2655 Sir Arthur Currie Way, Edmonton, AB T5E 6S8, Canada
Web: www.tallpinepress.com E-mail: tallpinepress@gmail.com

Cover photo: Staff & volunteers at iHuman, Edmonton, Canada.
Photo by Dustin Delfs, Laughing Dog Photography.
Book design: Jeff Sylvester, Cut & Paste Design.

Library and Archives Canada Cataloguing in Publication

Bellous, Joyce Edith, 1948-, author
Learning social literacy / Joyce E. Bellous, Jean M. Clinton.

Includes index.
ISBN 978-0-9810149-3-7 (paperback)

1. Social learning. I. Clinton, Jean M., 1954-, author II. Title.

HQ783.B39 2016 303.3'2 C2015-907011-2

CONTENTS

PREFACE

Jean and Joyce first met at a presentation on the nature of human spirituality that Joyce gave at a conference in Hamilton. It was one of those special moments when you realize you've met a soul mate, someone whose view of the world and of the nature of connection are as your own, yet these views were formed from completely different life experiences.

At that time, we agreed to an idea that's basic to *Learning Social Literacy*, which is that human spirituality, *as a sense of felt connection*, was our preferred way of describing the spiritual aspect of human life.

Our connection continued during our collaboration to bring a social and emotional skills development program to a Child Care Centre in Hamilton that has strong ties with childhood research at McMaster University. In 2007, that program, *Working With Others*, was adopted in Hamilton in cooperation with Dr Cathy Ota from Brighton University, UK, who is its originator. Joyce spent time at Brighton University becoming familiar with the program and it continues to be implemented in Hamilton.

A further opportunity to collaborate came as Joyce taught a program she developed called *Building For Resilience* (BFR) to a group of staff and volunteers at iHuman, which is a not-for-profit agency in Edmonton that works with youth-at-risk. iHuman is an arts-based drop-in centre in the heart of the city that engages with hundreds of youth who would otherwise have few places to feel at home in the urban streets of this city.

Jean continued to provide insight into human interaction that informed *Building For Resilience*. In the winter of 2014, BFR ran one day per week for 4 months as a training program with staff and volunteers. BFR focuses on seven competencies that enhance personal resilience and group collaboration. These competencies include: Connection, Courage, Mindfulness, Empathy, Life Satisfaction, Emotional Literacy and Social Literacy.

The experience of teaching, and learning with the compassionate, skilled people at iHuman was a career highlight for Joyce and it only seemed appropriate to have the team pictured on the cover of the book as a way to say thank you to them and honor their efforts to help young people find a healthier way forward toward a more satisfying life.

Building For Resilience is a hands-on, skill-based program. *Learning Social Literacy* offers theoretical underpinnings for the *Building For Resilience* program. We hope you find it helpful to reflect on these pages so that you may see new ways to understand yourself and other people in your efforts to make the world a better place, which we think brings people significant life satisfaction.

1

INTRODUCING SOCIAL LITERACY

INTRODUCTION

An adolescent was accused of murdering his girlfriend. As he sat in court, and a sentence was passed to convict him of guilt, he noticed the girl's mother in the courtroom. She was crying. He turned to his lawyer and said, "Why's she crying? I'm the one who's goin' to jail."

One morning on the *Go Train* from Hamilton to Toronto, Jean overhead a conversation between two men she often saw on the train. They both worked in foreign currency. As their conversation proceeded, she joined in. She had just heard about an event in which Georgians took over a school in Chechnya. They kidnapped (and eventually killed) all the kids. She asked the men whether they'd heard about the kidnapping. One responded by saying: "Oh well, it hasn't changed the Market." She replied, "There were how many kids taken hostage and you're asking about the effects on the Market." The other man was a member of the Knights of Columbus, a Catholic who's involved in his community. He, too, wondered if the kidnapping had negatively affected the Market.

On a major street in Montreal, on a wintry Friday night, two adolescent girls (dressed in t-shirts and jeans) moved swiftly down the street, dodging passersby. One girl grasped the other firmly by the wrist, holding her hand high in the air. The captive had the demeanour of a deer caught in the headlights. The girl who made them both move quickly, was shouting out: "She'll have sex with you for a dollar." She kept repeating the phrase, modifying it at times to yell: "She'll suck your cock for a dollar." She continued to holler as they moved quickly past shop windows. A man tried to avoid them and shifted out of the way, saying, "What's going on?" But at no point did anyone interfere with or stop them.

In a Bolivian hotel, Joyce was descending the stairs in a dark hallway when she stopped for a moment because she couldn't locate the next flight of stairs. Just then, a small Bolivian boy, about five years old, looked at her and pointed to the next stairway, which was to the left of where she was standing and not easily seen on the dimly lit stairs. This small boy read her body language, noted her confusion, and without either of them saying anything, knew what she needed and took action to point the way down.

The first three scenarios describe people who convey no sense of felt connection to one another. The last one depicts a (fleeting but real) felt sense of connection between two strangers. While you might think Joyce stumbled upon the only socially sensitive five-year old in Bolivia, that wasn't the case. She saw many Bolivians put people ahead of other concerns. For example, meetings, announced to start in the morning, often began in the afternoon. Why? People came before schedules. Meetings wouldn't begin until everyone was present. Because dependable transportation wasn't available for many who wanted to come, everyone else waited.

Why was the Bolivian so civil? What skills did he use to connect with a stranger? In contrast, the young man could make no sense of his victim's mother. The interaction on the train intimates a culture in which money trumps all other considerations, including the lives of school children in Chechnya. In the Montreal scenario, the connection between the girls was used to transmit radical harm—a possibility that built up slowly—due to injurious, repeated, small offences against her because she came to believe that she was without any healthy relational support in those contexts, perhaps at school.

The first three scenarios convey an absence of civility in a sense developed in the rest of the chapter. Civility is grounded on concern for others, often expressed by what's referred to as the Golden Rule: treat others as you want to be treated yourself. In the first three scenarios the most fundamental requirements of concern for others is missing. Its absence creates relational poverty, producing an atrophied sense of felt connection to others. This poverty is at the root of much school failure, yet it's one that school environments could alleviate. The Bolivian boy, in contrast, conveys the impact of living in a relationally rich social environment.

This chapter introduces social literacy by linking its motivation, civility, to a sense of felt connection[1] that keeps social connection vital and alive. Civility dissuades us from using that connection to intentionally harm other people. Our capacity to believe in ourselves is conveyed through that felt sense. It's a communicative conduit for human decency and civility each of us owes to every other due to the universal human need to feel viably connected to other people. That felt sense of connection secures the right of every person to enjoy benefits and accept burdens of being a citizen.

Social literacy relies on a sense of felt connection, on civility, social capital and social happiness as confidence builders that allow people to enjoy social security in a relational sense. In contrast to relational security, this chapter provides French sociologist Pierre Bourdieu's (1930-2001) description of a logic of insecurity that arises under current economic conditions, and American educator Vivien Gussin Paley's depiction of a culture of insecurity that shows up as she tried to teach school children to be inclusive of others. In contrast to security and civility, patterns that Bourdieu and Paley uncover privilege some people at other people's expense. They frustrate the development of social literacy and weaken its link to civility. Practices of insecurity diminish a felt sense of connection to others, produce alienation and may even result in self-abuse and suicide. A culture of insecurity forecloses on the possibility of creating environments that focus on what we refer to as relational habitat maintenance—the will to be inclusive—which is a sustaining intentionality that's organized around the rights and duties of civility.

Paley's experiment, as summarized in this chapter, shows that social literacy is a primary means by which we maintain a healthy relational habitat. Her case study uncovers an educational process best described as a movement from rules, to maxims, to life principles, although she doesn't use all these terms herself. This chapter also follows that movement. She demonstrated a human need to rely on rules and learn from maxims in order that children could become civil.

To establish inclusion as a life principle, the chapter includes a thought experiment using legal conceptions to undergird the ideal of inclusion as a universal right and duty of school children. After that analysis, a section describing Action Science allows teachers to be self-aware enough to become socially literate by helping them perceive their own behavior toward others. The chapter ends with a summary of the rest of the book as a way to support the point that social literacy is a means by which we make the world more bearable by enhancing social opportunities for those who are disadvantaged during social interaction—so they can come to enjoy a more robust sense of life satisfaction.

WHAT'S GOING ON?

As a species, human beings are wired to connect. As a necessary part of the reflective process implied in becoming socially literate, we gain an awareness of what's going on during social interaction as people connect with one another—in gaze behavior between an infant and his mother, in romantic glances between two strangers in a crowded room, in embodied messages between friends at school. It's our capacity to connect and use that connection to communicate intentions, desires, longing and expectations that's at the heart of our ability to be in human relationships. All told, people become socially literate by being with others who have already mastered the complex skills of social literacy.

Social literacy is composed of complex skills that are grounded on an ability to think on our feet. It relies on developing insight into what's going on during social interaction. We've all had the experience of walking away from an encounter and regretting a lost opportunity to improve that connection. Social literacy refers to an ability and willingness to participant in and/or repair an encounter while we're still engaged in it. It's characterized by giving full attention to another person and relies on civility for its motivation.

Working to improve a situation implies that those involved receive and offer respect to one another and aim to understand each other more fully through the encounter. Understanding doesn't necessarily imply agreement, but relies on mutual respect. Evidence of respect is expressed in the willingness and ability to state the other person's view or experience in a way that the other can acknowledge is accurate and fair.

In contrast, the Montreal scenario is an instance of bullying, an extreme form of social interaction that's devoid of respect. It's a kind of social illiteracy. Respect isn't only absent; something else is going on. Bullying gives evidence that social behaviour is out of control. Its prevalence—a fundamental breach of civility—is a social fact we can't ignore. It's pointless to ask whether schools have always housed bullies. Bullying is a social problem that's currently taking the lives of children and youth. Learning social literacy teaches people how to treat others with respect so that bullying is less likely.

Bullies use their sense of felt connection as a way to hurt others. While this book isn't about bullying *per se*, it's a troubling aspect of social life that reveals an absence of social literacy in the sense described throughout these pages. Bullying has significant impact on the possibility of learning social literacy. As an extreme form of rejection, it's devoid of empathy and humanity. It violates taken-for-granted social rules and rests its violence on social patterns people misuse to create radical harm. Bullying limits the social experience of those who are bullied and seduces bullies into self-defeating patterns. Because of their actions, bullies are held (hold themselves?) outside social relationships that have the power to provide them with respect, mutual affection and intimacy.

From Joyce's perspective as a transformational educator, four characteristics of bullying are relevant to social literacy:

- People who bully must be socially significant to the bullied person and generally valued
- They must appear able to put the victim under continual surveillance
- Bullied people internalize the harm and inflict (often) catastrophic harm on themselves
- As a consequence, those who bully may appear innocent of any overt wrongdoing

Bullying creates a culture of insecurity that draws resources away from learning social literacy. Margaret Atwood's book, *Cat's Eye*, is an excellent literary example of internalized aspects of bullying. In a context of bullying, those afflicted feel a deep and deepening sense of insecurity that annihilates their felt connection to others and makes it difficult or impossible for them to believe in the worth of their own lives.

These internalized aspects are troubling. A bullied person often carries out the abuse on himself or herself so that it's hard to track its source. Its traces are internalized so that others may even engage in victim blaming. Bullies may escape in a crowd of attention offered to victims, while their own inner wounds, accumulated through harming others, go unnoticed.

But if people acquire the skills of social literacy, they gain a vital felt sense of connection to others and realize they're not alone. The impact of bullying isn't totalizing. With the skills of social literacy, there's freedom to escape to safety and be oneself. Socially literate people learn to hear self-harm and self-hatred as inner voices that can be quieted and calmed by reason and by effectively conversing with people who care about them. As an outcome, bullies are welcomed back into community. But walls built by insecurity are thick—it's a fortress that isn't easily scaled by those who care about people who are endangered or by those who long to limit people that instigate the harm.

From Jean's perspective as a child psychiatrist and specialist in the early years, bullying is a relational issue that's invested with power and control. Some young people that bully others have relational struggles at home. Adults may be unaware that their parenting style contributes to bullying. It's common to think of children who bully as having an abusive home life, but the incidence of bullying is so high it can't be limited to kids who are abused by parents or siblings. What's evident is that the style of connecting among family members doesn't lead to empathetic responsiveness. As a result, the stress system children are caught in isn't buffered by a healthy sense of felt connection to family members.

It may be that these families spend too little time maintaining their relational habitat and may build a culture of insecurity at home, which makes them unavailable as a site of restoration and healing for those who return home from a culture of insecurity at school. As a result, an opportunity to learn social literacy, and its complex trust-building, communication and problem-solving skills, needs to be extended to families as well as school children if we're serious about living up to the ideals implied in civility and the human rights people have worked so hard to acquire over the last few centuries. Those rights depend on learning to be civil. They flourish in a civil culture. They flounder if social interaction is built on exclusion. Incivility manufactures insecurity. Given a human tendency to enjoy exercising power over others, as Paley's case study will show all too clearly, what will persuade us to be civil?

Who Wants To Be Civil?

Social literacy is a means for becoming a civil society—a just and fair culture in which everyone has opportunities to flourish because material and relational needs are adequately met. The four scenarios at the beginning describe the presence and absence of civility. The Bolivian boy is civil. His concern for a stranger implies a culture that enjoys social trust, skill and interdependence. The other three scenarios depict a remarkable absence of concern for others.

As mentioned, social literacy rests on an essential assumption that people will be civil; that they will work through a social encounter, while they're in it, in a manner that shows self-respect and respect for others. As Dan Goleman pointed out, social intelligence, the ordinary capacity we all have for being in relationship with one another, rests on caring about other people's needs in additional to our own. He notes that empathy by itself matters little if we fail to act on that concern.[2] He observed that social intelligence could be misused to produce behavior best described as manipulative if people feel no concern for others.[3] Social literacy develops through the use of social intelligence and relies on civility to be effective. What is civility? How does it fit our current circumstances in Western cultures? What impact does an environment of incivility have on people's ability and willingness to be civil?

The term civility has a number of roots, for example in Roman civil law where it implied certain duties citizens were required to fulfill, but its impact on modernity also has a source in the French Revolution (1789). As a consequence of overthrowing the monarchy, leaders of the rebellion required citizens to enact their newfound rights by swearing allegiance to the French state. That allegiance has the potential to motivate civility—an expression of citizenship that differs from military, religious or political allegiances and is distinct from our natural condition at birth and during childhood. Civility relies on duties that aren't military, religious or political and requires an education. Children must learn to be civil if a society is to flourish.

Civility implies that every person has duties and rights. What are the ordinary duties of a citizen? The first thing to note is that civil duties impact individuals and society as a whole. Let's take the mundane duty to care adequately for our own property. If I don't look after the weeds in my yard, my neighbor will have more trouble controlling weeds in her yard. If I let weeds grow, the city can warn and fine me, but by this time my neighbor has suffered considerable frustration, has had to do more work in her yard, has had to tell someone at City Hall and may have incurred costs specifically due to my weeds. Neighborliness is jeopardized.

Civil duties are often clear to us when we think someone else is at fault. They may be less obvious when it's our own behavior that causes harm. An offense is clear if my neighbor lets her weeds grow, but I may make excuses for the lively weeds in my yard. The implication is that there's a lot of wiggle room with civil duties. Civility is primarily about what I do when no one can prevent me or punish me for failing to act for the common good. That is, civility is a telltale sign of mature human character.

Ordinary civil duties might include observing traffic lights, paying my fare on public transport, driving with care, shoveling my walk in winter, sharing the sidewalk as people pass me by, moving out of a shop doorway while I'm texting someone so that people behind me can exit the store, greeting people on the street, managing my garbage, keeping glass off the beach, dressing appropriately in public, speaking politely to salespeople, waiting patiently in lineups, paying my debts promptly, smiling easily, consistently saying excuse me, please, thank you and you're welcome, calling 911 if someone is injured on the street and staying with them until help arrives and chewing my food politely in a restaurant.

The primary reason these behaviors are civil is that they convey a fundamental respect and concern for others based on a felt sense of connection to them. Civility is about what's good for 'us'; it's about paying attention to the common good, which in turn constrains how we think of and act toward others. If these are examples of civil duties, what rights are implied?

Civil rights are best understood as beliefs and actions that recognize and affirm the humanity of others and that educate and enhance one's own humanity. As a negative example, Shakespeare's play, *Othello*, illustrates a pattern of incivility that leads to abuse and murder in the words the character Iago uses to describe the people he eventually destroys. Like him, in order to rob others of their humanity, we first begin by talking about them as if they aren't quite human. The call to recognize the humanity of ordinary people was at the core of the French Revolution (1789), the Universal Declaration of Human Rights (UDHR, 1948) and extensions of rights during the last two hundred years. As British social theorist Edward Miliband observed,

> the eighteenth century saw individuals granted civil rights (equality before the law), the nineteenth and early twentieth century brought political rights (equality of the franchise), and the early twentieth century onwards, [encouraged] social rights

(based on principles of equal access to education, health care, housing, etc.).[4]

Miliband isn't naive in describing human progress. He refers to developments in human rights as a rough and ready assessment of this period of history. Previously to this development, duties were linked to privileges that went along with aristocratic wealth and class (e.g., *noblesse oblige*). Slowly, rights were associated with humanity itself. We have rights simply because we're human beings. Equality isn't yet secured in the West. The prevalence of sexism and sexual slavery are examples that more work needs to be done, but Miliband's analysis lays a foundation for two more aspects of human rights that influence whether or not we value social literacy.

In addition to advancements Miliband outlined and during their development, Marx recognized the need for humanity's material support. He saw that "the senses of human being can operate at a merely animal level—if they are not cultivated by appropriate education, by leisure for play and self-expression, [and] by valuable associations with others;" American philosopher Martha Nussbaum added freedom of worship to his list.[5] Marx supported Immanuel Kant[6] in situating humanity at the core of mutual responsibility but distinguished himself by "stressing (with Aristotle) that the major powers of a human being need material support and cannot be what they are without it."[7] Marx wrote the Communist Manifesto in 1848, when ⅚ths of the world's population lived in abject poverty.

Based on interactions with social theorist Amartya Sen (whose work with the United Nations has significant impact on promoting human rights) and by collaborating with women in Africa and India, Nussbaum designed a human needs theory that has further implications for social literacy. If Marx argued persuasively about the human need for material resources, her work implies a fundamental need for relational resources so that all people may live a truly human life. Her philosophical analysis is persuasive and clear, and is an antidote, for example, to instances of bullying.[8] In civil rights, relational resources play a pivotal role. It's more essential to get adequate attention than it is to have lots of money. Relational resources are felt primarily in adequate, appropriate attention that people freely get from their social world.

Just as we can see who has money and power, we value those with an ability to get and keep attention, which is a marker of wealth in human worth.[9] Inequality in public spaces isn't simply because some people have plenty in the relational equation, but rather, to get and keep their abundance, they feel justified in siphoning off attention from other people.[10] When that happens, essential human needs go unmet.

In addition to Nussbaum's assertion about religious freedom, every human being has a spiritual need to celebrate, mark significant moments, bear witness to truths learned about life, play, tell their story, grieve, mourn, lament, connect with the past, make significant journeys, express themselves symbolically, seek purpose and meaning, ask ultimate questions, have a satisfactory way to think and speak about the beginning and end of life, survive, flourish, experience longing and enjoy its satisfaction, relax, cope with life circumstances, be seen, be heard, have a name that's remembered, be part of a larger community, organize experience meaningfully so as to make sense of it, maintain human dignity and see the future as hopeful. Recognizing and meeting relational needs is a way to distribute appropriate attention fairly.

A fair distribution of attention builds social capital, a product of civility. With its increase, it becomes more and more effective as a vehicle for distributing relational resources. Social capital refers to the degree to which members of a community trust each other and engage in reciprocal relations based on trust. Physical capital refers to objects, i.e., tools that enhance individual productivity. Human capital refers to individual training and education that enhances productivity. Financial capital refers to the wherewithal for mass marketing. And social capital is familiarity, tolerance, solidarity, habits of cooperation and mutual respect.

It's a generalized willingness of individuals who trust others in face-to-face encounters that encourages reciprocity, which in turn draws people into common endeavours. Social trust is an embodied belief: 'I'll do this for you without payment in return because I know someone will do this for me if needed in the future'. Trust builds up slowly and erodes quickly; it must be caught from others rather than imposed from above. Bullies may make people fear and obey them. They can't *make* people trust them.

The degree of social trust among people is a good predictor of life satisfaction because the character of one's community is almost as important as personal circumstances in producing happiness.[11] Trust nurtures collective action and explains efficient government and competitive economies in terms of social bonds of association and interdependence. Effective institutional performance is a function of trust; it's an expectation that arises within a community that enjoys regular, honest and cooperative behaviour, based on commonly shared norms that are maintained by most members of the community. Trust is more essential to a society's success than are other forms of capital mentioned earlier because, during times of distress, trust is like glue that holds people together until disaster passes. Trust creates communities that empower citizens to engage in collective deliberation about public choices; its these choices that translate most fully into effective public policies.

Trust arises from and produces a felt sense of connection, is exercised in social networks and distributed through norms of reciprocity and cooperation. Trustworthiness grows through these connections. French sociologist Pierre Bourdieu saw that a network of connections isn't a natural given, or even a social given; it's the product of endless effort, investment strategies, individual or collective, consciously or unconsciously aimed at maintaining social relationships and transforming ordinary relationships (neighbors, colleagues, relatives) into bonds that imply durable obligations, subjectively *felt* in gratitude, respect, friendliness or friendship. In short, "the reproduction of social capital presupposes an unceasing effort of sociability, a continuous series of exchanges in which recognition is endlessly affirmed and reaffirmed."[12] An embodied form of social capital is knowledge that knows how to arrange for its increase. Historically, women were most active in establishing and perpetuating trust[13] and the collective and individual obligations that trust implies among neighbors, friends and family.

Social capital has roots in neighborliness.[14] At a time when force and family were the only solutions to dilemmas of collective action elsewhere in Europe, citizens of Italian city-states devised a way of organizing collective life. It was a richly religious time, expressed in pious works and devotional exercises that lay people (not only priests) carried out. Ordinary people connected soul care with social care so that religion upheld some of the spiritual needs outlined earlier. It was a time of unparalleled civic commitment.[15] Rich networks of associational life created civil community. That pattern of civility persists in many places, since a "successful neighborhood is a place that keeps sufficiently abreast of its problems so it is not destroyed by them."[16] But the effort to build social capital must continue from one generation to the next. As an example, while the U.S. enjoyed a high point of social trust at the beginning of it, by the end of the twentieth century its economy was healthy but its social fabric was weak.[17]

When trust flourishes, self-interest is alive to the interests of others. While civility isn't selfless, it regards the public domain as more than a battleground for the pursuit of private family interests. Social capital opposes itself to individual family systems that maximize their private, material, short-run advantages and assumes that all others will do likewise: a pattern that throws those who can't provide for themselves on the goodwill of the public purse. To be confident in collective action that could threaten immediate self-interest, neighbors assume that others will work for the common good as well. Collective life is eased by the expectation that others will likely follow the rules. Knowing that others will, neighbors are more likely to fulfill that expectation. They listen to one another and act on what they hear. In civic regions, light-touch government is effortlessly stronger because it can count on willing cooperation and self-enforcement among its citizenry, and *citizens are happier.*[18]

Bourdieu recommended an economics of happiness to motivate civility. He affirmed the value of social happiness. He observed the profits garnered from individual and collective sociability and material and symbolic expressions of support that build security and he contrasted these patterns with material and symbolic costs associated with insecurity. Security v. insecurity is his measure of an economics of happiness. Insecurity produces violent social interaction that conforms to a certain logic—a way of thinking about ourselves and others that perpetuates the ease with which we either care nothing for, or actively harm others. His analysis focused on employment, and its lack, but it's a heuristic for considering social interaction in general.

To Bourdieu, all violence is paid for: structural violence exerted by financial markets in layoffs or loss of security, is matched sooner or later in suicides, crime and delinquency, drug addiction, alcoholism, as well as a whole host of minor and major daily acts of violence.[19] He analyzed the logic of insecurity to say that,

> In the suffering of those excluded from work, in the wretchedness of the long-term unemployed, there is something more than there was in the past. The Anglo-American ideology, always somewhat sanctimonious, distinguished the 'undeserving poor', who had brought it upon themselves, from the 'deserving poor', who were judged worthy of charity. Alongside or in place of this ethical justification there is now an intellectual justification. The poor are not just immoral, they are stupid, they lack intelligence. A large part of social suffering stems from the poverty of people's relationship to the educational system, which not only shapes social destinies but also the image they have of their destiny (which undoubtedly helps to explain what is called the passivity of the dominated [and] the difficulty in mobilizing them).[20]

An ethos of insecurity is a systemic attack on human courage for those who suffer from it.

A culture of insecurity withholds from some people the "social entitlements which are...among the highest achievements of civilization...that ought to be universalized, extended to the whole planet, globalized."[21] Social entitlements include the right to work and a health and welfare system. People have suffered and fought for these rights. As important and precious achievements, they don't only survive in museums, libraries and academies, but are living and active in people's lives and govern their everyday existence;[22] they are relational resources that Nussbaum argued for as the essential means for living a fully human life. They're implicit in social capital. They're absent in a culture of insecurity.

A culture of insecurity generates anxiety, is demoralizing and promotes conformity. If people feel a profound insecurity about themselves and the future, they form a disenchanted image of themselves and their group.[23] Their loss limits hope, social trust and a felt sense of connection to others. They're unhappy. Bourdieu suspected that insecurity isn't the product of an economic inevitability, identified with globalization, but of a political will. He applied his analysis to economic structures, but the politics of insecurity, aimed at forcing people into submission and the acceptance of exploitation, is a mode of domination he believed was unprecedented, which he referred to as *flexploitation*.[24]

Resisting insecurity requires people to collaborate (charitably or militantly) against its destructive effects.[25] He wondered if those who suffer insecurity would waken to cooperate and end its power over them. While he remained hopeful, he identified individuals who perceived themselves as 'solitary and free' as part of the problem. To think of oneself as above community harms social cooperation and threatens people's happiness. We're all held by an obligation to consider the happiness of others. For all our individuality, we aren't free to do as we please.

Civility takes account of the human need to connect with others and acknowledges a right to relational resources. It's a hopeful way of thinking about social interaction. Neighbourliness is another way to speak about civility; it's created and sustained through conversations among people who understand reality differently but know their well-being depends on acknowledging significance differences that matter to others.

The following case study explores the dynamics of civility by revealing how five year olds employ social power as they establish their positions in kindergarten. Unfortunately, at the beginning of the year, they're entirely capable of creating a culture of insecurity. They don't start out as good neighbors. They support the suspicion that social insecurity is an outcome of the will to hold power over others, and, as the experiment shows, is expressed through an urge to exclude some people from play until their felt sense of connection to others is threatened with extinction.

SCHOOL AND SOCIAL LITERACY—A CASE STUDY

Civility is learned by teaching people to be fair. It slowly develops alongside healthy, respectful human character in an environment that provides rules, maxims, principles and social affirmation for respecting other people. Respect relieves insecurity. Civility counters the ease some have in treating others unfairly. In a classic study, Paley described struggles in her kindergarten group as she tried to teach students to be inclusive, as a sign of their respect for everyone in the class. Her analysis, like Bourdieu's, reveals the impact of insecurity and lays groundwork for understanding what's required to build social literacy on practices of fairness or social equity. This section examines aspects of the complex task of teaching children what's implied by inclusion, based on their equal right to education.

A central motivation for Paley's research was a vision in which it's less easy for "some children to limit the social experiences of other children."[26] She began one school year with the personal belief that children don't have a right to exclude others from play, since they all enjoy the same right to be in class. It is, after all, a public setting. In response to her concern for equity, she tried to help her class put into practice the rule "you can't say you can't play;" and, because she wanted them to learn it for themselves and so wouldn't coerce the children in any way, she recorded their tensions and challenges as they openly discussed its application.

Rules such as hers are foundational to social literacy. Applying them is hard. Paley became aware of risks to her own position as she introduced the expression, made it a rule and a maxim (although she doesn't use that term). Practices of exclusion are learned early. During the process she realized the importance of working with very young children if she hoped to instill a life principle of inclusion. When she discussed it with them, older children insisted the rule would work only if it was introduced in kindergarten, because, they thought, children still trust their teachers. Children in upper grades that she interviewed believed kids get meaner as they grow older.[27] Her effort suggests that, while it may be hard, it's possible to influence people later in life to become socially literate. Her experience is a good starting point for naming obstacles to adult learning as well.

While equal participation is a cornerstone most teachers may say they try to build upon,[28] Paley tracked the resistance to including others in play in her kindergarten group and discussed the concept with children in grades one to six (before making it a rule) to collect their views on the idea of becoming more inclusive. Several issues raised by her research offer insight into learning social literacy. I organized these insights around the expression *boss culture* (not her term) that emerged as an identifiable pattern as she encouraged learners to be more inclusive. Even in the milieu of five year olds, ideas and practices that allow one person to boss others are engrained. A boss is someone who tells other children whether and when they can play and uses social power to exclude those who don't have the boss's approval.

Boss culture is not created in classrooms. Children come to kindergarten knowing how to exclude others—even at two years old children will tell others they can't play or can't come into the room where play is happening. Paley's five year-olds were articulate as to why they excluded others. She pointed to strategies of exclusion that are honed early and continue to structure adult life at work and in social or domestic spaces. She noted that "the way we do it, exclusion is written into the game of play. And play, as [children] know it, will soon be the game of life."[29]

In the workplace, boss culture characterizes how we organize social interaction. A boss tells people where, when, how or whether they're allowed to participate. I use the word boss not bully because I don't want to cast all bossy people as bullies. In analyzing boss culture several observations show up. Bosses assign roles in a game and rely on materialistic assessments to do so: children are excluded if they have none of the right toys or right clothes. Further, "rejected children know who they are"[30] and don't forget these rejections. Later on, they speak of them with clarity, as if they had just happened,[31] a behaviour characteristic of traumatic events. [A trauma is an event that's too complex for a person to process successfully at the time it happens.] Children that are rejected are most often continually rejected throughout their school years.[32] As a result, they learn to be outsiders in every group, a status that influences their ability to learn and instills a growing sense of rage. Rejected children reject others, given the chance, even though they can tell adults how much it hurts to be left out of the game.

Exclusion is a game of power—children feel powerful when they exclude others. In her research, older children reported that they came to believe exclusion is part of life. Those who are excluded simply have to tough it out, like a lesson they need to learn so they don't get so down on themselves when it happens. But does it work to be tough while one is excluded? Isn't being tough another way to marginalize oneself? What do children learn by being tough, if they leave out others when they get a chance—though they recognize the pain it causes? Inclusion is the way we want to be treated. Exclusion is the way we treat others whenever we can.

Implicit beliefs about rights and duties in public space directed the discussions Paley had with children at all grades. Classrooms are public spaces. What rules should we observe? What relational categories should we apply there? How do these rules differ from those used in private space? Although not explicitly stated, Paley is aware school children have a right to Freedom of Association, a right also well established in the Universal Declaration of Human Rights (1948). In her educational approach, she didn't extinguish that right; children weren't coerced into being inclusive. Coercion would violate her educational principle and does violence to the practice of going from rules to maxims. Rather, she addressed their undisciplined, uncivil and unreflective freedom to exclude other children from social interaction that those who were excluded needed to access in order to get an education.

At first, some children discussing the rule 'you can't say you can't play' were doubled-minded: they thought it was fair but wouldn't work. Boss culture influenced their dilemma. Older children saw the rule as desirable but inconsistent with what they already expected from human behaviour. Paley asked them, "Is it fair for children *in school* to keep another child out of play?"[33] Their answers conveyed ambiguity. Friendship is important. Time at school cuts through boundaries around work and play; "free acceptance in play, partnerships, and teams is what matters most" to children.[34] Invitations home or to parties are highly significant. In order to learn social literacy, people must make distinctions among ideas such as bossiness, bullying, leadership, free association and conditions under which a child has access to education.

Confusion about rules in public space creates a double bind that has to do with feeling powerful or powerless. Boss culture is complex. Exclusion is the heart of its complexity. Paley's children were able to perceive its complexity in their own and other people's actions. On one hand, some wanted a boss because only that person kept others out. They reasoned that if only one person did the rejecting, children who were excluded could believe that others in the group wanted them to play, but the boss wouldn't let them.[35] They also reasoned that, without bosses, everyone might play. Children no one liked would be included. Desirable people might drop out of the play, either because there were too many, they no longer had control, or they simply wouldn't play with certain children. Some were concerned about those who became too bossy, but for children who take on a boss role, the point of play is to express the freedom to keep some people out. The power to control play—primarily to exclude—is its most important aspect.

In terms of the rule confusion Paley's children expressed, is social power bad and to be rejected as a pattern for one's life? Paley isn't making that claim. Using power is unavoidable. To unravel the relationship between habits of exclusion and appropriate uses of power, Paley discussed a dominant child in her class that she called Lisa.

Lisa learned to make accommodations as she applied the rule to her own action but was able to remain in charge. Other children welcomed her leadership as long as she didn't keep them outside the game.[36] Paley saw that every time children analyzed the logic of the rule, they analyzed the logic of their behavior,[37] and came to perceive their own learning. While the rule took a lot of getting used to, and at the start children continued to say no to inclusion, several fifth graders thought they "could get it into their brain to say yes"[38] to including all children in games and activities at school that constitute access to an education.

While she didn't use the term, by gathering the insights of fifth grade children, Paley introduced the role maxims have in cultural learning. She concluded that children need rules to learn how to treat one another. The rule she established became a maxim to direct their learning and helped them change behavior through analyzing and discussing its impact and implications. If we examine Paley's class, we observe how civility operates as the Golden Rule: treat others as you want them to treat you. Paley recounted a consistent pattern: they treated others as they had been, or feared they might be treated, not as they wanted to be treated themselves. They followed a rule—*I will hurt (e.g., exclude) you like I was (or might be) hurt (excluded),* a pattern endemic to bossiness itself. Paley wanted to replace that tendency with the Golden Rule pattern.

A child's character develops through rule following, as Paley's example implies, but her rule is not like rules that stop us from hitting other people or running in the hallway. Following a rule is about discipline: it's about learning to stop undesirable action. Applying maxims is about learning to think: it's about observing and reflecting on action, involves conversation and reflection, so that it allows a child to ask whether she or he wants to continue acting in the way they've been acting. Rules make us stop. Maxims invite us to stop, think and make a shift. While maxims look like rules, applying them isn't about obedience; it's about reflecting on experience and on the reality of other people, and allowing their reality to influence our own.

Maxims help develop character through a process of learning from the real world about what happens when we act in certain ways. Paley saw her rule/maxim as essential. She believed it must be presented when children still trust adults,[39] and as they're introduced to a new setting, i.e., public space, which is unlike home or neighborhood. In a new setting, children know they need to learn the rules. To fail to give them rules allows children to pursue patterns they already possess which weren't constructed to provide justice in public spaces. Paley struggled with setting up the rule because it violated certain freedoms children had already practiced in private, such as Freedom of Association. These practices permitted them to exclude others. She saw them learn how to act in public by interacting with others under the guidance of her rule/maxim.

Learning social literacy implies that working with others at school is different from being with family and friends. In public spaces, others may be strangers and may even seem strange. How should we proceed? Paley's rule advocates a bias toward inclusion in advance of knowing the other and engenders mutual respect by helping children sense that strangers have relational needs, even if they don't make sense at first glance. Respect is a Western cultural virtue, so her project wins our approval. But the issue of power is subtle. Her experiment explores power as much as it does inclusion and respect.

Two children in particular struggle with power, Lisa (as above) and Curtis. Lisa gave Paley and her teaching associate most of their opportunities to engage with the rule 'you can't say you can't play'. Lisa was first to resist the rule by complaining loudly that there's no point in playing at all if she can't control who can play with her and, most importantly, who can't. During an inclusion conflict, she conveyed an all or nothing strategy by saying, "But it was my game!... It's up to me!" [Red-faced and tearful she said] "Okay, I won't play then, ever!"[40] As mentioned, slowly, through many encounters, Lisa learned a great deal by trying, failing, but persisting in her attempts to follow the rule until she could play with other children, assume leadership in a game, but not exclude others.

Curtis, a tall blond boy, had a different experience. During an inclusion conflict, one girl complained that she was always left out. Another boy involved in the game responded,

> 'It wasn't me, it was Curtis....He's the boss. He says who comes in the club.' Curtis is uncomfortable. 'I don't want to be the boss. They say I am.' 'We call him the boss,' the [first] boy explains. 'Yeah, because I make up the game. They *wait* for me to make up the game. Then I have to pick everyone or say no.'[41]

Curtis's discomfort is interesting. He expressed frustration at having the role, as if he felt no freedom in it. Yet, even if it made him uncomfortable, he believed that being boss required him to reject others.[42] Unlike Lisa, he didn't have to work hard to be boss—he was offered the role. A child's personality is crucial in their opportunities to be boss, as is their social milieu if it privileges tall, blond, creative boys who are relatively fearless.[43] Lisa wanted to be boss. Curtis didn't seem to want the role. Yet they had the same sad idea about it. To learn social literacy, they both must learn to use power equitably.

Again, I'm not implying that it's bad to use power. If we treat power as bad, we lose the opportunity to help leaders contribute to the happiness of others. Justice in public space isn't about refusing to use it: power flows through every social relation, whether we're conscious of how we use it, or not. The solution for social literacy is to remain powerful but use social power inclusively in public spaces since it's how everyone wants to be treated. It takes strength and wisdom to be inclusive. The goal is to use power so that it lends itself to effective leadership and healthy group participation. To accomplish that goal, we distinguish leaders from bosses and bullies. Adults continue the worst practices of childhood if they think leading is a license to rank others based on whim and self-interest. No organization flourishes by trading good leadership for boss culture. Bullying is inhumane.

Social literacy has a central role in helping children learn to use power equitably as a means for building public spaces into inclusive, respectful, creative, empowering cultures, and for resisting boss culture that stratifies people's place and value based on whether a boss likes them at the moment, believes they are unquestioningly loyal no matter what the boss says or does (as happens in gang culture), or due to material possessions they bring to the game. The ability and willingness to lead rather than boss or bully takes special care and attentiveness.

Leaders listen and act on what they hear. Recall that life satisfaction is based on spiritual needs, one of which is the need to be heard. If power is used to get what someone wants at other people's expense, their need to be heard is unmet. Reasonable people don't have to get their way in a discussion. They need to know that what they say is heard, considered and acknowledged.[44] Leaders are people who act appropriately for the common good. They find wise ways to convey the value of every person and the talents they bring to the task. This doesn't mean leaders allow team members to take advantage of them. In a work environment, it's possible to fire someone in a humane way that reflects that person's best interests or acknowledges their refusal to work for the common good. We can confuse being nice with being a leader. Being nice is important, but not if we turn a blind eye or deaf ear to suffering, injustice or un-collegial work habits.

Working for the common good depends on paying attention to what's actually going on and attending to rights and duties like those that motivated Paley. At school, a duty to include others is based on a universal right of access to education. In the next section, I analyze rights and duties that pertain to everyone's right to access education to show that exclusion from classroom experiences violates the human rights of children who are excluded. In contrast to contexts in which exclusion is rampant, Paley's class eventually provides a culture of security and relieves the suffering of social insecurity. Children in many schools aren't so fortunate. The purpose of the next section is to provide a framework for a principle of inclusion that motivated Paley's research.

FAIRNESS IN THE CLASSROOM

Paley's experience reveals educational implications for teaching children to be fair by including each other at school, a public space every child has a right to enjoy, use and benefit from because every child has a right to education.[45] The UDHR established that right so that elementary education is free and compulsory; although parents retain the right to choose the education they want for their children. As a result, children are required to be in school and have a right of access to education that's offered in that public space.

As they try to access education, Paley saw that some children limit the social experiences of others—a situation she came to see as unfair. She grounded her belief on a principle that wins support from the UDHR, Article 26. The historical path taken by Courts of Law and Courts of Equity also supports her principle. Courts of Equity began in England, initiated by the king. They stood alongside Courts of Law, which drew their judgments from the strict application of a rule, versus the fairness concept that was the focus for Courts of Equity.[46]

Courts of Law and Courts of Equity merged in England in 1873, so that both are included within one judicial framework. Over time, equity was applied more inclusively in the sense that a widening group of human beings were given the status of persons under the Law—a historical process that opened up Courts of Law to the demands of Equity; a growing demand for fairness applied to people who previously weren't considered persons under the Law. As an example, women in Canada weren't recognized as persons under the British North America Act (BNA Act, 1867, now the Constitution Act) until 1929.[47] The collective rights of Aboriginal peoples in Canada continue to have a complex and contestable status, with frequent disputes concerning their existence and the ability of the rights of others to compete with or even displace those of Aboriginal peoples.[48]

It's in the context of equity's growing appeal that a conceptualization of legal relations formulated by Wesley Newcomb Hohfeld can be applied to a child's right to education. Hohfeld was concerned with equity as it impacted judicial reasoning. Relying on a long history of judicial thought, he provided a set of conceptions to act as the "lowest common denominators of the law, and argued that most, if not all, legal issues are clarified and resolved by using the terms in relationship to each other."[49]

What follows is not a legal argument. It's a thought experiment using Hohfeld's legal terms. Its purpose is to inform rights and duties contained in the rule 'you can't say you can't play'. My goal in using Hohfeld's framework is to establish philosophical groundwork for a life principle of inclusion as it's exercised at school. It's a thought experiment designed to contribute to the educational process of moving from rules, maxims and principles and as the basis for demonstrating that children have a duty to include each other in social experiences at school.

Hohfeld was an American lawyer. The essays that map these fundamental conceptions were published in 1919. He was interested in the impact of equity on judicial reasoning because he believed judicial reasoning was often inadequate, confused and unfair. To him, Courts of Law seldom took a clear and systematic approach to perceiving the consequences for both sides of a conflict. Decisions often failed to account for the complex set of rights and duties entwined in each particular case. He analyzed judicial problems from the perspective of each party and represented each side analytically—first by showing opposite terms and then by showing correlative terms.

He picked out eight words, seven of which were common in the history of legal discourse and one that he invented to complete his system. He organized these terms into opposites and correlatives to adequately represent the perspective of each person in a dispute. His terms included right, no-right (a term constructed for the purpose), privilege, duty, power, disability[50], immunity and liability, which he organized into a system of equitable human interests. As he placed the terms into jural opposites and jural correlatives, the eight words show up in different pairs, as noted below.

Hohfeld's system of legal conceptions that inform legal reasoning

Jural opposites: right v. no-right, privilege v. duty, power v. disability, immunity v. liability

Jural correlatives: right/duty, privilege/no-right, power/liability, immunity/disability

From the perspective of jural opposites, if John has a right to own a house, David has no-right to enter it. From the perspective of jural correlatives, if John has a right to own a house, David has a duty to not enter it. Rights, privileges, powers and immunities are benefits that accrue to groups or individuals. Duties, no-rights, liabilities and disabilities are burdens that obtain; but Hohfeld loosely applies the term burden because, at times, he thought that a liability was beneficial to a person or group.[51]

Hohfeld divided these eight terms into paucital rights (applying to one or a few people) and multital rights (applying to human beings in general). People have paucital rights applying only to them. E.g., Fred, a carpenter, has a right to enter John's house to refinish the basement because he has a signed contract to do so. He also has multital rights, e.g., to own, use, enjoy, alter and sell his own house.

Multital and paucital were terms Hohfeld used to clear up a confused belief that some rights attach to persons and some attach to things. He pointed out that rights attach to persons only—only people exercise a right. Rights imply human agency. The multital right to own land is composed of the complex set of rights to use, enjoy, rent, alter or sell it. The right to education is also a multital right, which, based on the UDHR, is free and compulsory.

In the analysis that follows, I discuss multital rights primarily—a general right of all children that pertains to their access to education, using Hohfeld's conceptual map. Through careful analysis, Hohfeld defined the eight terms in the following way:

- Right is an affirmative claim against another person
- No-right is the absence of an affirmative claim against another person
- Privilege is freedom from duty; it's the liberty or freedom that negates a legal duty
- Duty is a legal obligation—an action we ought to do or ought not to do
- Power is ability or volitional control to change a legal relation (e.g., someone else's)
- Disability is no-ability, the opposite of legal ability and a correlative of liability[52]
- Immunity is an exemption or freedom from someone's else's control so that another person can't change one's legal relation
- Liability refers to responsibility so that a person is bound or obligated in some sense

Those who are under a liability may have their legal relations altered in some way. The change might cause a loss of some kind, or it might be beneficial. As an example, a young man and woman want to be husband and wife (a change of legal relation signified by their new titles). The change of legal relations is accomplished by virtue of the power invested in the minister of a church, a rabbi of a synagogue, an imam of a mosque or a justice of the peace). With the benefit of marriage, each person now has certain rights and duties, spelled out in the ceremony.

At this point, I want to consider the eight conceptions as they apply to a child's right to education and make a connection to Paley's concern that some school children limit the social experiences of others. The legal relations involved at school have to do with access to education. I offer the following syllogism to express the link between access and social experiences:

- If all children have a right to education, where right equals a claim to access,
- And if access to education is secured through entry into social experiences at school,[53]
- Then every child has a right of access (entry) into social experiences at school.

As Hohfeld pointed out, a single right is always a legal relation between a person who has the right and another person who is under a correlative duty.[54] A right to education implies that each child in a classroom has a right of access and a duty (obligation) to access that education. If a child isn't at school, the State will follow up on the reason for the absence. It also implies that if children have a right of access, then others have duties that are picked out in what follows.

The idea that children have rights and duties is based on the nature of education, as the syllogism shows, which is composed of social experiences that fulfill educational requirements of schooling. Legal aspects of education include two documents: the Individualized Program Plan (IPP) designed for learners with special needs and the Report Card that conveys whether students have or haven't passed from one grade to the next. Passing a grade changes the learners' legal relation of access to education—they can now access the next grade's social experiences. These two legal documents are related to one another in that an IPP is an amendment to Report Cards and states why a child can/can't reach the outcomes contained in them.[55] In applying Hohfeld's conceptual map, it must remain clear that the issue is the right of access to education, not a right to Report Card outcomes. Assessment is the province of teachers.

This discussion focuses on students' social interaction and doesn't address the teacher and student relationship, except indirectly in terms of its implications for creating an educational environment in which children learn how to include one another. A limit placed on this thought experiment constrains its range to access to education and doesn't imply or intimate that learners have a right to pass their grade. A right of access is not a right to outcomes. If a child is sent home from school because of unacceptable behaviour, refuses to complete an assignment, or fails an assignment, his or her right to education isn't violated. The child fails with respect to a duty to access education, an obligation that's unmet if a child refuses to do schoolwork.[56]

Access to public education is built on entry into social experiences at school. As Paley's experiment shows, a child's access is affected by exclusion—an effect that lasts as long as children remain at school. As a consequence, bossiness may influence and bullying does influence a student's access to education by limiting a child's social experiences at school. Both patterns threaten a child's felt sense of connection to a school environment. The goal of teaching children to be leaders, not bosses or bullies, motivates the following discussion of rights.

Hohfeld's first category includes three terms: right and no-right (opposites) and duty (correlative to right). A right is an affirmative claim against another person. John (every child) has a right to education and a duty to access education, which implies a right to enter social experiences that comprise that education. Using the opposite term, no-right refers to the absence of an affirmative claim against another person. Jane (every child) has no-right (no claim) to interfere with John's access to education. Jane has no-right to prevent John's entry into social experiences at school. The correlative term, duty, applies to John's obligation to access education and Jane's duty to acknowledge John's right of entry into social experiences at school.

Hohfeld's second category involves three terms: privilege, duty (its opposite) and no-right (correlative to privilege). What privileges do children have in the classroom? A privilege is freedom from duty, the liberty or freedom that negates a legal duty or legal obligation. While John has a duty to access education, the implication of his multital privilege to education implies that he's free to enter, participate in, contribute to, complete, leave or abandon social experiences at school. In getting an education, John has to balance duties and privileges in order to achieve success. It's in the nature of privilege that John experiences ownership over his schoolwork. The opposite term, duty, signals what Jane ought to do (include John) and ought not to do (exclude John) in social experiences at school, in class and on the playground, which is also public space.

A privilege of free access to social experiences at school has a correlative that is a no-right: if John has the privilege to enter a social experience, Jane has no-right that John should not enter. Excluding John from social experiences influences John's access to education. Hohfeld noted that a privilege, in the sense of changing a legal relation, applies only to changes that are under a person's volitional control or human agency. Changes that come about in an educational setting due to events that no human being could control (flood or fire) don't apply to the no-right correlative of privilege. But including and excluding another child from social experiences at school is a volitional act under the control of a human agent. Since her no-right is correlative to John's privilege, Jane has no-right to exclude John from his privilege to enter social experiences at school.

Hohfeld's third category includes three terms: power, disability (its opposite) and liability (correlative to power). John's power (ability or volitional control to change a legal relation) is over his access to social experiences in order to do his own work, which in turn influences his grades and allows him to pass his year. He's under a liability (correlative to power) and may have his legal relations altered by his teachers, e.g., by failing, or beneficially, by passing into the next grade. In education, the only equitable way to fail students relies on personal responsible to do their own work. To use someone else's work is cheating. Not to do one's own work is to fail one's duty.

The opposite term to power is disability, an inability to change a legal relation. While John is responsible for his own work and is unable to change his legal relation with respect to failing or passing, except by using his power to do his own work successfully, Jane has a disability with respect to John's power: she has no power to change his legal relation. The correlative term to power is liability (i.e., responsibility) in which a person is bound or obligated to do something or not to do it. Because education is accessed through social experiences, Jane has no power over John's entry into them at school; she has a liability to not prevent John from entering social experiences at school. In terms of their liability (responsibility), John and Jane have no power to move themselves from one grade to another and no control over their grades on assignments, except by fulfilling their duty to access education and do their own schoolwork.

The final category of Hohfeld's system includes three terms: immunity, liability (its opposite) and disability (correlative to immunity). John has immunity, an exemption or freedom from another child's control over his access to education, i.e., his entry into social experiences at school. The opposite term to immunity, liability, refers to Jane's responsibility to not control John's access to social experiences. To interfere in someone's access to social experiences is to impact the legal relation implicit in a general right to access education.

In terms of liability, Jane is responsible, bound and obligated to do her own work and bound to not exclude others who are equally entitled to participate in social experiences at school. The correlative term to immunity is disability. As mentioned, correlative terms examine the legal relation first from one side and then from the other. If immunity is an exemption from Jane's control over John's access to social experiences, disability (no-ability) refers to Jane's absence of control to accomplish a change in John's legal relation (i.e., grades and passing) by excluding him from social experiences at school.

In summary, John has a duty to access education by participating in social experiences at school and by balancing duty and privilege to achieve success. His liberty allows him to realize ownership over his own learning. Passing or failing is a consequence of completing schoolwork. Jane has no responsibility over John's work or his success at school. Her only responsibility with respect to John is to not exclude him from social experiences at school. An outcome of this thought experiment provides a basis for a principle of inclusion in the sense that no child has the right to exclude another child from access to social experiences at school because access to social experiences at school is the means for getting an education.

In addition, free entry into social experiences at school encourages children to maintain a felt sense of connection to this public space. A sense of felt connection is a pathway along which a child's relational needs are met and the requisite resources are distributed fairly. When access to social experiences at school is unhindered, a culture of security allows every child to trust that the learning environment supports their equal right of access to education.

Social Literacy And Its Requirements

While Paley presents one way to aim at healthy social interaction by introducing her rule in kindergarten, I'm not suggesting her rule is the only way to accomplish that goal. Yet it's clear that children need free access to relational resources if they are to learn to be effective in building relationships, which is fundamental to their right to access education. Given the vast difference between the legal thought experiment just described and the social power evident in Paley's class, what needs to be done so that children can access education in an environment of relational security?

Children can be inclusive at school if they acquire good rules at the right time and if rules become maxims, and eventually, undergird a life principle of inclusion that directs behaviour toward an equitable way of being with others. This sort of cultural learning is the heart of social literacy. Teachers need first to see what's going on during social interaction at school so they can affirm the principle of inclusion, using it to shape social interaction among learners. If they're adept at creating inclusive learning environments, teachers notice the principles they live by that impact their expectations for and responses to exclusion/inclusion.

In a useful book on adult learning, based on work by Chris Argyris and Donald Schon, Anita Farber-Robertson[57] investigates an approach that's essential to understand as we consider social literacy. In *Flawed Advice and the Management Trap*, Argyris pointed out that a human mind doesn't produce concrete actions without having a theory to rely on. These are theories we espouse (promote) and theories we actually use. Argyris and Schon developed *Action*

Science as a way to show that people and institutions constantly make errors in action that go undetected due to what can be described as hypocrisy: errors arise because people don't do what they say. *Action Science* identifies gaps and inconsistencies in theories people use to inform what they do. These inconsistencies produce errors in the sense that people end up doing what they say they don't believe in doing, or fail to do what they say they want to and will do. Paley's children are a case in point. *Action Science* helps people discern gaps between what they espouse and what they practice so that what they say will align with what they do.

Robertson provides an important insight about *Action Science* that applies to learning social literacy. She identifies a human need to get better at recognizing the persistent lack of reliably clear perceptions of what's going on and to remove the blinders that prevent us from learning from the reality that stares us in the face. She points out that we're well advised to move beyond the specifics of our own experience to reach for more generic models to explain social interaction. If we get a glimpse of bigger interpretive pictures of the world, we can use them to help us understand other people and ourselves.

Robertson proposes that as long as we view each of our professional (practical) failures and errors (i.e., hypocrisy) as idiosyncratic, one-time events, studying them won't yield useful knowledge. We'll be caught repeating what we haven't yet noticed or understood. She proposed that most people's behaviour is governed by rules, values and meanings that can be unpacked and known, but that frequently we haven't done that work.

To understand our own behaviour, it helps to see general patterns in social interaction that also apply to us. Relying on patterns that describe human behaviour doesn't negate personal authenticity. [58] If there weren't common patterns among people, we couldn't make sense of each other. Identifying patterns of bossing and bullying is an example of what Robertson recommends if we intend to get smarter about being in relationship with other people. In chapters that follow, you'll find some essential human patterns that help people learn how to be socially literate.

CHAPTER SUMMARIES

In the first chapter social literacy is presented as a complex skill we learn by working towards stable complexity in human relationships so as to adequately maintain our relational habitat. Its goal is to be ourselves at the same time as we live and work collaboratively with others. This is achieved by being mindful of what's going on and deciding what sort of person we want to be—an aim of character education.

Mindfulness has to do with what the mind can do—its capabilities. The mind can focus attention so that learning occurs. Aspects of mindfulness include a capacity to expend energy to pay attention, to see what's going on, understand, reason, make decisions and put them into play, make new decisions and be conscious of past and present experience at the same time.[59] It's as a result of being tuned to what's going on that we're able to decide what sort of person we want to be. Yet socially literate character is authentic *and* well integrated in community. It's civil. As a consequence, authenticity isn't freedom to do whatever we like, as if we were solitary and free.

In the second chapter, I continue to develop an approach to character education based on civility and describe social intelligence as an ordinary human capacity we use as we learn social literacy. I then outline abductive reasoning as a way to explain aspects of mindfulness. Following that, I propose that successful learning depends on having appropriate approaches to mastering face-to-face complex skills and offer a method for learning mastery that's aptly suited to social literacy. In the last section, I describe some ways to understand personal styles that shape social interaction in order to enhance self and social knowledge so that we come to understand what's going on during our encounters with other people.

Social literacy assumes that we can't be ourselves without help from other people. To contextualize our need for others, in chapter three, I describe social capital fully and also build a framework for social literacy that relies on embodied learning, a process that grows out of a felt sense of connection that becomes effective as a way to be authentic and integrated as we learn to think on our feet. My purpose is to demonstrate that we need one another and that social literacy conveys a hopeful view of the future. If adults learn its lessons, children catch these insights so that the social world is able to supply them with relational resources that make life bearable. But where can these lessons be learned? Where will they be practised?

I begin chapter four by providing a meaning for the word context and contrast it with an idea for community. My purpose is to say that community is the foundation for learning social literacy. There's semantic overlap between the terms, but, as I use them in this chapter, while a context is dehumanizing, communities make us more fully human. Community becomes the site for learning how to foster relationships and encourage the development of social literacy in all members. As people become community, they do so by taking responsibility for the relational environment and by describing, interpreting and evaluating contexts that have shaped their lives so as to gain a fuller understanding of how they want to treat each other.

In chapter five, I continue to describe patterns in social interaction in order to improve our understanding of what's going on, by investigating four global patterns that are woven throughout the smaller-scale contexts described in chapter four. To distinguish these large-scale, trans-cultural ways of life from the face-to-face contexts, I refer to them as global patterns. They form a unique logic in cultures all over the world.

To provide background for depicting them, I analyze a version of community that has empathy and cosmopolitanism at its core. Following that analysis, I describe the four patterns along with their characteristic views of the world and valuation of persons. The logic in each one is laid out and compared to the others. After I describe the patterns, and point out their weaknesses in supporting social literacy, I offer an approach to relational habitat maintenance based on work Harvard professor Robert Kegan (psychology and education) takes to Piaget's stage theory of human development. Kegan helps to indentify essential features of what's required in doing the relational work of building community.

His perspective fits well with cosmopolitanism and empathy. He doesn't believe authenticity requires us to walk away from our commitments in order to find ourselves. While change happens as we learn social literacy, the purpose of this chapter is to say that change relies on reflection and relational work, not on a twentieth century tendency to walk away from family and community as a way to seek personal fulfillment—or to 'find ourselves' as was often said.

Building community relies on empowering social relationships. Chapter six expands a discussion of power's role in social interaction that was introduced in chapter one. I situate that discussion in a network of concepts and practices that include the nature of symbolic power, the art of using power, misleading effects of individualistic assumptions about power and an outline of power's patterns. At its root, social literacy assumes that others have a strong influence on us, an affect we carry within and that we can learn to read. As we learn to read social interaction effectively while we are engaged in it, we get better at making ourselves understood. If we get better at making ourselves understood, we enjoy more fairness and freedom as we exercise our authenticity while we're with other people.

But acquiring this skill of social literacy depends on seeing how power operates and decoding its games so we don't get trapped in them. Understanding how power operates allows us to be objective, in Bourdieu's sense described in chapter two. Objectivity increases personal freedom while we're in the presence of other people. My purpose in describing power is to name some of what we're up against as we're learning social literacy. Patterns of power inform us about opportunities we have to test our skill, strength and integrity as we develop social literacy.

In chapter seven, I outline a role memes play in social learning as a way to say more about civility, which can also be described as being a good neighbour. Debunking a twentieth century prejudice that disdained neighbourliness is part of understanding what's possible in achieving social literacy, which, again, is understood throughout the book as learning to be near (socially close and connected) and different (maintaining important ideals and ways of life). I say more about what's implied in social literacy by looking at the dynamics of a human capacity for change. I then offer a list of aspects of culture that increase the self and social knowledge that's implied in the idea of being near to yet different from others.

If we account for the range of cultural aspects outlined at the end of the chapter, it's easier to see how to locate changes that social literacy recommends. My purpose is to identify opportunities to make an impact on social interaction, make good sense of it and improve it while we're still engaged in it—that is, as we learn to think on our feet.

Up to this point, social literacy is described as a balance between relational closeness and intentional distinctness from others, i.e., nearness and difference. The complex skill of being near and different, promotes civility and allows authenticity and integration to flourish. Balancing those two potentially competitive aims, depends on interpreting others with accuracy and tact, i.e., keeping people close without foreclosing on authenticity and persisting in being ourselves despite pressure from those who may misunderstand us. The fulcrum of that balance is empathy. Skilful empathy allows us to be true to ourselves and remain well connected to other people.

Empathy is sometimes misunderstood because it has more than one meaning. In chapter eight, I define and explore its ambiguity and describe a pattern in human development that forms the foundation for learning empathy. This developmental process uncovers what can go wrong as we try to be empathetic and I specify some of the obstacles to its healthy expression.

Empathy is sign of mature human character. My purpose is to say that, while we have potential for empathy, we learn to be empathetic in the presence of those who know how to express empathetic responsiveness. In chapter nine, Jean continues to explore the early years to establish bases for civility and empathy in one-to-one relationships that shape the early development of a child. In this chapter, Jean proposes that learning civility depends on family and community environments that provide the young with basic relational needs.

Chapter ten links resilience to healthy civic environments in which stories we tell about the human value of every citizen, the quality of civic leadership and the meaning of work all contribute to the support that's necessary in maintaining a healthy relational environment. Social literacy depends on living in a healthy setting. As we will see, cities operate as both model and opportunity for serving the aims and functions of social literacy. My purpose is to reveal its relationship to human flourishing and say that if we foster the healthiest kind of citizen, we promote the life chances of all citizens and promote complexity in human relationships.

CONCLUSION

In the West we spend a lot of effort describing and allowing for cultural differences, so much so, we may lose sight of what makes people human. A significant number of theorists seek to rectify this short-sightedness. There have arisen numerous points of view that focus on what makes us human. The good news is that common patterns in social interaction help people learn social literacy by providing theoretical guidance as they try to make sense of what someone else is doing, and, what they mean by doing it. Social literacy can't get off the ground if we attend only to people's differences. Human commonalities inform the capacities to observe, interpret and understand other people.

Perceiving what's going on during social interaction takes considerable skill. It's central work for the human mind. The purpose of this book is to provide a theoretical framework for learning those skills and for helping people pay attention to social interaction as a way to improve it. The framework has civility at its core. As we observe the quality of social interaction, we notice when we're harming others or when they feel no compunction against harming us.

The book also addresses relational poverty that's evident in the first three scenarios at the outset of the chapter. The willingness to improve social interaction depends on the social trust and social happiness that allow people to experience relational security. Relational security is an issue of justice as a thought experiment about children in school aims to convey. The power to include others encourages a felt sense of connection that's the basis for remaining meaningfully connected to others. In the next chapter, I examine what makes us human and how our connections to other people create or frustrate our willingness and ability to learn social literacy.

2

FOUNDATIONS FOR CIVILITY

INTRODUCTION

In the introduction, I connected social literacy to character education. The motivation to work on relationships (relationality), while we're engaged in them, comes from a commitment to create environments in which people live fully human lives. Being fully human depends on being included in public life in meaningful ways at the same time that we feel free to be ourselves.

Using Paley's case study, I separated leading from bossing and bullying and suggested that social literacy helps us be inclusive when we're involved in public spaces. If we focus on our humanity, as the raison d'être for rights and duties, we will ask more questions about its common qualities and try to see how it functions to motivate civility.

When we consider humanity's role in civility, two questions arise as we reflect on the school culture conveyed through Paley's example: How is civil life possible? How do people learn to be civil? Both questions impact character education. Each one addresses bullying in its own way.

The art of including others is basic to civility. What do inclusion and exclusion look like? In his inclusionary-status continuum, American psychologist Mark Leary identified a range of inclusion and exclusion behaviours. His summary identifies the following:

- Maximal inclusion: others make an effort to seek out an individual
- Active inclusion: others welcome the individual but don't seek out him or her
- Passive inclusion: others allow an individual to be included
- Ambivalence: others don't care whether an individual is included or excluded
- Passive exclusion: others ignore an individual
- Active exclusion: others avoid an individual
- Maximal exclusion: others physically reject, ostracize, abandon, or banish an individual.[1]

Bullying is a form of maximal exclusion that violates the human need to belong to a group as well as the legal right children have to be in school. Leary noted that bullying may move some people to cling to group acceptance, while others become defiant, and, in reaction, increase their socially objectionable behaviour.[2] Others may give up on society altogether or find effective ways to maintain their marginality. In all of these reactions, their humanity suffers.

Yet acts of inclusion and exclusion may play some part in how we practice being ourselves and how we set boundaries around our identity, which is why friendship is such an important issue at school and in the workplace. As mentioned, questions of civility, of what it means to live well with others, are linked to human character. But the two questions about civility also raise the issue of individuality. If we ask how civility is possible, we're also asking why civil life is attractive. Why should people give up some of their rights and freedoms to live in close quarters with others? One response could be, well, we always do. It's just the way things are for human beings. We start out dependent on our parents and never lose our need for others, although our needs change over time. And this may be the best answer.

At this point, I want to explore the idea of humanity and locate its position in teaching people to be more inclusive. The purpose of the chapter is to provide a foundation for civil thought and action that allows us to learn to be inclusive in healthy ways based on an idea of humanity that holds together our duties and rights in classrooms and workplaces, as well as in our own homes.

In connecting humanity with civility, I propose that civility is based on stable complexity and that its purpose is to teach us how to be *near and different*. The model for stable complexity in social interaction is derived from biology and culture. Next, I outline social intelligence to show what's involved in learning to use a capacity that every human being has already. I then describe C.S. Peirce's theory of abduction as a pattern for thinking and acting that's well suited to learning social literacy. After that, I detail a remarkably useful 7 stage learning approach to mastering a complex skill, put forward by American philosopher Hubert Dreyfus. The last section explores Dreyfus's stage theory by unpacking several ways to understand personal style—ours and other people's—as a way to notice the principled way of life that has become a personal habit.

The outcome of social literacy, authenticity and integration, are linked through coming to see what's going on during social interactions that emanate from people's personal style, i.e., their consistent way of being in the world. My purpose in this chapter is to say that social literacy enhances authenticity and provides citizens with the complex skills for living fully human lives as they integrate into community.

CIVILITY AND COMPLEXITY

Human beings are utterly dependent on being with their own kind. There's something called the human family that links us to one another, and for example, allows us to comprehend texts that were written thousands of years ago in ancient civilizations. Yet we live in a historical period when individualism might eclipse the value we place on what's common about humanity.

Social literacy depends on reclaiming a sense of connection to all other human beings as a way to ground our obligation to them. To be fully human, relationships (or relationality—the adequate provision of relational resources) are at least as important as expressing an authentic sense of who we are as individuals.[3] The question remains: How can I be myself, yet live well with others? That question motivated French reformer Jean-Jacques Rousseau (1712-1776) as he devised social theory. Though he wrote in the 1700s, and inspired the generation that carried out the French Revolution in 1789, his question remains central for character education. The idea of social literacy is a response to Rousseau. We're still asking ourselves how to be authentic and integrated with other people that matter to us—which, in my view, is an outcome of evolution, but not one that's somehow automatic and achievable simply because we're human. It requires social/emotional skills development that we invest in learning social literacy.

For instance, if it's reasonable to say human life, people like us, developed 160,000 or 140,000 years ago in Africa (depending on how we calculate time) and progressed through various stages of development by evolving culturally and technologically, it's fair to ask what we must learn now to live well together in order to take advantage of what we've achieved in the past. The idea of evolution, in the sense I use it, implies support for an idea of progress—the idea that things move forward based on what's already happened and as a result of it. What does progress imply about the nature of our humanity?

At the outset of modernity, which some suggest began with the French Revolution, many social theorists focused on making life more comfortable. Their concern was understandable. As mentioned, in the middle of the 1800s, 5/6ths of the world's population lived in extreme poverty. The desire to alleviate poverty and human suffering drove modern reform that continued into the twentieth century, for example, by improving health care and by securing wider access to goods and services that make life more bearable, as well as by extending human rights, eventually to imply the ordinary human need for relational resources. But progress doesn't only make the world more comfortable. It makes life more complex. It's timely to ask what we need to learn to seize the opportunity to improve the human condition, based on what's happened in the past, an investigation that's the responsibility and task of every generation.

Human Progress And The Persistence Of Memes

The idea of human progress has been disdained over the last few decades due in part to disappointments humanity suffered globally during the twentieth century. It's not surprising, given its Holocaust, genocides and terrorisms, that people lost hope in humanity. Yet despair is to some extent a result of misunderstanding what progress implies. Modern reformers focused on the material acquisition of all things comfortable. Look at art from the Middle Ages in Europe. By comparison, furniture, homes, workplaces are more comfortable now. Invention was aimed at ending all kinds of suffering; but modernity developed comfort at the expense of spiritual and relational needs that sustain humanity. Or perhaps, meeting some of those basic needs opened us up to a call from deeper needs. In accumulating goods and services, we forgot that physical comfort isn't the only basic human need. Spiritual needs express a quest for meaning. Relational needs convey a longing for support from others. Material plenty, by itself, won't provide people with a fully human life. The task of each generation is to make the world more human by learning to be humane and contributing to the humanization of the whole community that makes up the world.

Many of us in Western society who enjoy more physical comfort than a human being needs, pay scant attention to those who have no comfort due to material, spiritual or relational poverty. In my own country, too many people go hungry, while some enjoy plenty. Too much physical comfort turns us inward. Inequality emanates from unequal distributions of human goods, which is a cancer in civil life. When those who have all they want keep emotional, social, financial, racial, gendered and communal distance from those who have little, civil life falters. Everyone is less human. The challenge materialism presents to character education isn't simply to question the accumulation of things. Its flaw is found in a loss of empathy that emerges if we pay more attention to material than to the spiritual/relational aspects of life. I explore the relationship between social literacy and empathy in a later chapter but, at this point, I suggest that materialism, by itself, creates relational and spiritual poverty through weakening empathy; eventually, someone else's body is nothing more than flesh, function and mechanical parts—whether one takes a strictly medical or a solely sexualized approach to the body.

Materialism spotlights poverty. Poverty intensifies inequality. Inequality is destabilizing. If civility is to flourish, if we are to evolve to meet the current demands of life together, we must be generous or else reject commonplace excesses of physical comfort for the few and realize that progress doesn't make life easier, it makes learning to live well more demanding. Given that many of us enjoy plenty of physical comfort, will we feel free to reach beyond the ease of living to seek well-being at a more spiritual and relational depth? I argue throughout the book that one reason we don't reach toward more in terms of spiritual and relational maturity, is that we don't know how. We don't have the skills required for living in the present moment—with its demands for enhanced meaning and generosity. Spirituality and relationality require us to address the complexity of our current circumstances as members of local and global human communities.

How can the complexity of human progress become more stable? To respond to that question, we can see that evolution itself "could not get going without some mechanism for the emergence of complex stability."[4] The role of civility is to ensure that complex social life in the twenty-first century is stable, at the same time that it allows for diversity and change. Can we learn to meet these apparently competing demands? Are there well functioning models that hold them together? I propose that a model is found in the functioning of a human body as a model for how to function within the social body. What is that model?

In response to British theorist Richard Dawkins who wrote the book *The Selfish Gene* in 1976, British author Kate Distin (2005)[5] outlined the nature of what Dawkins called memes, bits of data that reproduce culture similarly to the way genes replicate a human body. Genes and memes are like recipe cards that indicate how to do something—in one case the body *reads* them, in the other, people *read* them as they learn how to be part of a group. Memes are bits of cultural information that instruct us: they detail how to make cement, build a kite, raise a family, get your own way, play the violin, collaborate with others or use a computer.

Genes and memes make copies of themselves in order to pass on and preserve content on the recipe cards. While their processes of replication differ, the tendency for memes to survive and reproduce in a culture is supported by their capacity to get support from the environment—certain instructions survive because they're supported by others. Memes that are unsupported fail and seem forgotten. For example, the rules about how to wash dishes, or bake bread have largely been lost in North American homes. We have dishwashers and readily available stores that sell bread. In earlier times, daughters were apprenticed to their mothers to receive and practice those skills.

The way memes and genes function offers a model for maintaining civility, in the sense of learning to be *near and different*. Genes and memes make copies that persist. Regarding their capacity to persist, Distin showed that genes and memes are self-assertive, yet integrated in the human body (as genes) or in culture (as memes), a complex stability that constitutes a model for being authentic yet integrated in the social world.

The perpetuation and persistence of genes and memes has to do with their self-assertion and integration. When they enjoy support from the environment, they band together, yet maintain their own identity within the system. In reference to self-assertion and integration, she described successful replication by saying that "each [part] maintains its own identity in the assembly [and] each must be compatible with others in the assembly, otherwise the result would be unstable [which is why] each is self-assertive and integrative."[6] As bits of cultural data, memes reproduce stable complexity within human cultures. They do so by being precise, mostly. Like genes, memes reproduce exactly, almost. There's enough consistency to create stability and enough slippage to allow for innovation and change over time.

Being self-assertive (authentic) and integrative (relational) is a model for human civility. The purpose of this book is to reveal social patterns that conform to the possibility of being oneself while in the company of others. Civility depends on the health of authenticity and integration during all or at least most social interaction. But as part of that possibility, settings in which memes try to survive, or people try to flourish, are crucial to their success.

Let's use cultural synonyms for self-assertion and integration. Two patterns characterize aspects of the history of the human family. One is a tendency for social and cultural groups to be *near and the same*. People form community based on proximity that requires them to be like everyone else. In speech, dress, ritual, celebration, attitude and belief, deep-going and surface similarities unify communal life. This isn't only a cultural phenomenon, it's also sub-cultural, e.g., in groups and gangs. If people live out the implications of being *near and the same*, they might live amicably with others or they can be thoroughly oppressed, as they are in totalitarian societies, religious cults or street gangs. In *near and the same* settings, loyalty is expressed in practical and apparent ways: people speak the same language and value the same things, so that, in healthy situations, they share resources, express solidarity and social concern but in unhealthy situations, they aren't free to be themselves. To be different is to be unsafe.

The other broad tendency, sometimes described as secular,[7] views the human world as a site of competition requiring individuals to secure every advantage through being *distant and different* from all others. In this view, the social world is conceived as a loosely linked mass of people joined through temporary economic relations that last only as long as those who benefit from them continue to be involved. Privileged individuals rise above the mass because they're different from the herd. Difference makes them unique. Distance from other people (material, spiritual, relational) allows them to maintain their advantages. They're driven to keep up with being different to maintain their status above the crowd. Based on that uniqueness, goods and services are unevenly distributed so that privileged people have a better chance to get and keep resources. As a consequence, the world is rife with *have nots*—people who have no access to the means of getting and keeping valued resources. The unequal distribution of resources is justified by privileges based on differences that show up in those that *have* and don't show up in *have nots.* These distinctions are intensified whenever and wherever wealth allows the elite to increase their distance from the poor.

In contrast, social literacy implies learning to be *near and different*: socially close, interdependent, involved, compassionate, empathetic responsiveness and responsible, yet unique, authentic, different from other people who continue to matter to us. To be *near and different* is a way of being oneself in the company of others, whether they're friends, family or enemies. The complex skill of being near to others yet different from them promotes civility and allows authenticity and integration to flourish together.

Social literacy is a developed capacity to read the world in a way that enables people to achieve balance between their important differences and their human solidarity. Literacy, as a model, is more than reading words on a page. Likewise, social literacy implies a hermeneutic skill of interpreting social contexts and imagining other people's lives in a way that they would affirm as accurate. Learning social literacy depends on developing hermeneutical skill—a capacity to interpret others with accuracy and tact, to keep people close without foreclosing on authenticity, to persist in being ourselves despite pressure from those who would devalue us. If our genes must function in this way to maintain human life, surely we can learn the skills implied in securing civil life.

Underlying our capacity to be *near and different*, authentic yet integrated, are three complex, essential skills. To be near others yet different from them requires social trust, social love and empathy. Taken together, these complex skills allow us to interact without wanting to escape from others in order to protect ourselves, or to become invisible because we can't be ourselves while we're with them. Social trust, based on reciprocity, social love (acting for the common good) and empathy are the core of what it means to be civil. Social love is perhaps the least understood. It's defined as the willingness and ability "to act intentionally, in sympathetic response to others…to promote overall well-being;"[8] that is, to love is to act for the common good, [9]which logically includes loving oneself.[10] If we don't trust, love and empathize, we can't sustain our relationships in personal, social, economic, political, gendered, racial and cultural aspects of daily life. This book offers various perspectives on social trust, social love and empathy, all of which are grounded on capacities that develop as we intentionally develop our own social intelligence.

But why bother? It sounds like so much work! I suggest it's only under the conditions of trust, love and empathy that human beings can relax. To relax in the company of others is a deep spiritual and relational need. It's crucial for an infant's development to relax in the arms of its parents. Our freedom to flourish rests on our ability to relax in the embrace of the social world. This book is about realizing, to some extent, that possibility. If we acknowledge the significance of sharing the world, locally and globally, we realize that the poor aren't happy to be perpetually confronted by the humiliation of watching others enjoy excesses no human being needs, which are consumed because some can get them and others can't. We also see that relational poverty is equally humiliating and dehumanizing. A truly civil society aims to make life more human for all its citizens. The quality of civil life is measured by the way a society treats its weak members. Positive social interaction shapes a hopeful belief that the future is friendly.

Responding to these insights requires people to have a developed capacity for social trust, social love and empathy. What about people that don't have them yet? How does social literacy stabilize complexity and encourage hope? These are important questions for social literacy to face. I believe people can learn to work collaboratively to enhance civility. The book is a thought experiment on how to be more civil through becoming socially literate so as to promote stable complexity and hope. But I want to be clear that becoming socially literate isn't simply an idea to be discussed—it's a complex skill that must be learned in practice. Can everyone learn it? Before I outline some of the requisite skills, I will say more about the fundamental capacity each of us already possesses that can be employed to develop social literacy.

SOCIAL INTELLIGENCE

The possibility for learning to be socially literate rests on a foundation all people have for what American author Daniel Goleman calls social intelligence.[11] Goleman is well known for the book *Emotional Intelligence* (1997). Its influence is evident in business, educational, religious and popular culture. In 2006, he distinguished two ideas by saying that emotional intelligence involves the inner life of individuals: it's about self-awareness and self-management. Social intelligence is concerned with human relationships: it's about social awareness and relationship management.[12]

He wasn't the first to use the term social intelligence but built his view on current brain and behavioral sciences to insist on one aspect that sets his view apart. The original formulation of social intelligence was "the ability to understand and manage men and women," a definition that, to Goleman, allows one person to manipulate others.[13] He pointed out that some definitions don't distinguish the "callow aptitudes of a con man from genuinely caring acts that enrich healthy relationships."[14] In his view, "simply being manipulative—valuing only what works for one person at the expense of the other—should not be seen as socially intelligent."[15] His definition affirms the possibility of being *near and different* and supports the need for social trust, social love and empathy.

His support for social literacy is due to his focus on interaction as key to understanding social intelligence. He believes it refers to "being intelligent not just *about* our relationships but also *in* them." Social intelligence involves at least two people. His shorthand for the term is "acting wisely in human relationships."[16] Research on which he built the concept shows that we impact other people's emotions and biology, and they impact ours, every time we interact. As an example, American researchers Janice Kiecolt-Glaser and Ronald Glaser demonstrated that the effects of continual stress reach all the way down to the level of gene expression in immune cells that are essential for fighting infections and healing wounds.[17] Harmful social interaction makes us sick. As Goleman insists, stress is social. People may get sick and not heal well if their setting is stressful.[18] To Goleman, since we have so much impact on others, we're well advised to conduct "ourselves in ways that are beneficial even at [a] subtle level for those with whom we connect."[19]

Social intelligence is associated with what researchers call the social brain, which isn't a certain part of the brain; it's "a particular set of circuitry that's orchestrated as people relate to each other."[20] During social encounters, behavioral research reveals that feelings pass between us much the way we catch a cold: feelings are triggered by being with others who have that feeling. Social intelligence relies on a "reflexive, unconscious awareness that signals an emotion by priming the same emotion (or a reaction to it, such as fear on seeing anger) in us—a key mechanism for 'catching' a feeling from someone else."[21] Emotions, and our reactions to other people's emotions, are contagious and instantaneous. Social literacy involves reading those emotions *as* we are with others and learning to act appropriately during the encounter.

The idea that emotions are contagious isn't well understood. Suppose a woman, Sheila, is riding her bicycle and wants to turn on to her street at the corner farthest from her house. She sees two things at the same time: neighborhood children playing on the curb, walking along it and slipping off into the street, and a car careening around the corner just where the children are playing. The car comes to a sudden stop just in front of the children. The driver and passengers are laughing. As she rides by, she stops and knocks on the young driver's window to point to the children who might have been hit by his car. He opens his window and starts yelling. She yells back, feeling a sense of rage she seldom experiences. She rides away completely frustrated. Why did she get so angry?

Let's look at the scenario more closely. A theory associated with social intelligence posits that the human brain "has been preset for kindness."[22] If we see someone in distress, similar circuits reverberate in our brain. There's a kind of hard-wired empathetic resonance that's the prelude to compassion. To see distress readies us to do something about it. Compassion implies seeing it and doing something in response, as a sort of echo effect. If an infant cries, the parent's brain reverberates in much the same way and automatically moves the parent to soothe the baby.[23] As mentioned, we catch feelings from others. To Goleman, concern is expressed as empathy and action. Someone who has concern is most aroused by emotional contagion, most moved to help someone in distress.[24] As a consequence, Goldman believes we should foster young children's attention to and concern for others as a strategy for preventing misbehavior in their later years.

Concern reflects a person's capacity for compassion. For the cyclist, concern for children playing on the street sparked a desire to create a safe place for them. Concern for one group (the young children) brought the cyclist into conflict with another group (the young men) whom she saw as creating a potential hazard. But both groups are someone's children. How does social literacy help create safety and support for both groups? It helps us read complex situations, identify our own strong feelings, perceive another's feeling (rather than simply reacting to it) and leads toward declaring those interests in a clear manner.

To achieve social literacy, it helps to understand how the social brain works. Goleman[25] notes that the circuitry of the social brain includes two pathways that researchers call the low road and the high road. As we read the impact of whatever we perceive—a clipped tone of voice in the young driver, the anger around his eyes, the defiant posture of his upper body, a gesture of punching the air made with his fists—the low road in the cyclist picks up these signs and the corresponding emotion, below her awareness, automatically and effortlessly. It's as if the low road is wet, slick with emotion and composed of raw feelings that allow for immense speed in her reaction. The contagious emotion passes to the low road quickly. She acts first and thinks afterwards. The low road is quick. Emotions are caught. The high road is slower and arrives at a more nuanced reading of what's going on.

The low road makes snap decisions. The high road is deliberate, mindful, wary and observant—yet I suggest it might miss opportunities to act when required. The low road is a sixth sense, an early warning system to prompt us to feel with another person even though we're only vaguely aware of our attunement with them (attunement isn't always a happy experience). The low road triggers sympathetic emotional states without offering an intervening thought. It's what Goleman calls instant primal empathy. The high road offers choices to refine understanding of what's going on.

The low road is necessary in some situations but the high road opens up as we monitor low road reactions and fully attend to the person we're talking with, to understand better what's happening. If the low road offers an instantaneous emotional affinity, the high road generates a social sense to guide an appropriate response. For example, the cyclist might have asked herself: How will this young man act in front of his peers? Is this the best time to approach him? If I knock on his window, what's the look on my face? The high road runs through neural systems to work step by step, with deliberate effort and offers a measure of control over one's inner life.

Social intelligence relies on both roads. These roads use different parts of the brain but normally work seamlessly, since they depend on each other's strength and skill. In one sense, the low road is responsible for reactions; the high road for measured responses, as long as we recall that some situations call for a reaction, not a time-consuming response, such as when we see a young child tottering on the side of a busy highway, a short distance from the open front door of a nearby house. Social intelligence offers interpersonal effectiveness that includes high and low road awareness, such as in the talent a nurse has when calming down a crying infant by offering just the right touch without having to think a moment about it.[26]

Given the differences between low and high roads in the social brain, social intelligence research asserts that emotions are social. We can't separate the cause of an emotion from the world of relationships. Social interaction drives our emotions.[27] Further, we *can't not* express emotion: even if we stop talking, we can't stop sending signals about our feelings.[28] Social literacy depends on a human aptitude for comprehending what's going on as we interact.

Learning social literacy depends on the brain's capacity to learn from experience. In this regard, Goleman points to a remarkable research finding: the human brain is designed to change itself in response to accumulated experience.[29] It's this reality that enables us to achieve social literacy. To understand more fully what's involved, I cite his ground rules for relationship and his analysis of social intelligence, which include a distinction between the two complex skills: social awareness and relationship management. He refers to relationship management as social facility. I relate his ground rules and describe his complex skills to show how his view presents knowledge and insight that's central to becoming socially literate.

Searching For Patterns In Social Interaction

The human sciences and the hard sciences train researchers to look for patterns in data. Researchers sift through information until they see how to organize it in usable and transferable ways, whether they use inductive, deductive or abductive approaches in their searches. This insight connects with the idea that all learning is organizing experience, since the brain is set up to change based on the accumulation of experience, as noted above. The ability to see patterns in our own behaviour and perceive patterns in other people, depends on being able to sense pattern organization,[30] an ability that develops over time as we reflect on what's going on.

Learning social literacy requires us to find and work with patterns that exist in social interaction. The assertion 'stress is social' is one of those patterns; it says we impact each other for good or ill. The implication of this pattern is significant for people at work or at home if these sites intensify social stress through practices that dehumanize them. Social literacy implies learning to become wise about harmful social patterns by perceiving the pain involved in them so that we can respond in healthier ways.

Human wisdom refers to accumulated and generalized insights based on patterns people use to organize experience meaningfully. Wisdom implies that pattern recognition is informed and reflective—if we're wise, we've achieved mastery over the social world and our responses to it provide healthy alternatives to dehumanizing practices. As Goleman's concept of social intelligence asserts, socially intelligent action aims at increasing the common good rather than intensifying social harm. Social literacy relies on and contributes to the practice of a social researcher (teacher, leader) as he or she establishes what's going on and gauges what to do about it, while the interaction is taking place. As we learn to be effective during social interaction, we gain complex skills, which, again, are combined in the effectiveness of using the brain's low and high roads.

As he sets out to describe two primary, complex skills involved in social intelligence, Goleman identifies ground rules for interaction that children, youth and adults learn as they exercise social intelligence. His ground rules include how to:

- attend to another person
- pace an interaction
- engage in conversation

- tune into other people's feelings
- manage one's own feelings while you are engaged with others.[31]

The two aspects that distinguish social from emotional intelligence, social awareness and social facility, are the means by which we learn to attend to, pace, engage in, tune into and manage our feelings during an encounter. The complex skills he names are social awareness and facility.[32]

Social Awareness

Goleman points out that social awareness refers to a spectrum of comprehending and responding that includes instantaneously sensing another person's inner state, understanding that person's feelings and thoughts, to the point where we 'get' what's going on in a complicated situation, such as the one Sheila faced,[33] one she didn't fully understand. Given her social failure, she may decide never to interfere in situations like that one again. As a result, she may shut down her feelings and silence her concern. It's not that she would stop feeling deeply, but she would have to stifle her concern. She might even try to seal herself off from her feelings.

Instead of shutting down, social literacy helps to sense reactions and respond appropriately so that people continue to contribute to the common good. Social literacy involves social awareness that includes:

- primal empathy: feeling with others and sensing non-verbal emotional signals
- attunement: listening with full receptivity by attending to another person
- empathetic accuracy: realizing another's thoughts, feelings, intentions
- social cognition: knowing how the social world works.[34]

The first three aspects of social awareness develop through using normal human capacities that are enhanced through conscious and intentional reflection on what's going on, a skill that's often referred to as mindfulness. The fourth awareness arises through education and experience in which people come to perceive large-scale social patterns that influence their encounters.

Using the four points above, as one plausible application of social literacy to the cyclist's experience, she could attend to the following before she knocks on the car window. As soon as he sees her, his fists are in the air, his voice is strained—he's expressing anger. She asks herself: What's the look on my face? She might begin by saying, "Hi. I'm Sheila. I'm your neighbor. I live just down the street." She might ask a question rather than make a charge. She might listen first and realize he's been driving his friends around in the car and is a very inexperienced driver. He may feel embarrassed. He may want to protect himself. Young men won't easily back down in front of their friends. This is only one way for Sheila to respond. She must also remain herself in the encounter, but social literacy allows her to be civic-minded with the children and young men. Developing social intelligence helps keep in mind a dual concern for both groups and the common good. If the driver hit a neighbor's child, his life would be seriously altered, as would everyone's in the neighborhood, including his friends and the families involved in the incident.

Social Facility

Cognition (intellectual understanding) is essential for social literacy but by itself doesn't enable someone to be literate. Cognition builds on social awareness so that interactions become smooth and effective as we think about how to respond rather than being trapped in reactions to others. Relational management (not manipulation), also called social facility, includes the following abilities:

- synchrony: interacting smoothly at the nonverbal level
- self-presentation: effectively providing others with a sense of who we are

- influence: shaping the outcome of social interactions
- concern: caring about other people's needs and acting accordingly[35]

If Sheila developed these four abilities and had a strong social awareness, the interaction with the young driver might have gone differently. She might have identified herself as his neighbour and smiled. She would notice the young man's tone of voice and respond calmly. She would have paid attention to his body posture and assumed a position that didn't seem threatening, angry or judgmental. She might have chosen another time to speak with him.

She didn't have to ignore her concern but might have presented herself in a way that permitted her to convey she was listening, so he could hear her eventually, even if he did so grudgingly at the time, especially in front of his buddies. Social facility allows concern to be effective. She would have a better opportunity in the encounter if she knew the people on the street well and had a healthy connection to the young man because she was a good neighbour.

Goleman identified research, strategies and tests that increase social awareness, e.g., the PONS (Profile of Nonverbal Sensitivity) that measures interpersonal sensitivity.[36] These skills are learned in practice. People need training to increase their social awareness by identifying specific skills and practicing them. The section on Learning Mastery in this chapter outlines a useful way to teach someone to acquire a complex skill.

The fourth form of awareness, social cognition is the ability to recognize patterns in a given situation,[37] which is based on a general ability to perceive patterns in social life. Several chapters in this book enhance social cognition by explaining patterns that show up in exchanges between people and in groups. In the next section, I develop more of the cognitive underpinnings for social literacy, in particular, an approach to exploring what's going on in a given situation.

To recap, social intelligence supports civility by showing how concern is an essential aspect of its purpose, development and fulfilment. If people are free to be authentic in the presence of others, to be *near and different* (authentic and integrated), social literacy develops and civility can flourish. What sort of research helps us to achieve the goals of social literacy? The next section proposes that abduction is that approach to reflecting on what's going on.

ABDUCTION AND SOCIAL LITERACY

In the introduction, I discussed a process of learning in which children first obeyed rules that helped them stop undesirable behaviour and then acquired maxims to help them stop and think. The third phase of the process includes settling on life principles that guide our action in the world, and therefore how we choose to identify ourselves in terms of our character, i.e., what people can come to expect from us.

I want to introduce a way of reflecting on experience that's precisely right for this educational pathway. It's a research method called abduction. In a few television series, e.g., *Numbers* and *House*, characters use abduction to solve complex problems.

The term abduction is misleading since its common usage puts us in mind of child snatching, which isn't what I'm talking about. Abduction is a way of gathering data until it forms identifiable and applicable patterns. The approach is neither inductive nor deductive; it's both, and more besides. The term was coined by American philosopher C.S. Peirce (pronounced purse). He worked on abduction his whole life. The story of his starting point is helpful in conveying what abduction is about.

In 1879, Peirce[38] was travelling on a coastal steamer from Boston to New York. He went ashore only to realize he'd left his watch aboard ship, a Tiffany watch that meant a lot to him. He rushed back to his stateroom to discover that the watch and his overcoat were missing. To find them, he lined up suspects and asked if one of them had taken his belongings. No one admitted the theft. He was determined to find the thief. As he walked down the line, he stopped and stood before a man and accused him. The man denied it. Later, Peirce went to his house and found the watch and overcoat.

Reflecting on his experience, Peirce concluded that abductive reasoning relies on discovery, a logic of guessing that must be "fundamental to the acquisition of knowledge about all reality, not just the reality of crimes."[39] He conceived a process of guessing in which a seeker moves back and forth from induction (gathering data bit by bit to build a theory) and deduction (choosing a theory and then finding data to support it).

Abduction is a process of perceiving that relies on a theory to get started. As an example, Pierce might think 'the thief is someone who had quick access to my stateroom'. He might have this theory consciously in mind, or not. As he moves forward in his investigation, the theory gets support from his capacity for receptivity, the receptive submission to the situation in front of him. For example, he may have sensed "the thief paused before he answered my question in order to carefully compose a response while those who didn't steal from me spoke immediately, in a confused manner."[40]

In the first steps of abduction, suppose observers actively collect a likely group of people and line them up, so to speak. In the second, they suspend their theories and wait to receive from a person in the line-up some small evidence of calculation, purpose and planning. Pierce may have consciously realized only afterward (or not at all) what the thief did to trigger his guess. The seeker is using theory and being receptive. American author Malcolm Gladwell described this receptivity in his book *Blink* (2005), although he didn't use the term abduction.

Abduction moves back and forth from induction to deduction. It requires a theory and involves the suspension of theory. Suspending theory allows for observation to take place in small amounts or 'thin slices' of time. To Gladwell, "thin-slicing refers to the ability of our [mind] to find patterns in situations and behaviour based on very narrow bits of experience."[41] Gladwell relied on John Gottman's research, which used thin-slicing to investigate marital dysfunction.

Gottman acquired an ability to detect marital dysfunction with great speed. He taught his students to do the same. He identified the central indicator of marital dysfunction in a tone of voice and manner that conveyed contempt. Contempt is a thin slice of a bigger pattern. Through observation, Gottman noted that "having someone you love express contempt toward you is so stressful that it begins to affect the functioning of your immune system."[42] A contemptuous tone of voice isn't a one-off way to speak to someone—it's a way of thinking about the person that can't be disguised by a tone of voice. Through observing videos of couple interaction, Gottman predicted with remarkable accuracy the marriages that would last for the next 15 years and those that would break up during that period of time.

For those who want to learn social literacy, the example of a contemptuous tone of voice is instructive. The role of contempt is similar to disgust which has an effect of completely rejecting and excluding someone from community.[43] Through tone of voice, one member of a relationship is approaching maximal exclusion, as in Leary's inclusionary-status continuum, described at the beginning of the chapter. A tone of contempt means that someone is in trouble, since respect and its absence are most clearly communicated through tone of voice.[44] Tone of voice is caught in an instant and resides in most utterances. If marriage counsellors use abduction to identify patterns in a marriage, teachers can use tone of voice and gestures to assess stress between two students, one of whom bodily demonstrates effects of abuse. (Although someone who's skilled can shift tone of voice depending on who they're speaking to; and spouses seldom speak to neighbours and strangers with a tone of voice they've come to use with each other.)

As Gladwell put it, thin-slicing is not an exotic gift; it's a central part of what it means to be human.[45] Perhaps thin-slicing is more of a low road reading of the world, but using the high road helps to gain control of thin-slicing in an encounter with another person. Thin-slicing isn't a term Pierce used. Yet in abductive reasoning, people are receptive to the reality of those who stand before them. During receptivity, an instantaneous guess doesn't present itself as a thought, although later someone may realize that it works as a good theory and may organize their perception into a research framework.[46] In being receptive, an observer sets aside theory until she or he perceives a response that gives itself away. That theory is a hunch. It's verified by checking it against reality, in Pierce's case, by finding his stolen items.

Abduction involves activity and receptivity; the active initiation of theory and the active holding back of theory until one is receptive to the present moment and its meaning.[47] Abduction isn't a process of guesswork in which we act impulsively on a hunch; hunches appear and are checked-out by observing reality that's readily available. In abduction, researchers find patterns to explain what's going on. They can't let theory get in the way of receptivity but need theory to find a pattern in what they're seeing. There's an iterative relationship between theory and receptivity that builds toward eventually guessing what's going on—a perception that's checked against reality. Abduction develops through practising *Action Science,* as referred to earlier. And abduction is a humble process. It's based on the willingness to be wrong and to try again.

Identifying patterns that lie behind thin slices of experience, Pierce believed, led to a better understanding of reality. To explore his insight further, let's rely on a pivotal insight from French philosopher Michel Foucault's observations in *Discipline and Punish.* To show how power operates, he directed our gaze (and receptivity) to those who have been subjected to its use and abuse. He proposed that the effects of power reside in the body that experiences its impact. Let's look at an example.

The movie *Doubt,* with Meryl Streep, Philip Seymour Hoffman and Amy Adams demonstrates receptivity to abuse by using abductive reasoning, although no one uses that term. It's about a Catholic parish school in the 1960s. Streep is its Principal. She's an older nun who works with a priest (Hoffman). At one point, Streep comes to believe that the priest is sexually interfering with some of the boys. She confronts him with the help of a young nun (Adams), also a teacher. Adams recounts an observation she made of a boy in her class after he returned from a private session with the priest. She described the way the boy re-entered the classroom and put his head on his desk. The motion of laying his head down on his desk and his silence were evidence for her that something was wrong. Together, Streep and Adams confront Hoffman, who demands that Streep provide some evidence. She cited an observation of another boy who quickly pulled his hand away as Hoffman stretched out his hand toward the boy while they were both in the playground. During the movie, a third boy showed evidence of being uncomfortable at school. Streep saw in these gestures evidence of a larger pattern—action taken in private between a powerful and a powerless person. The privacy of sexual abuse withholds from public view evidence of its harm, but residual behaviour remains in the child.

The abuser may be skilled at lying, smooth in social interaction, talented at securing pity and support from a group of powerful people, as was Hoffman. As a result, his behaviour was hard for others to imagine. But observe the child, as Foucault told us. Abuse resides in the child's body. As Hoffman gestured toward him in public, the movement of his hand triggered a private offense in the boy. The body remembered. The boy recoiled. That movement, a thin slice, was enough for Streep to hypothesize that sexual abuse was going on.

The entire movie demonstrates abductive reasoning. Streep began to observe Hoffman at the beginning of the movie because of a sermon he preached—a thin slice that triggered her concern. The movie demonstrates that abductive reasoning is risky. There are many reasons why it's titled *Doubt*. It's only because Streep recognized a whole pattern in a small gesture that she carried out an inquiry into Hoffman's behaviour. She got little support from the social world in which she was trying to act. At one point, even Adams doubts her. It's isolating to see a pattern behind actions if you're the only one who sees it—as industrial whistle-blowers can attest.

As with any type of research, abduction seeks pattern among data. The search moves ahead by choosing theories and responding to reality. Researchers rely on theories they already have in mind or find, and actively hold back theory to allow data to speak for itself. How does a person acquire this insight into social interaction in order to become literate? In the next section, I describe an educational model that depends on face-to-face encounters, as one way to think about how social literacy is learned.

MASTERING SOCIAL LITERACY

Social literacy refers to developed capacities used in social interaction and adapted to authentic responses that move an encounter toward positive outcomes based on mutual respect and caring.

Suppose you are having coffee with a young mother in her kitchen. Her two-year old girl enters the kitchen, babbles something and looks as if she may start to cry. The mother quickly gets up, moves close to the child, bends down, smiles, and asks the child, "What do you want?" She realizes the child is hungry, shy because you're present and she doesn't know you. The mother doesn't want you to feel embarrassed if the child expresses discomfort, so she moves quickly. She gets a cookie, lifts the child to her knee while conversing with you. The child eats her cookie and slowly studies you from a safe place. The mother's response is a complex social interaction, performed smoothly—a demonstration of social intelligence. She shows concern for the humanity of her child and the humanity of her guest. Competent social intelligence enables people to make others more at home in the world.

American philosopher Hubert Dreyfus[48] identified 7 stages of learning that culminate in mastering complex skills. He believed that later stages depend on, and grow out of, earlier ones. Moving toward mastery involves instruction, practice and apprenticeship. Dreyfus wondered whether learning to be masterful could be achieved *via* computer-mediated-communication. He came to believe it couldn't. Mastery of a complex skill is achieved bodily, in face-to-face encounters. His approach is well suited to learning social literacy—which is learned face-to-face. For him, omitting the body from learning environments leads to a loss of ability to recognize relevance, loss of skill acquisition, loss of a sense of the reality of people and things and a loss of meaning.

Social literacy couldn't function well in the presence of these absences. The young mother applied her skill in a face-to-face situation by reading the faces of her child and her guest. What follows is a summary of how to master that complex task. I make reference to a young man who's learning to drive a car with a standard transmission to explain some of the stages. Recall that learning social literacy involves abduction, as outlined earlier.

Stage #1 Novice

Inexperienced learners are given *features and rules.* Teachers begin by decomposing the task to be learned into its context-free features that beginners can recognize from everyday life. Suppose a teacher wants to teach grade one children about parallel lines. He might take them outside and put them in pairs, each pair with a piece of string. Then he asks one child to walk along an edge of sidewalk and the other to walk along its other edge, keeping the string tight. Back in class, he points out that they walked along parallel lines when the string stayed tight. These children learned about parallel lines because they knew how to keep string taut, walk a straight line and talk to one another. These features are domain-independent.

At this stage, novices are given rules for determining actions based on context-free features like a computer following a program. *Walk at the same pace as your partner. Continue holding the string without letting it get loose.* Learners must recognize features, engage in drill and practice, and then apply these features to a new situation. For example, when learning to drive a car, learners recognize domain-independent features such as speed (speedometer) and receive and use rules, such as: *Shift gears as the speedometer points to 10 m.p.h.*

Stage #2 Advanced Beginner

Learners now have some experience and are given *maxims.* A maxim is a building block for learning principles of operation that eventually shape a person's chosen way of life, or character. Unlike rules, a maxim requires learners to have some understanding of the domain to which it applies. They become discerning by using maxims. As novices gain experience coping with real situations, they begin to develop an understanding of relevant aspects and note, or an instructor points out, fruitful examples of additional aspects of the situation. After seeing a sufficient number of examples, they learn to notice new aspects. Instructional *maxims* are used at this stage.

A maxim is tried out in new situations, recognized through experience and applied to objectively defined, non-situational features already known to a novice. An advanced beginning driver uses situational aspects (engine sounds) as well as non-situational features (speed) to decide when to shift gears. In addition to rules acquired by a novice, he learns the maxim: *shift up when the motor sounds like it's racing, down when it sounds like it's straining.* Since engine sounds aren't adequately captured in a list, at this stage of learning, features can't take the place of choice examples in learning to be discerning. The advanced beginner learns to drive by making mistakes such as racing the engine, until he recognizes the sound of a racing engine.

Stage #3 Competent Learner

Competent learners have experience and can identify the potential relevance of aspects of a situation. With more experience, the number of potentially relevant elements and procedures that learners can recognize is overwhelming. Since a confident sense of what's important is missing, performance is nerve-racking and exhausting. Learners wonder how anyone ever masters the skill or gains know-how. To cope with overload and achieve competence, people learn through instruction and experience to devise a plan, or choose a perspective that determines which of the situational aspects must be treated as important, which can be ignored. As they learn to restrict themselves to a few of many possibly relevant aspects, their understanding and decision-making become easier.

To avoid mistakes, the competent learner seeks rules and reasoning procedures to decide which plan or perspective to adopt. But rules such as these aren't easy to come by if the learner is expecting the ease with which features/rules, relevance/maxims were acquired at earlier stages—even though they weren't experienced as easy then. In learning a complex skill, there are many situations than can't be named or precisely defined. No one can prepare learners with a list of types of possible situations and what to look for in each one. Students must decide for themselves in each situation what plan or perspective to adopt, without being sure that it will turn out to be appropriate.

Given the level of uncertainty inherent in becoming competent, coping is frightening and exhausting. Prior to this stage, learners could rationalize that they weren't given adequate rules for doing what they wanted to do. When they have someone else to blame, they feel no remorse for errors. But at this stage, results depend on learners themselves. They feel responsible for their choices and the confusion and failures that occur. On the other hand, choices sometimes work out well and learners feel elation unknown to novices. The role of emotion in becoming competent is important. Embodied human beings take success and failure seriously. Learners are understandably scared, elated, disappointed, discouraged or inspired by outcomes of a choice.

As competent learners become more emotionally involved in the task, it's increasingly difficult to draw back and adopt a maxim-following stance, as advanced beginners do. The strangeness of this stage is felt deeply. Learners believe they're getting better, but feel worse about what they're doing. Involvement is upsetting. One response to this distress may be to withdraw from moving forward. This is the wrong move to make.

Unless learners stay emotionally involved and accept the joy of a job well done, as well as remorse for mistakes, they won't develop mastery. They'll burn out trying to keep track of all the features, aspects and rules that a domain requires. In general, resistance to involvement and risk leads to stagnation and ultimately to boredom and regression. At this point teachers matter a great deal. They influence whether students withdraw into dis-embodied minds or become emotionally involved in learning.

A teacher's manner and embodied perspective provides a model for learners. Teachers may be involved or detached: either way, learners pick up their approach, responses, hope or despair. If teachers are open and involved, if they take risks and continue to learn from their failures and successes, their courage is transmitted to learners. Courage constitutes the best possible embodied perspective for learners to experience in order to move on to mastery.

A competent driver leaving the freeway on an off-ramp curve learns to pay attention to the speed of the car, rather than whether to shift gears. After taking speed into account, surface conditions, criticality of time, he decides he's going too fast. He then has to decide whether to let up on the accelerator, remove his foot altogether, or step on the brake and precisely when to perform these actions. He's relieved if he gets through the curve without mishap and is shaken if he begins to go into a skid. In this way, he begins to acquire principles of action to replace rules and maxims. With principles, if he takes time to reflect, two questions are always necessary: e.g., what does good driving look like? Is the way I'm driving an example of good driving?

Stage #4 Proficient Learner

Proficient learners are involved. They see issues immediately but must decide what to do. If the detached, information-consuming stance of novices and advanced beginners is replaced by involvement, learners are ready to advance. The resulting positive and negative emotional experiences strengthen successful responses and inhibit unsuccessful ones. Learners' developed theory of the skill, as represented by rules and maxims, gradually is replaced by situational discriminations, accompanied by associated responses. Proficiency seems to develop *only if* experience is assimilated in an embodied, a-theoretical way.

Only then do intuitive reactions replace reasoned responses. Action becomes easier and less stressful as learners simply see what needs to be done rather than calculating among several possible alternatives. Students learn to act appropriately. There is less doubt about taking action. They learn to discriminate among options, even though they are deeply involved. They still need to decide what to do even though they're discriminating. They see goals and salient aspects of the situation but action isn't immediate. Though seeing what matters occurs spontaneously, they may fall back on detached rule following or maxim following at this stage.

A proficient driver, approaching a curve on a rainy day, may *feel in the seat of his pants* that he's going dangerously fast. He must decide whether to apply the brakes or reduce pressure by some specific amount on the accelerator. Valuable time is lost while he decides. A proficient driver is likely to negotiate the curve more safely than the competent driver who must consider speed, angle of the bank, felt gravitational forces before deciding if the car's speed is excessive.

Stage # 5 Expert

An expert sees what needs to be done and understands how to do it. The ability to make more refined, subtle discriminations separates experts from proficient learners. In situations all seen as similar, an expert distinguishes between situations requiring one response from those demanding another. With experience in a variety of situations, all seen from the same perspective but requiring different tactical decisions, the brain of an expert gradually decomposes classes of situations into subclasses, each requiring a specific response, that allow the immediate intuitive situational response that's characteristic of expertise.

In teacher-student relationships, observation and imitation of expert teachers replaces the random search for better ways to act. Simulations or case-study learning help make the shift from a classroom to real life. It's not sufficient simply to work through lots of cases. Case studies must matter to learners. Flight simulators are effective in learning to fly a plane because they create credible conditions that provide stress and risk. For case studies to work, students must be emotionally involved and identify with the experience of people in the scenario. The most reliable way to produce involvement is to be an apprentice. By imitating a master, learners gain abilities for which there are no rules, e.g., how long to persist when work doesn't seem to be going well, how much precision should be sought in research situations.

The role of a master is to pass on to an apprentice the ability to apply theory in the real world. Master and apprentice must be immersed in a setting. Suppose someone is trying to become a masterful medical doctor. In becoming a master at diagnosis, the instructor has learned to see an already-interpreted situation in which certain features and aspects spontaneously stand out as meaningful, just as when one is familiar with a new city, it ceases to look like a jumble of buildings and streets and develops a familiar face. A medical intern is trying, among other things, to acquire a masterful doctor's physiognomic perceptual understanding—that is, to recognize the pattern in what's going on. In transmitting an informed understanding of the domain, teachers can't help demonstrating the perspective they take that typifies the way they do things. As a consequence, apprentices pick up an embodied perspective. In addition to content, they adopt a personal style.

The expert driver not only *feels in the seat of his pants* when speed is an issue but knows how to perform the appropriate action without calculating and comparing alternatives. On the off-ramp, his foot slips off the accelerator and applies the appropriate pressure to the brake. What must be done is done simply. It's at this point that observers who haven't achieved mastery with his skill will fail to perceive all that's gone into making it all look 'so simple'.

Stage # 6 Being Masterful: Discernment Plus Personal Style (Authenticity)

For passing on style, Dreyfus thought that apprenticeship is the only method available. This isn't to say that teachers produce clones. Working with different masters (as musicians do) becomes a way of finding one's own style. To shift from the driving example to a musical one, it's not that a young musician should go to one teacher for fingering, another for phrasing. Skill components can't be divided this way. Rather, one master has a whole style. Another master has an entirely different whole style. When apprentices work with more than one master, they're destabilized and confused. As a result, they can't copy any one master so they must develop their own style. This is what's called mastery. Learners develop personal style to shape discernment they've acquired over time and through experience. If we think about our driver, at this point, he takes on a personal way of managing a car. As examples, he will change his own oil or he will take it in to get an oil change. He'll use every opportunity to speed or he'll obey speed limits whether or not police are present.

Stage #7 Acquiring Practical Wisdom: Discernment, Authenticity Plus Cultural Style

Practical wisdom is the highest level of mastery. This stage adds cultural style to personal style. Culture is learned by being among others who have already learned it. It's often invisible unless we experience a different way of doing things. Learning about our own culture is a bit like setting up house with someone who uses the toothpaste tube by squeezing it in the middle, while we always thought it could only be squeezed from the end, with precision.

As we notice our differences, we come to see how things are done and, as importantly, to see how we do things ourselves. Once we understand there's cultural style to the way people do things, a style that governs how anything can show up for what it is, we notice that a broad, cultural style shapes that society's members. As a consequence, practical wisdom allows someone to adapt her or his personal style to a specific cultural setting.

Learning practical wisdom requires being with others face-to face. Wisdom is learned in relationship. Other masters recognize the complex skill of social literacy for what it is. To get a better sense of practical wisdom, we might consider the way good driving would look on a Canadian or American highway versus the way it looks on the German Autobahn.

AUTHENTICITY AND PERSONAL STYLE

Social literacy is a complex skill to be mastered. If it's learned well, people engage with others in a healthy way: neither person dominates a social interaction nor gets lost in it. Dreyfus's last two stages require self, social and cultural knowledge. In terms of self and social knowledge, the next section outlines dimensions of personal style for stage six learning. The seventh stage requires that we perceive and achieve cultural style. The seventh stage is explored in several chapters, e.g., in "Culture, Memes and Social Learning" and "The Resilient City."

Social intelligence relies on abilities all people have due to genetic endowment and cultural learning, expressed in certain habits they develop. Before outlining personal styles, the philosophical idea of habit or *hexis* is a useful way to think about how we acquire the self and social knowledge that allows us to see what we're doing and to better understand what others do.

The idea of *hexis* goes back to Aristotle and plays a role in Western philosophy.[49] For Aristotle, habit (*hexis*) was an active tendency to behave in a particular manner. It's a way of being that becomes second nature and is expressed in a person's principles of action. *Hexis* is an acquired tendency to act and react in certain ways. To

Aristotle, some dimensions are acquired through cultural learning; some seemed innate. For Aquinas, following Aristotle, habit (which he called *habitus*) implied that principles of action enhance rational capacities and improve one's manner of acting so that *habitus* (habit) was understood as a tendency to act well, with strength.[50]

To Aquinas, habit gave perfection to one's original potential. Different theorists used the Greek *hexis* or the Latin *habitus* for habit, so that the terms were interchangeable, but a general understanding of the term meant that one's habits were a tendency to act in a way that became recognized as expressing strength of character.

In contrast to its previous development, French sociologist Pierre Bourdieu distinguished *hexis* from *habitus*. To him, *hexis* is personal; *habitus* is socio-cultural. That is, people *and* cultures have a way of operating that's characteristic of a given era. He pointed out that one's personal habits (*hexis*) must conform to dominant cultural habits (*habitus*) in order to find one's place as a competent individual, to secure, as he put it, a post in the field. This point is implicit in Dreyfus's stages and explicit in American educator Howard Gardner's analysis of intellectual styles (1983, 1993). Gardner[51] noted two aspects of intelligence: individuals who are capable of using an array of competencies in various domains of knowledge; societies that foster individual development through opportunities they provide, institutions they support and values they live out.

To be thought of as intelligent, an individual's *hexis* must match the dominant *habitus*. A distinction between *hexis* and *habitus* (whether or not the terms are used) is one root of post-modern criticisms of modernity. During modernity, following men such as Aristotle and Aquinas (whose *hexis* matched the *habitus*) many were unaware of the privilege their identities enjoyed. Theorists such as Franz Fanon, and feminists of many types, noted that privilege is socially constructed rather than necessarily inherent in the merit of individuals. That is, the *hexis* of men such as Aristotle and Aquinas was advantaged by the *habitus* of their culture—theirs was the preferred *hexis*, whether or not a match provides society with the most beneficial attributes needed at a particular time. A fit between *hexis* and *habitus*, at times, will simply confirm the *status quo*.

Social literacy acknowledges this insight about the match or mismatch between *hexis* and *habitus*. Those who gain competence in social literacy are people who decode a person's way of being (and their own), perceive differences between *hexis* and *habitus*, and apply a hermeneutical rigor that allows for individual differences to gain meaning, even if a *hexis* fails to conform to the dominant *habitus*. Interpreting *hexis* in the light of *habitus* is a complex interpretive skill that has become more necessary in this century, and is an essential feature of Dreyfus's stage seven.

An individual *hexis* develops from a set of beliefs that people acquire over time and that shape their principled ways of acting in the world. As Distin put it, "human minds are furnished with all sorts of mental states and events, including thoughts and feelings, attitudes and opinions, memories and skills; [each of which is] a 'representation'...some piece of our mental furniture which carries information about the world."[52] Representations, the content of mental life, are fixed as beliefs in the following way:

> Beliefs are those natural, internal indicators [that] have become representations with the function of controlling a certain behaviour, *because of* the information they carry about external situations, and *in order that* the behaviour may be produced whenever that situation occurs.[53] [italics original]

Once again, learning social literacy is related to a developing ability to perceive patterns that explain people's behaviour. These patterns form from particular beliefs people hold, based on the history of their experience. The goal of being oneself in the company of other people is, in part, realized through perceiving these social patterns.

For this reason, to acquire self-understanding as a hermeneutical skill, I list several dimensions of personal style that those who want to be socially literate aim to understand about themselves and others. The list isn't exhaustive. It's a useful tool for analyzing self and social knowledge. It helps us realize people differ from one another in legitimate ways and provides concrete patterns for those differences.

Whenever they remain under-analyzed, these differences in personal style thwart social interaction. This section is intended to whet curiosity for more ways of seeing that we're not the same as others, to help us notice when someone is making a contribution despite their differences from the dominant *habitus* and to increase the capacity to make good use of self and social knowledge.

Personal Styles

Plato and Socrates are at the heart of Western understanding of what education should be like. In the *Republic,* Plato wrote dialogues that Socrates had with those who spoke with him about what it means to be wise. To Plato and Socrates the essence of good teaching centered on observing the learner. In the *Republic,* Socrates told his hearers a story about gold, silver and bronze to say that teachers should observe what learners already are as they help them discover what they can become. In sharp contrast to his social world, Socrates asserted that we shouldn't put aristocratic children in aristocratic positions unless they have a gift for the task. He urged his hearers to look for the gold (rulers), silver (guardians) and bronze (craftspeople) in everyone so that the task and person would be a good fit. Many of his hearers were unimpressed with his story. The rich wanted their offspring to occupy places of power. They had no intention of doing otherwise, whether or not their children had a gift for leadership.

Yet his idea that we should attend to children in order to help them identify their future is imperative if we teach social literacy. I suggest it's not possible to teach social literacy unless we attend to what's already in students. I've taught education and leadership courses for many years and always ask students to assess themselves by using several tests. The aim is to build self and social knowledge. I want students to gain access to their own way of being and realize that other people are different. This sounds simple, but the depth of new insight graduate students gather about themselves always surprises me. The following assessments help explain social behavior. Over time, I've observed that many people come to identify overriding patterns in their personal style that help them manage social relationships more effectively.

As a backdrop to presenting these assessments, I assume that people are like soccer balls. We have flat sides sewn together to create the unity that makes up our identity. Each side can be assessed separately as long as we remember that the way we're stitched together is unique. Or perhaps we're more complex, like geodesic domes, with many facets glued together to make a sphere. The dimensions of personal style listed below are some of those facets. Two questions help to organize the pattern of our personal style: What do I bring to the table? What's it like for other people to experience me? These questions function within a framework mentioned earlier, of social trust, social love and empathy that motivate the development of someone's *hexis*, their principled way of being.

Action Style

The term action style is used by American management strategist Kathy Kolbe (1990; 2004).[54] She employed a Latin term *conatus* to convey a pattern that applies to the characteristic way people do things. She used the term *conatus* (which has to do with willing) to get a descriptor (conation) to describe every person's orientation to action. A conative style combines the mental domains of action and will.[55] Conation has to do with desire, volition and striving. Kolbe identified patterns that apply to how we carry out plans of action. Her categories include people who engage in fact finding, follow-through, are quick starts or implementation oriented.

These action styles express how people tend to expend effort.[56]

For example, some get off the mark right away to start the task while others take time to gather data before starting. Those who are oriented towards starting quickly may leave a task when others might think it isn't finished. Some people work through a task until all its aspects are tidied up. Kolbe found no correlation between action styles and social style (personality).[57] Teachers who understand individual action styles can put children in groups effectively and can encourage a well-rounded action orientation since they realize the young approach tasks differently. If teachers are aware of action styles, they can help children name their preferences and build good work habits. Her action style assessment, the *Kolbe Questionnaire,* is found on-line.

Attachment Style

Attachment theory is the result of initial research carried out by John Bowlby and Mary Ainsworth.[58] Goleman (2006) identified attachment's importance to social intelligence and referred to three categories established by Ainsworth in her *Strange Situation* experiment with mothers and infants in which she assessed how we relate to important people in our lives. Her findings were generalized to say that we may be secure, anxious or avoidant. Josephine Klein's (1987) analysis is also a full description of attachment behavior.

Attachment has to do with our link to significant people. Klein saw that attachment is based on biological needs that permit infants to survive. She divided attachment experience into two categories using playful terms: some people are home loving (homebodies) and some are space loving (spacebats). Homebodies tend to organize attachment around people. Spacebats tend to organize attachment around space, equipment and skill. Homebodies need to feel in tune with chosen people or attachment figures. They believe they can win the favor of their chosen people and need to be in contact (closely attached) so they keep in touch with them. Spacebats need to feel in tune with the whole world. They believe they can conquer the world without relying on anyone's favor. They tend to watch others from a safe distant and use their eyes and ears to be alert. They relate to others by making them safe by using their interpersonal skill. Homebodies and spacebats have something to teach us about the people we work with, and ourselves, that matters as we try to work together. At the present time, attachment theories are finding a place in discussions aimed at understanding addiction.

Emotional Style

Temperament (emotional style) refers to a tendency to approach or withdraw from new or foreign experiences and refers to how people tend to react to life in general. Temperament shows up in infancy, which leads to the conclusion that it's part of our genetic endowment. While environment influences it, temperament is somewhat stable over time. To psychologist Jerome Kagan (1998) temperament is a tendency to be inhibited or uninhibited. He acknowledged that temperament is multi-dimensional but its main description is seen in approach or withdrawal tendencies that appear in infants. We might use other words when speaking about temperament, e.g., extroverted or fearless, versus introverted and fearful. In addition to Kagan, Chess and Thomas developed an assessment of nine temperament traits: Activity level, Intensity, Sensitivity, First reaction, Adaptability, Mood, Frustration reaction, Distractibility and Rhythmicity (regularity) as components of temperament, which are summarized by Mary Gordon (2005).[59] Theories about temperament suggest that we learn to respond more effectively to others if we perceive these differences as part of someone's personal style, rather than as a personality flaw that can spark clashes between people who are very different from each other.

Intellectual Style[60]

To American educator Howard Gardner, intelligence isn't limited to the Intelligence Quotient (IQ) tests that were so popular in the twentieth century. Intelligence is an ability to solve problems or create products that are valued within one or more cultural settings.[61] Intelligence comes in various forms. The aim of presenting these intelligences, rather than presenting intelligence as one general category that some have and others don't, is to help us see—not whether someone is smart or stupid—but to discover particular ways in which everyone is smart. The theory of multiple intelligences is based on some assumptions: for example, not all people have the same interests and abilities; not all of us learn in the same way; no one can learn everything there is to learn. As with other personal styles that show up at birth (and may be genetic) the expression of one's intelligence is also strongly influenced if it receives support from home and educational environments. If we want to support and encourage a range of ways of being smart, social structures and institutions need to recognize and honor different ways of demonstrating ability.

Involvement Style

Involvement style has to do with a person's preferred way of working in human systems. As we become system thinkers, we learn to detect a web of influences that's impacting someone's actions and reactions, rather than thinking each event is random. *Involvement Style* assessments allow us to see the overall process that's taking place, rather than merely seeing each event as an isolated snap-shot. We learn to resolve issues rather than staying angry and withdrawing from a task and other people—physically or emotionally—because they're different from us. Over time, we realize we can choose to be angry and withdraw, or we can become systems thinkers. In addition, the assessment shows that an organization moves through a life cycle from birth to adulthood. Organizations grow old and die, depending on whether they take adequate account of four activities: visioning, relating, programming and managing.

American management strategist George Bullard identified these four activities and assesses organizations in terms of life cycle stages by showing whether these four activities are well-functioning or out of balance with one another. His insights are contained with the *Involvement Styles* assessment. Bellous and Bellous developed a self-assessment to measures the activities: visioning, relating, programming and managing, available at tallpinepress@gmail.com or www.tallpinepress.com.

Learning Style

A learning style identifies how people perceive and process data. While there are many models, the Kolb Learning Style Inventory is widely used. Kolb developed the instrument into a tool that's easily accessible and has other applications for helping people work in teams. The Inventory works well with the Involvement Style assessment. The Kolb Inventory divides learning styles into four types: learning through thinking, feeling (experiencing), observing or doing. In addition to gaining self-knowledge, the assessment helps people identify differences in the way others learn. As insight accumulates, groups or teams move away from taking differences personally or being negative toward those who have a different style. They try to ensure that teams have access to these different ways to learn and try to help team members understand each other's language and behavior. If we understand the different learning styles, we have a way of perceiving what others on the team are doing or not doing and why. For more information, see the *Kolb Learning Style Inventory* (LSI) *Workbook*, which is available through www.haygroup.com.

Social Style

The expression social style refers to human personality. Everyone has a way of relating to others based on patterns acquired through life. One well-researched personality assessment is the *Myers-Briggs Type Indicator*. If a group or team gathers self-knowledge through its analysis, it's important to share that information with one another and keep the differences that the Indicator identifies handy when a difficult situation arises. If people refer to their social style as one way to explain and negotiate their way through conflict, self and social knowledge builds and offers a way to make it easier to work together. Myers-Briggs isn't the only personality test.

Some of the other personality assessments include *Insight* (insightlearning.com), DISC Profile (onlinediscprofile.com) and *Enneagram* (EnneagramInstitute.com). In addition, there are sites on-line that allow people to assess their personality at a reasonable cost. A role personality plays in working with others is significant but it's not the only facet of personal style that's helps us understand how to collaborate with others and how to learn social literacy.

Spiritual Style

Spiritual styles describe how we try to make the world a better place or improve a situation. Four ways people typically try to improve a situation include: using words, feelings, symbols or by taking action. We rely on these four approaches to express our ultimate concerns. Spiritual style indicates how people think, act and speak about what really matters to them. How we try to make the world a better place is a deeply felt urge. Since these issues go very deep into one's sense of what's important, people may miss each other's meaning because they rely on different ways to express what really matters to them. The aim of the assessment is to enable people to work more effectively in settings where they talk about what really matters. A rich, supportive environment is saturated by exposure to all four of spiritual styles. For background information on spiritual styles, see Joyce E. Bellous, *Educating Faith* (Tall Pine Press, 2012) and Joyce E. Bellous and Dan Sheffield, *Conversations that Change Us* (Clements, 2007). The assessment tools, for adults and for children [Bellous, Csinos and Peltomaki] are available at tallpinepress@gmail.com or www.tallpinepress.com.

CONCLUSION

The primary purpose for taking self-assessments, such as those listed above, is for personal self awareness, team learning and trust building. In order for complexity to achieve stability in our complex social world, self and social understanding offers a way forward for those who take civility seriously. If we refuse to let social intelligence lie dormant or remain under-developed, we take up the challenge of civil personality that aims toward finding stability in our current complexity. Using abduction to undergird the research human beings are capable of, those who move toward a more civil character, learn to master themselves while they're with other people—not in order to manipulate—but in order to understand others as well as themselves.

In this chapter I present several ideas that are linked to the possibility of being *near and different,* which is the outcome of learning social literacy. In the following chapter, I develop more fully the relationships between social trust and civility and their connection to naming and maintaining one's own identity in the presence of those who matter to us. I add a dimension to the social literacy curriculum that focuses on our ability to think on our feet, which is an essential aspect of being with others and remaining true to ourselves while we're with them. Thinking on our feet allows us to reflect on our own experience at the same time that we learn to perceive the meaning that someone else is bringing to the encounter.

3

HUMAN CONNECTION

INTRODUCTION

An absence of a sense of felt connection to others is at the root of harm depicted in scenarios presented in the introduction. If you recall one of them, a young man couldn't see why the mother of a young woman he killed would be crying as they both sat in a courtroom. In the previous chapter, being *near and different,* made possible by a lively sense of felt connection in a healthy community, is cited as an outcome of learning social literacy. There's a vast distance between that young man's reality and the experience of learning social literacy. Could any human being traverse that expanse?

Well, there's Brian. When he was 2 years old, his parents packed a suitcase and took him to Yonge Street in Toronto. They sat him down on his luggage. Then they walked away. In his opinion, if you trace the approximately 5000 children who were abandoned by parents in that area around the same time, you'll find a connection between them and motorcycle gangs that spread across Canada in the last several decades. He was part of those gangs and ended up in prison for many years. When released, he was dropped off in a city he had never been to before, lived on the street and was sleeping rough for 3 years. He was one of the first people to be housed through a city program called *Housing First,* part of a 10 year plan to end homelessness. The day before I first heard Brian speak, he was baptised into the community of a local church where he's a valued member. He's very clear that he had to unlearn and learn many things as he became part of that community—not because he wasn't welcome but because his own demons continued to haunt him for a long time.[1]

In this chapter, I explore aspects of the glue that holds people together so that they feel authentic and safe in the company of other people. Respect is part of that glue, as are social trust, social love and empathy. Respect and trust are a focus for this chapter. Human connection is made possible and attractive if people are skilled at showing each other respect. Human beings need respect from others in order to live a truly human life. As Richard Sennett suggests, for respect to be persuasive, it must be "felt and convincing."[2]

The truth he conveys is that we don't feel respected unless the sentiment is genuine. We can't bestow respect on ourselves. We're respected, or not, by other people. It's a received assurance that requires us to trust that the sentiment is sincere. Simply put, our need for respect implies our need for other people. It's true that we must trust and internalize that respect. But perhaps the process isn't unlike bullying—the social world creates a setting in which we have no value and we eventually internalize the force of that belief. With respect, it's only if the social world conveys our value that we internalize it as the truth. Our need for others is very great.

In a society that believes strongly in individualism, as ours does in the West, the idea that we depend on others for respect may not appear to be good news. I disagree. It's good news if we learn to use the social power implicit in granting and getting respect in a wise and humane manner that builds character as we develop socially literacy.

Being socially literate includes making the repairs necessary during a social interaction if and when it isn't respectful. We exercise respect by reading other people accurately in terms of the meaning they convey verbally and bodily. We're able to read others because we're connected to them through a common humanity. This isn't to say we're all the same, but we have a capacity to relate that emerges through the social experience of becoming human in the presence of others—a capacity to be *near and different*. Respect is one of the messages we continually search out and (hopefully) receive during these interactions.

In this chapter, I examine our need for others, first by summarizing two educational projects that build trust and respect in the classroom, in addition to Paley's approach that was described in the introduction. These two programs enjoy success in improving social interaction at school, a Canadian program *Roots of Empathy* and a British program *Working with Others.* To contextualize our need for them, I drill down into social capital, a concept that was initiated by Pierre Bourdieu and developed by Harvard sociologist Robert Putnam.

I then offer a framework for social literacy that relies on embodied learning, a process that grows out of a felt sense or felt self, which develops from birth onwards as the structure on which we hang the meaning we make of life and that continues to be the place we work from as we learn to think on our feet.

In exploring a felt sense, I propose that we learn to feel trust and share respect by understanding our own situation more accurately—a situation dependent upon healthy felt sense experience, as described by American psychiatrist Eugene Gendlin, and by appreciating our own worldview more fully, as British psychotherapist Josephine Klein helps us do as she probes our need for others and its roots in infancy. At the end, I unpack Bourdieu's approach to social interaction in which he conveys the possibility of thinking about our own worldview so as to become critically aware of it, *while we are engaged with other people*—i.e., by getting better at thinking on our feet.

My purpose in writing is to demonstrate that we need one another and that social literacy conveys a hopeful view of the future. If adults learn its lessons, children catch these insights so that the social world is able to supply relational resources that make life bearable. But where can these lessons be learned? Where will they be practised?

School classrooms are the oft chosen site for endless reforms that harry teachers if those changes sweep over them like tidal waves. But literacy isn't a fad—social literacy is something everyone needs in order to be effective in human relationships. Classroom cultures inevitably convey how to behave in public, for good or ill. So we're well advised to teach social literacy at school.

SCHOOL AND SOCIAL LITERACY

In describing social interaction among kindergarten children, two common social patterns stood out, bossing and bullying as distinguished from leading. As noted in that chapter, perceiving common human patterns in social interaction is groundwork for learning to read and respond during social encounters to improve them. Paley's work, and two examples that follow, express the idea that learning depends on navigating social interaction with skill and confidence if other talents (academic and practical) are to find a secure place in the world. Through following rules and thinking through maxims, learners move toward the responsibility of deciding what sort of life principles they will choose to live by.

The following two programs are also compelled by a desire to teach children how to be effective relationally. They imply that, without relational skills, our contributions to society go unnoticed at best, or at worst, perpetuate social harm because we use social intelligence to satisfy selfish, isolating interests rather than working for the common good.

Roots Of Empathy

Roots of Empathy focuses on universal human experience and addresses spiritual needs we all have to be heard and understood. The program was developed by Canadian educator Mary Gordon. Her approach supports an essential human trait, one that's fundamental to learning social literacy. As with Nel Noddings' book, *Home School,*[3] Gordon points out that the primary adult activity of being in a family and caring for children receives little support in most school curricula. While schools pay attention to sex education, they may pay little or no attention to educating a child's capacity for extending to others the relational resources we all need in order to flourish. To amend that omission, Gordon's program links school children with a parent who brings her infant regularly to the class. School children experience an infant's development over the course of a year and learn what the infant can teach them.

Her program focuses on teaching parenting skills, and in its portrayal of empathy, she notes that the "ability to attribute mental states to others as a way of understanding their social behaviour is learned from infancy and enhanced by positive experiences in environments in which we grow up."[4] The program has anti-bullying outcomes. She notes that "many women who abuse their children lack empathy—the capacity to understand and respond to the feelings of others—and lack the ability to accurately identify... emotions revealed in facial expressions."[5] As an example, parents who abuse their children may confuse fear with anger, and react to what they perceive as anger with more anger. *Roots of Empathy* helps school children read a baby's emotional state and discuss it together so they become better able to distinguish and understand a variety of emotional states.

Gordon's program teaches emotional literacy, defined as the ability to recognize, understand, cope with and express our emotions in appropriate ways.[6] She points out that an infant's first language is emotion. Gordon's program offers children a first-hand experience in observing and naming an infant's emotional repertoire, with the result that the children in her program are more adept at reading emotional language generally.

Working With Others (WWO)

While *Roots of Empathy* is remarkable in its outcomes, I suggest the following program has advantages in teaching emotional literacy in that it can take a whole school approach to learning skills involved in successfully negotiating human interaction, although both create environments that promote and support character education. The British program *Working with Others* (WWO) is a positive, pro-active approach to social and moral issues involved in classroom interaction and group work. It focuses on teaching skills involved in emotional literacy. The skills are acquired through engaging in trust, communication and problem-solving activities, which are practiced in the classroom at least three times per week.

While WWO refers primarily to emotional literacy, its impact is felt on social interaction in the classroom and the whole school environment, so that it promotes social literacy and anti-bullying behavior. Core skill-building exercises—trust, communication and problem solving—are taught to all adults in the school (if a whole school approach is taken), through well-designed skill based activities rather than simply by talking about theories and ideas that undergird the program. Adults convey these skills to children and youth as they interact with them in class, in hallways, at lunch, or on the playground. WWO activities are built into regular classroom goals and enhance the motivation and achievement of students.

WWO grew out of four years of research (2000-2004) at three universities in England (London, Cambridge, Brighton) as the SPRinG program. SPRinG established evidence-based learning to form the basis for WWO. In 2004, a Brighton University group of researchers, led by Dr. Cathy Ota, entered into partnership with 6 schools to offer training to create and sustain respectful, collaborative classroom environments.

In 2006, membership for WWO included 65 schools and the program continued to grow at an astonishing rate. Schools or groups of schools signed on to the program of their own accord. It wasn't a top-down implementation of curricular change. Buy-in from teachers and whole school staff members was a central goal for WWO trainers. Participation was bottom up and paid for with in-service budget money. Dr. Ota[7] and her teacher trainers provided ongoing support for member schools in the Brighton area, as well as in one day care centre in Hamilton Ontario. Their support included providing well-designed, attractive materials to focus on what they referred to as emotional literacy.

Paley, Gordon and Ota developed approaches that give respect and social trust a central place. Their programs depend on and enhance a human capacity to relax when we're with other people. As Klein noted, "to relax into non-purposive activity (play), to be undefended and not on the watch...is a very rare state for most of us."[8] She explored this capacity to relax when we're with others by quoting American psychotherapist Donald Winnicott. He developed his notion of ego-relatedness by pointing out that the goal of maturity is "not whether you can be on your own, but whether you can be in other people's company, and yet be yourself, and feel comfortable and unthreatened."[9]

The capacity to relax with others is central to learning social literacy. It's built on a willingness and ability to trust people in general, part of learning to be *near and different.* It implies that we have a good sense of how to be ourselves while we're with others so that our capacity to be authentic and integrated allows us to be near to and different from them, even in important ways.

In a capacity to relax, distinctions between collegiality and friendship, work and play are relevant. Social literacy implies that we relax as we work playfully with colleagues.

Foundations In Social Capital[10]

If it's desirable to be authentic and integrated into social life, what can we use as a social glue to hold together our initial attempts to learn this way of being ourselves when we're with other people? Character education and the skill-based programs just described rely on a developed capacity to exercise social trust, in Pierre Bourdieu's terms, social capital.

Social literacy can't develop without a heavy investment in skills associated with wisely trusting other people. Social capital refers to the degree to which members of a community trust one another and engage in reciprocal relations based on that trust. Social capital may be high or low in a given setting. Bourdieu saw that social capital is the groundwork for all other forms of capital accumulation.

The idea of social trust isn't new. Communal contracts, dating back centuries, built social interaction on mutuality and reciprocity.[11] Reciprocal social connections are important rules of conduct. They create and sustain social networks and clarify mutual obligation. Reciprocity is generalized, in the form: "I'll do this for you without expecting anything back, in the confident expectation that someone else will do something for me down the road," or specific, by saying: "I'll do this for you if you do this for me." Social trust isn't about being friends, it's about being friendly, as is social love. Trust is based on social love[12] (*philia*), acting for the common good, which is an intentional, sympathetic response to others, because one comes to see in others the very things one clearly needs for oneself.

In the eighteenth century, David Hume offered a simple parable to capture the dilemma of refusing to act for the common good, thereby refusing to build social capital:

> Your corn is ripe today; mine will be so tomorrow. 'Tis profitable for us both, that I shou'd labour with you today, and that you shou'd aid me tomorrow. I have no kindness for you, and know you have as little for me. I will not, therefore take any pains upon your account; and should I labour with you upon my own account, in expectation of return, I know I shou'd be disappointed, and that I shou'd in vain depend upon your gratitude. Here then I leave you to labour alone; You treat me in the same manner. The seasons change; and both of us lose our harvests for want of mutual confidence and security.[13]

Social capital implies a lack of pretense. We're able to admit that we're sometimes in need—an existential inevitability in human experience that we deny to our detriment.

Social capital refers to networks of connection in which we build up trust as we *do with others not for them.* Reciprocity and an admission of mutual need are essential for trust to develop. Doing for others is laudable, but not as an aspect of social capital. A high level of trust is a better predictor of generosity and philanthropy than is a high level of financial capital because people who've been helped are more likely to offer help. With high social trust, giving time and money tend to go together. Social capital expresses itself in tolerance, solidarity, habits of cooperation and hospitable attitudes that create a generalized willingness to trust others in the face-to-face encounters we have at City Hall, in shops, at work, at church, synagogue or mosque, when we walk downtown or along the streets of our own neighbourhoods.

Social trust is built up face-to-face. It's a form of social interaction that engages people in common endeavors and nurtures their capacity for collective action, even at mundane levels, such as the implicit agreement to let the driver who saw it first have a parking spot in the supermarket lot. Social capital is productive and allows individuals to get work done with less physical capital (tools and equipment). It facilitates spontaneous cooperation and is a moral resource whose supply increases rather than decreases through use. It's an ordinary public good. Like all public goods it tends to be undervalued, undersupplied by, and under invested in by private agencies. Social trust develops in public spaces as a by-product of other activities. It lubricates social cooperation. Co-operation inspires trust.

Social capital expresses itself in dense networks of participation in voluntary groups and associations, where people absorb and maintain norms of civic action and engagement and the social structures that enable interaction to take place.

Do we have the right sort of practices to accommodate current expectations for involved social engagement? For example, *Robert's Rules of Order*, published in 1876 in the United States, was actively and widely used to accommodate the practice of social engagement during the early twentieth century. These rules were based on parliamentary procedures and adapted for ordinary societies, e.g., religious, educational or public meetings, so that people with different expectations and experience could make decisions together. The Parliamentary framework offered rules for presentation and argument, opinion and debate. Does that framework help our current circumstances? I'm not suggesting people still widely use the *Rules* in ordinary societies, although they may, but I wonder if we've found a better way to secure public involvement and conversation in this century.

Social literacy allows people to have their say, yet still make decisions and move toward the common good. Argument and debate are less of a focus. A distinctive feature of social capital is found in the creation of formal organizations that include local chapters where members regularly meet and have as their goal to benefit their cities and neighbourhoods. To Putnam, Rotary Clubs are a good example. A large stock of social capital makes for healthy and vibrant societies, robust democratic practice, effective and efficient economies.

But social capital builds up slowly and erodes quickly. It has the character of something that must be developed and absorbed autonomously, not imposed from above. Unfortunately, once mistrust sets in, it becomes impossible to know if trust was ever justified. Mistrust becomes a self-fulfilling prophecy. If someone tries to compel you, it's evidence they don't have your trust. Freedom is implicit in trust—or it isn't trust.

In building social trust, context matters. During his research, Putnam and his collaborators asked why some areas in the United States are high in social capital while others are low. They discovered that settlement from Scandinavian countries was a predictor of high social capital and the American system of slavery was a primary predictor of low social capital.[14] As he said, the more virulent the system of slavery was in the past, the less civil that State is today. He pointed out that slavery was a social system *designed* to destroy trust among slaves and between slaves and their white masters.[15] His research indicates that the slave system continues to influence the health of present-day institutions and limits their effectiveness in building social capital.

Effective institutional performance depends on and is a function of trust because it's an expectation that arises in a group of regular, honest, cooperative people who have common norms about how to treat one another and how to regard their own contribution to the group. In emotionally unsafe environments even trustful people eventually realize that trust is unwise. Trust is built up or lost through daily interaction as people do their jobs. For example, meetings are an opportunity to express and resolve conflict and allow trust to develop, or they are a place where people learn they have neither voice nor value—and mistrust grows.

Humane institutions *listen and act.* To Putnam, institutions are responsive by listening and effective by taking action. Trust lubricates the connections between listening and acting so that institutions with high social capital have the following summary of features:

- equality
- leaders who compromise

- just as prone to conflict but leaders are readier to resolve their conflicts
- openness to partisanship, i.e., to people who have strong, different views
- leaders who don't deny the reality of conflicting interests
- leaders who are unafraid of creative compromises
- dense local culture and recreational associations.

When leaders listen and act (based on what was accurately heard) they enhance social trust.

In the absence of trust there is no certainty in contracts, no force in laws. Listening and acting are divorced. Social trust calls attention to the fact that civility is most powerful when embedded in dense networks of reciprocal social relations. A society made up of many virtuous but isolated individuals is not rich in social trust.

What Is Trust?

Trust is a way of looking at the world. It's a disposition or attitude that encompasses risk and danger at the same time that it instills hope. Trust counts on people to be and do what they say. To understand trust more fully, we look at what it isn't. Trust is neither gullible nor cynical.

A gullible person gives away too much. To be gullible is to focus on the value of others, ignoring one's own. It's self-disregarding, giving another's voice more weight than one's own. The pattern of gullibility believes everything and jumps to conclusions. It's a character trait that shifts from one quick judgment to another, without counting the cost. It's rash, unpredictable, not grounded on hope. Its attitude is hasty, perpetually open, but unreflectively so. Gullibility doesn't take stock of its own reality and the actual situation of other people. It accepts any evidence, however small, for action it takes. Gullibility is anxious with worry and unwise. In terms of time, it's impatient and won't wait for evidence. It's an approach to life that creates an optimist who attempts everything and burns out trying to do it all.

A cynical person gives away too little. It's a character trait of the self-absorbed. A cynical attitude is self-preserving at other people's expense. It stubbornly refuses to be generous with others and resists attributing value to what they say. Cynicism refuses to be caught out as foolish or wrong and seldom takes action. It commits to nothing and never arrives at a final judgment. It feeds on sarcasm and contempt. It refuses to take risks. It resides in a heart that's hardened and lives without hope. Its pessimism is unmoved by human need. Cynicism is anxious due to anger and disappointment. It believes nothing it can't prove; yet no evidence will suffice. It treats all evidence with suspicion. In its use of time, it won't stop waiting for evidence before acting, due to its relentless skepticism. Cynicism solidifies into pessimism that attempts nothing. A cynic is stuck and rusts out in a refusal to live a full life or contribute to fullness of life for other people.

In contrast to gullibility and cynicism, trust is relational. It has a hopeful approach to life and other people. Trust is willing to converse and be wrong, but aims to make sound judgments. It revises its judgments in order to be reciprocal. It isn't hasty, but is willing to act on judgments and take risks. Trust is discerning and conveys a non-anxious presence. As a character trait, it's able to believe in advance on some basis but looks for evidence and interprets it effectively. Trust knows it has time; it isn't hasty or stuck. It recognizes and assesses how harm operates in people and in social systems and takes harm into account when responding to human behavior.

Trust is hopeful, not blind. Hope sees that life is complex. Not everything one wants can be accomplished. People of hope tell optimists there are degrees of accomplishment in what can be done—not everything is possible. A hopist says to pessimists that we have to try to do things that seem impossible otherwise we foreclose on these opportunities in advance. Hope relies on trust. Trust believes that the world is a beautiful, broken place. It offers love. It takes care of the essentials of social life.

Optimists try everything. Pessimists try nothing. A person of hope tries something. Hope increases in the presence of trust through effort expended by people who want to make the world a better place. Hope and trust make social life more civil.

Civil Life

In his analysis of social capital, Putnam points out that civility depends on people who try to make the world a better place. In uncivil societies, for all the politicking they do, citizens feel exploited, alienated and powerless. Uncivil society creates vertically structured, horizontally fractured patterns that produce exploitation, dependency, and frustration, especially at the bottom, but also higher up the social ladder. In an uncivil society, life is dangerous. Citizens are wary. Laws made by people higher up the social ladder are there to be broken. People are more likely to call for law and order since they expect others to break the rules. Because social trust is low, in the end, cynical expectations are confirmed by what actually happens. With incivility, people don't have access to the horizontal bonds that can be a channel for collective reciprocity.

Without solidarity and self-discipline, hierarchy and force show up as the only alternative to anarchy. The social climate leads to a demand for stronger government but makes it less likely for government to be strong *and* democratic. In uncivil settings, relationships are personalistic: people look out for themselves using economic transactions to secure material gain at other people's expense. Social relations are feudal, fragmented, alienated and isolated. People look out for their own family. Putnam calls this pattern amoral familyism: maximizing material, short-run advantages for a nuclear family while assuming everyone else does likewise. Uncivil regions see public space as a battleground for pursuing personal and family interests and family honor.

In civil society, trust is the glue that holds social interaction together. It positively affects the productivity of individuals and groups and is closely related to civility. The virtue of civility is most powerful when embedded in dense networks of reciprocal social relations—dense bonds of association. Civility implies honesty, trustworthiness and law-abidingness. Citizens deal fairly with one another and expect fair dealing in return. They expect government to follow high standards and are willing to obey rules they impose on themselves for the common good. They don't take personal advantage of public systems, such as public transit; they understand that freedom is a result of participation in making and acting out common decisions. There's greater confidence in others. As mentioned, citizens are happier. Civility is also good predictor of life satisfaction.

At the individual level, life satisfaction is best predicted by family income and religious observance, but a correlation with civility is almost as strong as family attributes. High social trust is not just a phenomenon of days gone by in rural areas. Based on Putnam's analysis, modern cities provide high social capital in strands of social interaction that include:

- repeated, face-to-face, multi-stranded networks: e.g., steel workers who meet for drinks on Friday after work, church on Sunday and the PTA on Wednesday
- episodic, single-stranded, anonymous interactions: the faintly familiar face you see in the checkout line at the grocery store several times per month
- formally organized groups, with incorporation papers, regular meetings, a written constitution and connected to a national organization
- informal interactions: a pick-up basketball game in the neighbourhood park
- explicit public-regarding purposes: membership on a volunteer fire brigade
- private enjoyment of members: a regular bridge club
- private and public interests served at the same time, e.g., regular Rotary Club meetings.

These strands are woven together in cities where people flourish, not on the basis of personal and family advantages alone, but because they live in an effective city with high social trust.

There are three related dimensions of social capital that explain how to increase its positive influence: bridging and bonding capital, machers and schmoozers, thin and thick trust. During formal and informal social interaction, bridging and bonding capital work towards different but interdependent goals. Bridging social capital is public, inclusive and outward looking. It draws people together across social divides, e.g., civil rights movements, youth service clubs, ecumenical religious organizations. It's good for linking people to external assets and information that are needed to achieve success in the social world. It's good for getting ahead. Bridging social capital generates broad identities and large-scale mutual reciprocity.

Bonding social capital is private, exclusive and inward looking. It reinforces close-knit identities to create homogeneous groups. It's good for undergirding specific reciprocity and mobilizing solidarity. Bonding social capital is good for getting by. It bolsters our narrower selves and group loyalties, but may have a strong out-group antagonism, which is why civil life needs both bridging and bonding capital. Bridging capital is a sociological WD-40 lubricant. Bonding capital is like sociological superglue. Both are good and necessary for learning social literacy.

Bridging and bonding social capital aren't interchangeable but neither are they always beneficial. As Putnam pointed out, Hell's Angels isn't the Rotary Club. We must ask ourselves whether positive consequences of social capital (mutual support, cooperation, institutional effectiveness) are maximized and negative manifestations are minimized (sectarianism, ethnocentrism, corruption) as we consider how bonding and bridging social trust operate.

If social capital is working effectively, cities are healthy. Trust makes us smarter, healthier, safer, richer and better able to govern a just and stable democracy because it operates to:

- resolve collective problems more easily
- grease the wheels for advancement
- allow us to see how we're all connected
- provide channels for information flow that help us achieve our goals
- work through psychological and biological processes to improve individual lives

Putnam also identified two types of actors that build social trust: machers and schmoozers. Both contribute to building bridging and bonding capital. Schmoozers develop informal connections: each link is an investment in social trust. Machers develop social trust through formal connections. Putnam concluded that more women are schmoozers.[16] Even as teenagers, they more likely express concern and responsibility for the welfare of others. They're avid social capitalists but, without support, the weight of these connections can be debilitating.[17]

While he names gender differences in machers and schmoozers, the third dimension, based on personal experience and early impressions, impacts men and women. Thick trust (confidence in personal friends) and thin trust (a tenuous bond between you and your nodding acquaintances at the grocery store) work together to shape expectations for how to treat people and how they might treat you. Thin trust is exercised towards a generalized other. It's expressed as fair play towards strangers and extends the radius of trust beyond people we know well to those we hardly know at all. Thick trust is based on personal experience and is embedded in relationships that are strong, frequently maintained and nested in wider, personally important, interdependent and affirming networks.

A healthy social world includes the development of bridging and bonding capital, machers and schmoozers and thin and thick trust. If early family experiences are unhealthy, people find it difficult to contribute in positive ways to these three dimensions of social life. What happens to people in the first few years of life impacts their skill for building social trust.

Trust is a civic virtue that influences home life positively because it provides a healthy model for social interaction. A society characterized by generalized reciprocity is more efficient than a mistrustful society, for the same reason that money is more efficient than barter. If we don't have to balance every exchange instantly, we get more accomplished. Social trust is a standing decision to give most people the benefit of the doubt, even strangers.

In high social capital environments children are better off, schools work better, children do better in schools and in later life, watch less TV and adhere to family values more readily. Mortality is lower, health is better and happiness is more prevalent. People are happier if they have a socially connected network and if everything doesn't depend on them alone.[18] Being well situated in families, institutions and organizations is the bedrock of social life. High social capital can repair damage done in broken families. Children of single parents do better alongside those from two-parent families if they have a rich stock of neighbourly social trust.

EMBODIED LEARNING

On the basis of social trust, developing the capacity to be effective during social interaction requires us to repair encounters that go off the rails. Conflict during social interaction is normal. We can learn to repair damage, from our side at least. In his analysis of social intelligence, Goleman gave an example of relational repair in a story about a little girl and her uncle. A three-year-old was distressed. As her uncle entered a room, she told him three times that she hated him. Each time, he responded by affirming his love for her. The third time, he swept her into his arms and said reassuringly that he still loved her. In his arms, she conceded softly that she loved him as well.

This sort of repair requires skill in some basic ground rules of relationship that Goleman outlined: attend fully to a person, pace the interaction, engage in conversation, tune into the other's feelings and manage your own feeling as you engage with the other person.[19] When relationships are repaired, both people feel good. If it remains disconnected, people feel fearful rather than courageous enough to initiate relational repairs.

Learning social literacy leads to human flourishing once we realize repair is possible and desirable. To Goleman, the "ability to repair a disconnection—to weather an interpersonal emotional storm and reconnect...—is one key to lifelong happiness."[20] The possibility for connection and repair has its ground in human spirituality. Human spirituality, *a sense of felt connection,*[21] arises multi-dimensionally from birth and develops through the following five processes: biological, cultural, sociological, neurological and psychological, as noted earlier.

On the basis of these dimensions, the formation of spirituality is a unified process linked through the fifth dimension, the psychological processes of object relating. As we consider the skills for exercising trust, remaining connected to others and making repairs during a social interaction, let's consider more fully Sennett's assertion that, for respect to be persuasive, it must be 'felt and convincing'. What does it mean for respect to be felt? How can we come to trust that we're in a situation in which it's safe to be ourselves? I pursue this question by describing *a felt sense*. After that, I link a felt sense to the formation of identity, and explore what it means to use a felt sense in the context of others because we've learned to think on our feet.

What Is A Felt Sense?

Feeling respected depends on trust. Trust is fragile. It evaporates if we perceive it was temporarily, conditionally or insincerely extended. Yet respect makes us more human. Its absence weakens our capacity to be human.

Trust depends on a spiritual connection we feel with others. In *Educating Faith*, I defined spirituality as *a sense of felt connection* and used faith in a broad sense to include a tendency to trust ourselves, others, God, an Ultimate Ideal, Rational Principles or the world in general. If a sense of felt connection is strong, people have faith to take action based on trust. Unless people exercise faith, they can't be well.

When I wrote *Educating Faith* I was unaware of Gendlin and his research into what he calls *a felt sense*. He uncovered a felt sense as he analyzed taped conversations of his clients. He began to observe a difference between those who made use of therapy and those who didn't seem to benefit from it. Through that research, he helped students predict who would and wouldn't benefit from counselling by pointing to an ability some have to focus on internal experience. He concluded that those who were conscious of a felt sense they had about the subject in question would be more able to make use of therapy than those who weren't self-aware.

As I encountered his philosophical and psychological thinking I realized I could define spirituality as *a felt sense of connection* but that's perhaps already understood by those who think about spirituality in light of that earlier work. A felt sense of connection makes trust possible. A felt sense allows us to perceive what comprises our worldviews—and make even slight shifts in how we understand the world, based on the accumulation of evidence and experience, a competence our brains are designed to help with. But what is a worldview? How do we come to have one?

A worldview forms as we make meaning out of life experience. Human beings make meaning. It isn't optional. It's essential to our humanity that we gather bits and pieces of experience that we weave into a story that tells us why we exist, who and what else matters, what might happen while we live and after we die. The story itself is made of threads that connect us to each other and to life. The meaning we create isn't only about things, nor is it merely a logical structure, it involves felt experiencing.[22]

Felt experiencing is hard to put in words but is partly an unformed and gradually forming stream of awareness to which we have access at every moment. It's an inward flow of feeling, concretely experienced. We can pay attention to it if we wish.[23] It's a flow of awareness that plays a basic role in behaviour as we form a narrative that waters root and branch of the way we experience the world, which to Gendlin, we can learn to cup in our hands and taste. It's deeper, broader than what can be put in words. Infants are capable of felt experiencing. It grounds their capacity to initiate, sustain, or end inter-subjective experiences with others long before they can talk. There's a relationship between felt experiencing and thought itself.

Thought, as we actually have it, always requires experiencing. Human thought is really a functioning relationship between mental symbols (words, images) and experiencing.[24] Felt experiencing always has an inward referent; it's always available if we attend to and concentrate on it. It's an ongoing bodily aspect of human living that's constant, like metabolism or taking in sensory input. It differs from intermittent actions we carry out, such as looking at a picture, moving our legs to run, thinking about a friend, speaking to a teacher or sleeping at night. These specific actions are events. Experiencing "underlies every moment's special occurrences of living."[25]

Gendlin points out that "nothing is as debilitating as a confused or distant functioning of experiencing;" if it's lost to our awareness, we search for it.[26] As we pay attention to this inner stream, we organize its content, although it's always partly incomplete and unfinished. To him, felt experiencing isn't only a capacity we use before we have words, it's pre-conceptual and complex. It exceeds our ability to create logical systems of thought. Its content is employed in the different logical schemes we use each day or in special circumstances. It lies behind the way we organize smaller systems of logic we believe determine our action, thought and feeling.

Felt experiencing contains the flotsam and jetsam of everyday life and is always at work in the following sense: we are affected even without noticing it by every response others give us. We experience these responses, slight though they may be. They change as we talk, think and feel because these responses are carried along the connections between us and others at every moment of our experiencing: they partly affect, produce, symbolize and interact with consciousness.[27]

Gendlin points to other theorists who've tried to express this reality and have described it as the feel of meaning that guides our inferential movements, as John Dewey did, or say that it's a *sens emotionnel* to guide us in speech, as Merleau-Ponty saw it. It's an experience of internal wholeness that supports the meaning we make of life, which we try to express in the words we use to convey that meaning. It's a capacity to perceive experience directly. Gendlin would say that before human beings cognize experience, their "observations are censored and selected by a little man [sic] in the machinery who also cognizes, and does so first, and often with more intellectual refinement than the conscious person possesses."[28]

This point needs more elaboration. I want to add to his understanding by describing Klein's contribution to an account of felt experiencing.

Identity And Human Connection

At this point the reader may say, I don't know what Gendlin is talking about. I see no such capacity in myself. Gendlin might respond by saying we're aware of felt experiencing when words fail to convey adequately what we're trying to say at a given moment to a particular person. At such times, a felt meaning is much more than words can express. If communication doesn't work, we may feel anger or withdraw into silence. That strong emotional reaction is due to the difference between what we mean and what we can put into words. Whether or not the reader is persuaded, I'd emphasize here that felt experiencing isn't determined by logic, yet it doesn't function arbitrarily. It's more fundamental than logic.

We try to make logic conform to meaning we feel deeply, even if we're unaware of it consciously. Logic is built on the basis of the meaning we've formed and continue to form through felt experiencing.[29] That meaning is capable of having one or more of its aspects schematized by other experiences;[30] its pattern helps us understand the world more adeptly. But it may also lead us astray, i.e., away from the reality that's in front of us. Freud categorized the meaning that's disconnected from everyone else's meaning as neurotic or psychotic. It's quite possible for ordinary people to create pet theories they refuse to let others challenge, which they impose on others and on the world.

Learning social literacy relies on perceiving how meaning made during felt experiencing directs our action, thought and emotion. At this point, I offer the working hypothesis that social literacy is the willingness and ability to read and understand what's going on and to interact intentionally and wisely with people while we're encountering them. It's learned through the human connection we have with others from birth. If we become socially literate, we're aware of the story we tell about ourselves, others, the world, God, our ultimate concerns, the meaning of life and realize the impact this story has on the way we think and act.

The idea of a felt sense may seem odd or difficult to understand but it's an experience rooted in infancy. Josephine Klein outlined the process of acquiring meaning through the use of felt experiencing.

At birth, an infant's experience is a stream of sensations, a felt sense or in her terms a felt self that's eventually organized into patterns that become concepts we use as we think, feel, investigate, decide, and that, taken together, eventually form a narrative we tell about the world and our place in it. The sensory messages streaming into an infant brain (cortex) create cortical effects that gradually work into shapes and patterns. Some form the concept 'me', some form the concept 'not me'.[31] Klein composes a picture of human identity to help us understand how we come to learn and express concepts such as trust and respect that are foundational to becoming socially literate.

As she explained it, identity slowly forms to include two aspects that together create the situation we find ourselves in as we interact with others. At the beginning, an infant fuses with its mother and doesn't distinguish himself from her. Over time, an infant emerges into a self. The term e-merge refers to coming out of this merged connection between mother and baby. As Klein put it, "somehow the baby has to e-merge—come out of the merge. As a baby e-merges, so does the (m)other, in the baby's experience."[32] If all goes well, a baby is accurately aware of itself as distinct from its mother, a foundational experience for comprehending all others. Slowly, a way of looking at self and others will form the foundation for a worldview. Two parts of a worldview that we form by early adolescence[33] include what Klein called a map and a model.

She identified these aspects and described what happens as a stream of sensations enters the cortex. These neural impulses have effects: they set off other neural impulses. To simplify, these impulses activate other impulses until the brain is an orchestra of effects. The orchestration eventually is tuned to convey patterns that are perceived and used by an infant. Babies eventually come to classify these effects until they build up into concepts—all of which happens through a baby's experiencing of people and objects in the world.

This classifying, conceptualizing process is meaning-making labor that everyone carries out. As mentioned, creating meaning is spiritual work—achieved through using a felt sense of connection with self and others. Object-relations work is the unifying activity that produces meaning. Its complex engagement with the world relies on a spiritual dimension of being human. To link Klein to Gendlin, I will say more about the map, model and human identity.

To situate the meaning making work that people do, and connect it to identity formation, let's go back to the idea of a felt sense. For Gendlin and Klein, a felt sense (felt self) indicates the innermost experience of a person. It's a stream of sensations (consciousness) organized into concepts and classified into patterns. One way to think about the process is to say that a map forms which consists of concepts and the connections between these concepts. Klein warns that it shouldn't be thought of as flat and two-dimensional. It's multi-dimensional. It defines the relationship of everything to everything else. It's like looking at a Google map of North America where we pinch in or pinch out to get a bigger perspective or to see the finest details. The mental map Klein is describing has that sort of complexity and depth.

At birth, there's no map. There's the human potential to make a map and create it out of incoming experience. There's a structure in place on which to build experience. While they don't have a map with self-identity inscribed as yet, infants have a mapped representation of their body on the cortex of the brain (called the *homunculus*).[34] Experience situates itself in relation to that representation of the body.

Infants can't organize their world in adult fashion, Klein explained, because not enough has happened to get more than a blurry picture of what's going on.[35] As a child has more of it, experience becomes "an internalized object-relation with potentially three elements: a sense of self, a sense of other people and things, and a sense of what goes on between the two."[36] As an inner map is built, children first experience themselves as a place where things happen—as an object of experience; if things go well, later on, they experience themselves as an agent of what's going on.[37] As a person learns social literacy, the movement from being an object of experience to being an agent of experience is a pivot point around which all other forward movement toward being oneself in the presence of others occurs. In bullying however, agency in the bullied person is threatened with extinction—except, perhaps, if they harm themselves; yet this would hardly be considered a healthy example of being the agent of one's own experience.

The second aspect, the model Klein talks about, is a representation of the present moment we find ourselves in. The map and model each contain a self-concept. The model is experienced with the map as its background. A person adjusts to elements of the present moment that are active in a social interaction. The map has a full effect on how the present moment is read.

Suppose an event occurs. Klein explains that a person tests incoming experience against the map and senses whether the current instance is congruous or incongruous with what the map has led her to believe about the world and her place in it. Next, she judges whether this event accords with how things should be or should be done. If an event is congruous with the map, that's the end of it. If an event is incongruous with the map, she senses something should be done about the mismatch. A process of testing and finding congruence or incongruity is carried out until the present moment matches the map. This checking and rechecking can happen in an instant. We might be quite unaware of what's involved as we react to certain situations.

Further, we're mysterious to one another. Every person is constructed from experiences that are unavailable to others, even those who are close. As a consequence, as we encounter people, we have no sense of the whole map that stands behind the model of the present moment *for them*. We can't see behind the back of other people to perceive the trajectory of experience that shapes their sense of what's going on. We gain reliable access to that trajectory only by asking them about it.

Over time, the map we're constructing will reify. It works for us—we make it work for us—and we come to believe in the way it represents the world. As it develops into a system of interlinking concepts, a new event is less likely to affect the map's overall organization, which is why a person's worldview is well established by early adolescence. The map is an internal organization based on past and semi-permanent connections composed of memories that create a personal meaning system that intimates what the future will hold.

Any new event encounters the whole construction and can only modify behavior in light of the whole. It's a relatively enduring structure that steers a person in one direction or another, based on past experience. A map has a self-concept embedded in it. My map tells me who I am. The present moment also says something about me. The map self and the model self interact in every social relationship. A model is the active part of the map involved in the present moment. Map and model selves, under favorable conditions, are closely linked, giving continuity to one's identity, direction and value to life in general.[38] Learning social literacy depends on a capacity to reflect on our maps and ask ourselves whether we want to continue to think and act in the ways that our history urges us to do in the present moments that pass before us.

Perhaps an example will help explain relationships between maps, models and reflection. In Junior High school, for reasons I can't remember, I knew the principal well. He knew me and respected my family. One of my grade eight teachers didn't share his view of me. I had this teacher for subjects in grades eight and nine. In both years he chose to find me impossible. He made me put my desk at the very back of the class, against the wall, where he could keep an eye on me, as he put it. On one occasion, he made me go out into the courtyard, where I could be seen from many of the other classrooms. He told me to stand there, while he yelled at me from his classroom window on the second floor of the school.

One moment in his class stands out in which I felt an incongruity between my map and the present moment. As I sat in my desk at the back wall, I reflected on what would happen if the principal were to enter the room. I felt I might split in two—one identity as my grade eight teacher saw me would face another identity that obtained when I was with the principal. I felt panic, believing that I wouldn't survive the confrontation. Something would happen to 'me'. My map self stood in relation to my model self and the two weren't getting along. This experience is one many teenagers go through as they form their own identity in the public world—the present moment in school culture conflicts with the map they built through family experience. They feel as if they might split in two.

What holds us together while identity is forming? In research carried out primarily with autistic children, Klein asked the same question. Based on work done by Frances Tustin, Klein pointed to *felt self* experience, the stream of sensations that needs to form into patterns. As she put it, at "first, the child is a stream, or the stream is the child, and the...mother acts as a skin might do, before the infant has developed what one might call its own skin—something to contain all its fluctuating rushes of sensation."[39]

If all goes well, the mother acts as a container, a primary nurturing containment for the child's stream of sensations until the child becomes aware of its own skin. If she is able, the mother holds the child until the flow of input is steady for long enough to allow "some pattern-making and pattern recognition, some organization and structuring, to take place."[40] The mother helps put things in perspective. This process takes place through affect attunement between mother and child[41] in which both are active agents. I sometimes wonder how my mother would have brought calm and perspective on identities that were splitting for me and the panic I felt at the image of having the principal enter my grade eight classroom.

The process Gendlin and Klein described is what I call embodied learning. As we learn social literacy, in felt experiencing, we become conscious of what has already accumulated in a personal worldview (map) that we work with in the present moment (model). Embodied learning involves the construction of the map and the model as well as the reflective checking back that goes on between them. Conversations between map and model take place as we learn to think on our feet.

THINKING ON OUR FEET

Bourdieu gave us a way to think about the map, model and reflection during social interaction. In establishing his insights, one of his first interests was the interplay between social honour and social recognition. He was fascinated by the idea that struggles for recognition are a fundamental dimension of social life. The high stakes in these struggles have to do with gaining and losing a resource he called symbolic capital. He came to believe social strategies that help to shape the accumulation and loss of symbolic capital are neither conscious and calculated, nor mechanically determined; they are the product of what he called a 'sense of honour' and a particular feel for the game of honour.[42] We learn these strategies by being in the presence of those who already know how to play the game.[43]

As he came to understand social interaction, he took what he called a reflexive sociological stance. To explain the term, he used the example of learning language. To get recognition, speakers have to situate what they say in a particular setting: competent people speak appropriately in the circumstances they face. In his view, this practical competence can't be derived from the written or oral utterance of an ideal speaker. Competent speakers embed sentences or expressions in practical situations that are tacitly adjusted to the relations of power between them and those who listen. Practical wisdom involves the capacity to make oneself heard, believed and respected. Those who have practical wisdom (stage seven in learning mastery) know when to speak and how to perceive whether those who listen reckon they are worthy of attention.

The right to speak, to Bourdieu, is grounded on an ability to use the right strategies, in the right way, at the right time, with the right people, for the right reasons. But right is ambiguous: entitlement to speak depends on effectively situating an utterance (orally and bodily) in a culturally savvy manner. In trying to situate speech, two common problems arise. The speaker may treat a linguistic exchange as an intellectual (i.e., cognitive) operation only and fail to notice the body's strategies that secure or lose the right to speak. In missing or misconstruing an opportunity, we miss the significance of associated forms of power and authority that shape all communicative situations. Secondly, speakers may allow a (so-called) right way of speaking to dominate so they never speak authentically: they may come to believe that they earn the right to speak in these situations only if they speak like other people. The power of authentic speech is unused by them.

In coming to his views about honour, social power and speech, Bourdieu took seriously J.L. Austin's work on words.[44] Austin described performative utterances, such as christening a ship, in which the saying of the ship's name and the smashing of a bottle of champagne on its bow is a ritual that changes a state of affairs. The ship now has a name and can begin its journey. Performing a wedding ceremony is another example: because of an utterance, two single people are married—a change in their social status. Performative utterances are carried out by those who have authority to do so. They get this authority from the institutions that give it. An institution to Bourdieu is any durable set of social relations that endows individuals with power, status and resources of various kinds.[45] Institutions *authorize* people to secure the efficacy of what they do.

Bourdieu used the term field to describe the context in which someone acts or speaks. As a sociological construct, a "field includes the people, institutions and award mechanisms and so forth that render judgements [sic] about the qualities of individual performances."[46] Those who are judged to be competent by the field are likely to become successful practitioners: they're seen to demonstrate practical wisdom. If the field isn't able to judge the work of a particular person, or if their work is judged to be inferior, opportunity for achievement is radically curtailed.

Based on his distinction, authenticity is shaped by interactions between intelligence, domain and field. Intelligence refers to the ability to solve problems, or to create products, that are valued within one or more cultural settings.[47] The domain is a subject area in question. As an example, a mathematics professor (domain) may speak to a high level conference of mathematicians (field) in a way that wins respect (intelligence). If she can't situate her talk appropriately, she won't be recognized as intelligent. However, it may be that a woman *per se* is perceived by the field as not being the sort of person who could be intelligent about the domain of mathematics, as was true for many women in the twentieth century.

Let's pursue this point by examining a role the body plays in thinking. Bourdieu made a distinction between the terms objective and subjective. Subjective, in his view, refers to an embodied intellectual orientation to the social world that seeks to grasp the way the world appears to individuals who are situated within it. Subjectivity presupposes the possibility of some kind of immediate apprehension of lived experience (ours and other people's) and assumes that this apprehension is by itself a more or less adequate form of knowledge about the social world.

Objectivity refers to an intellectual orientation to the social world that seeks to construct the objective relations that structure practices in, and representations of, the social world. Objectivity permits people to perceive patterns in social experience and presupposes a break with immediate (subjective) experience. That's, in part, what's going on when someone is using abduction to research a situation, as Meryl Streep did in the movie, *Doubt*.

The theory of the break is central. Objectivity, according to Bourdieu, places primary experience in brackets and attempts to perceive structures and principles on which primary experience depends, but that aren't directly grasped as we're caught up in subjective experience.

Bracketing refers to suspending judgment about the term (phenomenological object) that's put in brackets by suspending our current (enculturated) presuppositions about it. We suspend what we've come to take as the natural attitude to have toward what's in brackets so we can reconsider what to think about it. The aim of bracketing is to permit us to purify our perception of the bracketed item so we can sense what's really or essentially descriptive of it, and uncover some of its general aspects.[48] To break or pause in the midst of subjective experience allows us to consider what we're doing/saying/being in light of what we choose to be, do, or say—that is, to reflect on the map and model and the relationship between them. During the break we attend to what we're doing or saying so that it shows up for what it really is, rather than what we've always thought about it. During this process, we reflect on the map, model and the relationship between them that we've constructed over time.

Bourdieu thought that subjectivity and objectivity were inadequate on their own. Objectivity has the advantage of breaking with immediate experience. Objectivity allows us to take a step back. This move is necessary for inquiry to take place. The disadvantage of objectivity is that it can't sense the real world of the people it's observing. It always retains the danger of being imperialistic. Bourdieu wanted to take account of the need to break with immediate experience while at the same time doing justice to the practical character of social life. How can objectivity link with subjectivity so as to take account of the need to break with experience yet do justice to social experience? This question is a deeper probing of the issue of how we can be ourselves while we're with other people.

Bourdieu proposes the term *habitus* as a way out of the difficulty between objectivity and subjectivity. It's the *habitus* that provides people with a sense of how to act and speak. He identified *habitus* as a set of dispositions that incline people to act and react in appropriate cultural ways because they're perceived as legitimate in a given context. Dispositions generate practices, perceptions and attitudes that are regular without being consciously co-ordinated or governed by any rule. These dispositions, or habits, are situated within one's worldview and provide an explanation of them. We all have a story to tell about why we do what we do. An individual acquires a set of dispositions (*hexis*: a personal style with regard to map, model, talents, desires) that moulds the body and becomes second nature.

These dispositions are produced and structured by, and they echo, social conditions in which they're acquired: e.g., class differences are evident in the body.[49] In providing us with a sense of how to act and respond, the *habitus* orients our actions and inclinations without strictly determining them. It's not so much a state of mind as it is a state of being. It's not so much an attitude of the head as an activity of the body. In acting dispositionally, we may be unaware of what we're doing as we do it.

Bourdieu describes another dimension of these dispositions. Bodily *hexis* is the individual mythology of a particular group *habitus* that's embodied and turned into a permanent disposition and has the potential to engender trust. *Habitus* includes, for example, a durable way of standing, speaking, walking, thinking and feeling that's considered appropriate in a given situation and that shapes expectations for how members of a group will act. The importance of bodily *hexis* is seen in different ways men and women carry themselves—their personal styles must match the appropriate cultural style for them. As examples, there is a womanly way of walking for females and a manly way of walking for males in every culture or sub-culture. Patterns such as posture are enforced through social controls of various kinds.

To experiment with this point, try walking into a familiar group in a manner that's feminine if you're male, or masculine if you're female. Observe the responses. We judge the appropriateness of people's behaviour according to their bodily *hexis* by comparing it with the *habitus* of our cultural group. When individuals act, they do so in a specific setting. Actions aren't only a response to *habitus;* they're an interaction between *habitus* and specific social contexts or fields (influenced by sub-cultures) that shape experience. We walk differently, depending on where and who we are.

To summarize, the body is a site of incorporated history. The practical schemes through which the body is organized meaningfully are products of personal and cultural history, and, at the same time, reproduce that history. Dispositions give shape to a characteristic way of being a particular cultural member. Bodies have their own language. Attentiveness to the body helps to sense that bodies, not just words, tell the truth, or lie. We confer honour or insult, we harass and abuse, through the use of the body. If we accept Bourdieu's view, we acknowledge that human actions are only rarely an outcome of conscious deliberation or calculation in which pros and cons of different strategies are carefully weighed, costs and benefits assessed, or ethical principles applied to specific situations. People are conceived as fundamentally inattentive to what they're doing, according to Bourdieu, unless they're being objective. Social literacy improves as someone learns to be objective.

If I Were "Objective," How Would I Think And Act?

How does an objective break work? During a break, we essentially learn to be inside our own experience and outside of it at the same time, without devaluing either. Bourdieu was cautious about the ability to read others because he believed observation itself is limited. The observer of an action, particularly a so-called impartial observer, is excluded from the real play of social activities in which that action has meaning. The impartial spectator is condemned, according to Bourdieu, to see all practice as spectacle. As spectacle, the observer mistakes action that to the participant has a meaning that's invisible to the outsider's eye. Bourdieu saw subjectivist viewpoints as having their centre of gravity in beliefs, desires and judgments of agents who are endowed with meaning and empowered to make meaningful the world in which they act.

Objectivist viewpoints explain social thought and action in terms of material and economic conditions, social structures, or cultural ways of being (logics in his terms). From an objectivist viewpoint, given its tendency toward imperialism, the latter aspects of culture are more influential than are cultural agents themselves.[50] He explored weaknesses in both perspectives: objectivism depends on an understanding and orientation that it doesn't make explicit to itself. Subjectivism neglects to explore adequately the objective social conditions (broad cultural patterns) that produce subjective orientations to action. He thought that neither position entirely grasps social life.

Being reflective, in his terms, as mentioned, involves us in being subjective and objective at the same time. How did Bourdieu think an iterative relation (being outside and inside experience) was accomplished? The relation takes place through an objective break with subjective experience. The point of the break is to make what's unconscious show up to the agent who acts, speaks, and who's able to improvise. To Bourdieu, emancipation means grasping the meaning of our actions. Making the objective break requires that we understand human action in terms of its patterns.

Using his concepts of *habitus* and *hexis,* we're able to identify common cultural patterns for acting and speaking, and can sense how our actions and speech compare with cultural expectations, in light of our personal worldview. To think on our feet is first of all to break with experience and pay attention to what we're saying/doing/being, and to ask how we want to act, speak and be. As a second move, self-understanding based on an objective break with subjective experience enables us to recognize what other people are doing that overtly differs from the way we act, speak or are, so that we're able to pause, reflect and grasp the meaning of those differences.

Bourdieu believed his idea of *habitus* makes it possible to see and say things more truthfully. If we consider Paley's rule (that became a maxim) we realize she led children through a process somewhat like Bourdieu's approach. Cultural patterns brought to school—I exclude you like I was excluded—or, I exclude because it can—shaped children's expectations of how to act at school. (I intend no blame toward her children.) As Klein pointed out, we treat others, "for good or ill, in the manner and in the spirit we learned from others. *We do as we were done to* [italics mine]."[51] It's only as we reflect on our action that we can shift to a rule like *'you can't say you can't play'*.

The shift requires empathy, an imaginative consideration of what it might be like to be in another person's place; cognition, remembering that he or she is a person in a human body with feelings like mine; and then reflection, asking the question of how we would want to be treated if we were in that person's place. The freedom to '*do as we would be done to'* confronts the tendency to '*do as we were done to*', or perhaps, as we've always gotten away with doing.

The shift requires improvisation. To Bourdieu, action isn't automatic (people aren't robots). Action results from a process of improvisation that, in turn, is structured by cultural orientations, personal trajectories, and the ability to play the game of social interaction. Recall that *Action Science* holds as a fundamental assumption that no action takes place in the absence of a theory. To make use of Bourdieu, we think consciously about our theories and learn to work from inside and outside everyday experience without denigrating either.

Working from outside relies on knowing something about common patterns in human experience. Working from inside keeps us in touch with what we understand ourselves to be doing/saying/being as competent agents in our own cultural setting. Allowing the outside to inform the inside, and *vice versa,* helps to sense what we're communicating to others and opens up the space for reflection and change.

How can we learn to think on our feet? In schooling, if we're fortunate, we have teachers like Paley and programs such as *Working with Others* or *Roots of Empathy.* But how can adults learn to think on their feet so they will guide children toward social literacy? It's through insight and practice. Perhaps an example will help. Suppose I notice behavior between two people (Jill and Nancy) who I sense are in conflict. As I see how they speak to each other, I notice their actions intensify anxiety for everyone. Every time Jill speaks in a meeting, Nancy immediately speaks with a challenging comment that implies criticism. I observe this pattern: Jill speaks immediately after Nancy. Nancy speaks immediately after Jill. Each time the speaker implies weakness or inadequacy in what the other has said.

Later, during a meeting, I notice that I speak immediately after a colleague that I sense I'm uncomfortable around. Each time he speaks, I speak immediately after him. Even though I tell myself I'm only trying to be helpful and care about the project, I begin to feel suspicious about my motives. As I reflect on what I say each time he speaks, I realize my comments imply inadequacies in what he said or the way he said it. Further, I notice that if he speaks or suggests something I turn away, gaze somewhere else or look down. I don't look at him while he's speaking, as I do when others speak. Then I notice that I search out faces to see how others are reacting to him. I'm looking for evidence that they don't value what he's saying either.

I realize I'm trying to discover whether others support him. At times, I even look directly at others in the group, conveying bodily to them that he's speaking nonsense. In so doing, I hope to send influential but unspoken messages to convey the whole group's lack of support. I do this with slight movements: lifting an eyebrow, turning my head, frowning, being restless.

In this way, I engage in bodily practices that initiate a common human pattern that Mark Leary identified in his continuum of inclusive and exclusive behaviour. The motivation to act this way comes from the heart and is conveyed by the body, working as one. If I become aware of what I'm doing, I conclude I'm in conflict with this man and my behavior is an attempt to isolate him from the group so as to weaken his position and strengthen my own. Then I ask myself whether I want to be in conflict with him and whether it's right to treat him this way. Is this how I want to be treated? Is this how I want to impact group process, if I also say I care about it? The reader might think I should just talk to him.

I disagree. I need to change my embodied practice to prepare for that conversation. If I speak in a climate of disrespect, the conversation may never get off the ground. If I have more or less social power, the conversation may be ineffective. While speaking to him, I may miss an opportunity for empathy because, for a long time now, my body put the lie to any attempt to be sincere.[52] Contemplating these thoughts, and sensing what I'm communicating, I decide to convey openness rather than rejection. I look at him when he speaks. I don't pick away at what he says. I don't gossip about him. I don't garner support or weigh in if others oppose him. I don't try to isolate him from the group. I demonstrate respect in ways that don't require me to say anything about the underlying conflict, at least, not yet. This doesn't imply I support everything he says or does, but it compels me to show respect, even if we disagree.

CONCLUSION

In all of this activity, I keep in mind I have been applying only one plausible interpretation of this man. I haven't tried to understand him. Since I can't sense the map or model he relies on, I must choose to ask him about himself. I recall Bourdieu's caveat about being imperialistic. I'm well advised to hold my interpretation of what I think is his pattern (e.g., he's insecure or competitive) as a working hypothesis and remain ready to see him differently when observation and communication bring new data. I work from inside and outside my own experience. Realizing I may misinterpret the situation (e.g., I may fail to realize how he actually wants to be treated), I resolve to treat him with the respect I also wish to have in the group.

Why should I go to all that work? That's a difficult question in the current social milieu in which the most important part of being with others is the success of my own image, which, from my perspective, is different from my identity.

Why should I care about him? Social literacy calls on us to have answers to these questions. Throughout the book, I offer some possibilities and hopefully inspire the reader to arrive at his or her own way of thinking about being oneself in the company of others. But perhaps I can say at this point, that if I refuse to do the work of being respectful and trustful of other people, I may find myself alone. The game may turn against me. My spiritual needs will be unmet. I can never relax into the productivity that comes through focusing on the art of living authentically with myself when I'm with others.

Social intelligence, as described earlier, includes social cognition, or knowing how the social world works. Social cognition is an awareness that arises through education and experience in which people come to perceive large-scale patterns that influence the social interaction they experience day by day.

In the following two chapters, as part of the social literacy curriculum, I outline common human patterns in face-to-face encounters and in broad social, historical themes. If we understand and perceive them, these patterns help us become more objective in Bourdieu's sense. Unless we begin to see human patterns from a wider perspective, it's very difficult to extricate ourselves from the relational mistakes we make again and again—e.g., the mistake of disappearing in social interaction instead of allowing ourselves to show up for the person that we are, or the mistake of making war on others as the only way we can think of to be ourselves. Both tendencies foreclose on the social literacy project. Unless we use our experience to help us move toward a better way of working with others, we can't give and receive respect, offer trust, relax into trusting others or experience the hopeful anticipation of a future that social literacy aims to deliver.

4

CONTEXT AND COMMUNITY

INTRODUCTION

My husband grew up on a farm near the village of Hyas, Saskatchewan. After we were married, trips to the farm were frequent. His cousins filled me in on village folklore. Apparently, its name was supposed to be Hays, but the farmer assigned to the task of travelling to Regina to register that name realized when he got there that Hays was already taken. Rather than driving his team of horses all the way back to hold another meeting, he re-ordered a few letters and named the village Hyas. When he got home, his neighbours approved of his prudence.

In stories of Hyas, one character stood out. We'll call him Bill, not his real name. He was the son of a poor single mother. At some point in his life, while his mother still lived, he was taken to an institution because he suffered from significant mental limitations. I don't know when, no one was sure, he returned to Hyas to live with his mother until she died, and then he lived out his days in the village. Stories about Bill focused on his physical strength. Cousins told me of times when Bill would arrive on the scene if a tractor slipped into a rut or a car slid into the ditch. Sometimes he had ropes with him. At other times, he used strength alone. He would pull or push the vehicle to safety. These cousins told of a time when their own car hit the ditch.

When they came back in the morning with a tractor, it was back on the road. Many villagers had witnessed his feats, so they assumed Bill had come along and pushed their car out of the mud.

On one visit to Hyas, I was sitting in the driver's seat in the family's blue half-ton truck. Bill suddenly showed up at my window and pressed his nose against the glass and stared at me. Within moments, a man walking down the street stopped at my passenger window and knocked at the glass. I rolled down the window to hear him assure me Bill was harmless. "He won't hurt you," he said kindly, which also conveyed to me that he had regard for Bill. I guessed that Bill recognized the family truck and somehow knew of my arrival. On another occasion, I was in the village to buy a magazine. While in the store, Bill showed up at my elbow with a magazine of his own. He stretched open its pages for me to see. He spoke, while looking at me, in a rumbling tone repeatedly pronouncing the word *guns*. He waited for my response. I looked at him, smiled and said, "Yes Bill, I see the guns." He persisted, repeating the word again and again. This lasted for a few minutes. I smiled at him and assured him that I had seen the picture. He tried again. This time I looked him in the eyes, smiled, and asked a simple question about the picture. He paused a moment, then went away without responding. Perhaps he found me boring.

Hyas operated as an effective community with respect to Bill. His differences were accommodated and incorporated into village life without fuss or fanfare. Since he lived there, he belonged there. It was simple. Villagers embraced Bill. Those I spoke with respected Bill. They learned it from one another. They benefitted from a functional attribute he offered them, but he wasn't their equal in terms of his labour. Sociologist Richard Sennett asserts that respect is an expressive performance within a community. As such, it must be learned, as it was in Hyas.

Even if his ability didn't make him an equal to others in terms of his overall productivity, Bill was valued. Sennett put it this way: "While society may respect the equal dignity of all human bodies, the dignity of labour leads in quite a different direction: [it's] a universal value with highly unequal consequences. Invoking dignity as a 'universal value', moreover, provides in itself no clue about how to practice an inclusive mutual respect."[1] Sennett also noted that:

> Radical egalitarians have sometimes argued that if material conditions can be equalized, then mutually respectful behaviour will spring forward, 'naturally' and spontaneously. This expectation is psychologically naive. Even if all the unjust inequalities could be removed in society, people would still face the problem of how to shape their worst and their better impulses. I don't suggest accepting or accommodating inequality; rather, I argue that in social life as in art, mutuality requires expressive work. It must be enacted, performed.[2]

Bill's work was not valuable in itself. In another town, his efforts might have gone unnoticed or been suspect. In Hyas, he was valued because townspeople chose to offer him respect and trust.

In this chapter, I propose that the contexts in which we live shape life chances and life satisfaction, and in turn, impact social literacy. These contexts convey lessons that hinder the development of social literacy under certain conditions. It's not that we can't read other people in these contexts. What they lack is a fundamental regard for self and others that social literacy is built upon. As Goleman put it, we are "wired to connect," but if our context isn't grounded on satisfying face-to-face, nourishing encounters, its "toxic quality can act like a slow poison in our bodies."[3] People pick up attitudes and emotions from their contexts and weave both into the story they tell about life. Paying attention to contexts that shape our life narrative is an essential part of learning social literacy.

I begin the chapter by providing a meaning for the word context and contrast it with an idea for community. My purpose is to say that community is the foundation for learning social literacy. There's semantic overlap between the terms, but, as I use them in this chapter, while a context is dehumanizing, community makes us more fully human. It's more able than a context, as I stipulate the term, to encourage the full development of social literacy in all of its members.

If a group of people become community, they do so by taking responsibility for their environment and by describing, interpreting and evaluating contexts that have shaped their lives. During this reflection, it's possible for people to set their collective will toward reframing life together. While I don't discuss technology in any of the contexts I outline, it's one example of a context that's causing havoc in children's brains and social life. Many children (40% of toddlers in one set of U.S. data) spend too much time in front of television sets.[4]

In becoming community, as is the case with building social capital, adults turn off the tube and take time to play with their children. Many hours spent watching TV are lost to the experience of being with others who can help the young learn to get along better in face-to-face encounters. Some research indicates that the more TV children watch, the more unruly they are by school age.[5] We build community by refusing to exist in solitary technological ghettos that many of us inhabit for much of the time.

Our schools, classrooms, churches, community associations, workplaces and homes have potential to be community if we pay attention to what's going on. This chapter functions as a primer for social interaction to help identify aspects of social interaction that hinder community.

I started with Hyas to point out that social literacy skills aren't exotic attributes of a few special people. They're plausible, homey skills people learn in a community that focuses on offering respect and relational resources to everyone. In the next section, I distinguish between context and community and explore examples of contexts that fail to provide relational resources due to injustices that rage within them or because people falter in their commitment to address the living conditions that kill healthy interaction.

Common elements of these contexts reveal their inadequacy for teaching social literacy. In outlining them, my hope is to encourage readers to resist their power, to recognize how they limit people's potential to be fully human, and to realize that enjoying community is a viable, valuable alternative to contexts in which harm, dismay and exclusion are rampant. I begin by describing context and community in a general sense before I differentiate them, so as to emphasize a negative connotation for the term context.[6]

WHAT'S THE DIFFERENCE?

A society is an actual group of people and how they order their social relations.[7] Each group in a society is a subset of it, and is divided into smaller groups that look after the needs of everyday life. I want to explore the idea of a group to pick out two ways of organizing social relations by distinguishing contexts from communities such as Hyas. Both context and community refer to groups of people and the interactions that shape their experience. But each plays a very different role in the process of becoming socially literate.

As an example, consider Paley's class and the boss culture most children brought to school. My purpose is to show that people merely survive in contexts, such as boss culture, while they thrive in communities. But first a question: How did Paley justify requiring children to follow the rule 'you can't say you can't play'? At one point, a child asked Paley where she got her rule. She replied by giving the girl a rule and a reason. She quoted the Hebrew scriptures (Leviticus 19:34) to say that we should treat aliens and strangers as we treat our own people.

The reason she quoted is that 'you were strangers in the land of Egypt;' that is, everyone to whom the scripture is addressed already knew how it felt to be excluded. Her biblical reference and reason pertains to the people of Israel and refers to an historical experience in which they were enslaved in Egypt. Paley used it as a metaphor to express the reason for not excluding people. Other major World Religions provide a rationale for ethical conduct, practical compassion and justice in daily life. Many have a version of the Golden Rule,[8] though I'm not suggesting all versions are the same. There's also a strong secular rationale for providing relational resources based on the trajectory of human rights, outlined earlier, and motivated by human needs' theories.

Paley cited her authority for the rule and introduced a most complex and appealing aspect of what should motivate how we treat others. In taking leadership, she realized children need rules in order to treat others justly, which was also the way they wanted to be treated themselves, although they acknowledged they didn't adhere to that treatment when interacting with others (hence the need for rules). Secondly, she realized children need a reason for these rules. She used their insights, supported by an authoritative voice, to say that we treat others the way we want to be treated because we know how it feels to be hurt and we know we don't like it.

As mentioned, her rule functioned as a maxim because the children were drawn into consciously considering their behaviour in its light and practising the options of following or failing to follow its implications for how they treated others. They were encouraged to notice what happened if they followed the maxim, what happened if they didn't. The emotional and social work involved in their reflection encouraged their behaviour to change in ways they adopted for themselves, at least eventually: they chose to act intentionally and gave themselves socially acceptable reasons (i.e., that others could support) for carrying out these actions.

We wouldn't call Paley a relativist, but she was warmly open to each child in her class. She wanted everyone to flourish and be honoured for their particular talents and perspectives. She wanted to include everyone without devaluing anyone. But as soon as she aimed at inclusion, she limited the actions of some children. She was welcoming, not permissive. The culture she challenged and changed was a context of friendship modelled on disciplinary power (by this I don't refer to the teacher's power but to the power to create conformity exercised by certain children in the group).

While she doesn't say it this way, she's working from context to community, which isn't realized until the children actively create the welcoming, egalitarian, just and kindly ethos she wanted to foster. Community, as I use the term, is an outcome of genuine engagement, which contributes to inclusive, mutually respectful interdependence. Like Paley's children, most of us must overcome the effects of the contexts in which we were reared and where we work, if we wish to build community in the public spaces where we learn and labour.

But why is a context not a community? I want to expand on the general meaning for the word context. It originates from the textile industry, specifically, the craft of weaving and is related to the word text. There are two spheres in which the word text has taken on particular meaning: the world of weaving and textiles and the world of literature and composition, both oral and written. In each of these endeavours the idea of context implies the weaving together of separate elements into a whole entity, which acts back on each of its elements. In written or oral compositions, text is holistic. The meaning of one part is fixed or determined by its position in a whole framework, particularly by what immediately precedes and follows it. When we refer to social interaction, context is the milieu, surrounding, back story, situation, circumstance, setting or background into which people are woven, so to speak.

A context has a mood or ambience that it conveys due to the actual weaving together of its bits and pieces. If paintings have a particular look, cloth has a specific feel, food has a unique aroma—the settings for human interaction have an identifiable ethos. The history of social relations—the range of possible actions and tendencies to treat people in a certain way—are shaped by context. The weight of its impact can encourage conformity and they thereby hinder authenticity and integration.

When put this way, it almost sounds as if contexts have a mind of their own. To some extent, I do intimate that—a context shapes and constricts social interaction so that people treat others and themselves according to its script. However, nothing is inevitable if human agency is directed towards consciously describing, interpreting and evaluating the effects, assumptions and behaviour that characterize a context—that is, if people learn to think on their feet. Agency is foundational to being human.

A context may appear as compellingly attractive as boss culture did to some of Paley's children, or show up as a spectre to horrify and harm us, as it does to people who are excluded from or trapped in it. But when I refer to moving from context to community, initial steps of that movement produce the difference between being woven into the fabric of one's context, and stepping back to read its pattern, as one reads a novel. A point of awakening occurs if we see the contexts that shape what we think is possible and necessary.

What does it mean to be woven into a context versus stepping back to read it? As mentioned, the idea of writing and speaking derives from the situation of a weaving loom. The Latin word to weave is *textus*. When I write, I'm constructing, intertwining ideas on a page so that each word has a context that goes before and after it, which determines its meaning. Each word makes sense in terms of everything else, but may not make sense if taken out of context.

A word may be ambiguous (have more than one meaning). If I use the word light, for example, its context conveys which of its meanings I'm using, whether it's a reference to weight or brightness. Consider the following sentences:

- The picture frame was so light that, when I dropped it, it didn't scar the table.
- The morning light spread slowly across the surface of the table.

By analogy, just as light is an ambiguous word, it's also true that people may appear ambiguous and hard to read if they show up outside their normal context.

The difficulty of reading other people has to do with the function of contexts in which we form the story we tell ourselves and others about how the world works. Contexts are texts that make sense to those involved. I'm understood best if people are aware of my context. It's easier for them to interpret my behaviour if they know where I've come from. The affect of a context differs from the effects of personality, but impacts personality. Personality may show up in a given context ambiguously, the way the word light does—you don't know how to interpret someone until you see them in their own context, just as we may be unaware of ambiguity in the word light until we see both sentences together. Suddenly we say, that's right, light has these two meanings. We already knew that fact about the word, but weren't consciously using our awareness until we put the sentences together. If someone puzzles or disturbs us, it may be that we can't imagine their context. If people shift from context to community, they do so by coming to understand each other in terms of the history and experience of previous contexts. Contexts can become communities, but not without hard relational work.

Context has two dimensions, as I use the term, which are important to differentiate, although they influence each other. A context is a face-to-face setting that creates an overarching environment into which I am woven that I must come to comprehend by describing, interpreting and evaluating it, in order to read its logic accurately. For my purposes, a context differs from a community in that it weaves us in and forecloses on authenticity and integration. It's as close as the air we breathe. Community, in contrast, arises through relational work everyone does in order to form the group more intentionally. The contexts described below aren't an exhaustive list, but more of a social interaction primer. My aim is to pique interest in interpreting social groups so as to decode patterns in face-to-face interaction that do us harm.

FACE-TO-FACE CONTEXTS

I describe the following contexts to introduce a hermeneutic habit of reading social groups, their prejudices and practices. If we're able to read social interaction we gain agency for change that turns a social force like boss culture and bullying, as examples, toward building community.

First a point about order. The contexts are alphabetical to signify that they don't flow into one another, although each may shift into others. A group of people may live out several of these types. These contexts leave an indelible impression. They can be observed in the way people do or don't speak to one another, do or don't look each other in the eye. They're read in tone of voice, body language, facial gestures, flow of inclusion/exclusion. In spelling them out, I hope readers recognize their harmful effects. One more point. Some are described more fully in other chapters. The list is meant to whet appetites for finding a way out of groups of people that hurt each other or fail to live up the human potential to relate in healthy, hopeful ways.

An Abusive Context

In abusive contexts, harm is endemic. Isolation is profound. The movie *The Good Shepherd* conveys elements of a context that show up whenever people are abused. In the movie, actor Matt Damon joined a group of men that required him to go through a hazing ceremony in which he was urinated on during a mud fight with other men who were also trying out for membership. At the ceremony, he was placed naked on a slab in the middle of a large room that had a balcony. Utterly exposed, he could be seen and heard from all points in a large room. He was compelled to tell a secret about himself that he had never told anyone and still caused him shame. He did so. Through the rest of the movie, which claimed to be based on the formation of the C.I.A., he was reminded of his confession whenever he tried to withdraw from doing what leaders of the group told him to do, despite its illegality or cruelty.

I visited Bulgaria a number of years ago to attend a conference for Philosophers of Education, which was held four years after the Communist Party had been overturned in that country. After the conference, some of us were taken on a tour by faculty members from the University of Sophia. As part of the tour, we saw two communist retreat centers that were no longer in use. Our guide told us that, during Communist rule, if an ordinary Bulgarian so much as touched the wire fence surrounding the opulent spa, they would have been shot on sight. At dinner one evening with our Bulgarian hosts, we asked them why people in the restaurant were whispering to one another. In response, one Bulgarian told the following joke:

> When the Communists were in power, eight of ten Bulgarians informed on their families and friends. Now the Communists are no longer in power. Things are better. Only four out of ten would inform. But which four?

He punctuated his joke with a discomfiting laugh. Circulating suspicion and fear infused the Communist era and left a wound in its citizens that still echoed through their whispers.[9]

In abusive settings, fear, suspicion, cruelty, betrayal, conspiracy and isolation imprison individuals in webs of social harm that form an environment which appears inescapable. A sense that there is nowhere to turn, nowhere to hide, is typical of abusive settings. It was hard for me to believe that people could be physically trapped in a city—until I visited Monrovia, the capital city of Liberia, Africa.

Before I spent time there, I asked myself: How could people feel escape was impossible? In the remains of a network of checkpoints set up by rebel leader Charles Taylor, in a bone-shaking experience of driving over bomb-pitted roads, in vestiges of constant surveillance, in stories of capricious killings on public streets—in all of this—I finally sensed a web of tightly woven controls that prevented many Liberians from escaping the country. And I recalled Hannah Arendt's comment, as a journalist at Nuremburg trials, when she described the banality of evil.

Families, institutions and work places can be abusive. An environment is abusive if it dehumanizes people and remains unchallenged in doing so. People are trapped, paralyzed and silent. The most famous abusive context in literature is George Orwell's *1984.* The most renowned political examples include Nazi Germany, Stalin's reign in Russia and regimes in the twentieth century that carried out small and large-scale genocides, such as those in Rwanda and Liberia.

Whether an abusive context characterizes a country or workplace, its effects are similar. In the book, *Social Intelligence,* Goleman outlined the effects of abusive work environments on the body, beginning with his point that stress is social. His list included the following symptoms: rising levels of Cortisol (a hormone the body mobilizes in emergencies), toxicity of social insults that elevate a person's blood pressure, unfair criticism linked to hypertension, an increased rate of coronary heart disease especially for people that try to isolate or silence themselves as a way to reduce the impact of abuse and increased risk of susceptibility to other illnesses, e.g., the common cold.

In abusive contexts, a logic of insecurity produces ambivalent relationships that put an emotional demand on us. Each interaction is unpredictable, perhaps potentially explosive and requires heightened vigilance and effort,[10] that produces a logic of insecurity, as Bourdieu describes it.

Abuse is unhealthy. Even relatively minor upsets can trigger a mechanism that attacks the immune and cardiovascular systems so that these systems secrete body substances that form artery-clogging plaque. In situations where abuse is routine, people are at greater risk of heart attacks. Of all the sorts of stress that occur in workplaces, "the worst by far [is] when someone [is] the target of harsh criticism and [is] helpless to do anything about it."[11] All of these effects, over a period of time, produce ill health.

In abusive contexts, people are treated as if they have no value, no voice. Their value and voice are controlled through power relations that emanate from one person or from a gang of people that support the leader or take control themselves. In abusive settings, leaders have double-value; followers are treated as worthless. Abuse dehumanizes everyone involved, including those who carry it out from the top of the heap. In abusive settings there's another pattern that emerges: one individual is selected by a boss for special favour. This person is often held up publicly as a good worker or as highly valued in some way. However, the cost of the boss's favour is always paid for in that person's unquestioning loyalty. The victim enjoys no security and is compelled to harm or humiliate other workers as part of the pay he or she owes the boss. These people have no authentic voice; they're merely a mouthpiece, even if they get some benefit from being the boss's 'favourite'.

An Anxious Context

In a context characterized by anxiety, the voice and value of members won't flourish. In an anxious context, everyone is focused on something the group dreads, whatever that may be. As an example of the harmful effects of anxiety, suppose you're driving in traffic and a car in front of you is in an accident. What happens if you become anxious? If you're anxious, you stare in a fixed way at the accident ahead of you. You give full and fixed attention to the accident, and in so doing, hit the car ahead. What you dread takes place. We might call this a self-fulfilled prophecy but that expression fails to point out that anxiety itself led to disaster as it paralyzed the driver and created conditions that *became* inevitable.

Anxiety is like that. An anxious context is fixed on what it corporately dreads. No one is able to pull attention away from what the group assumes is an inevitable negative outcome. As a result, it often happens for the same reasons that you drive into the accident on the highway ahead of you if you refuse to look away from it. In this context, no one can see where else to go or how to get there. No one makes other plans—except those that lead to disaster. Dread might focus on an event from the group's history that people believe is likely to recur. It might be an event they believe is going to happen due to present or future conditions.

If we explore the driving example, we can always ask what to do if an accident takes place in front of us. What can we do if we still have time? Do we even perceive that we still have time? One correct action is to pull attention away from staring at the accident ahead long enough to choose a different path. In fixing one's eyes in the direction that leads to safely, the car tends to follow in the direction of the driver's gaze. While aware of the accident, and what's going on, drivers prevent themselves from becoming part of an accident by looking in a direction that will take them out of harm's way. But in anxious contexts, all attempts to divert attention from an accident that people dread is dismissed in advance or rejected outright. Hope is seen as foolish. Alternate paths, if they are spoken of at all, are seen as impossible.

A Coded[12] Context

Speech codes are used in every context. The dominant code is a speech pattern that characterizes a group. It's the right way to speak. Those who use it effectively are well situated in the group. There are two types of speech code that matter in a discussion of context: restricted and elaborated. To mark the difference between them, suppose three friends go for coffee. Two of them saw a movie the evening before and are still talking about it. They speak to each other in a way that leaves out the third person. This is because they saw the same show. They don't need to explain the plot or give details to each other. They make partial references to what happened and start to laugh at the funny bits. They don't even finish their sentences because they both know the story. The third person has no idea what the movie was about if the two friends keep using a restricted code—i.e., a way of speaking and acting when you have both seen the same show. If they switched to an elaborated code, the third person would get an overview of the plot and its characters so that he or she isn't excluded any longer.

Each code has its rightful use. A restricted code is appropriate if informal relationships call for a relaxed posture, free movement, casual dress and uninhibited speech. A group that knows each other well develops a restricted code based on common values, to create a common experience and commitment. Restricted codes internalize these elements in the process of social interaction and depend on shared experience. Elaborated codes don't depend on shared experience. They work well in a context that needs to be explained by laying out all its parts, defining its terms, and introducing outsiders to its way of being, for example, in an introductory lecture on mitochondria. Elaborated codes are necessary in any context when members want to welcome newcomers.

Only insiders understand a restricted code, while an elaborated code is open to anyone who takes the time to listen to an expanded, comprehensive representation of a subject, e.g., a public lecture about a city's transit system. If restricted code users enter elaborated code contexts and try to use a restricted code, their assumptions, body language, expectations and speech skills show up as naïve. They have to learn to speak in that context. If restricted code users want to open the group up to outsiders, they have to shift to an elaborated code. Discontinuity between code users and the dominant code stands in the way of full participation—if a setting calls for a restricted code and someone elaborates, or if it calls for an elaborated code and someone uses a restricted one, there's no fit between speakers and context.

Neither code is better than the other. Each generates its own matrix of social relations. Differences in the codes depend on the relationship between speech and the organization of social relations. Restricted codes arise in small-scale, local situations in which the speakers have access to the same fundamental assumptions and experience. Every utterance is pressed into service to affirm the social order. Speech has a solidarity-maintaining function and is deeply enmeshed in the immediate context so that utterances have a double purpose of conveying information and expressing (embellishing, reinforcing) social solidarity.

In restricted codes, maintaining the *status quo* takes priority. Speakers draw from a narrow band of language alternatives so that speech is rigidly organized and correct usage is enforced, whether it's a gang that peppers their talk with four-letter words, a group of Christians that use precise theological terms, or a group of scientists that use the same technical language. In restricted code contexts, status appeals tend to be formulaic and hierarchical and rely for effectiveness on the status of the speaker. Restricted codes transmit local culture to increase the similarity of those in the group. These codes produce people that know how to be near (socially close) and the same as each other. If members in the group rebel, they challenge the whole context. Others may react with punitive action. Restricted codes rely on *mechanical solidarity* (Max Weber's term) that's created when the sentiments people understand are the same.

Everyone uses restricted codes in some situations (e.g., family) but there's a significant difference between users who have access to more than one code and those who use one code only. Elaborated codes arise in social situations where speakers don't accept or know each other's assumptions. Its primary function is to express unique individual perceptions and to bridge different initial assumptions. Speakers select from a wide range of words and expressions that are flexibly organized. Elaborated codes require complex planning because they're adapted to make a speaker's intentions explicit and clarify general principles. Speakers are aware that other possibilities exist for fundamental assumptions and other ways of saying the same thing are effective, depending on the group.

Elaborated codes are the product of the social division of labour and produce *organic solidarity* (Max Weber) so that they organize thought processes, distinguish and combine ideas, in order to cross the boundaries of these divisions. An elaborated code eases the strain caused by diversity and complexity. It provides taken-for-granted knowledge insiders already have so that outsiders can gain access to the story insiders tell. Newcomers acquire the code in order to belong to the group.

Those who grow up with a restricted code are disadvantaged if society's changing quickly. Rapid change calls for elaborated codes to help newcomers catch up. In all groups, inclusion is based on knowing how to talk. People who switch codes appropriately can switch roles seamlessly and enjoy the ease of social mobility. But in code switching, there's always the risk of betraying one's roots and losing one's original identity. A context becomes a community in part if people learn how to talk together, yet also retain their authentic voices.

A Collapsing Context

Every group is a system. Nations, religious traditions, businesses are systems that survive and flourish if they account for human needs and respond appropriately. Systems aren't static. They move. But hopefully, they're healthy because their complexity is dynamically stable. If healthy, they convey a particular poise. Yet no dynamically stable human system lasts forever. If we think of human history holistically, dating from about 160,000 to 140,000 years ago (depending on how time is measured), large developments in human culture included the taming of fire and the perfection of hunting.

With the perfection of hunting, along with the gathering that supported its viability, humankind produced a crisis—the extinction of large animals. Hunting failed as a cohesive survival strategy because it collapsed in on itself. Just as cod fishing in Canada was endangered due to its productive success, the wholesale hunting of large animals no longer gave support to the human groups that depended on it for survival. The extinction of buffalo and bison herds in North America is a more recent example.

If we look at history from the perspective of World Religions and the development of cities, Karen Armstrong identified the following shifts in practices aimed at human survival that include the following general periods:

- Palaeolithic Period: Hunters—20000 to 8000 BCE
- Neolithic Period: Farmers—8000 to 4000 BCE
- The Early Civilizations: Cities—4000 to 800 BCE
- Axial Age: 800 to 200 BCE [Religion as a way of life emerged]

- Post-Axial Age: 200 BCE to 1500 CE [Initiation of the world religious systems]
- Great Western Transformation: 1500 to 2000 CE [Christianity in the West flourished][13]

As man the hunter and woman the gatherer perfected their crafts, they extinguished their food source. As a result, hunting developed into herding. Woman the gatherer found herself in cities and developed gardening skills, perhaps as a response to remaining in one place. The hunting era shifted into a farming revolution, typified by social practices associated with herding and gardening. Cities were sites for developing these strategies. The oldest known city, Catal Huyuk in modern Turkey, is believed to have flourished for a thousand years.[14]

Collapse occurs if resources a group relies on are undermined by the very productivity they deploy to get those resources. As with the perfection of hunting, conditions show up that end in collapse. These conditions undermine a group's habitat and threaten its survival. The signs that indicate a potential for collapse include the following:

- Soil problems (erosion, salinization, infertility)
- Water management problems
- Overhunting
- Overfishing
- Effects of introduced species that harm native species
- Increased per-capita impact caused by people
- Human-caused climate change
- Build-up of toxic chemicals in the environment
- Energy shortages
- Full usage of earth's photosynthetic capacity.[15]

Collapse is a consequence of not paying attention to messages a context is sending to the people that are accountable for its maintenance.

Every system provides data for self-correction. Just as socially literate leaders learn to read the criticism they get as a way to correct flaws in their leadership, natural systems provide data that operate as signals for self-correction. Although collapse is built into systems, survival seems to be as well. But people must read the signs and respond to them.

The data that systems provide to prevent collapse include the following: bifurcations [a fork in the road]; positive feedback loops (information a system reports and responds to); negative feedback controls and emergency adaptations. I explain these systems more fully in the last chapter, but what's essential to note at this point is that systems always give feedback to prevent collapse. The issue is whether or not people heed the information that systems provide. If data are ignored, a vicious circle emerges. Vicious circles are dead ends that don't correct the instability reported by the system itself. Rather, they intensify it.[16]

In a vicious circle, systems can't recover. Jane Jacobs identified what she called a Dark Age as a period in which a dead end leads to the loss of knowledge of ways that sustain life and the loss of skills that correct and re-stabilize a group, as happened on Easter Island.[17] One feature of a Dark Age is a loss of memory for a people's way of life. Indigenous populations that have experienced large-scale imperialism and conquest, lose the memory of their way of life, a loss that is recorded in stories they tell about the past. Their cultural stories often begin with and cluster around the coming of *The White Man.* These stories are kept secret but imply a lost way of life that pre-dated the appearance of men from Europe, and which is now beyond recovery.[18]

Jacobs also identified saving traits, bestowed by evolution as a means for self-correction if a system hadn't yet collapsed. To count as a saving trait, the attributes must cut across all cultures and persist over long spans of time. They mustn't be at odds with competitive success,[19] and are gifts of consciousness. While collapse is built into culture, because humanity has the capacity to perceive danger and reflect upon it, human systems can step away from a cliff edge, if they employ saving traits consciously and consistently.

Due to their agency and resilience, she believed people access self-correcting resources, built on overarching human traits that provide social complexity with its dynamic stability. These saving traits include:

- Aesthetic appreciation of art and its practice
- Fear of retribution
- A capacity to feel awe
- Ability to use language
- An inborn capacity to tinker and contrive
- A sense of morality that takes seriously how we treat other people and ourselves.[20]

The resources apparent in these saving traits are available if we're awake to patterns that typify collapse and if we respond appropriately.

A Global Context

The speed of transportation and the development of technology extend the knowledge we have about the world and make the earth seem smaller. If we compare knowledge now with data world leaders had when they met in Paris in 1919, to settle boundaries, debts and peoples after WWI—we know a great deal. The famous picture of earth taken from outer space persuades us we live on a little planet. Consequences of size contribute to the responsibility NGOs feel for justice issues in other nations, particularly in the last several decades, e.g., the way Western countries intervened in South Africa to put effort toward ending Apartheid. Some theorists are concerned with the flow of wealth among countries so that the idea of forgiving national debt as a way to encourage peoples deep in unresolved debt is a real global strategy and perceived as good for everyone. It's as if we have begun to take seriously implications of the *Universal Declaration of Human Rights* (1948).

Someone might argue that globality is not a face-to-face context as are others I explore. Yet shifts arising from globalization's features emerge to influence face-to-face encounters.[21] As an example, during the mass migrations of the last century, either willingly taken up or forced upon refugees, culturally different peoples were compelled to live in close proximity. As social theorist Zygmunt Bauman noted, "it is a grave mistake to locate the 'global' and 'local' aspects of contemporary living conditions and life politics in two different spaces that only marginally and occasionally communicate."[22] Local and global sites interpenetrate. Humanity as a whole is implicated. Actions in one place produce effects in another. Economic decision-making is a global responsibility. For example, if monetary traders decide that food is a Market commodity, people in some places on earth will go hungry. The advice to act locally and think globally is a rubric to guide a person's developing sense of what it means to be a good global citizen.

A Guilty Context

A context can be infused by guilt just as it can drown in anxiety. There are two types of guilt: what we might call real and false guilt. Real guilt is an awareness that we haven't lived up to reasonable expectations others have for us and that we have for ourselves. We feel guilty because we caused real harm, neglected responsibilities, or failed to follow through on our commitments. We're caught in patterns of doing something we wouldn't want others to do to us, or of not doing what we say we will do—of neglecting to do what could reasonably have been expected of us. With real guilt, there are good grounds, or reasons, for feeling guilty. If we feel guilt for an appropriate reason, there are always ritual ways to cleanse a conscience, for example, by asking forgiveness from others or by finding a way to pay our debts.

Ungrounded or false guilt arises when we have expectations of ourselves that aren't reasonable. For example, we may follow through on other people's expectations that aren't appropriate and that we never promised to carry out. In false guilt, we feel as if we're disobeying rules that have never been clearly stated. In some cases, we may have committed to a task or responsibility but aspects of it were based on unstated, unclear or far-fetched expectations. Other people's (or our own) expectations are inconsistent with what can reasonably be expected of us, or perhaps expectations fail to take account of reasonable differences in people's personalities, interests and talents.

If we have unreasonable expectations, either of ourselves or due to others, and if we can't or don't say these expectations are unfair and unreasonable, we swim in false guilt. It's a sense of being silenced and perhaps paralyzed by outrageous or uncalculated demands that pervade a guilty context. In a guilt-ridden context it's difficult to identify reasonable expectations. Every attempt to settle on what's reasonable may be ignored or punished, perhaps because those in charge don't recognize the problem false guilt causes, or because it serves their interests to keep people feeling guilty without offering to relieve that guilt by the ordinary means people have for assuaging their guilt through finding forgiveness.

A Liquid[23] Context

The expression liquid context is something of a contradiction. Because modern life tends to present us with contradictory experiences that we contend with somehow, it's a useful way to talk about our current circumstances. I've described a context as a framework that weaves us in and holds us firmly, until we step back and read it for what it is, to get perspective on it. The term context implies permanence. Even if I step back and am transformed through reflection, a context nonetheless has formed a background for my life.

In a liquid context, everyone is constantly on the move and on the make. So I wonder whether self-identity and self-reflection are quite the same in liquid contexts as they are in others on this list. Zygmunt Bauman (2003) described liquid love, which he thinks is the main game in modern human relationships. In liquid, nothing is fixed. It's a bit like writing the words to form *I love you* on sand at the beach. Attempts people make to relate are easily and regularly washed away by each wave of chance encounter and new opportunity. Despite the impermanence of the specific people in these relationships, in liquid love, it's relating itself that matters, according to Bauman.

In a liquid world, each individual is on his or her own to find and make connections with others so as to satisfy a deep need to relate. People are considered valuable if they make these connections easily and often. Connections must be easy to get and easy to set aside so they don't bind individuals too closely. Individuals must be left free to seek out new and better connections, if an opportunity arises. A genuine felt sense of connection gets in the way, although a practiced skill for seeming to connect is useful, e.g., as a means for flirting. Finding, relating, setting aside are elements of the game. The goal of relating is to have one's cake and consume it too.

The energy to seek relationships gives an aura of activity, speed and involvement. Until the fear of commitment and an aversion to feeling settled, paralyzes that activity. The passion in the game of liquid love is to relate—it's declared often—people say over and over again that relationships are important. Yet a closer look suggests that the driving force in this context is a refusal to let relationships go bad, which they must do inevitably since relating to other people is such hard work. In a liquid context, all relating is accomplished as an act of the will—the work of our hands, the effort of our skill. We must till the soil of relationship by the sweat of our brow, searching for relationships to sustain life. Even though people regularly feel lonely and alone.

To Bauman, relationships are what we say we want, but they stay pregnant, failing to give birth. Relationships remain big with "vague threats and somber premonitions," linking the pleasures of togetherness with the horrors of enclosure.[24] Every chance, disappointing encounter is washed away. People take a bath and begin again. They exchange the possibility of family commitments for this liquid motion of relating. They don't work hard to keep relationships. They exert themselves somewhat as they work these connections in order to keep themselves afloat.

As a result of one's efforts to stay open to every relationship and to consume them, in a liquid context, a "lonely, self-concerned, self-centred economic actor" pursues the best deal guided by his or her rational choice and is "careful not to fall prey to any emotions that defy translation into monetary gains," [by] populating "a lifeworld full of other characters who share all those virtues but nothing besides."[25] These consumers are men and women without social bonds. They're ideal residents of a market economy, even of a relational economy—based on straightforward exchanges of services. In a liquid context, there's an observable crumbling away of the ordinary skills of human sociality,[26] of the sort of daily offerings of care that one person makes to another because they know their partner will be there in the morning when they wake up. The idea of social literacy isn't easy to see as a social good in liquid culture.

A Material Context

In this context, the material world is all that matters. Goods and services that money buys are uppermost. Whether or not people are wealthy, the stratification of human value depends on what one owns, what people possess. A person is worth what they have. Their value depends on their possessions—those with more are worth more—and are treated according to the physical evidence of their wealth. In this context, people are obliged to show off wealth so they will be seen and heard. A material context is radically different from contexts in which privilege and prestige are grounded a person's social location in family hierarchies. Material contexts flourish alongside individualism, since getting possessions depends on money, attention and the status that's believed to be a reward for individual effort.

At the root of modern materialism is the belief that the world we see, taste, touch, feel and hear is all that's real. What's odd about material contexts is the lack of concern for those outside their borders. The focus is on conservation—building up, hanging on to what one has, so as not to risk loss. The fewest resources are spent on what can't convey wealth, in terms of money and time. Yet somehow having a great deal isn't comforting. By itself, wealth doesn't bring satisfaction.

A story is told of a group of wealthy individuals who were enjoying a Mediterranean cruise on a 40-foot yacht. They took in sun, food, scenery, until the day that a 42-foot yacht sailed by them. Two feet made a difference. Suddenly their boat looked small and ill equipped.

The trip lost its glitter. As the bigger boat sailed by, envy burned. Disenchantment grew until they couldn't recover their former enjoyment. They ended the cruise earlier than planned.[27]

The focus of material contexts isn't on enjoyment but measurement: on having accumulated the most. In a material context it matters very much that some people are poor or have less than the wealthy. It's only under these conditions that there's someone who's ripe for the envy that the wealthy want to sense in them. Others must have less for plenty to show up well. Those who have less are deemed unworthy. Poverty causes the wealthy no concern at all. Generosity doesn't flourish in material contexts, nor does hospitality. A material context isn't simply about possessions. In community, people who are wealthy are also generous, hospitable and serve the needs of the poor by sharing their good fortune with others who are perceived as equally deserving of basic material goods and services.

In community, humility and gratitude ameliorate the negative effects of materialism. What makes a context materialistic is its tendency towards dehumanization and the effort expended to keep separate the rich and the poor—although it's handy to have the poor available to witness that wealth, and therefore to affirm its value, as long as they don't get too close.

In this way, materialism shares something with the impact of scientific atheism, which also relies on a belief that the material is all that's real, all that matters, and that, as one example of its expression, views religion as *a mental virus*, a ridiculous delusion. This point of view is evident in Richard Dawkins' book, *The Selfish Gene* (1976), in which he proposed that material human bodies (and materiality is all there is to them) are a mere device to house a selfish gene. In his reaction to dehumanization implicit in scientific atheism, mathematician David Berlinski, a secular Jew, observed that:

> If nothing else, the attack on traditional religious thought marks the consolidation in our time of science as the single system of belief in which rational men and women might place their faith, and if not their faith, then certainly their devotion. From cosmology to biology, its narratives have become *the* narratives. They are, these narratives, immensely seductive, so much so that looking at

> them with innocent eyes requires a very deliberate act. And like any militant church, this one places a familiar demand before all others: Thou shalt have no other gods before me. It is this that is new (in twentieth century science); it is this that is important.[28]

A material context is exclusive of other interests, values and ways of life. Life begins at birth. It ends at death. The value of human life is based on calculation and accumulation. It might be that some would see an exclusively spiritual context as a happy alternative to a material context, but in community, spiritual and the material aspects of human life are taken seriously and prized.

A Narcissistic Context

In community, we get and give each other appropriate attention. With adequate attention, we're persuaded we have value. Giving and getting attention is an economy of esteem, which is won or lost during social interaction. The attention we receive from others is "one of the great generic currencies of social life."[29] As with money, attention is analyzed to establish the value of a person's life, and like money, some get too much, others get too little. A context is inattentive to a need for the equal distribution of attention, if that context is dominated by narcissism.

Narcissism is a tendency to regard oneself as superior to others and expect other people to treat one as special. A narcissist is driven by hunger for attention to steal value from other people. Their insatiable desire prevents them from being available to others, causing personal and social pain that endangers social life and produces a context of disregard and indifference.[30] These desires are unstable. Narcissists hold high opinions of themselves that fluctuate from day to day in response to ordinary events. They're self-centered, interrupt others in conversation, express hostility toward those who disagree with them and talk *at* rather than *with* people. In order to maintain center-stage, they do a variety of things to irritate and silence those around them. Narcissism is rampant in North American cultures. In modernity generally, individuals have received a burdensome gift of an overgrown self. They enjoy the positive, attractive features of this self-orientation, but fail to see how much it costs the whole society.

If narcissism is an excess of unstable self-esteem, self-negation signals its depletion. The two patterns tend to go together. If some people think too highly of themselves, they require others around them to think too little of themselves. In saying this, it sounds as if I'm blaming narcissists but that's not my intention. Both tendencies are built on a false assumption of how one achieves and sustains human value. People that suffer from self-negation, have, for various complicated reasons, no sense of personal value. They don't count themselves as important. In a narcissistic context, they don't receive the attention they need to challenge that low self-image.

The problem with narcissism is it's ravenous instability. It's very different from ordinary self-confidence, in which a person makes realistic assessments of his or her talents and abilities, has a stable sense of personal value, can resolve self-doubt, has no need to destabilize others in order to maintain their position, and has a sound commitment to the quality of life of other people. Self-confidence provides a secure foundation for being collegial, friendly and generous. In community, adequate attention is offered to the gifts, qualities and potential of all members of the group.

A Negative Context

A negative context is beset by ideas of hopelessness and despair. People think of themselves as a failed project. The focus is on what's missing, undone, not good enough. Regardless of what the group is or has, negative contexts tell a story of disappointment. This narrative measures the community by what it doesn't do, doesn't have, instead of what it does do and have. The focus is on what's lacking, not what's possible, on what's been lost rather than what's been found or preserved.

Every suggestion that doesn't support negativity meets with resistance and rejection. Each event is filtered through negativity. The group circulates and perpetuates some or all of the following messages:[31]

- All or nothing thinking: Life is described in black and white terms. All effort in the group is placed in perfection or failure categories. If performance falls short of expectations, it is a complete failure. There are no excuses. There's no middle ground. There's no hope or joy at small successes.
- Overgeneralization: A single negative event, regardless of how far back in history, is seen as a never-ending pattern of defeat. There's no other option but to continue failing in the way this one event captures.
- Mental Filter: A single negative detail overtakes the entire focus and all reality is dark. For example, suppose a group has limited resources or old buildings in poor repair. As a result, they act, think and speak as though their growth and develop are impossible. No one will want to share their space or join their endeavours.
- Disqualifying the positive: Positive experiences are rejected because they don't count. Some reason or other is found to dismiss anything positive or hopeful. People think they should be realistic and that means focusing on what can't be done. In this way, a group focuses on the negative even if it's contradicted by experience.
- Jumping to Conclusions: A negative interpretation is offered and is accepted even though there are no definite facts to convincingly support that interpretation. Jumping to conclusions can take two forms:
    - Mind-reading: a negative interpretation is offered and not checked out
    - Fortune-telling: a negative interpretation is anticipated and thought of as an already established fact
- Magnification or Minimization: People perpetually magnify the negative and minimize positive aspects of their experiences. Any counter opinions are rejected as unrealistic, without paying attention to the deep assumptions that drive the tendency to minimize success and maximize failure.
- Emotional Reasoning: It becomes a habit to base action, opinion and

expectations on what people feel. They fulfil the implications of the view by saying or thinking, if we feel this way, it must be true.

- Should Statements: Particularly in a tired or guilt-ridden community, all activity and planning is moved by what people think must or should be done. No one listens to the needs of the group. They follow a program of fulfilling expectations that have been handed down from the past or established by powerful personalities.
- Labeling, mis-labeling: If something goes wrong, a negative label attaches to the whole group. Everything the group tries to do is tarred by that label. Strong emotional language is often used to describe the group, such as, "We're just a bunch of losers. No one likes us. Everything we do is stupid and embarrassing."
- Personalization: Individuals are seen as the cause of negative external events for which they weren't primarily responsible. Sometimes someone is a scapegoat because the group tries to alleviate negativity. Scapegoating never brings about resolution to the real issue because an ordinary person, as a scapegoat, has no way to fix what's wrong.

Negative contexts are depressing. People drown in hopelessness and passivity. If people remain trapped and don't resist its influence, their speech and action are typified by negativity. They are negative about the past, passive in the present and cynical about the future.

An Oppositional Context

Honour is the most significant quality in an oppositional context. As French sociologist Pierre Bourdieu put it, honour supposes that someone "sees himself always through the eyes of others, [and] has need of others for his existence, because the image he has of himself is indistinguishable from that presented to him by other people."[32] Honour/shame contexts are generally found in traditional, hierarchical societies or organizations. In these settings, honour is granted or got through social games of challenge-riposte.

Social interaction is modelled on a fencing match of challenge and riposte, which refers to the action of giving a quick thrust after parrying a lunge. A riposte is a return thrust, a counter-stroke, e.g., an effective reply by word or action. To parry is to ward off a blow, ward off or turn aside a weapon, stop, ward off, or evade a challenge. The fencing metaphor conveys a type of social interaction in which people hassle each other according to socially defined rules.

In this context, honour is essential to survival and exists in limited amounts. There's only so much to go around and it can't be created or destroyed. Honour is passed around or kept. Almost every social interaction is perceived as a challenge. This context creates an agonistic or warrior culture. All social relations are contests for winning or losing honour. Challenge-riposte describes a constant social tug-of-war, a game of social push and shove. It's a type of social communication—a zero-sum game in which winner takes all. It's communication in which a challenger sends a message to a receiver in public. The perception of a challenge presents the following pattern:

- A claim: challenger claims to enter the space of the receiver; may be either positive (space sharing, in the sense of I belong here too) or negative (space dislodging)
- A challenge: a word, deed or both; threatens to usurp the reputation of the receiver
- A perception of the action that depends on the evaluation of the social position, power of the receiver and the public's view of both players in the game.
- A riposte: reaction to the message, which may be a positive refusal to act (expressed as contempt, scorn, disdain) or an acceptance of the message and offer of counter-challenge. If a receiver can't respond, fails or neglects to respond, he loses honour.

The pattern of challenge and riposte is most characteristic of male dominated cultures and is carried out among social equals. Only elite men are social equals.

The rules of the game stipulate that only equals can play. They must be recognized and recognize each other as such. There's no game between inferiors and superiors. In hierarchical cultures based on social power and gender, women serve the interests of these games but aren't players. They're spectators who cheer on their men and suffer if their man loses. An inferior doesn't have enough honour to resent an affront from a superior. An affront from an inferior doesn't constitute a challenge. A superior pays no attention to insults thrown at inferiors. An inferior person can't afford to feel the affront. A superior person can punish any impudence.

Each player is answerable for his honour only among his social equals. What he does to inferiors, regardless of its brutality, doesn't lose him honour. In this context, women are excluded or misinterpreted if their intention is to share space with men. The context isn't open to their involvement and doesn't understand their offer if they simply wish to collaborate.

I'm not saying women refrain from exchanging honour. But in oppositional contexts, women gain or lose honour through their connection/closeness to a dominant, powerful male. They fight with one another to establish, maintain or breach those associations. In this context, female honour is granted based on a woman's willingness to be submissive and show deference to men, especially to husbands, if they have them. Without a husband, women have little value or safety. As a result, while a bad man is shameful (to society and himself), a bad woman is shameless if she doesn't show deference to superiors due to their privileged social position. A genuine show of unscripted mutual respect is almost impossible to imagine between superior and inferior people.

Oppositional contexts characterize many ancient societies and medieval societies, e.g., pre-Revolutionary France. However, challenge-riposte patterns explain many social interactions that one might experience in modern cities, around the world, in Western cultures as well.

A Personal Context

Personal systems are generally initiated in families in which children are free from a system of rigid positions. Freedom is not absolute however. Children may become prisoners of an unstated system of feelings and abstract principles. In personal contexts, adults use talk as their primary means of discipline. The family celebrates not a fixed pattern of roles or duties but the autonomy and unique value of individuals. If a child asks questions, the mother responds with answers as fully as she can. The child's curiosity is used to increase verbal control, elucidate causal relations and teach children to assess the consequences of their actions. Control is exercised over children by developing their sensitivity to other people' feelings and learning to inspect their own.

A child's conduct is related to the feelings of the regulator: meaning is related explicitly to the regulated. As an example, a mother might say: "I want you to pick up these toys because I need help. I'm very busy. We're going out to dinner as a family. I'm in a hurry so please pick them up now." The child is motivated by helping mother, going out for dinner, keeping mother from being overworked or from getting angry. The child has a range of choices. Control is effected either through verbal manipulation of feelings (directly or indirectly) or through establishing reasons. A child has access to the regulator as a person and to the significance of child's own actions as they relate to consequences. Some of the control is in the hands of the child. In personal contexts, right and wrong are learned in response to feelings and needs of the family structure. Instead of internalizing a particular moral structure, a child acquires an internal ferment of ethical sensibilities.

In extremely personal contexts, it may be difficult for a child reared on abstract principles to draw moral lines or be bound by promises, since unquestioned boundaries never were part of his or her upbringing. In a strongly personal family, meals aren't held in common, hierarchy is unrecognized. Mother and father would attempt to meet each child's needs by creating an entirely individual environment for mealtime and bedtime rituals.

In personal contexts, there's a tendency to rear children using both restricted and elaborated speech codes, producing a child who's acutely sensitive to the feelings of others, interested in internal states, predisposed to ethical preoccupations and who can deal with changing social situations with less difficulty. Yet, while they're vocabularies are open to deep feeling, it also denies them a sense of order in social life—life is *ad hoc*—with the child at its centre. The young must search for a justification for their way of life and existence outside the performance of a set of rules. This can be found in good works on behalf of humanity in general, in personal success, or both, but children may become adults without any generalized sense of why they should do one thing rather than another.

A Positional Context

In a positional context, controlling children is accomplished by continually building up a sense of social pattern, of ascribed role categories. If a child asks why, a mother might say: "Because I said so (hierarchy), because you are a boy (sex-role), twelve years olds must do this (age status) and you are the oldest (seniority)." Right and wrong are learned in the structures set up by the family. Children see themselves in relation to that structure. In working class and some aristocratic families, a child is harnessed to the task of sustaining the family's social situation. Authority is clear-cut, unambiguous and reinforces solidarity: the child may not step out of line. Meanings are more likely signalled by bodily actions than by words. The child learns the restricted code of social requirements that are imposed by the family. There's a tight relationship between language, reality and perception. Choices and preferences are built into the family's language code.

Right and wrong are issues of obedience/disobedience to authority. All family practices affirm the hierarchy of rank and sex: places at the dinner table, the living room, every meal, every rising, bathing and bedtime is structured to express and support the social order. The oldest and therefore most important people eat first. Men may eat before women. In positional families, requests and appeals for compliance rely on differences in rank for their effectiveness. In a personal context, they rely on the manipulation of thought and feeling. The positional family pattern continues to form some families, but the personal family is more and more prevalent in the twenty-first century in Western cultures, and it sometimes creates a very great strain for migrants who come from cultures in which the positional family is the main model for social interaction at home.

A Resentful Context

Some contexts aren't what can be called abusive, but there's a pattern that consists of high expectations and low support. This combination causes resentment, a psychological state of feeling distressed and anxious because reasonable expectations and appropriate demands aren't met or even acknowledged by the treatment a person receives at the hands of others. It's a sense of moral indignation at a felt injustice in the behaviour of others toward oneself. There's a sense that one's situation is not in keeping with one's power, status and social role. If people feel trapped by high expectations and low support, resentment sets in—a feeling of not being recognized for what one has contributed or could contribute to the setting.

Resentment arises from not getting appropriate recognition. Every human being needs recognition, without which, we can't identify our contribution to a group or value in it. The value we enjoy confirms our self-worth. We need to have our value affirmed and echoed in everyday experience. People in a resentful context may work extremely hard but not receive even the most basic form of support. Normally, unresolved resentment can erupt in revenge. Resentment arises due to a loss of face—a sense of not being seen or heard accurately. Revenge appears as a solution because loss of face drives people to try to regain face by punishing someone else, even someone outside the offending context, by damaging property or harming those in positions of power. Unresolved resentment is a social poison infecting all social interaction if unaddressed.

A Stymied Context

The power to stymie can infest a context. This is the power that always says no, or always says wait, without giving specific boundaries around its command to wait. The power to stymie is incapable of doing anything itself, except to render what it dominates incapable of doing anything, except for what this power allows it to do with permission that's measured in small doses. People are stymied if those in positions of power reduce them to obedience so that they're kept from thinking on their own and compelled repeatedly to ask for permission. Regardless of the manner of asking or frequency of the request, or the posture they assume as they ask, they don't get a positive, affirming response. Sometimes, a tidbit is offered but never without strings attached. A stymied context is unproductive. Even the interests of those who stymie others can't be realized, if one is measuring the stated goals of an organization. The power to stymie is extremely wasteful of human ingenuity and effort.

A Tired Context

A tired group is one that's spending too much time on things that aren't consistent with its giftedness and goals. The context is bogged down by reproducing practices and patterns that have been part of its history perhaps, but whose value to the current group is questionable. Tiredness is contagious, like yawning. One solution is to re-evaluate what the group is currently doing and ask whether all these things are the right things to do. How much can a healthy organization do effectively? A tired context creates apathy. Group expectations eventually become very low—even if people say that they have a lot to do. What's done is incomplete, ill-conceived. No one expects productivity to result from their effort.

Members can address their tiredness by asking themselves: What are we now doing? Why are we doing it? How does what we do fit with being the organization we say we are? To re-evaluate, a tired community asks: How is the system working? Are there gaps in communication that require people to do too much unnecessary work? Are people redoing work that has already been done? Is there sufficient support for leaders?

CONCLUSION

Many social groups are held together either by coherence or regulation. With coherence, through internal agreement or cultural heritage, members hold important values and practices in common. As mentioned earlier, they get along on the basis of being near and the same. Given the diversity of most social groups in the twenty-first century, coherence won't provide enough social glue to hold them together. Social groups that encompass diversity and difference must be held together through trust-based forms of regulation: through learning rules, trying out maxims and adopting principles that enjoy moral persuasion and legal support.

Contexts described in this chapter fail to fulfil the hopes of social capital and are held together by various kinds of force. They are rife with injustice. As a result, they distort the growth of social literacy. Some people have less value, a condition that limits personal reflection on one's circumstances because the cost of seeing what's going on is too hard to face. If members critically reflect on their circumstances, those who suddenly become aware of injustice may take action through resistance, rejection and revenge. These reactions to injustice are understandable, but often futile, due to the socially well-situated conditions that surround those in the habit of using force.

The outcomes of these contexts include a range of experiences that are dehumanizing. People feel exposed, isolated and can't enjoy ordinary social engagement, which involves being vulnerable and safe in a group of people who matter. There's generalized betrayal and entrapment in this contexts that spark biological and chemical harm in the human body. There's intensified anxiety. Exclusion may be based on encoded talk that disallows full participation for new members, or 'foreigners'. These contexts are frequently on the verge of collapse. In them, people are riddled with false guilt, feel helpless and worthless, since they lack adequate attention. They may be oppressed by the narcissism of their leaders and feel unable to genuinely commit to a setting that's pervasively painful.

In these contexts there's an overarching and unrelieved isolation and relational poverty. Negativity dominates. All effort to improve a situation is met with negativity. There is, generally, perpetual conflict among those who must cope with these circumstances, which shifts from one set of individuals to another without rhyme or reason. In addition to conflict, there's misunderstanding that's difficult to pinpoint and resolve. There are outbursts of sensitivity to what's said and done—to what's unsaid and undone. These contexts perfect the tendency to pinpoint individuals for humiliation. In many of these settings, everything is personal, due to an overall sense of isolation. In some situations, rather than oversensitivity, there's vigilance toward the potential of chaos—perceived disorder that hovers at the margins.

In general, resentment, frustration and fatigue characterize these contexts with the result that, at best, people are passive and bored. Community isn't possible, as it was in the village of Hyas. Being in community might not show up as attractive if these contexts create an overall sense of individual isolation and slavery. It's essential to perceive and resist the effects of a context, if, and as, we're learning social literacy.

In the next chapter, I describe large-scale global patterns that influence social literacy. The description of these patterns is based on a different frame of reference than the one used to describe contexts in this chapter. Yet, unless we get good at reading these global patterns as well, we won't recognize their impact on our willingness and ability to create communities that allow us to be near to other people, yet distinctly different from them.

5

GLOBAL PATTERNS AND LIBERATED PRACTICES

INTRODUCTION

If contexts create unhealthy settings for learning social literacy, what's to be done? Can people who've been schooled in passivity create community as an intentional enterprise? I propose that people can create and enjoy community, otherwise, we wouldn't have communal possibilities in our consciousness, even as an ideal.

If creating community is a goal groups take on, one element stands out. A community cares for all members. Community membership is based on common humanity and commitment, not on privilege or competence. Membership based on competence creates a guild. Membership based on privilege forms a club. In contrast, communities establish rules, maxims and principles to ensure every member enjoys inclusion. But members aren't free to do whatever they like. They accept their communal obligations. They learn social practices that are humanizing and use social power to empower, which means they encourage all members to develop a fully human life. Forming community isn't based on exotic social skills. It's an intentional response to a particular kind of environment.

All this isn't to say communities are idyllic. They don't set out to produce something—not even perfection. Rather, people expend relational effort to create and repair social encounters so that life satisfaction is realized to a great extent and levels of trust increase within the group. Recall that, if social trust is high so is life satisfaction. In this chapter, I include meeting one's own and other people's needs (as far as one is able) as a central aspect of community obligation; offering and receiving relational resources is essential work in building community.

Turning a context into a community requires members to step back and see what's going on—to be attentive enough so that self and social knowledge increase. Taking a step back means describing, interpreting and evaluating a situation in order to become conscious of assumptions, expectations, practices and beliefs about what's possible within it. Reflection replaces passivity. Being community is relational work that moves against the grain. Like any good exercise, it's uncomfortable at times, yet satisfying. Community arises through relational work members attempt in order to form the group intentionally. Relational work is carried out on a foundation of understanding that enables people to read social patterns as well as the people that convey them.

In this chapter I describe four global patterns that are woven through the smaller-scale contexts described in the last chapter. To distinguish these large-scale, trans-cultural ways of life from the face-to-face contexts, I refer to them as global patterns. They form a unique logic in cultures all over the world. In multicultural societies, they shape interaction in extended families, schools, universities, churches, temples, synagogues, mosques and public institutions. Each pattern has telltale signs.

To provide a background for depicting them, I first outline a version of community that has empathy and cosmopolitanism at its core. Following that analysis, I describe the four patterns along with their characteristic views of the world and valuation of persons. The logic that inheres in each one is laid out and compared to the others.

After I describe the four patterns, I offer an approach Harvard professor Robert Kegan (psychology and education) takes to Piaget's stage theory of human development and outline his view of what's required in doing the relational work of being family and building community. His perspective fits well with cosmopolitanism and empathy because he articulates a view of how liberation works that doesn't require walking away from one's commitments. He believes being integrated with and differentiated from people that matter to us, doesn't require leaving them in order to find ourselves, a tendency, as mentioned, that doesn't work well for mothers or members of strong group cultures. While change happens with social literacy, it's the purpose of this chapter to show that change relies on reflection and relational work, rather than a twentieth century tendency to abandon family and community as a way to seek personal fulfilment.

But someone may ask, why do I need to know about global patterns? My response is that they build barriers to community if they're misunderstood. Each one represents a different way to envision community and social obligation. When they co-exist, but are under-analyzed, people find it hard to get along. Social literacy itself is at a loss.

One more point before moving to empathy and cosmopolitanism. In describing face-to-face contexts, I used what's called a deficit model. I outlined what they lack, fail at, or can't offer in terms of meeting human need. The four global patterns in this chapter aren't described using a deficit model. Rather, they convey the way things are in social relations that have been worked out historically and continue to influence what we expect and demand from social interaction. Learning to read them, as they show up in experience, is part of a social literacy curriculum, not so much to alter them (although it may) as to negotiate them in our attempts to build community.

I don't rely on a deficit model because each pattern makes a worthwhile contribution to our understanding of human community and captures something that's true about the human condition. In outlining them, my purpose is to help interpret social interaction and its underlying expectations so that readers can decipher some of the reasons why people do what they do. Building community in groups we inhabit, or choose to join, depends on getting insight into motivations, expectations and aspirations of the people with whom we interact, which means we need to understand the way they understand how the social world works.

COMMUNITY, EMPATHY AND COSMOPOLITANISM

What is community? The word is a noun, an adjective and an activity. One may live in an urban or rural community, one may part of a community group, but community is also something we create together. In one view,[1] communities are smaller groups within society made up of people and things that share a common space and engage regularly and predictably in social interaction. Members offer each other mutual aid, but most communities rely on some self-sufficiency in family units that form part of them,[2] which is why family culture is important to understand as people build community.

A community is distinguished from a formal organization, though it has degrees of organization in order to fulfil the needs of its members. As an example, a hospital is a formal organization designed to restore people to health. People enter, get well or die. Whatever the outcome, patients leave the hospital. Hospitals aren't communities in the sense I'm developing here. Neither is a business an apt model for a community. Businesses have organizational goals.

A community isn't an organization in that sense. Although it may be highly organized, it's more than what it accomplishes; it's a way of living together. Unlike organizations, a community isn't primarily defined by a set of goals,[3] (although it may have some). Its goals don't define it; being together defines a community. Living and dying are part of life together. Some communities are together simply because, like a village, they find themselves in the same location, sharing the same resources over the course of many life times. But their communal quality is measured by the way they treat each other, in particular, how they treat their most vulnerable members—the sick, infirm, aged and the young.

The difference between communities and formal organizations is picked out in the following comparison:

- Formal Organizations: Have sharp, recognizable goals. Members recognize and contribute to their achievement. Other goals may exist but they mustn't detract from attainment of established goals that mark the group off as an organization. Social value and a sense of belonging are based on one's contribution to these goals.

- Communal Groups: Have no goals that apply to the whole group. Social relations form around the cooperation of members and families. No goal is given priority so that specific goals don't interfere with the aim of living together. Social value and a sense of belonging are granted based on an inclusive group membership.[4]

Formal organizations function around their ability to meet their goals. Goals don't hold a community together, people do. In community, families matter. They're foundational to the possibility of staying together for a long time and prevent collapse. In formal organizations, the family is a side interest; time spent with family may be seen as getting in the way of successfully meeting organizational goals.

The use people make of space, time, cooperation and integration are significant while building community. Since it's a complex interplay of social interaction carried out by a group, every community is unique. In community, the aim is for people to come, stay and have their needs met. They remain because they belong to it. They have similar and diverse needs that they expect community to address. If a religious group, village or city operates as community, the needs of everyone are addressed for as long as they're involved. Their lives continue to influence the community after they die as part of the corporate memory of the group. If cities, religious groups or villages act like formal organizations, many human needs are unrecognized, dismissed or postponed.

A crucial factor that turns a context into a community isn't that people stay a long time, but that they hold values, interests and their humanity in common. Needs are acknowledged and met, merely because they exist. If people belong, needs are addressed or the group suffers. In community, there's no favouritism in whose needs are met and whose are ignored. To be left out is to be excluded. Exclusion isn't simply a problem for community. It prevents a context from becoming a community and from shaping a communal sense of mutual obligation.

All practices of exclusion foreclose on community. This isn't to say being community is an ideal in which everyone gets what they want. Being community derives from perceiving common relational needs that must be met for justice to flourish. A community is a local group that enjoys mutual respect among its members, responds positively to felt needs, holds some rules, maxims and principles in common, honours the humanity of everyone and has members that are good neighbours. In terms of social literacy, it's an aggregate of people who are learning through experience to be near and different; community operates within a framework of nearness and difference, as I use the terms.

To recap, in learning social literacy we acquire skills but also require a type of social milieu in which these skills can be learned. We enjoy an environment in which we read other people's body language and meaning, realize how they impact us and perceive that everyone has value. A group is a community if people are learning these lessons. If they aren't, it may be because some individuals believe they have more value than others and hold onto that double value forcefully—only their needs are seen as important. Learning social literacy enables people to realize what's going on so they can enact changes in themselves which allow them to alter a context in the direction of community. To move from context to community, a set of practices and an attitude are necessary. That attitude is built on empathy and cosmopolitanism.

Empathy[5] encourages the freedom to tell other people the truth about who we are. It's an attitude and set of skills that develop if people are free to exercise voice and value in the group. It's an aspect of social literacy that hears what other people say and reads behind the lines of what's presented to interpret accurately what others are trying to convey. It allows people to tell stories of personal and communal harm that waylay their efforts to join fully in community. It meets relational needs. Empathetic people allow others to tell their story without interjecting descriptions, interpretations or evaluations of it, while it's being told.[6] Empathetic settings offer opportunities to witness exuberance, sorrow, success, failure and leave time to celebrate victories as well as grieve and lament losses. While there are other kinds,[7] relational empathy offers a set of affective (feeling), conative (willing) and cognitive (thinking) skills that are at the core of building community.

Empathy has the overall affect of allowing people to relax. When we're understood, the anxiety-produced and producing strategies we use to calm ourselves down are unnecessary. If the truthful story of our lives is heard and comprehended, we no longer feel compelled to endlessly repeat it. There's a sigh of relief. With empathy, there are slight or significant shifts as people interact. Messages are sent and received. A sender senses that the message is understood. A receiver's perceptions are conveyed in body language and words capable of winning approval for their accuracy from the sender. With empathy, community flourishes. Building community needs more than empathetic skill, but these skills provide a solid foundation. To build community in our current circumstances, I suggest we also need to be cosmopolitan.

I want to wed empathy to a description of cosmopolitanism that moral theorist Kwame Anthony Appiah (2006) offers as an antidote to social dislocation, competition and isolation. His view isn't synonymous with multiculturalism or globalization. At its center are two interwoven strands of thought. One thought is that we have obligations to others that stretch beyond kith and kin and that ground citizenship. We share a common humanity that can't be set aside to secure private interests. The second thought is that this obligation isn't meant to neutralize important, particular values, beliefs and ways of life.[8] Cosmopolitanism, as he invents the term, challenges our need to live together in local and global realities and offers support to the project of being near and different. Community obligation derives from the thread of common humanity that unites the human tribe. Respect for difference arises from the commitments, values, practices and concerns that people take on and that shape their personal worldviews.

The first thought, Appiah's idea that the earth's citizens are connected through their common humanity, is congruent with philosopher Immanuel Kant's (1724-1804) modern moral framework. Kant thought that "obligation applies to all of us since the earth is round and connected. As a consequence, every part of the earth affects other parts and people cannot escape these effects without leaving the face of the earth."[9] To ground moral obligation, Kant made a model for humanity *as a sensible being* and *as a free being.* In so saying, he shaped our modern idea of humanity. Appiah doesn't reject Kant's modern individual. Rather, like Kant, he marries the individual to obligations that accrue because of membership in the human family.

Appiah's second thought is necessary because people live in proximity to those who are very different. In working out his second thought, Appiah doesn't fall prey to racism and sexism Kant failed to count in his own view. To be cosmopolitan is to be a world citizen as well as a citizen in one's own hometown. The perspective Appiah promotes is more of an attitude than a solution. Cosmopolitan people belong to their own city and to the universe, to humanity as a whole and a particular community. As he put it,

> Each person you know about and can affect is someone to whom you have responsibilities: to say this is just to affirm the very idea of morality. The challenge, then, is to take minds and hearts formed over long millennia of living in local troops and equip them with ideas and institutions that will allow us to live together as the global tribe we have become.[10]

The reader might respond by saying, well, we all know that—so we say 'think globally and act locally'. But Appiah observes that during the twentieth century, it became common practice among liberal members of Western cultures to distance/disdain their own religious or cultural tribe as a way to accommodate the difference of strangers. In his view, this move is a mistake.

World citizens don't denigrate their own people in order to appear magnanimous to those who are different. Cosmopolitanism's dual claims require loyalty to one's own tribe—culture, race, gender, class—at the same time that one is loyal to and supportive of humanity itself. To Appiah, "no local loyalty can ever justify forgetting that each human being has responsibilities to every other;"[11] yet in saying this, he doesn't minimize the importance of local loyalties.

The pattern of knowing *one's own people only* is a unifying feature of the harmful effects of contexts described in the previous chapter. In contrast, community is guided by empathy and cosmopolitanism. We aren't authentic if we disdain our own tribe. We aren't integrated unless we support our common humanity. We live in complex settings. It's essential to develop social literacy to the full if we want to manage twenty-first century social complexity successfully. Empathy and cosmopolitanism help resolve conflict as it erupts in complex social settings, but we also need to perceive the global patterns that shape social interaction if we want to enjoy life satisfaction in the midst of complexity.

The confusion created by complexity is relieved to some extent if we understand patterns that co-exist around the globe, since our cities, towns and villages are populated by people from everywhere. Some of the ways people act conform to patterns that, if understood, allow us to see their behaviour from their perspective, whether or not we would behave in those ways ourselves. Seeing these patterns helps to make sense of what we observe and allows us to sense what's unique in others, i.e., their authenticity.

It helps us to see that each global pattern has its own logic. Identifying each logic permits us to gain insight into the media rich, technologically linked, culturally diverse environments we're trying to comprehend. Getting this understanding also depends on developing the human capacity to care that others survive and thrive—a capacity that must be addressed directly, rather than left to chance. But caring for others doesn't require us to abandon ourselves or our people. Learning to notice the diversity that exists among our own people is part of learning to welcome and include those who differ in ways that tend to surprise us.

FOUR GLOBAL PATTERNS THAT SHAPE COMMUNAL EXPECTATIONS

In an essay,[12] Canadian philosopher Charles Taylor describes three global patterns that shape Western culture. I expand on a fourth pattern that pre-dates these three, which he mentions in the essay. The oldest pattern is the logic of honour/shame. The other three, which in some way attempt to address inequalities that are perceived in the oldest one, are the logic of equal dignity, the logic of difference and the logic of recognition.

My aim is to enable readers to notice and understand the characteristic way each pattern shapes expectations for how social interaction should work. While my goal isn't to suggest these patterns should change, the differences they create are so disruptive that, when under-analyzed, repairing conflict is extremely hard to accomplish. They also influence family dynamics, so that intergenerational family conflict is also hard to resolve if these patterns are misunderstood. As mentioned, healthy communities take adequate account of families. Honour/shame dynamics typify what we might think of as the traditional family model.

The twentieth century tendency to reinvent the family is a result of choices made during modernity as techniques were developed to track the masses of people. Over time, nation-states gave attention to populations, rather than extended family systems[13] that were root and branch of social life in pre-modern Europe. With a modern capacity to control the masses (using techniques invented during outbreaks of the plague) nation-states grew adept at simultaneously tracking people-at-large (the masses) and individual citizens. In that milieu, families seemed too small as data for the statistics-gathering machinery that developed and too large to provide the state with information it wanted to collect about each person. (Gathering and recording information about people allowed for the worst excesses of fascism in the twentieth century.)[14]

The need to learn social literacy derives from these very changes in social history that the four patterns pick out, in particular, the human need for recognition that's comprised of spiritual needs outlined earlier. Taylor proposed that the patterns (omitting honour/shame) are linked by a modern desire for recognition. The need for recognition arose due to a breakdown of hierarchies that supported pre-modern social arrangements in Europe (i.e., honour/shame). Recognition wasn't a new human need, but was felt to be new because modernity opened up the possibility of its failure.[15] Unlike lifelong, pre-modern European social hierarchies, in a modern world that gathers statistics about people, a holistic human sense of each person and the essential quality of a social group can easily, and often does, go unrecognized.

A breakdown of social hierarchies associated with the medieval family meant that people no longer knew their place in society. Social location had previously been guaranteed by family structures. Everyone knew they were a pauper or prince based on family of origin. They knew the first son got all the property, the second was sent away with very little. Girls had none. Or, if they had an inheritance, they turned it over to husbands when they got married. People knew in advance of living it out how the script of their lives would read. Recognition was guaranteed by one's place in a family and by that family's position in the social milieu. Once those social arrangements broke down, recognition was a pressing human need, and showed up as a surprise.

The Logic Of Honour/Shame

The pattern of honour/shame is a backdrop for the other three patterns. I spend more time on it because it's the least understood, yet perhaps the most pervasive, in, for example, gang cultures and at the core of bullying. One way to understand tensions between East and West, and among so-called developed and developing worlds, is to see in strong group cultures[16] the pattern for honour/shame that's central to them, based on a cultural/religious ethos that puts family at the core of social life. From its centrality, families shape social interaction on concepts such as filial piety or ancestor worship, and assume that family solidarity is a person's most vital link to the rest of the social world.[17]

Individualism makes little sense in strong group cultures. While the concept of person obtains in them, personhood is based on dyadic group membership, not on rights, individual identity and authenticity—as these concepts were worked out during Western modernity among solitary men who were loosely linked through minimally interdependent economic transactions that continued only as long as benefits from these exchanges flowed toward those whose interests were served by them. Freedom to walk away is for individuals only. Leaving one's family in strong group cultures, in contrast, is dangerous if not impossible, because one's family is one's only social safety net—a net to be trapped in, if the family is the Mafia, as an example.

Honour/shame shapes social interaction in stable, traditional, hierarchical societies and influences infrastructure, institutions, roles and the value of every person. All members of the social group occupy a social location determined by family of origin, or, as in the case of the Mafia, a family they join. Honour is the positive value of a person in his own eyes plus the esteem he has in the eyes of the group. His honour is recalled and remembered after his death and has value as long as his family lasts. It's a claim to positive worth and is acknowledged as such by others. It's public. Members are seen and recognized as having honour and being honourable. The worst fate is to be called a fool. To have no honour is to be worthless.

In the first pattern, honour is an abstract concept that's made concrete in a particular society's understanding of power, gender and precedence. Precedence refers to being ahead of others in rank. Those at the top of the social ladder hold the most honour. Measuring honour stratifies one's position in the group. In terms of family, father is at the top: a male (gender), head of a household (position), whom wives and children obey as a demonstration of his capacity to control them (power). If they disobey, he's shamed and loses honour.

It's honorable to maintain one's social location and act according to its script, even if that location is low down in the hierarchy. A servant is honorable if he or she conveys an appropriate deference to those above, a posture the other three patterns began to see as a contradiction of human worth. Clothing and manners express social stratification and the division of labour is based on social stratification (e.g., caste). Some work is dishonourable. Those who enjoy privilege don't do it. Those lower in rank carry it out. The television series, *Downton Abbey*, demonstrates how work was ranked in pre-WWI Britain. When everyone cooperates, a sense of honour in serving is equal to a sense of honour in being served. The television series shows how this global pattern was challenged in Britain after WWI and produced the middle class.

In the honour/shame pattern, privilege is based on family of origin because honour is passed through birth as a family endowment (as is inherited wealth). It's also acquired or actively sought and won from someone else (as is acquired wealth), although honour is associated with land rather than money. Honour always implies that some have it, some don't. If someone wins honour, another loses it. Public space is characterized by games of opposition, competition and rivalry. Endless win-tie-lose contests redistribute social honour. As a result, one must defend one's honour during every social interaction. A man's reputation is made and maintained by his ability to dominate inferiors and challenge his equals.

Strong groups are agonistic. Social interaction is organized around public contests of honour in which one warrior (*agon*, the Greek term for warrior) challenges another for precedence, i.e., to move up in rank. The public world doesn't only refer to encounters that happen for everyone to see. Gossip functions effectively to make a challenge public. Conflicts amount to a clash over space. If a dominant warrior holds a particular place, another warrior may enter and attempt to knock the first man off that space to position himself in it. Every challenge, all confrontation is perceived as an attack. In these games, space isn't only physical. It's a metaphor based on fencing matches. In a match, winning and losing have to do with the effective use of challenge and riposte—which may be carried out as a war of words.

Dyadic members wear honour and shame bodily. The effects of winning or losing honour create a socially shared map that enables people, and urges them, to put members, things, events in their proper place. A social map is condensed, expressed and carried in the physical bodies of people so that, dishonour, as an example, is conveyed in expressions such as: 'lick the dirt off my feet' or 'kiss my ass'. Honour is conveyed bodily in eye contact or gestures that signal respect or its lack. Looking down on someone is a gesture that's easily read. Tension here can be analyzed using Klein's description of map and model from the chapter on Human Connection. In public, for the man of honour, an encounter must conform to his map self appropriately. If not, conflict is inevitable. He must force map and model selves to conform or he loses honour.

To dishonour someone, a person higher up the ladder enters that person's space without permission. That entry produces resentment in social equals. Those lower down the ladder have no right to feel resentment.[18] Dishonour is communicated by boundary crossing, trespassing into someone's space or speaking in a contemptuous tone of voice. In games of honour/shame, how one speaks matters more than what's said. In honour games, it doesn't work for a speaker to say he didn't mean what he said. It doesn't erase the challenge.

Only equals play honour games. Women aren't equal to men. In honour/shame systems, families protect female honour by being vigilant over women's lives. Its pattern creates a male/female divide. Precedence in men, called honour, is referred to as shame in women. For women, shame refers to sensitivity to what others think, say and do with regard to their worth. Their shame is expressed as deference to male honour. Female shame means having shame, e.g., looking down in the presence of men. It's a positive attribute of a good woman. Young girls are explicitly taught that women have little value; an unruly daughter is a scourge. Insubordination to fathers, brothers and husbands is punished. To be a shameless woman has the same effect that being shamed has for a man. A good woman isn't shameless; a good man isn't shameful.

Shame for males is a loss of honour. For women it's the right attitude to take towards themselves and their value in the group. Educating girls is an apprenticeship that teaches them the superiority of men and the necessity for women to prepare themselves for harsh constraints that nature, men and God have decreed for her. Mothers treat girls harshly. Even though they prepare the meal, women are given less food than men and often eat what's leftover (if anything) after men have had their fill.[19]

In honour/shame systems, rearing boys involves a special combination of lavish love and physical punishment and pain.[20] To begin with, mothers pamper sons until the age that fathers take over: boys tend to be breast-fed twice as long as girls. A small boy's every wish is a command to his mother. She responds immediately. The boy that results from this treatment can be over-dependent, powerless, helpless and self-absorbed. Growing up in strong group cultures, boys may feel smothered by mother love when young but tossed into an aggressive, violent male world when older—an approach that's evident in gang culture. Boys learn to dominate women and weaker men in response to this seesaw of love and violence.

At age 7 or 8, boys pass into an adult male world and learn to cope with its harsh, hierarchical setting. They must scorn childhood and repudiate femininity to become men. They mustn't walk, run or play sports like a girl. To accomplish this separation from childhood, boys may become hyper-male or *machismo*. Physical punishment forces the shift from childhood to manhood, a transition that can take years. The point of punishment is to cement family loyalty and a father's authority. Family loyalty is also group loyalty. All misbehaviour shames the entire group. A child is taught to submit to the will of the head of the household. Children are to serve their parents. From the perspective of honor/shame, good outcomes include:

- a father's benefit of joy when he's old, material support from his sons
- a father that gains honour if his son takes up his trade or profession
- a sense for parents that death isn't sad; it's not the end if there's veneration of ancestors
- the obedience of sons that can be counted on if the father faces conflict with his equals

Bad outcomes include the

- stubborn, disobedient son who's uncontrollable, particularly face-to-face
- son that can't learn wisdom (in terms of the ways of life that the group values)

An authority structure is embedded in strong group family relations. Wives are submissive to husbands. Children are submissive to parents (especially fathers). A child may respect family authority outwardly by feigning obedience, which doesn't cause a public loss of face for the father, but remain inwardly rebellious. As modern Western readers note these details, it's easy to feel critical. Popular culture doesn't support automatic obedience or hypocrisy in children.

Honour/shame is an ancient pattern. It characterized Hellenism. In the Roman Empire, power and honour had their source in Rome. Outside the city, there was little honour. At that time, honour was grounded on the nation, the Roman people, the empire itself. It pertained to the Roman state and its relations to other peoples. To have honour was to be related to the Emperor or the aristocracy. This emphasis was a shift from family honour (in which knowing a family name meant knowing the person's value) to national honour (from a Hellenistic to a Roman perspective).

Glory, honour and prestige were secured through war and subjugating foreign peoples, rather than through heritage. The Emperor was linked to various parts of the empire through personal loyalty. He was the source of honour, which he distributed to cities and peoples as he pleased. The social relation between Emperor and people was a model that echoed through the Empire in the form of a common bond between client and patron. A client was obliged to show honour to his patron. In return, he received honour, perhaps as praise from his superior, which increased his value in the social world. Honour/shame has different features in the various global settings that conform to some of its central aspects: countries as different as China, Viet Nam,[21] Russia, Africa and Italy share aspects of its logic.

In the three patterns that follow, we see the emergence of individualism as a dominant value in the West. Its trajectory doesn't apply in societies that remain strong group in their orientation to family solidarity—yet individualism creates tension even in these cultures. In multicultural environments the tension increases unless we understand how to read the significance of a person from the cultural point of view in which a person makes sense.

The basic unit of social analysis in strong groups is a dyadic member. Dyadic implies more than one. Members are always in relation with and connected to a social unit, mainly the family. As a member, one is embedded in 'an undifferentiated family ego mass'.

This relation is caught in the expression, 'You are because we are'. Without one's group, one ceases to be. Internalizing the social idea of membership is necessary to being mature and shapes dyadic identity. To be human is to live up to group expectations: I means We. Members are singular persons but are embedded in the group identity. Social power is exercised through granting or withholding social honour based on living up to that identity. The group's perception enables members to live well in society. If modern individuals ask themselves: "Who am I?" strong group members ask, "Who do you (my people) say that I am?"

For dyadic members, identity is sociologically constructed: conscience implies relationship. Conscience is sensitivity to a public ego-image and has the purpose of striving to align personal behaviour and self-assessment with the publicly perceived group-image. As well, a member's conscience internalizes what's said and done to him or her; one's people are the appropriate witness and judge of a member's success in being mature.

For a strong group person, there's nothing on the inside that doesn't register on the outside. Emotional language is expressed in surface terms; e.g., anger is a gesture. It's evident in the ancient literature of some strong groups, e.g., Greek myths, that there's no evidence of mind-body dualism and little evidence of critical distance or critical reflection on events, and perhaps, no distinction between fantasy and reality. For dyadic membership, the world one inhabits is whole—the material and spiritual are unified—and these dimensions freely communicate with and influence one another. Individualism appears lonely from a strong group perspective. Dyadic membership appears oppressive from an individualistic point of view.

Moral identity in strong group members is drawn from the external bonds of attachment with other members in a relationally generous world of interdependence. Individualistic moral identity works from the inside. It's contiguous with the outside of each psychophysical entity in a materially scarce, hostile and competitive world. In a strong group context, loyalty to the group is absolute. Insider/outsider distinctions are essential to the maintenance of healthy group boundaries. For individuals, loyalty to oneself is paramount.

The Logic Of Equal Dignity

It's more than authority struggles that separate strong group societies from those based on individualism. The value of the individual is the pivot point in the shift to the next global pattern, the logic of dignity. For Taylor, social recognition shifted its meaning due to another change, the change from a concept of honour to a concept of dignity and a drive for identity. A modern ideal of equality was built on those two concepts and that drive. Honour/shame societies distributed honour unequally. Dignity, in contrast, was designed to apply to all. The insistence that identity was to be authentic was another modern urge. With the breakdown of medieval hierarchies, people were free to be equally valuable, but they had to invent themselves.

Taylor proposed a "balanced reciprocity" among people to underpin equality.[22] He said that the sense of being that was lost, and the need to invent oneself, meant that human beings remain remarkably dependent on the opinion of others. If personal dignity and identity are indelible modern contributions to living a fully human life, reciprocity among human beings was supposed to ease our isolation and permit us to connect authenticity with people that matter to us. To Taylor, balanced reciprocity takes the sting out of our dependence on opinion. In his view, reciprocity, along with a unity of purpose that makes it possible, ensures that, in following opinion, I'm not in any way pulled outside myself. I'm still obeying myself (my authenticity), yet I remain a member of the common project or general will.[23]

To him, the purpose of society is to offer resources for collaboration that a balanced reciprocity aims to achieve. I agree that we can unite these purposes but I think we must consider carefully what to make of global patterns that shape many of our expectations for what's possible to achieve in public life. Under what conditions do groups offer balanced reciprocity to their members? I'm less confident than Taylor that we've turned away from honour/shame in the West. I think we've shifted somewhat as to who does or doesn't receive a full measure of social honour. We may have turned away from the Roman ideal of social honour (the willingness to die for one's country) but the logic of honour/shame is discernable in many aspects of our complex global environment. The North American public world doesn't yet grant citizens equal dignity, even though it's the logic that challenged honour/shame after WWI.

Rather than saying honour was replaced with dignity, I think we emphasize dignity when it comes to whether or not we'll put our lives at risk for the state, as people refused to do during the Viet Nam war in the United States. But if we consider prestige, privilege, power and social value, all four patterns presuppose a system for distributing honour and shame that still shapes public life. If we survey human suffering, particularly the pain of exclusion and the withholding of recognition, we observe people caught in social contradictions[24] that, in part, result from, and accompany, a loss of social honour. As a consequence, honour/shame still functions in the three logics that supposedly took its place. All four logics operate in places where we live, work and learn, which is why they're on the social literacy curriculum.

The idea of personhood is a substantial difference among these patterns. In societies that grew out of modern reform—individuals live from the inside. There are two beliefs at the core of the modern liberal view of individualism. One belief holds that people should lead their lives from the inside according to their own beliefs about what gives value to life. A second belief posits that people are free to question beliefs and examine them in light of whatever information, examples or arguments society can provide.[25] Each person is an individual in terms of unique developments in his potential that are marked off by bodily or mental capacities. A modern individual is the basic unit of social analysis and is seen as capable of independence, self-awareness, self-consciousness, self-control, personal responsibility and autonomy. Individuals live in a social world of others who are autonomous, capable social agents.

The aim of an individual life is to seek the fulfilment of one's own interests. These interests include material necessities plus what that person thinks is worth having. Public space is a site for competition between equally competent moral agents. Instead of honour's scarcity, material resources are seen as scarce. Competition is unfriendly, potentially hostile. Individuals are self-conscious, self-aware and aware of themselves as the object of other people's observation. For each person, individualistic identity is shaped through self-consciousness: the self is a filter through which identity passes. Individualism assumes each person is in control of her or his life and must remain in control of self-images and self-concepts. A self-image is the picture I have of myself. Self-esteem is the value I place on that picture.

Autonomy (choosing one's own rules)[26] and self-control shape individualism. If anything goes wrong, individuals must find the cause in their own early development. They go back and fix it if they want to be well. They may get help, but ultimately only an individual can find a way to be well. During modernity, following Kant's lead, the model for humanity was an autonomous, rational subject, the 'man of reason'. Eventually, humanity was expressed in terms of emancipation from the old order (pre-modern medievalism in Europe and the honour/shame pattern). A modern person sought emancipation from that old order (including the Church), the free play of the mind (so that people could follow their thinking wherever it might lead), a belief in progress and the assertion of individual worth. Christopher Marlowe's *Doctor Faustus* examines the glory and flaw of this modern project.

As mentioned, in modern individualism, the rationally autonomous subject can always step back from any particular project and question whether he wants to continue pursuing it, since every end contains the potential for revising oneself. The modern self is free to revise projects, commitments and goals in the light of new evidence, a process in which human will and choice play central roles. The following list isn't only attributed to Kant, though much of it flows from what he inspired. At its core, individualism implies that people become mature *on their own.* Human will is future-oriented, action-focused. The modern philosophical notion of voluntarism, which Kant and others inspired, includes the following ideas:

- All action is voluntary
- Agents act on their own accord, without compulsion, constraint, or undue influence
- Willing implies independent action: in willing we determine our own destiny

- Free will is at the core of the general conception of voluntarism
- Voluntarism requires separating oneself from others to use reason to make decisions
- Decisions flow spontaneously from character or situations in which one is involved
- Acts are understood as voluntary if they are motivated from within, free, unprompted from without and unconstrained, deliberate and intentional
- Adults are mature agents if they have a developed capacity to act on their own volition
- When we see people act, we generally presume them to be acting voluntarily
- We believe that people, especially children, can have too much will so we domesticate the will, at the same time as we believe that mature people should decide and act voluntarily
- Voluntarism assumes a solitary decision-making agent who is self-conscious[27]
- Man is free in regard to the unfolding of his consciousness
- For a long time, his freedom was believed to be exercised within the freedom that God has to design the larger context in which human activity has meaning
- With the rise of atheism in the twentieth century, when half of the world's populations lived in atheistic regimes, the connection between human and divine will was minimized or lost.[28]

Given these features, the contrast between individuals and dyadic members is sharp. Twentieth century feminist theorists noted that voluntarism doesn't apply to women who do domestic labour and care for the young.

Identity in individuals is psychologically constructed. Conscience is an internal, personal voice, driven by autonomy and self-control. Being mature involves being sensitive to one's inner voice in the midst of many other voices as well as striving toward autonomy. An individual is his own witness and judge.

One source for emphasizing human dignity in the West is located in reactions to WWI[29] but a negative reaction to an honour/shame pattern, which compels us to work for our own honour at another person's expense, is ancient. Dio Chrysostom (1200s) argued that autonomy, together with working for the common good instead of one's personal honour, relieves the social burden of disharmony. He believed if many people failed to work for autonomy as well as the common good, many others would feel resentment, which he regretted in his own society. His perspective didn't win support in the mainstream of thought, until it resurfaced in the 1700s.[30]

French social reformer Jean-Jacques Rousseau (1700s) abhorred the practices of honour-getting that encouraged men to dominate other people. He made it his goal to oppose the pattern in his writings. His work opened a door to the equal distribution of social honour for all men and he influenced the generation that carried out the French Revolution. He also addressed conditions for women but perpetuated a strong group female identity that kept women from coming into their own. His reasons for hindering women are complex, but he may not have imagined a world of equality for women given that social shame was still a positive value for women at the time—a value that women themselves supported.

British author Mary Wollstonecraft made inroads for women by writing *The Vindication of the Rights of Women,* a book inspired by the French Revolution (1789)[31] that erupted after Rousseau's death. As a consequence, the initial notion of equal dignity was designed primarily for men, to extend their value beyond the elitism that characterizes the honour/shame pattern.

The pattern for equal dignity can be traced through Rousseau and Kant to John Rawls in the twentieth century—to mention three of its pivot points. Rawls (1971) established justice as fairness at the heart of equal dignity for the male heads of households. He criticized the political philosophy of Utilitarianism and asserted that:

> Each person possesses an inviolability founded on justice that even the welfare of society as a whole cannot override. For this reason justice denies that the loss of freedom for some is made

> right by a greater good shared by others. It does not allow that the sacrifices imposed on a few are outweighed by the larger sum of advantages enjoyed by many. Therefore in a just society the liberties of equal citizenship are taken as settled; the rights secured by justice are not subject to political bargaining or to the calculus of social interests. The only thing that permits us to acquiesce in an erroneous theory is the lack of a better one.[32]

The logic of equal dignity assumes that human beings are universally the same in important ways—everyone has an identical basket of rights and immunities. In particular, Rawls's thought experiment based on his Veil of Ignorance,[33] was a guarantee that people would offer equal, fair treatment to others as an outcome of the rational capacity each person has, i.e., as a function of their humanity. His view is grounded on sameness (our common humanity) not on difference.

With equal dignity, justice is done if people are treated as though they're the same. In its logic, one fights for non-discrimination that's *blind* to the ways in which people differ. The logic of equal dignity may permit reverse discrimination as a temporary measure to remove inequalities that result from historical disadvantages such as poverty, race or gender. But at some point, justice requires difference-blindness to take over. Those who support equal dignity see all forms of discrimination as a problem unless they're temporary. An equal dignity perspective may, for example, accuse a black (e.g., African American) leader of discrimination if he wants to hire only blacks for a project he's initiating in a black community, as his way to address radical poverty in that predominantly black area of the city.

A deep assumption for equal dignity sees all humanity as of equal worth. For Kant, our status as rational agents, capable of directing our lives and carrying out action by following principles, was a common human potential that was the same in everyone. For him, it was a capacity all human beings have and share (he's not always clear about women). It's this capacity that ensures the worthiness of persons and secures their respect. Equal respect amounts to treating people in a difference-blind fashion. Its proponents see it as unjust if some people are given special treatment. This sentiment arises from its opposition to the honour/shame pattern in which some people enjoyed personal benefits due to their position in the social hierarchy.

With the development and spread of equal dignity, new groups (in addition to all white men) began to question whether the pattern adequately accounted for their experience and the need to be included as those who deserve equal respect. In many ways, it's the shift from rationality at the core of dignity to the concept of humanity that opened a door to the next global pattern in the mid-twentieth to late twentieth century.

The Logic Of Difference

Whose lives did equal dignity proponents care about? In honour/shame, only elite males enjoy privilege, precedence and honour. Equal dignity expands that focus. But did the pattern accommodate everyone? Further, does difference blindness produce justice? In response to limitations in the equal dignity pattern—as it applied to more and more people and as these questions were raised—it occurred to many that being treated in a difference-blind fashion failed to provide them with mutual respect. An analogy may help. Suppose you have two glasses of juice, one is half full and the other is almost empty. You add one half cup of juice to each glass and offer them to two children. The children complain. Equal amounts added to unequal amounts won't produce an equal amount of juice for each child to drink.

If equal dignity requires us to treat everyone the same, the logic of difference requires us to notice and support human differences. While equal dignity emphasizes common humanity, the logic of difference prizes authenticity. There's an echo of Existentialism as well in its assertion that existence precedes essence—what's unique to us is more important than what's common among us. Equal dignity focused on the essential humanity that Kant prized. With the logic of difference, being one's own self matters most and implies living from the inside rather than being an outer-directed person. The pattern asks us to recognize what's distinct about people and to take that difference into account during social interaction.

Difference proponents accuse equal dignity of glossing over authenticity, ignoring it, or worse, trying to assimilate authentic identity into a mainstream culture that equal dignity itself established—sometimes described as the privileged culture of Western white-skinned men. The logic of difference asserts that, when equal dignity proponents look at the less powerful, they see people who aren't yet or who are less than they are. There's a standard of measurement implied in equal dignity, one that belongs to the powerful. Equal dignity uses a perspective employed by Plato—one common element offers itself as the measure for everyone's value. People inevitably end up judging that some have more, some have less of that one attribute. A concept of humanity itself is in danger of succumbing to a judgmental reaction, in which some people are seen as 'more human' than other people.

The logic of equal dignity and the logic of difference both affirm universal equality. Yet meeting that ideal is expressed through different solutions. Logic of difference proponents would add unequal amounts of juice to each glass to end up offering equal amounts to the two children. Their demand is for specificity. The complaint is that the less powerful person is dismissed by or assimilated into the dominant culture. Assimilation is the cardinal sin of authenticity because it opens a door to discrimination and establishes first and second-class citizens. Those who fit feel at home in the social world, those who don't, never do, and, as a result, don't flourish.

The difference pattern implies that identity is dialogical—personal identity is formed with others who have an impact on its formation. A difference pattern challenges the idea of individualism itself because the sense of who we are can be thwarted through social interaction that fails to recognize and accurately interpret important differences in individuals and groups. Franz Fanon made this point when he said that a normal black boy becomes abnormal as soon as he steps out his front door and enters the white world.[34] Guatemalan social theorist Rigoberta Menchu[35] realized the nature of mis-recognition when she spoke of the Indians who come down from their mountain homes to the city and are seen, at best, not as people, but as interesting costume wearers to the urban Ladinos who hold precedence and power.

The two patterns offend each other at their most sensitive point—human equality. The difference pattern urges people not to be blind to difference but to make these differences the basis of differential treatment so that justice can be realized. Unlike equal dignity, the logic of difference wants to maintain distinctiveness forever. Uniqueness forms and defines one's identity, as a person and as a culture. Mutual respect means rewarding people for expressing their potential to be different. The logic of difference gives equal respect to actually evolved cultures rather than seeing them as inadequate or not yet like the dominant one. A core assumption is that each group produces an equally worthy product in terms of culture—a view that's the result of cultural relativism.

In contrast, the logic of equal dignity is constrained to offer equal amounts of juice to the children's glasses as a way to perform a just social act. Its focus is on what a society is doing, or not doing, to alleviate injustice. It's less concerned about the disparities that come through one's family of origin or life experiences. There's a tendency to ascribe personal or family merit to these disparities—a move that the logic of difference can't countenance, and one that Putnam called amoral familism. The logic of difference wants to include all the ways we've come to be ourselves in the project of finding and securing equality—a tendency that the logic of equal dignity finds too costly for scarce resources, and, more significantly, a form of inequality itself. As an example, affirmative action, if it's used at all, should be a short-term solution to social inequality from an equal dignity perspective.

The Logic Of Recognition

As is evident, the patterns of equal dignity and difference offend each other—they're opposed at a pivotal point. Proponents find each other hard to tolerate, difficult to understand. Since they grew out of unfolding ideas (equal dignity needed to emerge before difference was seen as a problem), the patterns don't cross over the generations. They cause dissonance in families and institutions, a conflict that's addressed by Appiah's view of cosmopolitanism, which is a response to the twentieth century cultural relativism that motivated the logic of difference.

The vitality of cultural relativism waned during the 1980s, with the fall of the Berlin Wall and global practices of sanctioning countries that violate human rights. South Africa is one such example. Sanctions imposed on South Africa were an expression of resistance to Apartheid, a social system internal to South Africa that's unacceptable in the rest of the world. The global mood in the 1980s affirmed a responsibility to support human rights everywhere and step in where they were violated, although that sentiment can be used to open up opportunities for imperialistic greed to insinuate itself along with an outward show of justice. My experience in Liberia (2007, 2008) revealed that imperialistic opportunism is always ready to give support as a way to get a country's resources.

The logic of recognition is grounded on the kind of responses that motivated sanctions against South Africa. It's an attempt to balance being ourselves in the presence of other people, at the same time that we're constrained by common humanity. The logic of recognition depends on the skill of perceiving humanity in others, even those who differ, and realizing how their practices are expressive of that humanity. It calls on people to notice when social practices are dehumanizing—when difference is inexcusable—such as in instances of slavery, child abuse and rape. The logic of recognition is an attempt to bring together demands of dignity and demands of difference. The project sounds like the right move to make, given our current circumstances, but the idea needs support from social literacy, if it's to be understood and put into practice.

The logic of recognition aims to resolve tension and points to a few, deep-going common human themes as a way to escape the stalemate between the previous two patterns. Relational work is an embodied practice that acknowledges differences and permits recognition to be realized. Recognition grounds a possibility for learning social literacy by providing a framework that's flexible enough to include essential human features while prizing the authenticity that modernity made possible. A proponent of recognition engages in relational work before adding juice to the two children's glasses and seeks to know more about the children before juice is offered, for example, to discover whether one of the children has just had a big drink of juice.

There are similarities between Appiah's cosmopolitanism and Taylor's logic of recognition. I don't mean to imply that either is easy to work out in practice. It may seem harder to do relational work involved in the logic of recognition than to stay in old patterns, even if they're personally and relationally harmful. Sometimes people prefer to remain harmed and harmful rather than to do the hard work of figuring out how to be more effective during social interaction. But those who prize social literacy can't be indifferent to its potential. In learning social literacy, we first notice how the body operates personally/socially and recognize how face-to-face contexts and under-analyzed global patterns threaten our hopes for being community.

LIBERATED PRACTICES

If contexts are settings we're woven into, as we try to build community, authenticity and integration take conscious effort. The co-existing needs to integrate and authenticate ourselves within a group (at home, school or work) are a modern existential necessity. If people want to learn to be themselves while they're with others, their future flourishing depends on a developed capacity to be themselves when they're with others in the contexts that are a present reality for them—which include the influence of global patterns that cut a broad swath through our complex societies.

If we see the need to resist injustice in contexts that harm us, what motivates us to meddle with the logic of four global patterns? I have already said that they aren't constructed on a deficit model. In one sense, they aren't in conflict. At least, the first logic isn't in open conflict with the others if I also argue that we've not put away the need for social honour as an element of public and family life. Again, changing that pattern wasn't the goal of trying to understand it. However, change itself isn't so easy to ignore these days.

Decades ago it was commonplace to say that people don't like change. It was an enemy of personal happiness—something to be resisted at all cost. That's no longer the way people talk about change. Now it's normal. To resist change is to fall behind. But what do we know about it? How can change be healthy and actually work towards developing authenticity, integration and social literacy? What else do we need to learn in order for change to be healthy?

Given intergenerational differences that tend to go along with global patterns, the current complexity of public life demands that we learn to be empathetic and cosmopolitan, two terms I outlined earlier. Conditions that arose with the logic of difference, e.g., based on race, gender, wealth, have increased the complexity of modern life. Further, we're thrown together at home, work and school with people whose experience is grounded in contexts and patterns very different from our own.

American psychologist and educator, Robert Kegan, identified this situation in his book, *In Over Our Heads*, in which he argued that complexity in modern and post-modern life requires the development of relational skills and social insight that enable us to get distance from the contexts into which we're woven when we're young. But to him, unlike influential theorists in the early twentieth century, such as Sigmund Freud, getting distance from an at-home world doesn't mean abandoning it.

Getting distance allows us to see a context or social pattern for what it is and to, in his terms, dis-embed ourselves from it. If you consider the weaving metaphor used to describe a context, we need to see how we're woven into a context clearly enough to notice its weft and woof—to see why we think what we think and do what we do. With that insight, we acknowledge its uniqueness and decide what elements we want to keep, what we what to unpick and remove, what we'll recombine to give our identity a new look. In all this personal work, we use materials we got when we were young, granted to us through tradition and heritage, as well as bits and pieces, or whole frameworks, we pick up by being with others who have known a very different way of life.

Getting distance is like the difference between looking through eye glasses and taking them off and looking *at* them—or having them analyzed—to see how they impact what we see. As mentioned, Kegan isn't proposing that we walk away from commitments and communities in order to redesign ourselves. He's not suggesting we walk around without eyeglasses. He's suggesting we do the relational work of being with those who matter to us in a way that's congruent with the personal worldview we each form over time.

Personal worldviews are formed from experience from the time we're born. As we grow, we're influenced by people, objects and conditions in the world. Parents, siblings, extended family, material objects, wealth, poverty, gender and race impact us as we make up our minds about what the world's like and what we can expect from it. We record and use our experience in the essential human project of making meaning. In psychological terms, everything we interact with is an object of experience that gives meaning to our lives.[36] According to Kegan, forming a worldview includes moving through a first and second stage of consciousness to a third stage, at which point the self is organized as a system. The meaning system formed out of this process is a worldview. The stages are an ongoing process of loss and recovery that move a person forward developmentally and meaningfully. Relying on Piaget's work, his stages include the following:

- Sensori-motor: embedded in reflexes, then reflexes show up to the child as perceptions
  - Mother shows up as separate, lose-able; infant expresses separation anxiety
- Pre-operational: embedded in perceptions, then perceptions show up as concrete
  - Self emerges as an object
- Concrete-operational: embedded in the concrete, then concrete shows up as thought
  - Self emerges as a role
- Formal-operational: embedded in thought, then thought shows up as an organization
  - Self emerges as a system [What Kegan means by third order consciousness]

That third order system, a personal worldview, lasts into adulthood.[37] It's a meaning system constructed through relational experience that informs character. To address the complexity of modern life, Kegan believes we need to allow change to move us beyond a third order of consciousness to a fourth—a shift that requires the skills of social literacy, although he doesn't use that expression.

How do worldviews change? Changing a worldview comes about through alterations in meaning. A worldview formed when we're 11 or 12 becomes relativistic for a period of time—like the cultural relative phase mentioned earlier. In this period, thinking and acting differently opens up a worldview to new ideas. But relativism operates on the meaning we've already made through memory.

Meaning is not the same as truth. Truth is something else. A problem shows up if we assume meanings we've made are exactly the same as truth. If we're relativists about truth rather than meaning, we're locked in little relativistic merry-go-rounds. We're trapped—there's nothing outside our worldview that allows us to get off—no truthful reality to challenge our settled ideas. Our own thinking is all there is. Some people seem happy to remain on a merry-go-round—but to stay there is to be stuck in third level consciousness. Reflection leads us out of our worldviews by truth itself—by directly observable data, by an education in reality, by the way others explain themselves, rather than by sticking with our interpretations—as Action Science teaches us to do.

The motion of meaning-making is necessarily relational and builds up through giving and getting attention, by attending to ourselves and others because "meaning depends on someone who recognizes you."[38] Recognition is attention that meets relational needs. If needs are met, we have the courage to come out of our tight-fitting, sealed-off fortresses (to become more open) or to get off a relativistic merry-go-round (to become more committed to a chosen way of life).

Giving and getting attention is paramount to moving from one stage to another. We learn as infants whether or not we're the sort of people who get and keep attention. Those unable to secure it are impoverished by their lack of skill. The greatest human inequalities come from a diminished skill at recruitability. That poverty goes deep—creating an expectation that we'll neither be heard nor seen: that we're invisible and no one cares for us.

Recruitability is the term Kegan uses to describe the capacity to attract and hold other people's attention. It's an ability that develops as we make meaning from experience. Healthy community redresses that poverty and teaches the skills of recruitability to the young so that insufficient attention doesn't limit life chances. But attention getting has other extreme, a lust for unlimited attention, which is addictive. In community, attention is equally distributed. If we get sufficient attention so that we're heard (and hear ourselves) a worldview relaxes into curiosity. Growth arises as we realize sensations and memories are interpretations not sense perceptions, i.e., the absolute truth about the world. It's in realizing that memories form interpretations of the world that we're able to mature. Growth is upsetting and disturbing—but relief isn't achieved by abandoning the world we made when we were young.

To Kegan, we're compelled to revise worldviews as we grow up, not reject them. As he asserts, "every one of us grows up with... an orthodox faith."[39] Transformation from third to fourth order consciousness comes about as we step back from family religion *without* believing that we have to abandon it.

While all reflection requires us to step back from experience, the difference between socially literate people and those inspired by modern reformers such as Sigmund Freud (for all his immense and valuable contributions to human understanding) is expressed by the reflection Kegan recommends. He doesn't require people to reject childhood concepts and the systems of families of origin, as Freud did; nor does he insist that we reject God in order to grow up, as did Freud. He invites people to observe how at home systems of thought and action have shaped us, and decide what parts to keep, what parts to release our grip upon.

By family religion, Kegan doesn't mean formal Christianity or Judaism. Rather, it's "a deep idiosyncratic belief system about what the world is really like;" a "constant minute-to-minute foundation and guide to the purpose of life and the meaning of realizing that purpose,"[40] which we learned at home. Moving from third to fourth order consciousness occurs as we're no longer held in the grip of family religion and become its conscious adherents, so that it no longer holds us, but we hold it. We're aware of what we do and think and what we intend to do and think. Family religion isn't formal religion. It may be that authentic Judaism or Christianity could hold the very means, by comparison, for revising family religion.

The point isn't to reject family religion so much as to realize what it means for us to hold it, rather than to be under its influence without realizing it. To Kegan, the idea of family religion is meant to direct effort away from a tendency "to demean, belittle, undervalue, indict, or pathologize every aspect of our heritage" and he "bids us... to take a respectful and appreciative inventory of the life-sustaining, significance-bearing elements of our upbringing."[41]

The metaphor of family religion, as a way of speaking about worldviews and the motion of meaning-making throughout life, "does not mean that the move to modernity...requires us to leave that family or the religion. What it requires is that we construct a new relationship to our family and its religion."[42] An at-home inner world (what Kegan calls a family religion) is confirmed by the language and experience of memory-based, memory-transmitting communities. What do the young hold in memory that forms their first faith system or picture of the world? How might they differentiate from, yet feel at home with that family religion?[43] Kegan's view of our relationship with kith and kin is congruent with Appiah's cosmopolitanism—with his belief that we can prize both our common humanity and our own people.

Kegan knows that the complexity of modern life requires relational work[44] because we haven't yet caught up with the requirements of modern/post-modern life.[45] (It's complexity that creates the need for social literacy—a skill set that allows us to learn how to do relational work.) How is this relational work to be done? To Kegan, object-relating holds an intrinsic interest for human beings: ego activity *is* object-relating and begins at birth.[46] He organizes psychological development and educational transformation around the meanings made through object-relating.

We make meaning through encountering objects in the world as we organize experience. What every organism does is organize; "what a human organism organizes is meaning."[47] In offering his claim about identity, Kegan re-interprets Jean Piaget's stages of human development to reveal an omission that matters if we believe children are capable of empathy and insight that Piaget didn't seem to think possible. While being faithful to Piaget's stages, Kegan focuses, not on the developmental plateaus Piaget described, but on the process of moving from one plateau to the next. Kegan emphasizes making meaning and thinks that the plateaus aren't the main point of our attempts to understand human development, although he doesn't criticize Piaget's stages.

In exploring human development, Kegan thinks Piaget described the achievement of meaning-made, not the dynamic self engaged in the struggle "to make meaning, to have meaning, to protect meaning, to enhance meaning, to lose meaning and to lose the self along the way."[48] Kegan focuses on dynamism: a self in motion—the ebb and flow of loss and recovery regarding the meaning attached to various assumptions we hold to be important. Hard relational work moves us through loss and recovery so that meaning is re-organized sufficiently for life to be hopeful and to help build community based on being near and different.

Meaning making implies change. If a worldview is seen as a static, unchangeable state of mind, the work of meaning making is undermined. This is true on two counts: firstly, learning social literacy allows us to genuinely encounter other people's worldviews; secondly, learning social literacy requires us to perceive our own worldview accurately. Making meaning is a process in which new experiences inform a worldview that's already in place. Integration (fitting in) plus individuation (distinguishing one's self) constitute our relational work. The individuation that achieves authenticity isn't separation. To fit in and be different is to be authentic and realize one's innate capacities,[49] a process that's interactive. As an example,

> We cannot integrate the potentially enriching experiences of others into our own self-understanding unless we first have a self; to gain a self, we must first relate to and then differentiate from community. It is a continuously enriching circular movement of interaction and definition. Once one is able to accommodate to new configurations of self, the personality remains open to alterations and enrichment.[50]

The interactive involvement between our worldview and the active presence of those who differ from us is a skill to be learned by the socially literate.

Social literacy, then, is a complex set of skills that includes a capacity to read the body, generate appropriate actions and reactions within one's cultural environment, decode contexts, notice global patterns, perceive differences between one's own typical way of acting and the way required by a new, perhaps foreign, context or pattern. Social literacy develops a capacity to realize that ineffectiveness in a given context is both personal and public. It's personal because the mis-communication belongs to an individual speaker; it's public because a mis-match is constructed in a given setting. An ineffective speaker in one setting may say exactly the same thing in the same way in another setting and enjoy audience acceptance.

In the chapter on Human Connections, I discussed Bordeau's notion of thinking on our feet, which is central for learning social literacy. He was effective in a working class setting in his youth. He reflected on the use of those skills so that eventually, he fit in an elite French school culture and achieved the most valued intellectual position in France. The way he used his skills are like advice given to beginning writers: Know your audience. Teachers ask students to consider their audience as a primary means for deciding what to write and how to write it.

Social literacy is as hard as learning to read and write, but we have less practice with it. It actually gets off the mark when things go wrong and we learn from our mistakes. If our context doesn't change, we seldom learn social literacy, since we already fit that *ethos.* If life circumstances continue to support the worldview we created in adolescence, social literacy seems unnecessary. But few of us live in a world that's just like us. In multi-cultural societies, we can't escape diversity. If our setting is a mix of working, middle and elite class sub-cultures, we need to adjust to it. Face-to-face contexts and large-scale global patterns have rules of the game that differ. For change to be healthy, we need to address the whole picture of someone's worldview and take it into account, at least by understanding that it holds together as a meaningful way of life.

CONCLUSION

The aim of this chapter is to help people get distance from global patterns that shape thinking and acting, to reflect on thought and action, and decide how we want to live, act and speak in the future. Bourdieu and Kegan thought we could integrate into community only if we understand its logic, exemplified in embodied social practices that help us stay with people rather than walking away from them. Social literacy relies on our capacity to observe what we're doing, what others are doing, and choose approaches and responses that enhance social interaction. Since we're agents in these actions and reactions, we're able to change what we're doing, if we want new outcomes from the social encounters in which we play a part.

In the next chapter, I point out that the use of power in social relations is a feature that must be understood if social literacy is to flourish. Doing healthy relational work, learning social literacy, and figuring out how we want to live when we grow up, are all significantly impacted by the way we use power. The way others use power also shapes our expectations for the way social interaction will go. As a consequence, power is on the social literacy curriculum.

6

POWER AND SOCIAL LITERACY

INTRODUCTION

Charles Taylor's notion of reciprocity is a basic social equation that encourages mutual respect. Socially literate people show respect, with the result that everyone in a community is integrated with others yet remains authentically themselves. In this chapter, I explore a role social power plays in mutual respect. My purpose is to show that power can interfere with or support social literacy. If it's used to create reciprocity, people are free to be themselves as they integrate with others. If power is misused, people are neither authentic nor integrated. In analyzing power's role, I assume that power operates in every social interaction. Learning to perceive the patterns of its operation is part of a social literacy curriculum. The goal is to understand how to exercise power so that reciprocity creates and sustains mutual respect.

Canadian author Margaret Atwood gave CBC[1] radio lectures on debt as part of an *Ideas* series. It received more online hits than most *Ideas* presentations. Debt's a big deal. As I read her text, I realized she was describing reciprocity—what she called *tit for tat*—an expression most of us picked up on the playground. She gave two examples, one from nature and one from computer programs, to illustrate a sense of justice she thinks is deeply embedded in our expectations for social interaction. I agree. Without justice, life is, in the words of Enlightenment-era philosopher Thomas Hobbes, "short, nasty and brutish."

Atwood's first example was an experiment with capuchin monkeys.[2] Primate researcher Frans de Waal and anthropologist Sarah F. Brosnan taught capuchin monkeys to trade pebbles for slices of cucumber. At one point, the researchers, knowing the monkeys saw grapes as more desirable than cucumbers, gave one monkey a grape for the same amount of work that previously had earned a slice of cucumber. As de Waal noted, the monkeys were perfectly happy getting cucumber twenty-five times in a row, but when only one monkey received a grape for work of equal value, the rest got upset, started throwing pebbles out of their cage and eventually refused to co-operate. The majority of monkeys got so upset if only one of them was given a grape for equal work they stopped eating altogether. Brosnan and de Wall pointed out that, while trading pebbles for cucumber slices had to be learned, the sense of outrage that the monkeys expressed at inequality appeared to be spontaneous.[3]

In Atwood's second example,[4] computer programs were designed to test what sort of behaviour patterns would prove to be the most robust in helping to survive the longest in a series of encounters with other programs. The experiment was designed so that when a program "met" another it had to "decide" whether to co-operate, be aggressive, cheat or refuse to play. The programs tracked each other's actions and stored each previous response. The winner was called *tit for tat.* Its winning strategies were the following: on a first encounter, co-operate; after that, do whatever the other program did on the previous encounter. *Tit for tat* won because it was never repeatedly victimized—"if an opponent cheated on it, it withheld co-operation next time—and, unlike consistent cheaters and exploiters, it didn't alienate a lot of others and find itself shut out of the play."[5]

The computer programs operated on a level playing field. None were advantaged in terms of power or weaponry. With *tit for tat,* one good turn deserved another, as did one bad turn. *Tit for tat* showed cooperation the first time but played by the rule "do to others as they do to you," a rule used by Paley's kindergarten children, except that, unlike the school children, *tit for tat's* first move was always to cooperate. It's second move was to withhold co-operation, not to instigate harm. Monkeys and computer programs demonstrate a pattern that sheds light on human interaction. We expect fair play. We know something's wrong if others get unjustified special treatment because they use power to create and sustain inequality. To survive in social groups, we expect fairness partly because we sense how easy it is to hurt and be hurt. Fairness is an antidote for evil, but, unlike computer programs, people don't live on a level playing field. This is why theorists refer to justice as a deficiency concept—it's required due to a human tendency to initiate, sustain and be caught in situations of circulating harm, for example, in abusive families. As some of the children in higher grades had learned, if they couldn't win at social interaction games, even if they tried, they stopped playing. They withheld themselves, not their cooperation. They were marginalized in the group, or marginalized themselves. Unlike the computer game, they lost their power to play the game that was directed toward their academic achievement.

A sense of always losing was stored in memory, which is why Paley saw the Golden Rule as necessary. Differences between computer programs and people have to do with how power is exercised for or against us and how it accumulates in the meaning-making activity that creates and perpetuates everyone's view of what she or he can expect from life. Because human beings are meaning-makers, the effects of power reside in body and heart, persuading some of us to live in a way that's barely tolerable, rather than integrated and authentic.

This chapter describes the power that's exercised during social interaction in order to spell out some of what can make us human in terms of integration and authenticity. I situate the discussion in a network of ideas that include the nature of symbolic power (of which monkeys and computers programs are examples), the art of using power, the misleading effects of individualism on how we learn to use power and an outline of power's patterns to uncover some of what we're up against as we're learning social literacy.

The patterns of power inform us about opportunities we have to test our skill, strength and integrity as we develop social literacy.

At its root, social literacy assumes that others have a strong influence on us, an affect we carry within and that we can learn to read. As we learn to read social interaction effectively while we are engaged in it, we get better at making ourselves understood. If we get better at making ourselves understood, we enjoy more fairness and freedom while we're with other people.

But skill in social literacy depends on seeing how power operates so we can distinguish the nature of its games and respond appropriately without getting trapped. Understanding how power operates allows us to be objective, in the sense worked out by Bourdieu and described in chapter two, and helps to increase personal freedom while we're with other people.

THE NATURE OF SYMBOLIC POWER

What traps are at play when people use power? While a traditional view of power situated its use in position and privilege, twentieth century thinkers began to describe power as energy that moves among everyone, everywhere. Power came to be seen as more pervasive than influence that's attached to a privileged position. In this view, described by French philosopher Michel Foucault, power is symbolic—it's felt, and it has effects. It's circulating energy that compels and constrains action. We see its effects in the monkeys' reactions to unfair treatment. Something got them started, kept their protest going and changed the way the researchers had to treat them in order to regain their cooperation.

Seeing power as energy is a new insight. Traditionally, power was thought of as the willingness and ability to get what one wants—a definition that sounds negative, self-absorbed and gives power a bad name. Recall that the monkeys were reacting against unequal treatment. Power is expressed if people get their way easily, but we want to understand how power operates more broadly than that. Why do some people get what they want so easily? People who seem to have this power often speak of it negatively themselves, as if sometimes they feel badly about having it. Perhaps they can't repress what even monkeys know about fairness. Yet power isn't only negative. If power were always bad or negative, the ethical response to having it (if one wanted to be good) would be to throw it away. That option has incalculable hazards that I point out later in the discussion of power's patterns.

At this point I want to dislodge a belief that power is only negative. I want to dispute the traditional way we've described it. Power isn't negative. It's ambiguous and therefore leads to ambivalence in social relations: power may be beneficial, harmful, enervating, energizing, productive or paralyzing. Its effects are complex and relational. If power operates in every social interaction, and if it's always bad, every encounter would be irredeemably bad. This isn't the case. The power a parent exercises to develop competencies in a child might be beneficial, energizing and productive in one case, or harmful, enervating and paralyzing in another. One needs to observe the child to see how power operates in her home. Foucault believed we couldn't assess power unless we observe the people on whom it's exercised. For example, if a guest speaker enters a classroom, attentive to its ethos, she's able to tell, by observing students' expectations and habits, whether the teacher wields power abusively, is neglectful, or uses power wisely. The effects of symbolic power reside in those who experience them; they ground one's expectations about life, the self and other people.

Symbolic power is not a specific type of power. Rather, it's driven by energy that runs through all social interaction to compel or constrain action. When it's negative (harmful) it forecloses on negotiation. If it's violent, it may still appear quiet or it may be carried out on inanimate objects. For example, a teacher may slam a door on the way into class to signal to students he's in a dangerous mood and isn't to be approached or bothered. A parent may break a glass to get a partner's attention or throw dishes across the living room, narrowly missing her children. These acts convey symbolic power. Even people who aren't touched physically are affected by its symbolic impact. They get the message and feel its effects. We can't ignore symbolic power. Those affected may not be conscious of its effects, but will express the impression it leaves on them if they fail to challenge its legitimacy. For example, they may adapt to violence and construct a life story in which bad treatment is all they should expect from other people. Or perhaps, they act rebelliously but are unable to say why or identify what they hope to accomplish by being obstinate. Further, effects of symbolic power show up neurologically and biologically.

Remember, though, symbolic power isn't only negative and harmful. Love is powerful. It leaves its health-giving impressions on the body and in the heart.

Symbolic power always requires either passive or active co-operation from those on whom it's exercised. We can't love fully those who refuse to be loved by us. We can't harm completely those who refuse to be harmed by us. Something in the human soul either resists or capitulates to power.

Pierre Bourdieu describes capitulation as passive or active complicity.[6] People co-operate in a power relation (albeit to the smallest extent) in a life story they tell about themselves. In passive complicity people seem not to notice injustice, or they tell themselves they're the kind of people who should expect to never get what they need or want. In active complicity, people agree (even if to only a small extent) that some people have a right to use power to hurt them and that they can't do anything to resist it—either because they believe that power is legitimate or necessary, or because they're afraid powerful people will create harm that's too expensive for them to endure. They express active complicity in the fear they feel that they'll be harmed if they complain.

Fear of symbolic power may be expressed in senseless reactions to social life, whether through acting aggressively or feeling invisible—as though no one can see us at all—hence there's no point in taking action to resist. If people are hurt by symbolic power and are complicit, they carry out daily rituals to affirm their insignificance, for example, by demonstrating a slavish attitude. When they speak to others, they seem always to be asking for a favour rather than acting in freedom to negotiate basic needs and interests. They remain an object of experience rather than its agent.

Harmful symbolic power is often unrecognized. Suppose a third party observes a young boy's behaviour at a given moment and doesn't account for the way power has been operating in his life, and as a result, judges his behaviour as proof that there's something wrong with him. Bystanders can strengthen passive and active complicity by supporting an apparent lack of value in a victim if they think something like, "If this is happening, there must be something wrong *with this person.*" Over time, people may comply with this tacit social judgment.

Many of us are accustomed to thinking of power as it applies to questions of gender, race, poverty, or physical and emotional abuse as extreme examples of its harm. Certainly we need to give attention to these instances, but in ordinary daily life, power can be used to withhold human value from some people.

Workplaces, in their continuation of boss culture, seldom exercise overt force. Bullies can be quite charming. They have to be charming at least some of the time or they wouldn't have the influence they need to misuse power—others would simply ignore them. Their symbolic power is embedded in hierarchies that serve their interests, but no one else's. I'm not saying hierarchical structures are bad. I'm suggesting we need to perceive how power operates in them so we learn to counter its *unjust* use. We can learn to say *ouch* if someone insults us, just as we would if someone stomped on our toes.

When symbolic power is strengthened by active or passive complicity, oppressed individuals *agree* to some extent with its exercise, even if their complicity isn't obvious to them. I don't intend to blame victims in saying this. The point is that people can learn to stop agreeing to bad treatment. If recipients weren't in some way implicated in the injustice, there would be no escape. I suggest victims can refuse to see themselves as deserving of rude, unequal, unjust treatment—even if they can't see an immediate way to alter the situation. The first step is to *disagree* that it's okay for some people to disrespect other people.

When power is misused, symbolic violence is a necessary and effective means for its exercise. Even mild misuses of power have the strength of violence, thinly veiled, lying behind them, but those on whom power is exercised feel it keenly. This type of power has the attributes of a so-called smart weapon. It can be aimed precisely at one person in a group and miss all others. As a consequence, the targeted person gets no emotional support from those who don't feel the impact. Isolation strengthens the harm of abusive power—separating out the victim is essential to its effectiveness as a social weapon.

The negative effects of power, expressed by foreclosing on negotiation, enable imbalanced, dehumanizing systems to be established and maintained through strategies, softened and disguised, to conceal abuse beneath a veil of what's permitted to be said and done to certain people. In industrial societies, symbolic violence is built into institutions themselves—workers are spoken to in ways that managers aren't. Negative uses of power dehumanize people and foreclose on negotiation and genuine involvement by those held captive by them—both those who harm and those who are harmed. A harmful use of power is essentially self-destructive for those who carry it out. It takes a lot of energy to maintain unjust relationships; that energy turns in on itself. Those who abuse become self-absorbed. As Goleman points out, "self-absorption in all its forms kills empathy, let alone compassion."[7] If empathy dies, those who harm others no longer sense when others are hurt by what they do. I don't say this to make an excuse for abuse, but to describe the deep pit abusive people dig for themselves. The human spirit is an agent of communication that's crushed by abuse—in oppressor and oppressed.

An abuse of power invests the body. We wear its effects. Suppose that you've learned to be enslaved. That diminished value feels so familiar you don't perceive it as unjust. On the other hand, suppose you've learned to say and do whatever you want, without restriction. In neither case would you understand nor practice social literacy. Collaboration is its primary outcome. Social literacy teaches people to use power in healthy ways. As part of learning social literacy, we come to notice if power is used to negate human value. Socially literate people know that power is ambiguous, they perceive the ambivalence it creates and choose to use power in healthy ways.

Ambivalence, Freedom And Power

If freedom and authenticity are to be learned through social engagement, we must be willing and able to contemplate what's going on around and within us. As an example, it might be justifiable to stratify academic achievement in school, but the system collapses if we think some children can be socially literate while others aren't.

By its very nature, social literacy involves everyone. As we establish networks for learning how to improve social interaction, no one can be left out. We fail to meet a fundamental democratic goal if some people marginalize others during social interaction, simply because they can.

Democracy aims at being classless. Learning social literacy involves working effectively with everyone, or at least expecting to do so. At home or at school, social literacy helps identify assumptions we hold about fairness and challenges our assumptions about exclusion. I pick up threads of this point in the section on empowerment, but for now I want to say that social systems fail to be inclusive if they stratify human value by using power negatively. Power's misuse stymies our freedom to be authentic and integrated into community.

Many questions face us as we consider power, freedom and social literacy. Prior to the post-modern era, Western modernity held several assumptions about life that impacted our expectations for social interaction. Modern theorists asserted that people were individuals, human progress was possible, human thought was free to go wherever it wanted and human associations should be terminated if they no longer provided satisfaction for one of those involved. As an example, if a marriage wasn't providing what one party wanted, divorce was reasonable. This view was in sharp contrast to pre-modern views of marriage that stressed the duties married people had to one another, to children and society as a whole. Modern freedom held few limits and wasn't impressed by dutifulness.

In the post-modern era, theorists saw that power operates during social interaction in ways that mean people aren't as free as modern theorists supposed. Further, they argued, we mislead ourselves if we believe that some people can act as solitary individuals. Other people constrain us. In addition, a modern belief in human progress was challenged by observing the cruelty and despotism of the Holocaust. Modern human beings didn't become more humane. It has also become apparent that human thought has a trajectory rooted in childhood and can't simply go whenever it pleases. People are situated within the cumulative effects of their life histories. And further, psychologists can calculate the harm done to families when parents leave. In post-modern critiques, power plays a central role in explaining why freedom doesn't conform to modern assumptions. Some questions about freedom also challenge the idea of social literacy. For instance, if we accept neuroscience's view of social interaction, are we acting freely when we respond to someone or to ourselves? When is action free? When is it constrained by people, assumptions, habits or the environment? The extent to which people act freely may be impossible to measure, but learning social literacy is a positive move. It makes conscious our intentional decisions and allows more freedom than we have if we don't read social interaction very well (which often means getting trapped or trying incessantly to elude commitment).

I want to show that freedom is limited within human encounters, but that understanding social literacy, like being able to read a book, opens a door to seeing what's going on. Freedom in social interaction is based on a developed capacity to perceive what's going on. What's going on may be unique in a situation you find yourself in, but generally, people exercise power in discernible patterns. We can be freed up, to some extent, by perceiving and negotiating these patterns and resisting their harmful effects. Freedom is an outcome of acting wisely in the moment, as we engage with others, if, at the same time, we see what's going on. But it takes hard relational work.

Freedom has limits. Recent philosophers and researchers have noted its limitations as they became more aware that people act in systems of social interaction—they don't act alone. Individual action takes place in living systems, for example, in political systems in which people have degrees of freedom, even if they're in positions of leadership. Ordinary people "buy or sell, vote or [do] not vote, speak up or remain silent, support or criticize leaders" yet "there is an overall tendency to 'submit to the ordering restraints' of the whole" and "behave in ways consonant to the maintenance of the social order."[9] If citizens don't conform to democratic behaviour and expectations, the outcome is that they degenerate into tribal warfare, whatever those tribes might be in a given setting[10] (for example, rule by the Mafia in some cities).

The insight that people act within systems provides a framework for examining patterns for the use of power. While freedom is an outcome of wise action, wisdom is learned through a developed capacity to read social interaction, and the power exercised through it, so that action is appropriate within a given setting. Freedom isn't only choosing to act in a certain way. It's also ensuring that actions fit well in a prevailing pattern for power so that our intentions are conveyed as clearly as possible. Social literacy is learned during encounters with power—its excesses as well as its tendencies to reward creativity and freedom.

Whether or not power is used to excess, it's always characterized by ambivalence, a condition that pulls people in two opposing directions at the same time. And because it's also ambiguous (has more than one meaning), more than one thing is going on as it's being used. I will examine this ambiguity and ambivalence, but first I want to say something about the slavery that can result when people are using power, even if they don't intend to harm others.

Analyzing power is a means for reconsidering the boundaries around freedom in contrast to being enslaved. Slavery has two forms: we're enslaved if we're unable to master ourselves or if we carry out plans that others set for us in which we have no interest. The word interest refers to material needs plus values and practices that express our ultimate concerns. Addiction is slavery in the first sense. If we're addicted, we can't manage ourselves. Abusive families create slavery in the second sense: parents degrade the personal value or deny the material needs of their children.

Slavery isn't easy to detect. People don't begin life as the enslaved. It's something they learn. Newborn infants aren't slaves. They hold the attention of a room of sophisticated adults who find they're gazing exclusively at the child, making silly, encouraging noises at a baby or getting down on the floor in their good clothes. In addition, our power may be invisible to us. Perhaps you've heard a woman claim to have no power but you watch her shut down a whole group of people by saying so. Maybe you thought your boss demanded your silence, even though he never uttered a threat aloud. The penalty for speaking out was vague but frightening. You didn't ask what would happen. You believed he had power to carry out a threat that would have too high a price tag for you to pay. Unlike the baby's situation, in these instances, power is misused; people feel trapped. They're caught between a rock and a hard place. Ambivalence is expressed in this feeling of being caught between two equally disastrous events that have an equal pull on us. If we consider power's symbolic effects, ambivalence and ambiguity are its defining features.

Decoding ambivalence and clarifying ambiguity are some of the essential skills involved if we want to maintain our freedom. But if it's misused, ambiguity and ambivalence characterize a situation in which power contains a double bind: it compels people to do things that violate their will and their interests. Power traps can be sprung; we can consciously interpret intentions and feelings of others and be aware of our active or passive complicity in feeling cornered. Traps hidden in power's misuse have a unifying purpose of refusing to allow some people to enter a social interaction as a full partner. If power is misused, it sets up a system in which *implicit* consequences appear too costly for one of the would-be players. If consequences are *explicit,* it isn't an exercise of power, it's a show of domination. If interaction degenerates into domination, any attempt to initiate co-ordinated action and resistance[11] is hazardous and might mean life or death for those who choose to rebel.

Traps that hide within the misuse of power tend toward domination if left unchecked. They are ambivalent situations that exert pull in two opposing directions. As an example, on one hand, a worker might feel drawn toward being seen by her boss as a productive worker, and, on the other hand, by the need to preserve her employment no matter what unjust demands are made of her. Learning social literacy offers insight into that ambiguity (i.e., work/ life balance). Social literacy doesn't prevent traps from showing up during social interaction; it reveals their presence. Freedom is an ability to see what's genuinely required of us, what isn't, and suggests a response to us that supports our genuine personal interests, and affirms physical and emotional well-being.

Ambiguity and ambivalence carry emotional and physical demands: "each interaction is unpredictable, perhaps potentially explosive, and so requires a heightened vigilance and effort."[12] Research on those caught in ambivalent social interaction shows that people experience bodily harm if they're being pulled in two competing directions. In a study of 100 men and women, participants experienced a significant rise in blood pressure when they were with people who troubled them, such as an overbearing parent, a volatile romantic partner, a competitive friend or an unpredictable boss. A rise in blood pressure and its effects on the immune system were related to ambivalent feelings and put them at risk for heart disease and other illnesses if they responded with passivity and silence,[13] especially if they also marginalized themselves due to the loss of value they felt during these harmful social interactions.

But why would some people respond to harm with passivity and acceptance? What have they learned to expect from life?

THE ART OF USING POWER

Power is learned through living with other people. As mentioned, "we do as we are done to." In community, we acquire a way of being that can be identified, described and expressed bodily. A Serbian friend told me that, while he was in Russia, he approached an auditorium where a lecture was about to begin. Two men stood in the doorway. As he paid attention to them, he thought to himself, *these two men are Serbian*. He was correct. He assessed their origin by observing their physical stance. When I asked him how he knew, he told me that they stood like Serbian men—they were physically disposed to be Serbian.

A disposition refers to a way of being we can depend on. Water is liquid at room temperature, solid at freezing temperatures and vapour at high temperatures; we depend on its disposition to be so. Human dispositions (habits expressed in personal styles or cultural patterns) are learned through experience in the presence of others who are disposed to be a certain way. Power is learned and embodied through that process. Human habits, however, have potential for change. In order to make the point, I expand on the terms *hexis* and *habitus* that were outlined in the chapter on *Human Connections*.

Aristotle observed the dynamics that my friend saw in those Serbian men. Dispositions create what Aristotle referred to as *hexis*, the root of which is "to have" or "to be disposed to"; the Greek term carries the sense of a good or bad condition, disposition or state.[14] To Aristotle, *hexis* refers to "a state of character or mind that disposes us to deliberately choose to act or think in a certain way."[15] It becomes part of our character. To him, it referred, for example, to what a man could be counted on to do during battle. If he could be counted on to remain in his place even though he felt fear as the enemy approached, his *hexis* was characterized by the virtue of courage. Aristotle attributed conscious intention to *hexis* and thought of in an active sense, although not all dispositions are good. Cowardice is a disposition some people can be counted on to demonstrate as well. He didn't think of *hexis* in personal versus social terms. His culture was the only one he considered: people lived up to it or failed at it. He wasn't comparing his culture with others. If he reflected on it at all, he thought of his culture as representing the right way to be. A tendency to think of one's own culture as the one right way to be has a long history—for example, in modern imperialism, until cultural relativism challenged its chauvinism.

Pierre Bourdieu drew a distinction between social and personal habits, which I want to distinguish by using the Greek word *hexis* and the Latin word *habitus*. He downplayed the role of intention that Aristotle attributed to *hexis*, and suggested we learn certain habits by being in the presence of others who already have that habit. To him, the body is a repository of ingrained habits (dispositions) so that certain actions eventually seem altogether natural. Childhood is an important time in forming these habits. Through ordinary processes of training and learning, instructions are given. *Sit up straight. Don't talk with your mouth full. Don't shuffle your feet as you walk.* Children acquire habits that literally mould the body and become second nature. They form a durable way of being that reflects their social condition. In the workplace, employees know how to act and recognize the meaning and intention of their actions when they're together. They know how to distinguish themselves bodily from their managers. Gender also creates an embodied set of dispositions. Why was Bourdieu so observant of the body's habits?

He came from a working class French background and won a place at an elite French school. When he entered the school, he was taken aback by the elite culture he met there. During childhood, the men he knew spoke with what's called "a big mouth"; that is, the lips and mouth are wide open as words are pronounced. In elite

French culture, he saw that men spoke with "a small mouth": as they produced words, their lips were close together rather than round and open. In order to fit in and be accepted as an intelligent man, he learned to produce his words with "a small mouth". While he succeeded at doing so, he saw that the change brought about two losses: he lost an important link to his working class roots and lost something of his maleness. When he was growing up, it was working class women who spoke with "a small mouth."

In a struggle to fit in, he became aware of embodied class differences and identified a connection between personal habits (*hexis*) and a field of interaction that characterized his social world (*habitus*). He observed that his *hexis* and *habitus* converged when he began to speak in a different way. He generalized that, if the personal fits well in the social, individuals are seen as powerful. But if these two worlds diverge, a person is seen as powerless and ignorant.

As we acquire a personal style that has cultural patterns embedded in it, we're invested with and by symbolic power. Since the West privileges modern individuals, a fit between the personal and social gives merit to people who appear to flourish in their own strength. If we're misled by the myth of individualism, we don't see the function that symbolic power has in conferring value on some people. We miss the significance of class, race, sex, temperament—dimensions that dis-privilege people who don't match the dominant attributes of their group's *habitus*. If we miss seeing the mismatch between *habitus* and *hexis,* and don't realize the reasons for it, we fail to accurately perceive the value of many people.

Bourdieu recognized a mismatch in his behaviour and changed his way of being. He was passively complicit at first, until he perceived the mismatch. He was actively complicit each time he spoke with "a small mouth" and made changes he thought necessary to success. He eventually won the place in French society that had been held by intellectuals such as Jean Paul Sartre and Michel Foucault. He followed a path established by Sartre and Foucault and became the central intellectual in his nation. French culture still regards intellectuals with the enthusiasm that North Americans reserve for movie stars and sports heroes, so his success was remarkable. He was liberated by being admitted to an elite school and, once there, learned practices of freedom as he acquired a new way of speaking. His accommodation allowed others to perceive his intelligence.

Is everyone able to do what he did? Does everyone want to do it?

Bourdieu taught himself to be effective in a new social world. He analyzed forms of capital that one must accumulate in order to flourish[6] and pointed to family, particularly mothers, as the source of social capital (trust) that's at the heart of every other form of capital accumulation. He was fortunate; not everyone is. Those caught by symbolic power may come to see it for what it is and challenge its legitimacy. In doing so, they liberate themselves from unjust uses of power.

But, like Bourdieu, after liberation, people who have been disadvantaged by the cultural ethos must learn to live with the freedom they've won. The knowledge and skills of freedom differ from those that secure liberation in the first place. To spring a power trap, we exercise certain skills—the power to resist, for example. But once liberated, the power to resist would be misapplied to living well with freedom. People who have expressed the social pattern of the disempowered must revise their way of being in order to live freely after that freedom has been won. Dispositions that empower people in their new-found freedom are acquired through gradually learning to notice the way of life that has one trapped in its grip and to imagine a new way of life that's thought of as possible to gain. In summary, springing power traps involves a process in which we:

- understand our own feelings of rage and resentment compassionately
- notice our own active and passivity complicity
- learn self-trust and self-regard
- name and practise new rituals that encourage personal efficacy and hope

These elements of unlearning and learning are implied in social literacy. Reading power and finding suitable ways to negotiate the dance of integration and authenticity gain, for the dis-empowered, a more equal advantage. But these people have to learn, as adults, ways of being that privileged people learned as children—ways of being they didn't have to think about or judge between. The socially literate person, as part of learning to practice freedom once liberation is won, must calculate the losses and decide what is and isn't a good fit for them.

In order to reveal practices of freedom, I unpack three patterns for the exercise of power that Foucault analyzed, and on which my own research and experience elaborates. Foucault was right to describe power as he did. While he doesn't say everything that can be said about power, perceiving the truth in his analysis is central to being socially literate. He noted how power infects us: we embody it as we interact with others. He identified a modern prejudice to hold individualism in high regard, which fails to reveal how deeply affected we are by other people.

Although individualism answers some questions about why we do what we do, social literacy cautions a modern urge to believe that individualism explains everything.[17] Foucault's view anticipates brain and body research that identifies how we impact one another for good or ill that's at the heart of social intelligence research. The next section criticizes a modern belief in individualism and offers perspectives on what believing in individualism has done to us, an insight that's prerequisite to perceiving the patterns of power in social interaction.

MISLEADING EFFECTS OF INDIVIDUALISM ON HOW WE LEARN TO USE POWER

If we accept social literacy as a viable educational goal we may be frustrated in its achievement by modern prejudices that privilege individuals over groups. Radical individualism marked the modern period and held assumptions about social interaction that are inconsistent with current research on human interaction. If social literacy refers to a developed capacity to read people's intentions and feelings, and to respond to and repair interactions as they're happening, it relies on the assumption that we're part of a human family that has deep-seated consistent patterns which are revealed across human populations. On its strength, we try to, and do, make sense of others.

Radical individualism assumes we're unique and different from others and emphasizes difference as a way to protect individual autonomy. Radical individualism is a consequence of Enlightenment principles that prized a solitary individual who could choose to limit and leave his associations when they no longer held value for him, and who would do so in order to secure the freedom to follow his thought and lifestyle wherever they might lead. The assumption that we can enjoy limitless freedom typifies this approach. The worst fate to befall a modern man is to be constrained by life experiences because he failed to realize his full potential. Feminists point out that this type of autonomy has been unavailable to almost all women historically.

Modern ideas about freedom[18] were challenged in the mid-twentieth century, particularly in the United States, by the empowerment movement. Its central and unifying theme was human maturity, which wasn't thought of as a static state of being complete or perfect. It had more to do with one's readiness to deliberate over problems and to seize opportunities so that outward action corresponded to inner-directed ideas about what makes life good. Empowerment was an outcome of living from the inside, so to speak, on the basis of highly prized, carefully considered personal values, and was married to a belief in human freedom and the responsibility to carry out one's personal values. The empowerment movement operated on an individualistic point of view—it was psychological not sociological in its interpretation of human potential and maturity.

In this way, empowerment emphasized subjective experience, if we recall Bourdieu's point about thinking on our feet, outlined in an earlier chapter. The movement didn't teach people about the patterns power tends to take. Empowerment taught people to live from inside experience, but it didn't teach them to think on their feet by perceiving what's going on around them. Empowerment advocates began to see the effects of the social world on the disempowered, but retained an individualistic ideal for human maturity.

Social literacy is an aspect of human maturity. But what does it mean to be mature? The overwhelming bias in modern thinking is to situate human maturity in one's capacity to act on one's own, seeing oneself as the primary motivating locus of attention. In a critique of these assumptions and their psychological implications, Foucault showed how power played out in social interaction. His views are confirmed by social science research: we affect and leave effects in each other. Although he had no access to brain research,[19] through observation and suffering, he noted the dynamic effects of social power. He was particularly interested in the relationship between social power and maturity.

The question of human maturity is not new. Immanuel Kant wrote an article (1784) to answer the question, "What is Enlightenment?"[20] To Kant, the motto of the Enlightenment was: "Have courage to use your *own* understanding." He believed Enlightenment ideals assured man's [sic] emergence from self-incurred immaturity and defined immaturity as the inability to use one's own understanding without guidance from others. He taunted his audience by suggesting that men remained immature because they were lazy or cowardly, or because it was convenient to be immature. He identified books, spiritual advisors and doctors as guardians who took it upon themselves to supervise and see to it that men remained immature [we might say dependent]. He thought the largest part of mankind, and all women, would find stepping toward maturity to be difficult and dangerous; thus, he thought people avoided moving in that direction.

Kant's influence is immeasurable. His work grounds most of modern philosophy and impacts how we think about ourselves psychologically. Foucault analyzed this essay and connected it to Kant's other work by noting that, according to Kant, maturity is made possible through the use of reason, as Kant depicted it.[21] Foucault thought that, for Kant, reason was a way out—a release from immaturity by "linking will, authority, and the use of reason."[22] For Kant, reason was a phenomenon and an ongoing process; it was a task and an obligation, because each man is responsible for his immature status. Enlightenment was a passage from immaturity to maturity, an outcome each man was responsible to initiate and complete. Rather than following Kant in saying that maturity is achieved through rationality, Foucault revealed various ways power obstructs maturity as we interact with others. He maintained some continuity with Kant by arguing that immaturity was due to being subject to other people's authority, but disagreed with Kant's notion that we're free to be what we intend. He moved beyond Kant's analysis by insisting that modern power made us subject to ourselves.

Foucault's analysis raises questions about whether people can be held individually accountable for their immaturity, as Kant would have us believe. Foucault welcomed maturity, but on a different basis, saying:

> I do not know whether we will ever reach mature adulthood. Many things in our experience convince us that the historical event of the Enlightenment did not make us mature adults, and we have not reached that stage yet. However, it seems to me that a meaning can be attributed to that critical interrogation of the present and ourselves which Kant formulated by reflecting on the Enlightenment....The critical ontology of ourselves has to be considered not ... as a theory, a doctrine, nor even as a permanent body of knowledge that is accumulating; it has to conceived as an attitude, an ethos, a philosophical life in which the critique of what we are is at one and the same time the historical analysis of the limits that are imposed on us and an experiment with the possibility of going beyond them.[23]

If we are serious about learning social literacy, Foucault's perspective on power is key to seeing how human interaction influences and shapes the possibility of reading people more accurately—including ourselves.

Foucault challenged a modern view that individuals are free (unlimited) in their goal to find a satisfying life because he observed that we're held in networks of power that shape action. His observation explains why children who are excluded will exclude others even though they can say how much exclusion hurts. They're infected with boss culture; they can't escape its influence over them.

In coming to this point, he didn't ask what power is, but how it operates. He investigated its effects. Power is energy flowing through every social interaction, leaving effects in environments and people to perpetuate a particular way of being powerful. He identified three patterns to reveal how power operates:

- sovereign power
- pastoral power
- disciplinary power

Each has characteristic strategies. To Foucault, they constitute a form of struggle, war games we engage in, even as they alter us in the process. Power isn't an add-on. It's in the very nature of human interaction: every social relation is a power relation.

OUTLINING POWER'S PATTERNS

Every human being exercises power, but that's not to say people are free. Every social encounter opens into an exercise of power, but that doesn't mean we say and do whatever we like. Power and freedom are in a complex relationship.

As mentioned, power traditionally referred to getting one's own way or doing what one wanted, whether it's good for other people or not. There's a compulsive core in power relations. If I have power, others must do as I say. The word "must" is ambiguous; it may mean people are compelled or they are well advised to obey powerful people because a negative consequence is hanging over their heads.

I use a king metaphor to capture the nature of the first pattern for power relations—sovereign power. It's useful because it crops up in so much literature, but I want to be clear that men and women may act like kings despite gender-exclusive language, for which I apologize to those who are distracted by it.

While Foucault analyzed three patterns for power's exercise using the terms sovereign, pastoral and disciplinary power, I use three other expressions to describe these patterns because it might be easier to relate to power's current exercise by referring to power exercised by:

- a king over subjects
- an expert over clients
- a friend over friends

Each pattern is characterized by ambivalence and ambiguity. Liberation comes about as we recognize the patterns and apply them to our own situation. Practices of freedom are learned as we decode ambivalence, clarify ambiguity and reclaim a sense of authenticity as we integrate effectively into an environment. Trying and succeeding, of course, aren't the same. Sometimes attempts to integrate and differentiate ourselves don't lead to success. But in the effort of trying, a measure of freedom is always to be gained, at least in the sense that we now see what's really going on around us and within us.

A King Over Subjects

A king is a person who has double social value.[4] I use male gender language to refer to a sovereign power that both men and women exercise.

What do I mean by a double social value? For the sake of argument, suppose we say that every human being is born with a value of one unit of humanity, whatever that might mean in a given society. I think that's what Kant meant by humanity in *The Metaphysics of Morals*.[25] Although modern individualism introduced problems associated with individualism, the idea of an essential unit of human value, applied to everyone, everywhere, is a contribution that shouldn't be lost. Foucault's analysis depends on it. Power plays with the basic mathematics of one unit of social value per person. Around the world, from Egypt and Greece to China and Mexico, a belief that a king's life is worth far more than the lives of other people shows up again and again.[26] The king exercises his double value whenever he likes, because he's in the best position to constrain his subjects. They must do his will.

Symbols and artefacts confirm his double value. He's at the top of a hierarchy of value and power and bestows value on—or withholds it from—others. He has an incontestable right of access to land, property, his subject's bodies and their lives. He appears legitimate because of his double value. Yet his power is discontinuous. It's exercised on those in his presence and through his agents—those he delegates to do his biding. As a result, it's possible to hide from the king under certain conditions. But the cost of doing so must be calculated into that choice.

All social rituals support a king's double value. Losses of social honour to the king matter more than losses of social honour to subjects. A king wins social support for his excess value but he needs to replicate his value throughout the kingdom. He relies on this replication so that all his subjects anticipate his freedom to act on whim. The king's men and women copy the way the king treats his victims as an expression of loyalty. In this way, his behaviour doesn't stand out; it conveys the way things are, even to his subjects. To prove his legitimacy to mistreat subjects, everyone learns to be worthless in advance of his action. Individual worth and worthlessness are established socially. Once people lose their value, they tell themselves it must be so; their loss is explained by the mathematics of social relations as they are and as they must be. As a result, they acquire personal bodily habits that confirm society's view of them and express evidence of their lack of value in the way they walk, speak, cower before the king or bully others in the king's stead—simply because that behaviour pleases the king.

In contrast, the king is capricious. He does what he wants, when he wants, to whomever he wants. To Foucault, a king's first impulse is to gratify his own wishes. If power is used violently, it takes the form of invading, grasping, withholding. It's a form of conquest grounded on winning and losing. The central aim is to get enough of what he wants to satisfy desires that are limitless, despite what others need or want. A central challenge to kingly power is resistance from his subjects (even in terms of their not responding immediately to his wishes). That resistance is a sign of a potential loss of power, and worries him as to whether he's failed to threaten his subjects adequately. He perceives resistance as a threat to his extravagant value.

Sovereign power is energy but (like electricity) is also a commodity. It's bestowed, withheld or withdrawn by the king. He delegates power under the condition that its distribution serves his interests. And it's a precious commodity. Privilege is attached to having it. People who enjoy privilege are driven to keep it. Power is scarce. If kings give up any, others will get some of what they believe belongs to them alone. The game extends to all his subjects and is echoed in every social interaction.

Sovereign power assumes that people who are lower down the social ladder will fight for the king's favour because that's the only currency that counts in the kingdom. The king is skilled at handing out grapes in place of cucumbers. All who are deemed worthy to be his delegates and make him look good by practising the belief that their lives have little value, compete with all others for what's scarce and desirable.

Conflict among subjects enhances the king's currency and security. But, if subjects unite in opposition, their unity is a threat to him. The king remains vigilant for signs of resistance or rebellion. He watches for evidence of collective action. He works to ensure that they dislike each other and remain preoccupied with currying his favour at each other's expense. It's to his advantage if subjects spy on and betray each other. Mistrust is thereby generalized and distracts subjects from realizing the potential of uniting to oppose him.

Although subjects engage in these activities and appear busy with them, the king renders them all victims of his power—even if some feel privileged for a period of time when they're elevated above all other subjects and treated as the king's favourite. All subjects are potential victims. Their bodies aren't respected as human. The body of a subject is a mere *thing* with symbolic significance because it's useful to the king. In sovereign power, a victim's body is like a movie screen on which to show the king's power. The display, whether it's to confer temporary privilege or carry out torture, turns a victim's body into a spectacle to celebrate the king's power. All who see what happens if subjects step out of line are controlled by what they believe is inevitable.

Sovereign power traps subjects in the ambivalent position of being both a witness and a participant. As witnesses, they affirm a king's double value to do what he likes. If they side with him they devalue the people he chooses as his victims. Their participation is two-edged: on one hand, they help the king victimize one of their own; on the other, if his behaviour appears blatantly unjust, solidarity might spark sympathy with the victim, ignite resistance and explode in rebellion. When subjects move toward solidarity, the king's power is revealed as an outrage.

The French Revolution (1789) was Foucault's chief example, one that revealed the ambivalence of sovereign power. As witnesses, subjects supported the king's right to treat victims however he chose—to keep out of trouble. Once the king chose a victim, he left others alone. They choose silence to avoid punishment.

But as participants, as his potential victims, these others sometimes perceived the king's injustice. Their ambivalence as witnesses and participants created ambiguity, if they ask the question: What's really going on here? At times, medieval subjects expressed aggressive hatred toward the king's victims. They turned away from them, or celebrated their punishment. At other times, they felt a link with victims that erupted in resistance and rebellion—a pattern that continues to exist if kings get their own way at other people's expense or when, for example, bullies are given license to exercise sovereign power over their victims.

In discussing power, I want explore its ambivalence from another perspective, to provide a fuller picture. Foucault isn't the only theorist to describe ambivalence in king/subject relations. Sigmund Freud analyzed the king/subject relation, and, while he too saw ambivalence and ambiguity, he described them differently.

In *Totem and Taboo,* Freud used anthropological data to note that kings must be both guarded and guarded against—this is the tension at the core of his description of ambivalence. Like Foucault, he thought subjects were drawn powerfully in two opposing directions. Subjects believed kings were bearers of mysterious, magical power communicated by contact, something like an electric charge, bringing death and destruction to anyone not protected by a similar charge, i.e., by anyone not having equal social value. People avoided direct or indirect contact with a dangerous but sacred king. Where contact couldn't be avoided, ceremonies emerged—as much to protect subjects as to celebrate kings.

To Freud, a king's power had healing effects. Accounts exist of healing powers in kings and queens. Kings of England were thought to exercise healing power over the disease scrofula. Queen Elizabeth, Charles I and Charles II are three examples that were said to have exercised this power.[27] Rulers were thought to have the power to regulate the course of nature: wind, rain and crops. They had a wealth of power and the ability to bestow happiness.

But they were watched over as well, to see whether they exercised power in the right way. Subjects weren't persuaded of their good intentions, so they kept vigil. In Freud's analysis, mistrust is mingled with taboo rules for the king. He said that the king/subject relation existed for subjects. A king's life had value as long as he discharged his duty by ordering the course of nature for the subjects' benefit, something like football coaches today. If a king fails to benefit his subjects (if a team loses too many games), the care and homage lavished on him would cease. Those who once honoured him now hated him and aimed to get rid of him.

Freud proposed that this shift in subjects' behaviour was consistent. A king is god and preserver. If he won't preserve his subjects, they make room for someone who will. As long as he answers their expectations, there's no limit to the care they take of him. Therefore, a king is hedged in by ceremonious etiquette—a network of prohibitions and observances—whose intention isn't to contribute to his dignity or his comfort, but to restrain him from conduct that, by disturbing the harmony of nature, might involve his people in a catastrophe. As an example, a political leader isn't free to say whatever she or he thinks. Their words have power. As a result, they have less freedom to say what's on their mind. To Freud, such prohibitions annihilate the king's freedom and render his life a burden and sorrow to him.

Freud acknowledged that rulers are granted great privileges, but thought such privileges were practically cancelled by taboo prohibitions. Kings were privileged; they could and did enjoy what was withheld from others, but were restricted by taboos that didn't affect subjects. To him, kings experienced an ambivalence of privilege and constraint that subjects didn't perceive. Yet subjects were caught in a different ambivalence. They expressed trust and mistrust toward rulers: they might express extreme tenderness on one occasion and hostility on another. These competing emotions could war with one another.

Freud and Foucault analysed the king from different points of view. Taken together, their analyses offer insight that one view alone can't provide. Foucault analyzed sovereign power from a victim's perspective (as the son of a father he hated). He was sympathetic toward victims. He attended primarily to the subjects' ambivalence, but saw that kings are trapped in maintaining privilege and fending off resistance and rebellion. Freud showed what it felt like to be the king (perhaps based on his own suffering). To him, kings and subjects experience different patterns of ambivalence but his sympathy was primarily with the king.

If we recall the two kindergarten children in Paley's research, Foucault and Freud capture differences in the children's experience of being powerful. Lisa was in the position of having and enjoying a double value when she could successfully shape the experience of other children. It seemed normal to her to control access to games and play. There was no point in playing if she couldn't say who was in and who was out. Curtis, in contrast, felt burdened by his assignment of power. He was uncomfortable and saw it as something imposed on him by other children. He felt controlled by the other children and limited in his freedom to play at school.

As we try to understand connections between power and social literacy, it's crucial to get clear about ambiguity. During social interaction, becoming aware of feeling trapped is important in learning to practice freedom. Yet having freedom doesn't mean we can say and do whatever we like. Everyone involved in social interaction is tainted by ambivalence and ambiguity. Action has direct impact upon the life satisfaction of other people.

As we talk about power, many tell Foucault's story. Others convey Freud's narrative. The reader can appreciate how hard it is to settle conflicts between people if one side tells Foucault's story while another tells Freud's, without realizing the difference. How can we tell a story about power that's actually liberating? How can we sense the advantages on each side so there's more freedom for everyone? How do people win freedom from traps that lurk in social interaction? Those questions move the inquiry of this whole book. It's my hope that readers are better able to answer those questions at the end.

An Expert Over Clients

Foucault used his analysis of sovereign power as the basis for two other forms that rely on it. The other two patterns emerged during modernity. They're linked, but I discuss them separately to make clear how they differ. To Foucault, the second pattern for power had roots in the organization of churches. As the State gained power over the Church, forms of control were available as the political assimilated the religious into public life. Foucault saw that Christian rituals exercised power over individuals and a group at the same time. The State swallowed up this pattern, spewing out a form of power that had control over, as he put it, "each and all."

In the State's hands, pastoral power focused on salvation here and now in terms of health, well-being (sufficient income, standard of living), security and protection from accidents. State police were its first agents. The aim was to gather data about individuals (as separated out from the group) and populations (as a mass statistic). Amassed data revealed normal and abnormal behaviour, and was applied to individuals by observing and reporting their conduct.

While one could hide from sovereign power (at a cost), this second pattern for power was ubiquitous, influencing the development of health clinics, prisons, schools, insane asylums and hospitals. Neither individuals nor the mass of people could hide from pastoral power. Human life was recorded in minute detail.

This power was exercised over private life, was burdensome, and earnestly enforced. He called it pastoral power because he saw, in the practice of confession, a pattern he wanted to unpick. He observed that a Christian "in confession does not know something, what he doesn't know is not whether X is a sin or not, or what kind of sin it is, *he doesn't know what takes place within him.* A [Christian] says: 'Listen the trouble is that I can't pray at present, I have a feeling of spiritual dryness which has made me lose touch with God.' The director says to him: 'Well, there is something happening in you which you don't know about. We will work together to find it out'."[28] To Foucault, this power assumes that ordinary people don't know themselves as well as an expert does.

As a result of pastoral power, people mistrust themselves. Not knowing what's within compels people to stay in relationship with those who apparently know how to make sense of their lives. This pattern for power continues to shape doctor/patient, psychiatrist/client relations and was at the core of the empowerment movement in North America. The idea that one person had advantageous knowledge was built into the helping professions in the 1960s and up to the present.

Pastoral power is a public form that entered into the inner life of individuals, creating an internal dialogue that becomes self-dominating—as an echo of external social relations in which an expert "knows more about me than I know about myself." As a client of expert power, people become the person they're perceived to be and exercise control over themselves to conform to expectations that are externally imposed. This view of power challenges the idea that we're individuals in the modern sense. Its pattern is intensified in what Foucault called disciplinary power, or what I refer to as the power of a friend over friends.

A Friend Over Friends

Disciplinary power is relational. Along with sovereign and pastoral power, it's exercised during social interaction but its quality takes on a tone of friendliness, rather than the force that typified the other two patterns. It's a form of power that, unlike sovereign power, emanates from everywhere, through everyone, to everyone because it has no central locus. There's no throne room. Anyone may pick up its pattern and carry out its threat, as happens with bullies on school playgrounds. Disciplinary (friendly) power isn't top-down; it's horizontally constructed. If it's used to negate human value, it's exercised during social interaction in which significant people in a group gain control over others, who eventually are perceived as having little social value.

If kings are capricious, friendly power knows how to be charming. It works according to certain aims and objectives that someone learns to master. Those who carry it out are relationally close to those they control. While a king was a different sort of being than subjects, friendly power relies on proximity and sameness—almost; it's exercised on people precisely because someone who seems like them knows how they think, feel and act. If a king was relatively ignorant of his subjects because he was protected from needing information about them, the personnel of friendly power are skilled in human interaction but choose to use that knowledge to control others, simply because they can. It's the current pattern for bullying.

To Foucault, this pattern for power[29] was directed toward securing productive obedience in the work of modern capitalism and industrialization. As it developed, it absorbed pastoral power and unveiled its capacity to make workers productive. People in advantageous positions observed the industry of all workers. With the invention of photography and cameras, a powerful observer could put mechanisms of surveillance in every conceivable location, for example, in modern factories.

The pattern is portrayed in literature and film, notably in the novel *1984* and in Charlie Chaplin's film, *Modern Life*—a must see, if readers want to watch modern machinery at work. Foucault unpacked that machinery and noted its effects on those subjected to it—in the production of their passivity and their usefulness to those in charge.

The agents of disciplinary power were responsible for watching others to make them good (i.e., productive) workers. Their strategic advantage allowed them to set up surveillance to ensure productivity.

Surveillance fitted in with training modern workers to expect that someone they couldn't see would see their every action. There was nowhere to hide.

Yet bosses might be outwardly friendly. They would imply, "Trust me. I know what's best for you." Their friendly tone appeared to make it unnecessary to create and sustain rules and regulations to ensure justice. Workers often came to think, "*Since my boss is so friendly* (the pattern implies) *I don't need to fuss too much about just and mutually beneficial rules.* Or they might simply think: *I'm sure my friend will look after me.* This pattern for power shows up in Steven Watts' analysis of the Henry Ford phenomenon in North America.[30]

In sovereign power, subjects protect themselves from the king by keeping out of his way. The recipients of pastoral power protect themselves by being invisible or by leaving the group or remaining outside of it. But disciplinary power established itself through the continual outbreak of plagues in Europe. During a plague, as was realized in Toronto, Ontario, during the SARS epidemic, everyone's existence is a potential threat to the social body. Disciplinary power is skilled at tracking and recording people's whereabouts, and assumes a right of access to data about them. But the pattern doesn't merely gather data; it assumes a right to declare that someone is a good person, depending on data gathered. Goodness doesn't refer to morality. It indicates a person's compliance. A person is good if she's normal, not good if she's abnormal, or in the case of SARS, is sick. A person is good is he's healthy and productive, bad if he's not. A person is good if he's passive and useful for his boss's purposes, bad if he tries to resist the system.

Consequently, disciplinary power turns some people into powerful, competent workers and others into incompetent ones. It produces abnormal subjects—people that don't fit the norm. I'm not claiming that disciplinary power made people normal. Rather it focused on a data gathering approach that categorized people based on what came to be thought of as normal. Those who can't measure up to an average stand out in the crowd. Standing out is dangerous.

Furthermore, disciplinary power makes people productive; its primary function is to make people do things; bullying is a good example. Through its exercise, those in charge take over the right to say how much others should accomplish. Output is meticulously monitored. Disciplinary power is characterized by one person who can bully another to do what the bully wants, or not do what the bully doesn't want done, merely because the bully says so.

An underlying structure of disciplinary power is negation. While it compels people to produce, it also strangely restricts them. I say strangely because it's self-defeating for people to exercise this form of power over others, but they do so anyway. A story may illustrate the point.

> A scorpion was a very poor swimmer so he asked a turtle to carry him on his back across a river. "Are you mad?" exclaimed the turtle. "You'll sting me while I'm swimming and I'll drown." "My dear turtle," laughed the scorpion, "If I were to sting you, you would drown and I would go down with you. Now where is the logic in that?" You're right," cried the turtle. "Hop on!" The scorpion climbed aboard. Halfway across the river he gave the turtle a mighty sting. As they both sank to the bottom, the turtle said, "Do you mind if I ask you something? You said there'd be no logic to your stinging me. Why did you do it?" "It has nothing to do with logic," the drowning scorpion replied sadly. "It's just my character."[31]

Bullying always has the quality of being self-defeating for all involved. While disciplinary power may have a friendly façade, it retains its potential to sting its victim. The power to sting or stymie is peculiarly unproductive, despite the intention of this pattern to focus on productivity.

The power to stymie reveals an aspect of disciplinary power, not as a separate dimension but as a core motivation. It has the force of negation on its side. It's not really productivity that disciplinary power aims to produce; it's control. Workers can't think for themselves. Individual creativity is brought to a halt. This point was especially troubling to Henry Ford and he wrestled with the nature of work he required of assembly workers. While the first workers were independently creative thinkers, assembly lines eventually reduced them to people who must stop thinking for themselves. Thinking for oneself got in the way of production.[32]

Tension in this pattern is fascinating. While power is energy that flows through social interaction, the power to stymie is anti-energy. It can't inspire work. It posts limits and micro-manages work, producing an inhumane system in which workers fulfil the boss's demands without having any say. The boss alone identifies work that matters. Innovation and independence are ruled out. The power to stymie is incapable of doing anything itself, other than to render those it compels incapable of doing anything either, except for what it allows them to do. It operates on the law: "You must do this because I say so!" Its effects produce submission and subjugation and reduce workers to mindless obedience: "Obey me or else!"[33] But compliance doesn't tap into creative potential. Productivity eventually collapses. Even though Ford's initial inventiveness depended on craftsmanship, working on an assembly line replaced the craftsmanship that his earliest workers demonstrated. The power to stymie never engenders a fully human life in workers. It rests on an underlying potential to turn to violence and domination in which injustice is allowed free reign.[34]

Foucault distinguished power and domination. To him, power games imply two (or more) players engaged in a struggle in which each has value and from which each has an escape. His model for power relations is like the computer programs described at the beginning of the chapter. Power games depend on a value of one unit of humanity for each player. He didn't claim the social world was equally represented in players—perhaps they came from different social locations, or enjoyed a different fit between *hexis* and *habitus*—but to him, for it to be a power game, players had to see themselves as equal in value, with an equal opportunity to win or escape. If these conditions are absent, it's no longer power, it's domination, a social relation that promotes and perpetuates injustice.

What turns the game into domination? This question points out what's complex about social interaction. At the beginning of the chapter, I said that individual action takes place in living systems. Artfully living with others draws people toward learning to be integrated within that system, yet differentiated from it. In domination, one player in the game finds a way to close down options for all others; winning and escape appear too costly. In domination, players lose voice and value. Other characteristics typical of bullying can also be picked out.

In order for the personnel of disciplinary power to compel people and bully them, a bully must be significant. A good example of disciplinary power is depicted in Margaret Atwood's novel, *Cat's Eye.*[35] The story is about the social world of four girls and the power one of them has over the others. It's a classic case of relational bullying. Atwood's novel captures the bullying behaviour of children at school and applies to adults in institutional and work settings. In the book, one girl of the four is wealthy and attractive, conditions that give her an advantage. The other three girls feel compelled to be her friend. Over the course of the novel, the main character, a relatively poor girl, is bullied to an extreme and endangers her life—an action that might look voluntary, unless one reads the whole novel.

In what I call *friendly power,* bullies must have charisma, charm and excess value (for example, wealth or social prestige) in order to succeed. They achieve the requirement for friendly power with support from onlookers, until victims internalize *friendly power* over themselves. In this way, victims appear to act of their own volition. The bully doesn't literally cause them harm, but rather, creates inescapable conditions in which harming themselves feels like a relief from the mounting, all-encompassing pressure to do or be something someone else wants them to do or be. Once the game is accomplished, bullies turn a charming and apparent innocence to their advantage. To meet the conditions of friendly power, a friend must achieve:

- significance: exercising the power to stymie due to a double value, ascribed socially
- surveillance: watching unnoticed, in a way the abused person senses but can't escape
- self-domination: internalizing abusive power to *produce* self-abuse, self-harm

The third condition is an outcome of bullying. The hero of Atwood's novel jumped off a bridge into an icy stream. The jump was a reaction to internal pressure, an echo of pressure exerted externally. This characteristic of bullying is completely devastating. A victim hurts herself due to hurt she experienced from others. This is Foucault's point about self-domination.

Learning social literacy aims to alleviate external and internal pressures of domination and friendly power. By reflecting on ambivalence, ambiguity and power, we uncover its traps and exercise power to limit domination over ourselves and other people, in order to achieve balance between important differences from others and social solidarity with them. Social literacy is a developed capacity to identify and counter friendly power and social practices that have broken down into domination.

To point to what social literacy needs to understand, I outline two practices that rely on friendly power and are carried out by someone who is proximate and important to those who are harmed. They're contrasted by their use of force and neglect and connected by dehumanization, ambivalence and ambiguity. If force is used, practices are coercive. If neglect typifies social interaction then the practices are laissez-faire. Both patterns thwart life satisfaction. Each practice damages social interaction and leaves its negative effects in victim and abuser.

Practices That Subtract Human Value—Force And Neglect

Foucault developed the term sovereign power by analyzing social interaction that typified the medieval period in Europe. The pattern is built on relationships between kings and subjects, but he saw that sovereign power continues to exist in institutions, classrooms, social agencies, churches and families.

Consider the following scenario.

John and his two sisters grew up in a home with parents who were preoccupied most of the time. John was fairly quiet. He liked reading books, watching TV and playing with his dog. On one occasion, his family was having supper and his sisters began fighting at the table over who had to clear off the dishes. They didn't fight openly but they were kicking each other under the table. One kick must have landed a serious blow because one of them started to scream. John's father had been eating his dinner and reading the paper at the same time. At the sound of the scream, he leapt from the table and grabbed John by the arm. He dragged the boy to his room, hollering that the boy was nothing but a troublemaker. The family sat in silence as they heard the man beat the boy. Later, while John was in his room recovering, his father stood outside in the backyard where John could see him. The father held up his dog by the scruff of its neck. John heard the dog whimpering and ran to the window in time to see his father let go of the animal, take a rifle and shoot his dog.

Like John, victims of a king's wrath stand out or get out of place by doing something the king thinks is wrong—even if he misreads the situation. The body of a victim expresses no value in contrast to a king's double value. John has no power, no voice and no value. He's empty in the sense that his father feels free to do whatever he likes to him. Members of his family also appear to believe the father can do whatever he feels like doing. They support his violence and absolute cruelty by their silence. Family members protect themselves by being distant from John. They could have, and should have, interfered as he was being beaten and before his dog was shot. Power that negates human value relies on force, whether it's physical, emotional, psychological or epistemological. I'm not suggesting every use of force is negative. Yet if people use force to withhold human value, it's coercive. To prevent a child from running into a street full of busy traffic is to use force that doesn't negate the child's value but affirms it. Parents employ epistemological force if they lie to children and try to keep them fearful and dependent. Psychological force threatens their self-esteem, rendering them helpless and passive due to their accumulated feelings of worthlessness. Physical force makes threats against a person's body. Emotional force creates relentless feelings of self-doubt. These forms of violence render a child unable to be authentic. The child becomes a stranger on the margins of the social world.

In coercive practices, powerless people mistrust themselves. They become silent, passive and useful for another's purposes. Coercive practices are characterized by an absence of love and safety. They prepare people to expect and tolerate abuse. Those who experience coercion are hard to draw out, find authentic disclosure difficult and express passive resistance, which may be followed by anger or aggression. Their actions are attempts to hide their longings from a social world that hasn't met their basic needs for security, love and recognition.

Coercion subtracts human value. Power exercised through these practices may be direct, through domination, or indirect, by manipulation. When power becomes domination, it separates people and creates dividing walls between them. If we take an individualistic approach to explain how power operates, and deny the explanatory impact of social intelligence theory, we intensify human isolation. If people aren't seen as operating within social systems, self-esteem is perceived as a personal problem, which implies that if people wish to succeed they only have to get their act together. Individualism assumes some people are deservedly rewarded because they are gifted and others are deservedly inadequate so that their lack of opportunity is legitimate.

In domination, getting power over others is an end in itself and establishes asymmetrical social relations. Any attempt that powerless people make to balance the asymmetry is open to a cycle of harm. The rule "do to others as they do to you" becomes "I hurt you as you hurt me." As the oppressed get angry and try to repay an oppressor by breaking the machinery of production or destroying property, they simply reveal the evidence of their disadvantage and poverty. If they're caught in a cycle of harm, they have no access to equal force. Attempts at retaliation are impotent. The disadvantaged seldom succeed at trying to equalize harm since the weight of privilege works against them. Workers must unite to have an affect on domination but an ongoing cycle of harm pits each against the other and tends to foreclose on collective action.

In general, coercive practices are characterized by the absence of love and the presence of violence. Abuse is often expressed in a "love/remorse/violence cycle. The abuser hurts someone, and even if he says he's sorry, isn't compelled to change his behaviour and remains free to abuse in the future. Abused people develop a tolerance for outbursts of violence. Coercion produces a bodily *hexis* in the oppressed that shows up as an opportunity for other people to treat them with disrespect. They don't become agents of their own experience; they remain an object of it and feel little or no responsibility for what's happening to them. Coerced people express an absence of will and come to believe others are responsible for their situation. They have an underdeveloped sense of personal efficacy and slavishly conform. They may have difficulty acting without asking permission. They don't practice self-trust or self-reflection and may over-control themselves. They have a low self-image. Life is infused with discouragement. Anger and hopelessness are at its core. They're perpetually dependent. Those who grew up under coercive practices must become socially literate to participate meaningfully in community.

A second type of practice that's typical of the power to negate human value has different outcomes and expressions, but is also based on dehumanization, ambiguity and ambivalence. Consider the following example.

Suppose you're walking through a shopping mall. Just ahead of you is a family consisting of a mother, father and little girl, about three years of age. The mother and father stop to talk to two other adults. It looks to you as though the four of them are friends. At any rate, all four are engrossed in conversation. Next to the spot where they're visiting, the child is playing by a fountain. It's surrounded by a foot-high wall with water that's about one-half metre deep toward the middle. You stop and watch. The child plays along the edge of the wall and tries to climb up on it. As she tries, she speaks loudly to her parents. You wonder whether you should do something. The mother turns from her conversation and says to her: "Get down from there." You look back at the child and somehow you don't think she'll get down. The mother looks at the child's lack of compliance and returns to the conversation. This happens two or three times. The father looks up once and raises his voice. The child stops for a moment. The father waits. The child bends down to get off the wall. The father returns to the conversation. The child straightens up, climbs onto the wall, turns toward the water, slips and falls into it. Everyone is upset and the child's parents are very angry.

In this second type of practice, rather than using coercion, people are laissez-faire. They take a hands-off approach to responsibility and exercise neglect. Agents of laissez-faire practices are like absentee landlords—they're emotionally absent, which has serious negative effects on children. They may absent themselves because they learned to be insignificant during childhood, but laissez-faire practices eventually erupt in anger. Initially, these parents convey a belief that their needs, actions, feelings and thoughts don't count, so they don't follow through on limiting the little girl's access to the fountain. They tolerate disrespect. Eventually, they erupt in anger that has force at its core. This is because it's not possible to suppress our own human value indefinitely in the opposition the little girl exercises when they tell her to get down.

Laissez-faire practices are the flip side of coercion and build on similar assumptions about the social world. If parents exercise neglect, a child has most or all the power for a period of time; the adult has little or none. Children develop a bloated sense of self-importance and become uncontrollable and condescending toward their parents. In some cases of divorce, parents reduce their value by trying to buy a child's love at any cost. From the parental side, the aim is to avoid conflict and appear sympathetic to the child's wishes, which allows children to express wilfulness. If laissez-faire practices shape a child's expectations, no one else wants these wilful, uncontrollable offspring around. Laissez-faire practices produce a child that's constantly "in your face."

Laissez-faire practices are characterized by a neglect/anger cycle. Neglected children can't respect other people. Neither can they get the ordinary human satisfaction they crave. They use body language to manipulate people and find it impossible to ask for what they want in a reasonable manner. They don't practice self-trust or self-reflection. They have little self-knowledge or self-discipline. Rage is at the core of their reactions. Perpetual opposition and their incapacity to be interdependent drive their social interaction. As adults, children of laissez-faire practices must learn to be socially literate if they want to participate meaningfully in community.

CONCLUSION

Skills involved in healthy, reciprocally satisfying social interaction depend on the use people make of power. Its patterns are sometimes hard to analyze but are always felt by those who experience them. Unless we perceive these patterns, it's easy to be trapped in social interaction that constrains our very being. This is because power informs us about our human value. As we reflect on power, social literacy encourages freedom by helping us notice if we don't feel free to be ourselves. Perceiving the patterns of power offers us a break in the flow of a social interaction that lets us pause to decide how we want to respond to constraints we sense. Power is liberating. Social literacy implies that we're powerful enough to be fully present during social interaction, at the same time that we're becoming freer to be authentic and integrated into community—through the judicious use of reciprocity.

Practising reciprocity remains complex. If people misuse social power and thereby mistreat us, as we learn social literacy, we retain the Golden Rule as our default strategy, but employ the *tit for tat* strategy as we counter the harm that surfaces if power is dehumanizing. In being mistreated, we learn to observe power's misuse and assess why, when, how and for how long we will play *tit for tat*. The Golden Rule is our default, being cooperative is our first move. But *tit for tat* applies a limit to unjust uses of power. Once its communicative influence is established with the other, we choose to return to being cooperative. In one way, this proposal is an elaboration of treating other people as we want to be treated ourselves. Those who are socially literate want to know if they're misusing power themselves—and, if they are, to stop doing so. This is always possible during human interaction. Including *tit for tat* strategies is a way of seeing that social literacy builds up concern for others that's balanced by mutual reciprocity and by taking our own humanity seriously. This chapter proposes that justice is served if we follow a pattern of doing to others what we want them to do to us—almost. The point of providing relational resources at home, school and work is to address a human longing picked out at the beginning of the chapter in Atwood's example of capuchin monkeys, and balanced by her example of computer games that play *tit for tat*. As we engage in social interaction, by aiming to be ourselves in the presence of other people, we learn a complex game and learn to play this game at the right time, for the right reason, with the right people, for the right duration, as Aristotle said. It's a game with two rules—a Golden one and *tit for tat*.

It's a game in the best sense. It's wisely responsive to what's actually going on. Social literacy requires us to listen, observe and think before and as we take action during social interaction. It isn't about simple rule following. It's a practiced, thoughtful response that's motivated by the demands of civility—which we apply to other people and to ourselves.

How are these lessons to be learned? In the next chapter, I explore the requisite education by looking at cultural learning, an informal process that takes place while we're with other people who are also culture members. I want to connect a healthy use of social power with the practices involved in learning to be human and humane.

7

CULTURE, MEMES AND SOCIAL LEARNING

INTRODUCTION

Learning about power and its influence on how we think about ourselves and other people is central to social literacy. The point of being literate is to use power to offer and receive relational resources while we're with others. The willingness and ability to be authentic isn't a license to do whatever we like. We employ social skills to build a civil world that consistently enhances life satisfaction for all members.

It isn't a small point to say that being this kind of person is learned through being with those who have these skills already. In this chapter, I describe social learning, as it applies to acquiring practices of social literacy. I want to bring this chapter in line with previous ones that say social literacy improves relationships and supports authenticity. The expression 'near and different' describes its goal. An acquired ability to be authentic with others, (whether in marriage, family, school or at work) while working toward the common good, depends on learning to think on our feet. Thinking on our feet relies on abductive reasoning. It may help to refresh what's meant by abduction.

An abductive approach uses induction and deduction to perceive what's going on. It's built on a developing capacity for perceiving and receiving. In practice, it allows someone to perceive whole patterns by seeing small slices of evidence that indicate those patterns and by checking out whether that hunch matches reality. In being receptive, observers start with a theory and then set aside theory until they perceive a response that suggests a pattern. Abduction is activity and receptivity: moving forward and stepping back. It's an active use of theory and an active holding back of it until someone is receptive to what the present moment is conveying.[1] If abductive observers are accurate, they might see a slight shift in someone's facial expression or body language, hear them take a breath, or say "Yes, you understand what I mean."

Earlier I said empathy and cosmopolitanism are part of a social literacy curriculum; so is abduction. The three work together. Empathy allows us to hear what's going on in someone else's experience, as well as in our own. Cosmopolitanism relies on being true to commitments and open to the humanity of others. With empathy, cosmopolitanism and abduction, we act on appropriate obligations to ourselves and others, and provide appropriate relational resources because we accurately interpret social patterns that operate in a given situation. But how do we learn to be cosmopolitan, empathetic and abductive? We do so by learning social literacy.

In this chapter, I outline the role memes play in social learning. I also say more about common humanity by describing a twentieth century emphasis on un-neighborliness that shifted us away from civility—a trend that produced and perpetuates memes that tell us what's possible and not possible in community. The impact on the West of un-neighborly memes is weighty.

Unpacking twentieth century Western un-neighborliness is part of understanding what's possible in being near and different. I say more about what's implied in being near and different by looking at the dynamics of our human capacity to change. I then offer a list of the aspects of culture that help us situate the idea of being near yet different. If we see the range of cultural aspects outlined at the end of the chapter, it's easier to see how to locate changes that social literacy recommends to us.

My purpose in the chapter is to help people grasp opportunities to make an impact on social interaction, make good sense of and improve it, so that we improve our willingness and ability to be near and different.

MEMES AND SOCIAL LEARNING

Social literacy is informed by realizing how social learning works. The preceding chapters detail dimensions of experience we take into account as we try to gain self and social understanding by realizing that everyone has a worldview shaped by specific contexts, particular global patterns and 'family religion', in addition to the personal attributes they bring to life experience. Because a human brain is wired to change based on the accumulation of experience, all learning involves organizing. What human beings organize is a meaningful worldview that has the potential to change over time as we learn, unlearn and relearn many things. What we accumulate and organize becomes obvious to us as the way things are, and therefore, the way things must be.

Perhaps a scenario will help depict relationships between culture, memes and social learning. Mary[2] grew up with mentally ill parents who self-medicated with alcohol. Childhood was unpredictable and frightening. At 17 years old, she was left alone with 4 younger siblings in a dilapidated part of town. She was starting her first year of university, yet felt responsible to feed and clothe the younger children by holding down 2 jobs. For 3 years she supported her brothers and sisters with food and shelter while continuing her education, yet graduated as Valedictorian of her degree program. She got an excellent, responsible job and was successful at it. At 27, she married a man who also grew up in an abusive household. They had two children.

When her daughter was 14 years old, a family conflict erupted that had been brewing for several months. Police were called in. Mary was taken to jail. When police entered her home, they saw no evidence of harm she'd done to family members and told her she'd be home within hours so didn't need to take any of her belongings. That's not what happened. Three days later, she telephoned a neighbor while she was still in jail. She told Martha about her predicament. Martha checked with her husband Dave and their three teenage children. They agreed to let Mary live with them. She moved into their home, with only the clothes on her back. She stayed for a year and continued to work at her job and develop new friendships.

After about 6 months, she confided to Martha that, before she lived with them, she didn't know spouses could welcome each other home in the warm way Martha and Dave did. She hadn't known that parents could argue with teenage children and resolve conflict effectively, so that they could all relax in each other's presence.

Mary named a number of emotional and social skills she'd never seen before she came to live at Martha's house. She described her relationships by saying that, even if someone was nice, inner voices bombarded her by telling her that no social interaction was safe. She didn't feel safe until she'd lived with her friends for 6 months. In was the first place where her spiritual needs were met. It was a long process of recovery. A sense of not being safe still shows its face at times, but she's remarried and lives successfully with emotional and social skills she's adopted for herself.

Martha and Dave didn't possess exotic skills. Clearly, Mary was bright and hard working. Martha and Dave's competencies seemed obvious to them as appropriate ways to interact with others. But if someone lives with emotional poverty and abuse, what becomes obvious to them—about themselves and the world in general—is that it isn't safe. Its dangers lurk everywhere. If someone uses substances or excessive work as a substitute for meeting their own and other people's spiritual needs, then emotional and social skills atrophy or don't emerge.

Mary wanted a better life but didn't know how to get it. She had to see it in action before she realized it was possible. This is how social learning works. As we gather experience into our worldview, meaning becomes a reality that acts back on how we experience the world, until that worldview is disrupted by experiences that don't easily fit into the framework we've constructed. One of the most difficult moves we make as we converse with another person is to state what, to us, is obvious. It's equally hard to figure out what to do if another person isn't prepared to agree that it *is* obvious.

I want to pursue what's meant by social learning. Social literacy refers to what we can do in practice. It aims to help individuals perceive and respond so that responses are well suited to a situation and increase social power that's available to everyone, which is the primary meaning of empowerment. A few more definitions might help. By the term society, I refer to "an actual group of people and how they order their social relations;" by culture, I refer to "the collective product of human activities and thought" of a group."[3] Cultural evolution takes place through social learning.

A meme is cultural information passed around through these encounters. The word meme was introduced by Richard Dawkins to explain how cultures evolve.[4] His view demonstrates how social learning takes place. His meme theory was grounded on gene theory. A meme is a bit of cultural data, acquired through nurture, in the same way that a gene is a bit of biological data, acquired through nature. The following list indicates the relationship between them:

- Genes are inherited bits of DNA
- They form chromosomes: chains of molecules that are instructions (rules) for how to make a human body
- Memes are inherited bits of cultural data that tell us how to live, work, make things
- They're passed on to children by members of the group they're born into
- They're instructions for how to live as a member of a cultural or sub-cultural group
- Culture is a human product; it's something people make by transmitting memes

As a committed Darwinist, Dawkins described genes as replicator mechanisms that survive if they're selfish—if they behave in such a way as to increase their own survival chances in the gene pool, at the expense of all their alleles (competitors). He concluded that "the gene is the basic unit of selfishness."[5] He didn't mean genes consciously secure survival at the expense of others,[6] only that those that survive do so because they succeed at doing so—which is (perhaps obviously) a tautological argument. His meme concept is so influential, it makes a good starting point for describing how social learning works.

But here's the issue. His meme theory could lead people to think selfishness is inevitable. If that approach is taken, we may come to believe that selfishness drives social interaction and dictates what can and can't be done while we're with other people. If selfishness is somehow necessary to survival, we begin to think it's beneficial. We might say to ourselves: I need to learn to be selfish in the best way (whatever that might include in our understanding of 'best'). Social power is implicated in these beliefs. With selfishness, having power means being free to get what one wants regardless of others. In contrast, *Tit for Tat* followed a cooperative not a selfish script for responding to other computer programs. With selfishness as our guide, we're less effective during social interaction than a computer program.

Social learning fits in a pattern identified earlier in which we follow rules and use maxims that form life principles. Let's examine Dawkins' meme theory more closely. His view suggests that selfishness is beneficial to survival. Memes like this are acquired through social learning—by seeing/hearing how others live them out and what happens when they do, and what happens if we do or don't live them out ourselves.

If the meme 'selfishness is beneficial to survival' takes the form of a life principle, it might be expressed as follows: "Look out for No.1 (oneself) because no one else will do that for you." Life principles shape social interaction as they form and affirm expectations and skills that are congruent with them. We sometimes say a life principle is self-fulfilling. By that we mean it creates the world it names. If we compare Dawkins' meme to a principle at the root of social trust, which is, "I'll do this for you now because it's likely someone else will do that for me in the future," we get a sense of how his meme differs from those that sustain social trust. As mentioned, there's reliable evidence that life satisfaction is higher when social trust is pervasive.

Life principles are indicators of a meme environment. Likewise, environments are crucial to the success of individual memes. Memes may be successful whether or not they foster a healthy culture because their success derives from a fit within the meme environment itself. The ecological crisis at the start of the twenty-first century is a case in point. Let's suppose, as a thought experiment, that gene-based selfishness fit easily into a mid-twentieth century milieu that privileged individual survival and self-interest over global well-being. Selfishness showed up as a necessary, natural, justified impulse. As a result, it held sway over social/global concerns and foreclosed on cosmopolitanism and empathy, neither of which can survive on selfishness.

Research on social capital affirms that individualism and self-interest influence social interaction.[7] So if this thought experiment is accurate, one outcome would be a lack of concern for the environmental impact of economic decisions made by particular individuals. Dawkins' meme, based on the way he understands Darwin's theories, supports an absence of concern for maintaining a global habitat. Recall though that concern for others is essential for learning social literacy. So what do we make of his theory about the selfishness meme?

Canadian urban theorist Jane Jacobs addressed his theory in *The Nature of Economies*[8] to make the point that Darwin and Dawkins provide too simple an analysis of competitive success. Using the natural world as an example, she noted that a plant that's successful at squelching its competitors depends for its survival on drawing from the accumulated richness of the soil where it grows. That soil is formed by other plants that grew there before it. The more efficient it is at dominating its space, the less it leaves for its own future. She argued that individual survival and habitat maintenance are directly related to the plant's success.

Why didn't Darwin emphasize habitat maintenance? Jacobs proposed that he promoted his views during the heyday of empire building, when having plenty seemed obvious to him. We no longer take material plenty for granted. We face the extinction of many species, the depletion of land in some areas and the earth itself. To link her point to the case for social literacy, we can see that social literacy is about *relational habitat maintenance*—paying attention to a human environment—to perpetuate its health. How well situated are the memes that currently circulate in our culture at promoting relational habitat maintenance?

The way we depict public space influences the selection of memes people take on and practice. Theorists who work on the social brain or social intelligence report opposition to their ideas from those who describe public space using individualistic methodologies[9] that privilege self-interest at the expense of others. If we learn to be the people our social world promotes through its network of memes, and our memes privilege selfishness, becoming socially literate requires mindfulness. It needs active, intentional reflection to consider memes that might help make the world a better place if dominant memes create a fit for selfishness.

From birth, we take on the world as it's presented. Later on, we reflect on that first world's taken-for-granted memes. The worldview we keep is one we consciously choose if we want to be mindful. Social literacy compels us to consider conscious, intentional aspects of how we want to be identified as human beings. The role memes play in the process is instructive.

Relational Habitat Maintenance

If Dawkins was right, and if genes are mechanisms that attend primarily to their own survival at the expense of alleles (competitors), and the human body houses these genes, but genes themselves have little interest in their housing, it's not unreasonable to position personal survival as a driving force for action. Other people, competitors, are not my concern. Neither is the environment, so long as it survives relatively intact if and when I need to make use of it. It's easy to note that, if this thought experiment is at all descriptive of the last century, social literacy would have difficulty fitting into our current meme environment due to its emphasis on social responsibility rather than individual competitive success alone.

Two questions arise. What memes contribute to relational habitat maintenance? How do memes operate to reproduce themselves in a culture as it evolves toward relational health? To respond to specifics, in light of these questions, I first ask how memes operate. The question of memes that contribute to relational habitat maintenance is a larger issue pursued throughout the book.

Yet in responding to the second question, I want to be clear how I use the term evolution. I agree with Distin that evolution doesn't create something out of nothing,[10] yet, if requirements are met, evolution seems bound to happen.[11] Requirements for an evolutionary process include:

- Replication
- Variation
- Selection

If organisms reproduce, passing their character almost (but not quite) accurately on to the next generation, and if the environment doesn't supply them with unlimited resources, they evolve. There will be a struggle for survival. The organism is preserved whose traits best fit a given environment.[12]

Distin points out that in two works, *Origin of Species* (1859) and the *Descent of Man* (1871) Darwin picked out patterns he expressed in the following ways:

- All organisms are engaged in a perpetual struggle for existence
- There are limited resources
- Organisms are naturally selected which have the optimum fit to conditions of existence
- Human beings are subject to evolutionary processes
- Our unique mental features are explicable by natural selection
- Natural selection can account for human social and ethical behaviour.[13]

The last pattern is problematic for relational habitat maintenance. In natural selection, if there's a struggle for limited resources, organisms with slightly advantageous variations have a better chance of survival and replication. Those with variations that aren't in sync with the environment find their survival threatened.[14] At present, social trust and social literacy are in that camp.

In analyzing Darwin's and Dawkins' theories, Distin asks if a meme is the mechanism for cultural evolution and argues that it is. Natural selection consists in the differential survival of genes, i.e., replicators—things that make copies of themselves. Genes are composed of content plus effects. They preserve and store biological data in DNA and occupy a particular place (locus) on a chromosome (a structure within a cell nucleus). A chromosome is made of DNA. Genes may have alleles: alternative forms of the gene in the population that occupies the same locus on the chromosome and controls the same sort of things the gene does (e.g., eye colour). Eye colour, for example, is a gene's phenotypic effects. Certain genes have blue eyes effects; others have brown eyes effects. If they make exact copies, an effect is transmitted exactly, but genes don't always make exact copies. They're selfish in the sense that "they cannot survive if they are inefficient at self-replication."[15] With longevity, fecundity and copying fidelity, some genes have a better chance of survival than others.

What's the equivalent of cultural DNA? Information must be preserved in a form that allows it to be copied so that its phenotypic effects can be selected. As an example, I might want to learn French but if there's no one to speak with, the meme is less successful. However, if I live in Ottawa, where there are plenty of bilingual people, learning French is a more successful meme (recipe for speaking it) than, perhaps, if I live in Calgary, Manchester or Dallas.

Dawkins (1976) coined the term meme to explain the development of culture as the distinctive feature of the human species—to him, culture makes us human. A meme is content plus effects: it's a unit of cultural data residing in the brain that has typical effects. Bits of cultural data produce effects characteristic of the information they provide. For example, the memes 'look out for number one!' or 'don't get involved' have effects on social interaction. Effects are the external consequences of that piece of information. As noted in earlier chapters, Paley's meme, 'You can't say you can't play' produces unique social effects.

Memes might be expressions, skills, music, advertisements. They're outward, visible, audible manifestations of data in the brain, transmitted between persons *via* sense organs. What they leave on the brain isn't an exact copy necessarily, but it can be transmitted again. Memes have two types of effects: on people and in the world. They use their possessor's communication and imitation skills to replicate themselves, to have effects on the world, and influence their own survival chances—a success that depends on the environment into which they settle.

Memes act together. As sets of memes cooperate, new ones find it more difficult to penetrate the environment that earlier memes established, unless they slip easily into the environment without making too much fuss. A complex set of memes provides protection against invasion from memes that do violence to those already in existence.[16]

The advantage a meme confers on itself must in some way be better than its rivals, but it may have nothing to do with the quality of effects it has on the people that own it. Abusive memes survive in an abusive environment. Memes survive within a complex of other memes primarily because they fit well, not because they contribute anything positive to human beings. They are effective, not so much because of their content, but due to their fit.

Memes are about the things they affect; they're representational content. A representation is a piece of mental furniture, so to speak, a state, event, thought, feeling, opinion, memory or skill that carries information about the world.[17] Distin pointed out that representations may take one of three forms: as icons which resemble what they represent (a drawing of a tree), as indices that are co-related with what they represent (a fuel gauge), or as symbols that represent *via* social convention (a white figure walking or a red hand upheld at a crosswalk).

Symbols represent each other and things in the world.[18] Symbolic content depends for its meaning on its relationship to other symbols, not just on the symbol itself or the object/idea it represents; it depends on the setting supplied by a meaning system. For example, if we're travelling abroad, we may see advertisements we can't interpret because we don't possess the right meaning system to explain them. Memes are interdependent; we must understand a whole representational system before we can interpret each symbol accurately.

As representational content, memes must be able to determine which representations count because they function to preserve information between generations in an appropriate way. Not all representations are memes: emotions and beliefs are not memes. They are responses to memes. A meme is a bit of data—you can't say you can't play—we respond to that data based on our understanding and interpretation of it.

Memes spark emotional reactions. Lisa responded to Paley's meme with outrage. In her anger, she got red faced and visibly emotional, in the same way people in the U.S. may get if the issue of gun control emerges. There's a strong set of memes associated with guns. People attach beliefs to these memes and have a strong emotional response to those beliefs. A belief is a natural, internal indicator that functions to elicit particular behaviour, such as getting red in the face or shouting. Due to beliefs about a meme, a reaction may be produced whenever the meme is referred to or shows up.[19] A meme doesn't 'contain' that emotional response, but sparks one reaction in some people and a different one in others.

The key ways to transmit memes include imitation, intentional work, formal teaching and learning a general method. Distin suggested that complex replication is more successful if the complexity involved is hierarchical, not in an authoritarian but in an educational sense. To learn successfully, a task must be broken into reasonable parts.

Suppose two watchmakers reassemble a watch that has 1000 parts. One watchmaker puts 1000 parts into groups of 100 and assembles each group. After assembling each set, she assembles the sets into a watch so that her work is hierarchically structured. Another watchmaker works with 1000 parts at the same time. At each mistake, she must begin at the beginning. The first watchmaker works with 100 pieces at a time. At each mistake, she has only 100 to fix. Learning to master a complex skill depends on learning to work with all its component parts by organizing them effectively. This is similar to the process outlined by Dreyfus in his approach to learning mastery that was outlined earlier.

Successful replication is particulate (authentic, so to speak) because each part has its own identity in the assembly. Each must be compatible or the result is unstable. In terms of the watch, each tiny piece is self-assertive and integrative.[20] It has its own identity that fits in with other pieces in the assembly. Memes work the same way. Distin saw that memes are self-assertive and integrative and noted a rule that emanates from each part's identity (authenticity) and fit (integration) in a system. To be acquired, memes must slide into a fitting place in an established assembly.[21]

To be transmitted in social interaction, they must fit into an assembly that's being replicated as a whole.[22] To be accepted, an idea (meme) has usually to be compatible with those already in existence; it needs a receptive environment *and* an external world that accords with its effects,"[23] i.e., perceives it as valid. Fitness is influenced by a meme's ability to gain and retain attention (from a human brain) which doesn't necessarily mean people are constantly or actively aware of it, but the existence of a meme assembly increases each new meme's chance of sticking with existing memes, and that process in turn builds up the assembly.[24]

Successful memes gain and retain a lot of peoples' attention. Recessive memes are passed on, but with a difference. They're not taken on board in a way that shapes action. Not being taken on board by people is what's meant by a meme being recessive. It resides in the meme complex but its effects aren't apparent in the behaviour of those who've acquire it through social learning. Distin made it clear that particular memes don't stick with us because they're beneficial to us. They stick because they fit the larger system.

Memes that affirm social responsibility don't integrate easily into environments that prize selfishness, so how does social learning explain what we need to do to support relational habitat maintenance? How can we teach people to care about the human world at the same time as we try to teach them to care for the earth?

Dynamic Social Learning

In social learning, there are three ways to create an artefact, i.e., a new product, complex skill or way of thinking. I may:

- Work from an idea I invent myself (like Socrates did when he invented authenticity)
- Work from instructions, for example, if I make a cake
- Copy a product someone else created[25] (when I learn to speak French in Ottawa)

In the second case, cake making, instructions include how to make a cake and give data on its essential features, which is an important part of new learning.

Suppose I try to make a cake but don't understand the chemistry behind baking it. I add ingredients but I'm not careful about measuring them. I can't observe the essential features of baking if I've only seen a finished product. To replicate a cake, I need to follow instructions that reveal what's essential to the quality of a final product. No amount of observing the final product or eating it will help me understand the role of measurement in making a cake. I must learn to follow instructions. As I follow them, and sometimes fail to do so, I learn that measurement is essential. This is the type of learning Paley led her children through. Lisa copied a surface form of 'you can't say you can't play' and acquired skill in its deeper structures so that she could still use power, without being exclusive of other children.

As people engage in social learning, they may copy the organizational structure of a behaviour or its surface form. Copying surface form is a lower level activity, but in either case pattern recognition is central: "it appears that the capacity to organize one's behaviour into patterns, and learn those patterns from others, is a hierarchical process that depends on the ability to pick out the structure of a pattern's organization."[26]

Self-awareness is pre-requisite for copying at either level. In order to copy behaviour, we must meta-represent it,[27] i.e., recognize/depict what we're imitating. The process includes three parts:

- Imitate the details of individual actions
- Copy the structure of more complex behaviour patterns
- Meta-represent the structure (non-linguistically or linguistically)

In meta-representing, a child recognizes what's been imitated and represents it in some way.[28]

Distin identifies a capacity for meta-representation as integral to being human and believes that modern human beings are born with a degree of mindfulness that's developed by existing memes to the extent that a fully fledged mind may, itself, create new memes.[29] That is, there's a meme (recipe) for being mindful.

Being mindful is built on the ability to represent. To decode a representational system, one needs first to look for the structural features beyond the details, before adding details and complexity later on.[30] Is it reasonable to think children are able to meta-represent? Distin argues that human infants can focus on overarching structures rather than on fine details. They do so when they learn language and even before that, a claim supported by observing their developing perceptual skills. Infants can recognize 'cat' in countless concrete and abstract forms and persistently know it's a cat. Human beings "cannot help but see the world in symbolic categorical terms, dividing it up according to opposed features, and organizing [their] lives according to themes and narratives."[31]

The mind of a child develops through this innate capacity to represent, to abstract information from the environment and realize it in a different, more concrete form: "At the heart of human culture lies our ability to meta-represent. The cultural equivalent of DNA, a meme, which all cultures use to replicate themselves—is not one, but a whole range of systems of representation.[32]

Take for example, memes for farming. The human family began farming about 11,000 or 10,000 years ago, depending on how one counts time.[33] Therefore, its memes should be stable. Farming is complex and allows for change and innovation. In a farming town, new memes fit into a meme environment townspeople understand. Advertizing and other more direct forms of instruction rely on that environment so that a specific meme is understood immediately due to its relationship to memes already there. But those same memes would be incomprehensible in a city today. Memes for fixing a pump, haying or 'splitting a tractor' are incomprehensible to most urbanites, and perhaps to most readers of this book.

Yet farming memes were so essential, and now so absent, that Leonard Sax, in *Boys Adrift* (2007), notes the difficulty professors have in teaching medical students about the heart. Faculty describe the heart as a pump but few students have hands-on experience with pumps so the metaphor isn't useful to explain how a heart works. We can't access what isn't well situated in our own meme complex. Instructions for how to use a computer, email, Google—all depend on practical experience that builds an environment that allows someone to extend, innovate and create new memes for the overall use of computers. Those who know little about computers find it impossible to make use of instructions (memes) just as non-farmers would find it hard to know how to augur grain.

I want to be clear that memes are a theory, conceptual possibilities rather than literal entities, although Dawkins's meme theory is a successful meme itself.[34] Memes explain an observable tendency people have to learn patterns from one another and to change these patterns when they learn something different as new elements are introduced into a culture. Social learning is, therefore, a mechanism of cultural inheritance.[35] We don't learn to be human as isolated individuals, by trial and error, we learn culturally to be the people that we become. It's not that we learn by imitation and copying only. We also learn by having new ideas that we find ways to fit into the existing meme environment.

Memes are a useful shorthand way to say that culture is an evolutionary system that involves inherited 'know-how' and depends on spirituality, *a sense of felt connection*, as the bedrock for all social learning. It's through a vital sense of *felt connection* that a child learns to be a healthy member of a given culture. If that sense of felt connection falters or withers, a child may be lost, either through despair or suicide. An active *sense of felt connection* makes survival and social learning possible. Memes are replicated among human beings by means of *a sense of felt connection* that's necessary for that transmission to be completed.

In discussing symbolic power in the previous chapter, I noted it requires people to believe that it's legitimate for some people to have more power than other people. But this isn't the only way to think about power. An empowering meme describes power as cooperative energy every human being is able to exercise. When power is perceived as the energy of negotiation, when everyone has the right to hold others accountable and learns how to do so effectively, power is no longer the bad energy of force or neglect. It's perceived as a giving, receiving, sharing, nurturing partnership among people of equal value to one another.

In this view, people are powerless, not if they can't get their own way; they're powerless if they're unable to manage emotions, skills, knowledge, material and relational resources in a way that provides life satisfaction through valued social roles (as worker or parent). This concept for power assumes everyone is gifted. Gifts need support and recognition. In this view, power refers to feelings, beliefs and behaviour that convey that I'm someone who can say and do what's congruent with an idea I have of myself and support my important interests; it assumes my important interests will be met as I help others satisfy their important interests. This power meme environment has effects on those who exercise it as well as those who benefit from its exercise.

Empowering practices are grounded on different assumptions about the social world than those characterized by force or neglect that focus on scarcity not relational plenty. Empowerment is grounded on relational generosity not fear of material scarcity. Within this meme environment, relational values are a basis for economic decisions. People that empower themselves and others believe there's enough relational support to encourage everyone to be fulfilled as human beings.

Empowering practices assume the equal worth of each person. The social world isn't conceived as a place of essential conflict over scarce and valuable interests. Time is plentiful. Decisions aren't made hastily by a few in the inner circle at the top of a hierarchy of decision-makers. Knowledge is shared. Decisions are negotiated on the basis of involvement among the players who are affected by a decision. Empowering people are capable of social trust and a willingness and ability to be near and different. In this setting, to be powerful refers to the ability to work cooperatively with others to achieve shared goals by being good neighbours.

Theories about other people

It makes good sense to treat others the way we want to be treated. It makes good sense to assist the disadvantaged if we want to live in a healthy society. These are the most basic bargains of being a good neighbour. As Robert Putnam pointed out,[36] earliest neighborhood contracts constituted a bargain based on social trust. These contracts were based on 'collective solidarity' and 'horizontal collaboration'; they created a "significant network of social and economic obligations...by recognizing the ability to be a good neighbor [sic] in each other.[37] Being neighborly, Putnam argued elsewhere, is the root of economic viability because it builds a solid base of social capital or social trust, which in turn produces a healthy environment for everyone. In his research (2000) he stacked up evidence to reveal social trust as the glue that holds society together. Social capital refers to connections among individuals, social networks and the norms of reciprocity and trustworthiness that arise from them.[38]

The underlying sentiment for social capital is captured in the meme "I should help others when they need it, without expecting anything in return because it is likely that if I need help someone will do the same for me." Kant put it this way: To be beneficent... to promote according to one's means, the happiness of others in need, without hoping for something in return, is everyone's duty."[39] Happiness to Kant referred to continuous well-being, enjoyment of life and complete satisfaction with one's condition;[40] it wasn't so much a light-hearted mood as it was a desire that life should go pretty much the way we want. Its opposite isn't unhappiness, i.e., down heartedness, but rather intense and continual frustration with trying to have one's most pressing needs met within a context that one can't escape. The conditions of extreme poverty are an example of unhappiness, if we take Kant's point.

In short, Kant thought we should be good neighbours. But there was a strong counter-argument to neighbourliness that influenced the twentieth century. It's misleading to suggest the last century developed theories of justice on the model of fairness without noting opposition to its altruism and generosity. Sigmund Freud, for one, proposed that it wasn't rational to love one's neighbour. As one of the most influential theorists in the last century, particularly in North America, in *Civilization and its Discontents,* he argued that the idea of loving neighbours should cause surprise and bewilderment if we reflect on it rationally. Since, he said, my love is valuable to me, I shouldn't throw it away without reflection. Love requires a sacrifice, he continued, so that "If I love someone, he must deserve it in some way."[41]

He said that a neighbour deserved his love if he was "so like me in important ways that I can love myself in him; and he deserves it if he's so much more perfect than me that I can love my ideal of my own self in him."[42] If the neighbour was his friend's son he would love him because he would share his friend's pain at seeing a friend fail to love a member of his own family. But if a neighbour was a stranger to Freud,

> If he cannot attract me by any worth of his own or any significance that he may have already acquired for my emotional life, it will be hard for me to love him. Indeed, I should be wrong to do so, for my love is valued by all my own people as a sign of my preferring them, and it is an injustice to them if I put a stranger on a par with them. But if I am to love him (with this universal love) merely because he, too, is an inhabitant of this earth, like an insect, an earth-worm, or a grass-snake, then I fear that only a small modicum of my love will fall to his share—not by any possibility as much as, by the judgement of my reason, I am entitled to retain for myself. What is the point of a precept enunciated with so much solemnity if its fulfilment cannot be recommended as reasonable?

Loving one's neighbour, to Freud, was unreasonable.

The Christian principle to "love one's enemies" was incomprehensible and roused nothing in him but opposition. In a passage where he talked about loving one's enemies, he revealed his suspicion of others and his dislike for them. He thought it more likely that neighbours were moved by sexual desire, greed and aggression than by love. For him, an ideal of loving our neighbours was an illusion (meme) to eradicate. To him, humanity is aggressive.

He said it might be possible to "bind together a considerable number of people in love, so long as there are other people left over to receive the manifestations of their aggressiveness."[43] His view of human nature was negative. He proposed that if the cultural ideal was: "Love thy neighbour as thy neighbour loves thee," he would have no opposition to that prescription.[44] In this way, he offers his support for the meme environment Paley's kindergarten children brought to class. It's fair to imagine that Freud would find her meme to be nonsense and a waste of her time.

From another perspective, Freud's neighbour principle leaves the model and method for social interaction in my neighbours' hands. His or her behaviour directs mine. To sum up, Freud believed we have no obligation to love neighbours. People are aggressive. We have no duty to them. I agree people can be aggressive and self-absorbed, e.g., Mary's family of origin. Freud was onto something. Suppose you have a friend who's a seamstress. She sets up her shop in your neighbourhood and you want her to succeed. One day you're in a local store and see posters for another seamstress who's setting up her business a few blocks from your friend's shop. You look around to see if anyone's watching, then pull down her posters. You feel justified in doing it, let's say, for the good of the neighbourhood. After all we can't have too much competition or no one will succeed. Your act is aggressive, unjust, whether or not you feel guilty about it. Of course, you wouldn't have looked around to see if anyone was watching if you felt no scruples. So I agree. There's a strong tendency in people to be aggressive. There may be a strong tendency in some people to commit murder. Does the presence of a human tendency legitimate its support? Do we give up on maintaining a relational habitat simply because it's difficult?

The role memes play in learning what's culturally expected is central. Freud's memes permeated the twentieth century, especially in North America, even though people who espouse them have little idea of their source. What's to be done to teach people otherwise? The entire point of this book is moved by that question. I want to say more about memes to point out how they shape expectations and experience and what they can teach us about change.

CHANGE AND SOCIAL LEARNING

In an earlier chapter I outlined two successful programs offered in Canada and Britain. *Roots of Empathy* and *Working with Others* (WWO) provide emotional literacy training for students. One difference between the programs is that WWO trains adults in a school setting. Adults use their knowledge, skill and insight to teach the whole curriculum. While both programs are laudable, teaching adults and students is preferable for learning social literacy.

While *Roots of Empathy* demonstrates emotional literacy skills, and teachers observe skill acquisition in their learners and gain insight from their observation, teaching adults directly helps them identify what it's like, first-hand, to learn the skills for themselves. If teachers understand how change happens in them, they have insight into how to help their learners face change.

Teachers who know how it feels to learn social and emotional literacy skills, what it's like to practice them with other people, and record how they think about learning them, are better able to pace and tailor a program of skill acquisition to learners. Their sensitivity to the learning environment is informed by what they know first-hand. They teach these skills from personal experience. This is the best preparation for teaching others complex, face-to-face skills of social literacy. If teachers practice first what they expect others to accomplish, they understand more clearly and respond more effectively to difficulties learners have in acquiring these skills. They understand from the inside why some learners may resist or struggle with learning.

The WWO approach uses the relational quality of teacher-learner connection that's already operating in a classroom and strengthens that link by training the teacher. Training the teacher allows an already existing support system to be better. This point is crucial for learning social literacy. It's a backdrop for what I want to say about social learning.

In the earlier section of this chapter, I used Dawkins's description and Distin's analysis of memes. Mihaly Csikszentmihalyi[45] developed the idea further in *The Evolving Self* (1993).[46] Beck and Cowan rely on his analysis to extend the role memes play in worldviews people hold, or that hold them, in order to talk about how people change. They unpack the function of memes in the way people feel about change itself.

Beck and Cowan are interested in how lasting change comes about. They focus on change in individuals and organizations. To them, change requires six conditions to exist before it can be counted on to endure:

- The potential for change is present
- Unresolved issues are acknowledged
- Dissonance is *felt* between the way things are and the worldview someone holds
- Significant insight is gained into that dissonance, with an awareness of alternatives
- Barriers to change are identified and eliminated, reframed, bypassed or neutralized
- Consolidation occurs, but not without confusion, false starts, long learning curves and assimilation into a new way of looking at the world.

If someone wants lasting change, they first must see where they are currently before setting out for a new place to be. They need to unpack their own worldview to see what it contains. Further, "if there is no culture of nurturing support during the transformation, new memes rarely germinate, much less bloom."[47]

This is why we teach teachers social literacy skills first so they create an empowering learning environment on their own. Given a supportive, nurturing setting that neighbourhood friends provided to her, Mary's experience fulfilled conditions Beck and Cowan identified as necessary for lasting change. If we recall Bill's experience in Hyas or Mark's experience in his church as he received housing, these people found a nurturing setting that provided the support they needed to survive and even to thrive.

Beck and Cowan say a great deal about change,[48] which is too extensive for my purposes at this point. But I want to explore the first condition, the presence of a potential for change, to show how social learning gets off the ground. People who offer nurturing support must have emotional/social literacy skills in order to see the dynamics involved in the human potential for change. Beck and Cowan acknowledge that not everyone has the same potential for change, although that situation isn't necessarily permanent. A socially literate person reads these differences and adjusts to people with tact.[49]

In terms of the first condition, the presence of a potential for change, Beck and Cowan posit that most people live with needs, values and aspirations that direct their lives. The interplay between these dynamics provides impetus for change. If the smoothness between the way we think and the way we live is disrupted, we're readier to accept change. If the way we're living is disrupted, three types of change potential show up: people may be open, arrested or closed to change. If someone wishes to teach someone something, these three states must be identified, in addition to the worldview that a person holds.

If people are open to change, they can deal with complexity. This is the healthiest response to opportunities for change and relies on someone's personal history and capacity to move forward by accepting the challenges that change presents to them. They're able to be flexible throughout change and remain open to its realities. They deal effectively with barriers by stepping over, removing or going around them and convey a sense that more than one option is available and attractive to them.

There are several attitudes that characterize openness: people strive to remove barriers and allow for the expression of individual differences. They don't get locked on habitual patterns that are rife with unexamined assumptions. They believe change is inevitable, show flexibility and seldom jump on the current bandwagon. They understand there are external conditions that complicate change. Accepting that reality, they work with it. Openness is typified by good listening skills, a non-judgmental approach, tolerance of difference and emotional availability in the face of complexity. An open person is able to accommodate surprises and disappointments without being stymied by them.

In the second state, if people are arrested, their forward movement is hindered by the way they currently operate. There's a way forward that remains available to them, even if it's uncomfortable, but they aren't taking that path. The barriers in a situation, which they believe can't be overcome, ensnare them. They may lack insight into what's going on and be unaware of what's in the way of progress.

With an arrested state, it's always a question of whether more dissonance would break up the logjam they're stuck in. It's typical for those who are arrested to give excuses and rationalize the *status quo*. Change may appear too costly. There's a desire not to rock the boat and to live with obstacles that hurt—like a stone in the shoe they don't take time to remove. They keep hobbling along. In an arrested frame of mind, people do their best with circumstances that face them. They run in their own lane and adapt to people around them, regardless of the personal cost of doing so. People that are arrested may shift a little here or there under the weigh of these encroachments but won't expend very much effort to move them out of the way.

They may say things such as: "It's just the way things are. You can't fight city hall. It's just the way the cookie crumbles. I'll deal with it one of these days." Emotional resignation is unchallenged. Others may look at a person who's in an arrested phase and say: "He just doesn't get it. He doesn't see what's going on. He doesn't care."

Being in an arrested state is common under certain circumstances. In an earlier chapter, I described the way people tend to operate in systems they don't question. Becoming open takes courage and effort. But there's also a cost to remaining stuck: "inability to adapt and change things leads to frustration, denial, anger, resentment and a leading malady of our age—stress."[50] Those in an arrested state have related problems: undue stress, gastro-intestinal disorders, passive-aggressive behaviours and other forms of personal and social frustration. Instead of being hopeful about the future, they reject transformational models of change and focus on patching-up their current circumstances, all the while refraining from upsetting anyone. Such people are hard to work with. From an outsider's perspective, the tried and true ways they deploy to relieve stress are blatantly ineffective.

The third state Beck and Cowan describe is one in which someone is closed to change. These are people for whom psychological blindness[51] keeps them from seeing alternatives to their current situation. Due to past experience, often trauma (or a family pattern that failed to help them be empathetic) and to a view of a future that has little hope in it, they're unable to recognize barriers that have them trapped, much less overcome them. Trauma triggers closure and is characterized by an absence of empathy.

The dynamics of abduction aren't available to someone who's closed. Abduction requires a flexibility that's unavailable to such a person—due to effort they expend to remain in a fortress that keeps things the way they are and under control. Seeing what's really going on would help them move out of a closed state—but a sense that this move is too costly keeps them where they are—even if they're increasing the emotional distance in relationships with people they say they care about. Their growing isolation produces strategies for staying closed and is a consequence of being closed.

People in a closed state are threatened by change and fight to stay put. They may lack the neurological equipment to consider change, according to Beck and Cowan. From another perspective, they might be mired in negative thinking they can't seem to counter with logic or to balance with positive thoughts.

Beck and Cowan identify certain signs they associate with a closed state. Such a person is inappropriate, with little or no ability to adapt to a changing milieu. They have an insatiable desire for more and more of what they want. For this person, there's never enough of what they value. They reject other possibilities in advance. Only a few people are in their inner circle—others are cut off and marginalized. They have an undue response to frustration, get irritable quickly and frequently blow up. Often this person is a perfectionist. They compulsively and constantly check and recheck a situation to be certain they're right. Closed people live in a shell. They may hide or destroy information if it doesn't fit their agenda. They command censorship and thought control from others, if they're in a position to demand it.

Given this description, it's evident that such people expend great effort to prevent themselves from moving toward conditions identified as essential for lasing change to take place. Their isolation as a solitary individual is profound. At the outset, I described social literacy as an idea that doesn't sit well with many of our memes about individualism, e.g., the social intelligence meme that stress is social and the insight that people operate in social systems and tend to perpetuate those systems rather than challenging them. Using Beck and Cowan's three states, how might we think about people, say for example, in a University College setting?

Suppose the Dean of the College, Tom, is in a closed state. Given indicators above, how would he influence others? Let's also consider Ted, the Associate Dean. In the milieu of a closed state, what can we expect of Ted in terms of his view of change? Would he be open at work? Even if he were open at home, in his neighbourhood, religious community or with close friends, it would appear unsafe to be open with someone in a closed state who has control over his academic and vocational future. Imagine the stress he'd experience if he were open everywhere except at work.

So what's to be done? As a socially literate person reads the three states in a work setting, she might begin with open people—if there are any such people there. Perhaps seeing others open up to change and enhanced life satisfaction would persuade those who are arrested or closed that change offers benefits worth having. But if closed individuals are the boss, they tend to close down on every opportunity, however slight, that's discordant with the *status quo.* A closed boss is Foucault's king. Their social interaction relies on sovereign power. So what's the next move for the socially literate?

Suppose Ted's wife has a rare disease. Her treatment is only available in the city where he works. His options appear limited. His life is complex. Under these conditions, how might he act so as to be near and different at work? Are there heroes to help him out?

Socrates is a hero, due to the way he thought about life. As Foucault put it, he was all about button-holing people on street corners and urging them to consider the condition of their own souls. He understood the human condition and paid a high price for his insight. As Freud and Foucault noted, social power is ambiguous and those who exercise it live with ambivalence. Socrates was loved by the people and killed by the people. It's dangerous to be heroic.

His insight about the human condition is captured in the *Apology*, a speech he gave at his trial, as he said goodbye to those he served and loved. It's likely a speech that's a fairly accurate record of his thought because Plato was at his trial and would have grasped, and maybe gasped, at every word. Socrates said something like this: What my accusers say about me isn't true. Let me tell you why. The oracle at Delphi declared me the wisest man. I think I'm not. So, I sought to discover the reason for the words said about me. Slowly, I realized that, if I'm wise, it's only because I know what I don't know and I never claim otherwise.

And so, said Socrates, when the god ordered me, as I thought and believed, to live the life of a philosopher, to examine myself and others, I didn't abandon my post. Even if you acquitted me now, Gentlemen of the jury, and say to me, Socrates, we don't believe your accusers, we acquit you, but only on condition that you spend no more time on philosophy. If you're caught doing so, you'll die, I would say to you, Gentlemen of the Jury, I'm grateful and am your friend, but I'll obey the god rather than you. As long as I draw breath and am able, I shall not cease to practice philosophy, to exhort you and in my usual way to point out to any one of you whom I happen to meet: Good Sir, you're an Athenian, a citizen of the greatest city with the greatest reputation for wisdom and power. Aren't you ashamed of your eagerness to possess as much wealth, reputation and honours as possible, while you don't care for, nor give thought to, wisdom and truth, or the best possible state of your soul?

If, Gentlemen of the jury, he continued, you wish for my exile rather than my death, be assured that I know that Socrates is the same man in public as in private. He would be the same man in exile as in Athens. Even in exile I'd go around doing nothing but persuading both young and old among you not to care for body or wealth in preference to (or as strongly as) the best possible state of your soul. And therefore Gentlemen, since my questions anger men and make me unpopular, and since I would be Socrates wherever I go, I'd accept the hemlock before I'd betray the god and myself. Which is, as we know, what Socrates did.

Clearly, Socrates' memes didn't fit his environment although he altered the environment for all who follow him. In this amazing set of assertions, he established authenticity: the heroism of knowing and being oneself despite the circumstances. Social literacy depends on authenticity. A socially literate person refuses to participate in power that kings initiate and spread through the kingdom. Acting behind the king's back to build opposition isn't in sync with social literacy; oppositional contexts fail to provide relational resources that are each person's due.

Ted must search out his alternatives. Recall that arrested individuals have alternatives, but aren't taking them. Having alternatives differentiates arrested from closed states. He might ask himself questions: What's holding me in place at work? Is the work worth what I'm paying for it? What does remaining here cost me elsewhere, since my stress is intensifying? Are there alternative treatments for my wife? Is there another job in the city that would be more bearable? Is desire for wealth and prestige sickening my soul? Is my stress harming my children? What's happening in my relationships? What do strength and weakness look like? How can I work for the common good in a place like this? Is my anger justified? How do I treat faculty members? How's my overall ability to trust others? Are there legal aspects a labour lawyer could address? What do I want from life? What are the principles I've chosen to live by?

If Ted fails to follow his own principles, the mark of Socratic authenticity, he's at risk of being caught in Tom's enclosure, with few chances to escape. From the beginning of their work relationship, if Ted violates his principles, the trap tightens. If Tom sees Ted violate his own principles, he can use that knowledge to cement Ted's loyalty to him.

Could his quality of life in other areas provide sufficient relational resources to live up to his own ideals at work? Why do we assume work should exert the most pull on us? Isn't life more than work? What if he just left? Leaving could be the right decision. But bad leadership is ubiquitous. If everyone left because of bad leadership, very few jobs would be filled. Suppose Ted chose to live in an open way. Perhaps, its attractiveness would appeal to his boss. Perhaps. If maintaining his own position is what drives Tom, Ted's social and emotional skills will show up as a threat and a challenge that Tom could read as a loss of his power.

Well then, do socially literate people drink the hemlock? That seems extreme. Socrates left behind a wife and two sons when he drank his potion. Is there something about integration even he failed to grasp? Earlier I distinguished liberation from practices of freedom. Once people are free to be authentic, what are the practices that daily inform how to integrate in a culture or sub-culture? This is the hardest question we ask ourselves or ask of ourselves. In response, I suggest we focus our gaze in more than one direction. What's to be done about Ted's anxiety?

Let's look at a healthy response to anxiety. An anxious context is like driving down the street and suddenly seeing an accident happen right in front of you. What do you do while you have time to avoid it? You turn your gaze in the direction you want your car to move in. You shift your focus. Your car follows. How might this practice inform Ted's response to his College context? How might his examination of his work's meme environment help him appropriately situate new memes he wants to uphold? At its root, his response requires him to look closely at authenticity and integration, what each signifies, how he's currently measuring up to each and what he might emphasize at the present moment, in the present moment, so as to lead a fuller life, whether or not he leaves his job.

Authenticity and integration are composed of different social and emotional skills. Ted could analyze the field they create together and assess his current position in that field. Rather than remaining stuck on coping at work, he might focus attention on what it looks like to be authentic and integrated in the context with which he has to contend. He might ask himself how this context might become more like a community. Without consciously shifting our gaze away from the accident in front of us (and being isolated in the privacy of our own vehicle) we tend to automatically reproduce an environment's memes, even though we find them offensive as we observe them in someone else.

The skill of turning our gaze in another direction, as we evaluate our behaviour, depends on developing an ability to read and detect memes that create an environment. Meme detection offers a certain kind of distance. We step back from a culture or sub-culture in order to remain authentic within it, identify memes that satisfy our own life values, and look for a place to fit them into foreign cultures, for example, the strangled culture of those who live in a closed state. The analysis of culture that follows is a menu for this enterprise. Culture operates everywhere. We can't become human without acquiring it. If we seek self and social insight, a socially literate person becomes adept at reading cultural aspects that contain memes he or she learns to sort through to improve an environment so that new memes might emerge in it.

WHAT IS CULTURE?

If Ted has courage to sort through memes in his work environment and imagine new ones that might create a more open environment, where would he look for information? In what follows, there are categories of culture that contain specific memes in a given environment. An overview of culture helps to provide places Ted might look as he investigates his work setting. As part of the process, he needs to ask himself what he brings to the table and what it's like for others to work with him—that is, he must examine his own work culture meme environment.

To examine his context, Ted needs to understand culture itself. The word culture, as we use it, isn't old,[52] though records of cultural interchanges are as old as the inquiries of Herodotus (c.484-425 B.C.E.), the first Greek historian. The traditional meaning had two roots: from the Latin *cultus* (worship) and *colere* (cultivate), the second from a Latin word *civis,* (civilization, civil). From its origins, it has two dimensions: appearance, dress (external, outward, material) and improvement, refinement of life (internal, spiritual). Both contain the idea of betterment, improvement toward perfection, which acted as a standard a group would use to measure its members.[53] Culture retains a sense of measurement; e.g., Ted feels measured by Tom regarding his fit in the current work setting.

English anthropologist Edward Tylor proposed the first scientific definition for culture in *Primitive Culture* (1871)[54] and acknowledged his debt to its German development. In Germany, the scientific concept had two branches: Geist, by using a deductive approach, identified general patterns for universal human culture that were typically based on Western rationality; and Kultur, which, by using an inductive approach, produced specific, ethnographic sets of customs, beliefs and practices of a local group of people.

Tension created by the two branches poses a problem for social literacy until we trace the idea of culture into recent times. Social literacy invites reflection on what's common and what's unique in people. Rather than gathering universals deductively and particulars inductively, we work abductively. While Kant (one of the researchers into Geist) doesn't use the term abduction, it's harmonious with his claims about conceptual analysis, in which he says that once we arrive at a theory, we're compelled to go into the world to find out if it's true to life. Theories we get by studying culture are no exception.

Culture is everything except our genetic heritage. It's the whole of a society's beliefs, knowledge and practices (available in a society's memes). Culture operates as a set of control mechanisms, plans, recipes, rules, instructions for governing behaviour and it guides symbolic-expressive aspects of social interaction. Meme theory post-dates this analysis, but explains how culture operates in a way that's congruent with this analysis of aspects of culture.

Culture grows out of patterned selections a social group makes over its history. Individual action alters a culture but only if many people take it on board. A friend told me the following story, which I have no reason to disbelieve, since her uncle was a skin specialist during this era. Apparently, Christian Dior went skiing in 1958 and came back with a tan. Prior to this, dark skin was associated with poverty, hard work and outdoor labour, an association common in Western white cultures. For example, in the movie *Fiddler On the Roof,* Tevye's daughters ask the matchmaker for a fair-skinned, learned man. Fair skin was associated with wealth and education. In contrast, Dior introduced tanned skin as a fashion statement, a sign of wealth, leisure and privilege. If significant cultural shifts of this kind occur, few remember who introduced it, but its effects spread widely. Getting a tan as a way to convey wealth and leisure is recent, as an effective meme, it took on significance and altered culture.

Human beings cannot not learn culture; a person is a human animal desperately dependent upon extra-genetic, outside-the-skin control mechanisms, such as cultural programs, for ordering behaviour. Humankind is incomplete or unfinished and completes itself through culture—not in a general way but through specific forms. This is because there's a distinction between *being a human being* and *being human*. Everyone is human at birth, but becoming fully human is worked out in primary and secondary socialization. By analogy, a woman may be a doctor upon graduation from medical school but it will take her years to really be a doctor. She becomes a doctor by practising medicine.

With this analogy, I'm not suggesting all cultural ways of becoming human are equally admirable simply because they exist. If women live in abject poverty and filth because they don't have the relational resources to make a better life, and can't imagine a better life because no woman they've ever known has a better life, it's not reasonable to expect them to think of becoming a doctor. Their environment fails to support that possibility. A culture that fails with respect to more than half its population can't be justified merely because it exists, as it still does, in places like Mahabubnagar, Andhra Pradesh, India,[55] to name one current example. Human beings become what they are within cultural systems of meaning that give form and point to life. Culture gives identity and place. In every culture, there's pattern and meaning, even if these Indian women take as their meaning that they have little value and their hunger is normal.

Culture shapes expectations. A human being is defined neither by innate capacities alone, nor by actual behaviours but by a link between them, by the way the first is transformed into the second, by the way general potentialities focus into specific performances.[56] What human beings have in common is that they can, and must, become human by experiencing particular cultural meaning-systems. Without humanity there's no culture; without culture there's no humanity.

With the German development as a reference point, since the 1800s, the emphasis has been on outward conditions of culture, i.e., an anthropological notion (Kultur). As a balance, Clifford Geertz

(1973) focused on universal effects of culture while observing different cultural contents. In his view, humankind is incomplete or unfinished and completes itself through a particular culture.[57] He described internal culture as a web of meaning, as socially established structures of meaning in terms of which people do things. To link Geertz and Dawkins, we could say cultural webs are woven out of meme threads.

To Geertz, culture members are suspended in webs of significance they spin collectively. The image of a web informs our idea of the relationship between specific memes and dominant cultural trends. Meaning in his view refers to the significance of a group's beliefs, values and practices. An individual belief or practice may be either a bridge line (from which everything hangs) or a foundation line (which gives shape and limit to a web). It may be a belief from which hang all other beliefs, or it may set boundaries for a cultural meaning-system. Damage to bridge or foundation lines is destructive to an entire web. Other threads comprise the tangle of silk that forms the most visible parts of a web. Plucking out one of these may be less serious to the web's integrity. If particular beliefs of a group are questioned, we must realize their significance isn't contained in an isolated description of that belief.

Each belief is linked to others. As an example, even though Apartheid was unacceptable, outsiders can underestimate the labyrinth of attachments that fixed the policy to its historical context. This is a similar point to the one Bourdieu made about subjectivity and objectivity. Culture members make sense of their own patterns and construct reality in terms of them. The way they make sense of their culture is seldom as clear to outsiders as it is to insiders. In finding a concept for humanity, we look for systematic relationships among diverse phenomena, not substantive identities among similar ones. Cultural analysis is like looking at the underside of a weaving to guess the design on the right side. A basis for understanding what it means to be caught in a cultural web is the recognition that individuals and groups need to work out relationships among past, present and future meaning-systems to live well with differences that they are now facing, due to a time of change.

What permits cultural reflection during a time of change is implicit in a theoretical framework for the culture concept developed by two anthropologists, Kluckhorn and Kroeber[58] in 1952 (pre-dating memes). Common aspects include descriptors, forms, experience, features, givens, limits and concept-categories. In examining them, it's possible to map differences that people bring to the common project of living a fully human life. They provide a road map to help navigate cultural change, while remaining true to our own convictions.

Aspects Of Culture

If we're trying to understand worldviews and webs of memes that shape people's way of being, the following aspects of culture function as a guide. They form a cultural checklist for questions we can ask as we aim to make sense of cultural and sub-cultural (e.g., work) settings. It's also useful as we unpack memes that shape our own expectations and experience.

Descriptors: universal (generalizations about the human condition) or particular (specific customs of a group). They're further divided into internal culture (care directed to refinement of life or the inner logic or meanings, significance or rules that shape culture) and external culture (general appearance, clothing, stance, or habits of a group, recognizable by other group members).

Forms: implicit (unstated patterns; conscious, partly conscious, unconscious designs for living) or explicit (actual observable patterns). Implicit forms of culture are invisible, like an architect's plan for a building. Forms are learned through primary socialization or picked-up through participation. They are values, rules, beliefs not expressly stated that are the basis for behaviour and belief. The important thing is to know what someone takes for granted, i.e., what seems obvious. Explicit forms are visible like the actual girders of a building. They're what outsiders see as they enter a society: clothes, rituals e.g., queuing up at subway train in Britain as opposed to cramming into the train in Japan.

Experience: insider (participant) or outsider (observer). The insider participates; the outsider observes. Each has a particular kind of knowledge: the insider has "know-how" and may know-why but may not be able to say why and might say: We've always done it that way. Outsiders know-that and perhaps know-why and may make certain connections based on knowledge they gain consciously. Observer knowledge is dependent upon insider insight for its validity, but an outsider may know things an insider doesn't (e.g., being an expert historian of a country in which many are illiterate). Outsider's theoretical knowledge may go well beyond an insider's cultural know-how, yet, when outsiders observe action they must understand that each thread is tied to many others that may be invisible to them, as Bourdieu made evident.

Features: integration—every culture possesses a degree of coherence to hold a society together under normal conditions; historicity—every culture is a precipitate of history that gains influence in shaping traditions and rituals, making life predictable and secure, which acts as a precipitate over time, a drift in one direction to create cultural poise; selective orientation—future choices and selections are constrained by that precipitate;[59] uniformity because all human beings become human by experiencing particular meaning systems they adopt.

Causality: how and why societies come to be in their present shape: natural environments, inorganic or organic; organic factors, e.g., Shakespeare in England. Social factors: size, location, increases or decreases of population; cultural factors: what's already in place culturally (television, technologies) or organizing principles, philosophical or religious systems.

Significance and value: the most distinctive properties of culture, the essence of its organization. Human endeavour is always directed toward ends; those ends are shaped by values in a culture that are felt as intrinsic. These values aren't means to an end; values are mental content (ideas) and are primarily social and cultural. They reside in individuals, but become a group value through collective participation. Relying on a value may become automatic. They provide the only basis for fully understanding a culture because the actual organization of culture is primarily in terms of its values. If the essence of cultures is patterned selectivity, the essence of this selectivity is found in a cultural value system expressed by its memes. Significance refers to the degree of importance that's placed on a value.

Values and relativity: show up by comparing cultures. Cultural relativity suggests that values have to be understood within the cultural meaning system of a given group. Relatively refers to these inter-relationships. Cultural relativity implies that we only understand a value by seeing how it's related to the others that surround it. Yet true universals or near universals exist between cultures as well. They may be few in number, but are as deep going as they are rare. Relativism was prominent after the 1950s but Kluckhorn and Kroeber saw that relativity exists within a universal framework. Universals and relativistic autonomy remain valid principles. Just as each person is unique but resembles all others in certain respects, cultures have unique as well as common elements. Otherwise, cross-cultural exchange couldn't occur and multicultural states would fall apart. After the end of the 1980s, countries were less willing to accept some types of behaviour toward those who were marginalized within a culture on the strength of cultural relativism alone.

Givens: exist in every culture because all human groups must provide sanctioned and approved ways of dealing with the:

- existence of two sexes
- helplessness in infants
- need to satisfy elementary biological requirements
- presence of individuals of varying capacities and varying physical and mental capacities

Social needs are derived from givens and vary over time and place, e.g., education for women, health care insurance, dental care, compulsory education.

Limits: constrain every human group because no culture tolerates

- indiscriminate lying
- stealing
- violence within the in-group
- incest
- suffering as an end in itself

No culture denies an after-life officially. Even atheistic regimes ceremonialize death and no culture defines as normal individuals who are inaccessible to communication, or who fail to maintain some degree of control over their impulse life. Ideals are notions of the way things ought to be and a concept of the way things actually are—that shape how one person interacts with others. Every social system presupposes basic moral axioms because human life is and has to be social. Groups that fail to incorporate certain limits dissolve as societies or perish without record. The need for limits is rooted in the interdependence between people who live in a group.

Concept categories: exist in every culture, e.g., for rights, duties, justice, amity (friendly relations), respect, wrong (action that's not right, true, just, good, correct or okay and which may occur through ignorance or inattentiveness and sin (action purposefully done, intentionally by violating a rule or standard that's deserving of a punitive response. Behaviour that goes along with these concepts varies among cultures. While each culture will have a concept of fairness, an observer may find it hard to recognize an action as falling under the category of fairness.

Processes: shape every culture since all infants enter life in an unfinished condition. Humanity is unique in the length of time it takes a child to stand on his or her own feet. Culture completes the development. Processes of socialization act as a backdrop for cultural expectations. In becoming socially literate, we can begin to sense those processes and distinguish their role in an attempt to make sense of people that differ from our own primary and secondary socializing processes.

CONCLUSION

The checklist helps interpret and predict difficulties we have as we try to understand one another. An example might help. An elementary school principal, John, entered a grade two class and asked to speak to Ti, a recent immigrant from southern Asia. John asked Ti if he had a new bike. His face beaming, he looked right at John and said yes. John asked Ti if he could see the new bike. Ti told John that it was at home with his grandmother. John knew that she was blind. Later that day, John and Ti visited her and John took the bike back to its owner. Ti grew up in a refugee camp where people frequently shared belongings. He saw the bike in a neighbor's driveway and took it home. John could have accused Ti of stealing. Every culture has a concept for stealing. But he knew the specifics of Ti's refugee camp. He'd been there himself for a summer. If Ti tried to conceal the fact that he had a bike, it would have indicated behaviour that fitted in the idea of stealing (knowingly taking something that belongs to someone else). Because of John's cultural know-how, this little boy didn't start life in Canada labeled as a thief.

All action is theory laden. The term theory is ambiguous. It may refer to personal preferences. But understanding culture is open to advantages and shortcomings of all theoretical investigation. Theories orient our thinking; every time we act, we do so on the basis of a theory we have about life and our part in it. It's not that something is true merely because someone calls it a theory.[60] The outline of culture that's included above is meant to provide cultural pegs on which to hang memes that make up a cultural context. It's a list of possibilities for thinking about what we're compelled to think about because we're human in the presence of other people. But there are choices to make as we reflect on enculturated thinking, e.g., the choices Freud made about neighborliness were based on his life experience.

Choices Tom and Ted make about how to work together impact faculty and students too. American theorist Reinhold Niebuhr had a theory that applies to the cold war between these two men. Writing in the mid-twentieth century, Niebuhr noted that "[t]he 'winner' of the Cold War will inevitably face the *imperial* problem of using power in global terms but from one particular context of authority, so preponderant and established and unchallenged that its world rule would almost certainly violate basic standards of justice."[61]

Social literacy draws us toward a different set of choices—in which we're willing and able to offer relational resources to others because they're human, just like us. Is offering people relational resources the same as loving our neighbors? It is in the sense of social love, defined as acting for the common good and logically including love for oneself.[62] Once again we're faced with the difficulty of teaching social literacy because it's only as we practice what we teach that we build a social environment that demonstrates how to offer relational resources to people that cross our path, and care for those we've never seen, yet remain true to ourselves. Perhaps it's a high calling. Perhaps it's precisely what it means to be human.

8

EMPATHY AND SOCIAL LITERACY

INTRODUCTION

I recall the day I lost my innocence about women. Up to that point, I thought women were kind, warm, compassionate, available, supportive people, quick to sacrifice their interests for others, particularly husbands and children. I had a wonderful mother. As Freud told us, our concept for women finds its root in experiencing our own mothers.

I woke up from that concept while watching a television documentary on the *Khmer Rouge.* As the screen revealed row after row of hard, round faces of men who tortured others with ease, even pleasure, I suddenly saw that same hard expression on the faces of women. I was aware they could be unkind, thoughtless, unfair, but I didn't know women could be cruel. Since seeing those faces, I've known of many women who are capable of great harm.

My early view of women unraveled from many points of view. I question the ease with which some make unnecessary sacrifices and deny their dignity because they practise a belief that a man's life is more important than their own. Human dignity posits the opposite: women are equally important to men—their lives are neither less nor more significant. I'm aware that we have few examples of people who live out gender equality in daily life. As Martha Nussbaum pointed out, no country in the world treats its women and well as it treats its men.

Prejudice against women shapes female perspectives as much as it governs male chauvinism. The idea of empathy explored in this chapter grows out of self and social respect that makes equality possible as a foundation for social interaction. But to get there, we have to examine obstacles in our path, as we learn social literacy. This chapter isn't focused on women's issues, *per se*. Rather, it's an inquiry into how we can hear the humanity in other people, without getting sidetracked by apparent and implicit differences that show up as we interact with them.

Up to this point, social literacy is described as a balance between relationally closeness to and distinctness from others, i.e., being near and different. The complex skill of being socially near and different, promotes civility and allows authenticity and integration to flourish. The balance that social literacy requires depends on learning to interpret others with accuracy and tact, on keeping people close without foreclosing on authenticity, on persisting in being ourselves despite pressure from those who misunderstand us. The balance achieved with social literacy has empathy as its fulcrum. It's empathy, as spelled out in this chapter, that allows us to remain true to ourselves and yet remain well connected to other people.

Empathy is often misunderstood. In this chapter, I define and explore its ambiguity. I offer a model for learning empathy in the process of ordinary human development; a process that also uncovers what might go wrong as we try to be empathetic with others. I then discuss some of the obstacles to its mature expression. My purpose in this chapter is to say that, while we have the potential for empathy, we learn to be empathetic by being in the presence of empathetic people. It's a human virtue, but may be the least understood, most ineffectively practised one. I also believe that, if we were more empathetic, we would be better people. Social interaction would improve. Social literacy rates would climb. When empathy is engaged, everything changes.

THE EMPATHY CONCEPT

I admit it's still hard for me to believe women find it easy to be cruel. My assumption has to do with a prejudice about empathy. I always thought women were naturally more empathetic than men. Non-verbal sensitivity research (PONS) indicates a solid basis for believing women in general are better than men at reading non-verbal communication.[1] Since the bulk of domestic labor and primary childcare remains with women globally, I reasoned that children wouldn't survive or thrive unless there was something about being female that enabled women to place themselves in other people's shoes, perceive their needs and respond to meet them. My prejudice was based on being unaware of many people's experience—those who struggle to thrive and survive because their mothers abused them.

The twentieth century focused concern on abusive men—fathers who abandon and harm their families and fail to maintain the relational habitat of their own home life. That research is significant. But I've also witnessed women being violent to their husbands and children. While spousal abuse statistics are lower among women aggressors, it happens more often than I imagined. All of this experience caused me to question the idea of empathy. As mentioned earlier, Goldman argues that, as an aspect of social intelligence, we have a pre-disposition to respond to the cry of an infant and meet that baby's needs. A capacity for social intelligence implies that people are hard-wired for offering an empathetic response—women and men. Yet this capacity can be used to mistreat other people as well as to be kind to them.

Empathy is an act of perceiving and an art of imagining that relies on self-understanding. This point picks up what I said earlier about women. Two problems frustrate the development of empathy: being unconcerned about others or being dismissive of one's personal needs and aspirations.

When people exercise empathy, they show understanding in two directions—toward themselves and toward others. In empathy, they attend to their inner state, reading their thoughts, feelings, needs and desires. As people speak, out of a depth of self-understanding, they remain available to others and listen attentively to their own inner state. Empathy is proactive. It relies on developing the capacity to see what's going on. Empathy focuses on someone else's experience in a particular way. During a moment of full attentiveness, it isn't judgmental or concerned with whether an incident is in the past or present of someone's experience. Whatever the event is, if it's alive for them, it remains in the present *for them*—their feelings about the incident are current—even if it took place many years ago.

To be empathetic is to realize that a person's anxiety doesn't distinguish between past, present and future. Feelings are resolved or unresolved. A person is either anxious or at rest due to feelings about what they're still experiencing. This principle applies when we're listening to someone recount a traumatic event, such as a Holocaust survivor who is retelling his experience, or listening to an adult child of divorced parents say that the divorce continues impact her. Being allowed to retell a traumatic event provides a sense of healing. Empathetic encounters enable people to be less anxious about what's happened to them.

In an empathetic encounter, two people discover and name truthfully what's going on. Empathy is based on telling the truth. The kindness of empathy is expressed by telling the truth in a setting where it's safe to do so. Telling the truth makes us anxious because the truth about us seldom lives up to our ideals. An empathetic person recognizes anxiety in another, even though anxiety wears many disguises, such as arrogance, indifference, busyness or lust. Empathy offers to listen to the inner state of the other person by sensing what's presented and *what's behind what's presented* in someone else's experience. In sensing what lies behind the presentation of self in ordinary life, empathy uses intuition, imagination and its own experience. But empathy always remembers that the experience is foreign and not the same as one's own.

Suppose I see a friend who looks sad. He tells me his brother died. I become aware of his pain. What kind of awareness do I have of my friend? While important people in my life have died, *it's not my brother who has just died.* I'm not in that sort of pain. As I look at my friend's face, which is pale and disturbed, and listen to his voice, which is toneless and strained, I'm in pain of a particular kind that I need to understand.

My pain comes as I gaze at my friend's face. If I don't turn away, my pain continues. Anxiety is painful and contagious. It doesn't arise from outside me (something that's happened *to me)*, yet it does. It comes from gazing at a friend's face and from an interpretation of what it might mean to have a brother die. Empathy is in the gaze. It isn't yet knowledge, since gazing at my friend's face won't tell me what the death of his brother means *to him*. As I gaze (without staring) empathy waits. Empathy might remain silent. It might ask questions or pose possibilities, which my friend is free to accept as true or reject as failing to describe his experience.

Empathy gazes at someone's experience but doesn't stare. Empathy isn't rude. It's not an intruder. Its aim is to relieve anxiety, not to intensify it. The aim of empathy is to establish a meaning for the inner state of the other person, when the time is right. An empathetic person may try to convey his or her feeling state eventually in order to expand the self-understanding of both people involved in the encounter—if the timing is right for both to listen and hear what's going on. Empathy sets up conditions in which it's more likely that I will eventually come to understand my own inner state as I offer empathy. For instance, Marshall Rosenberg[2] tells a story that happened when another man got into a taxi with him. Rosenberg is Jewish.

After the man was settled, a message came over the cab's loudspeaker to ask the driver to pick up someone with a Jewish sounding name at a local synagogue. The man sitting in the back seat with Rosenberg said: "These k…s get up early in the morning so they can screw everybody out of their money."[3] Rosenberg felt enraged. He sat quietly, mulling over the extent of his fury. Then he followed his own first principle for empathy. Stay conscious of the violent thoughts that arise in my mind without judging them. Use empathy on myself. First, gaze at my own heart. A few minutes passed as he pondered his feelings and then he began a non-violent conversation with the gentleman that eventually enabled him to convey his initial feelings, without anger, and only after helping the other man identify feelings that lay behind his comment on Jewish people.

So what is empathy? As a concept, empathy is ambiguous. Ambiguous terms have more than one meaning. With empathy, there are two well-defined camps and I expand on them as I continue to define the word. My aim is to sort through the concept in order to provide a working hypothesis. To begin with, there's a range of empathy definitions, which include the following:

- The power of projecting one's personality into (and so fully comprehending) an object of contemplation.[4]
- The power of identifying oneself mentally with (and so fully comprehending) a person or an object of contemplation.[5]
- An act in which I 'feel with' another person. I don't 'put myself in the other's shoes.' I don't say, "How would I feel if this happened to me?" I set aside my temptation to analyze and to plan. I don't project. I receive the other into myself. I see and feel with the other. The sort of empathy we're discussing doesn't first penetrate the other but receives the other....I receive, communicate with, work with the other. Feeling isn't all that's involved, but it's essentially involved.[6]
- The capacity to conceptualize the impact—on ourselves and other people—of what we do and to feel appropriate and genuine sorrow and regret without thinking of ourselves as irredeemably bad. Empathy gives us the necessary mental and emotional climate to guide our behaviour in a moral and self-enhancing manner without being harsh and mean-spirited to ourselves or to other people.[7]
- An act in which foreign experience is grasped; in which we sense what's presented, and what's behind what's presented as someone else's experience.[8]
- A response when someone attacks or criticizes you, in which you can be *sad* (flee, hide, avoid) or you can be *mad* (fight, protect yourself from criticism, reestablish your ground) or you can be *glad* (empathize, ask questions until you understand and attend to what the other person is trying to say to you).[9]
- Feeling one's self in another or in another's experience; knowing and being able to express what someone else is going through.[10]

According to these definitions, empathy between two people is defined as an act, a feeling, a response, a capacity and a power of perception. In gathering up threads to use as a working hypothesis, empathy is an interpretive act focused on thinking and feeling, in which complete attention is paid to another person's experience until he or she realizes that one who empathizes actually does understand the essential quality of that experience. Empathy creates a safe place for the experience of another person and releases people from feeling alone and strange.

There are several types of empathy. There's aesthetic empathy in which we approach an art object and try to make sense of it. Literary empathy attempts to get at the meaning of a text and realizes there's more to its meaning than words on a page. Relational empathy is a cognitive, affective and *potentially* sympathetic encounter with foreign experience, i.e., the experience of someone else. Ethical empathy is an ability to visualize behavioral consequences of our action and imagine its impact. In being appropriately and genuinely regretful, we feel no need to see ourselves as irredeemably bad. We're responsible for our behaviour without being harsh and mean-spirited to other people or to ourselves.

In all types of empathy there's an affective and a cognitive aspect. A difficult issue in empathy is connected with the ability to distinguish feeling from thinking and show how they work together. In all types of empathy, we face what's foreign—art, books or people. In considering the relationship between empathy and social literacy, I focus primarily on relational empathy, but the other types are instructive. A fundamental problem in trying to be relationally empathetic is to accurately interpret foreign experience, at the same time that we perceive how other people experience us.

So, what's essential to an act of perceiving what's foreign if we want to be empathetic? If empathy involves an imaginative act—we imagine the other person's experience to some extent—what keeps empathy truthful? What's the relationship between perception, imagination and truth telling if the experience of another person is foreign? By foreign, I simply mean an experience that isn't ours because it isn't happening directly to us.

Relational empathy implies that foreign subjects (other people and their experiences), present themselves in a certain way. We can understand them, even though the experience isn't ours. Empathetic people are able to enter into or come along side experience that's foreign, yet describe or narrate that experience in a way another person recognizes and acknowledges as accurate. I will describe relational empathy and mark out boundaries around the essence of empathy as well as what I call full empathetic participation (i.e., empathy plus sympathy). Both are models for relational empathy.

Two Camps

Two verbs predominate as people try to explain how empathy works. The first group of verbs defines empathy as an act of *projecting* oneself or one's experience into someone else's experience. This is the definition in the *Oxford English Dictionary*: empathy is the power of projecting one's personality into (and so fully comprehending) an object of contemplation.

The second group of verbs defines empathy as *receiving* another person's experience and suggests that full comprehension of the other is very difficult. As an example, empathy is an act in which I feel with another person. I don't put myself in the other's shoes. I don't say how I would feel if this happened to me. I set aside the temptation to analyze. I don't project. I receive the other into myself. I see with and feel with the other. Empathy doesn't penetrate. It receives the other. It communicates with and works with the other. In the second group of verbs, feeling isn't all that's involved, but it's essentially involved.

The first group conveys empathy as projection or as entering someone experience. The second group conveys empathy as receptivity. The two groups are often expressly contrasted with each other, particularly from the receptivity side, which tends to react against the idea of projection. From the perspective of receptivity, projecting is a mistaken way of talking about empathy. From the projecting side, receptivity might come across as entrapment.

Each camp offers important insight about empathy, but each also carries potential harm to a relationship. If empathy is *projecting* my experience into someone else's experience, I must come to realize that those who describe empathy as receptivity hear projection in terms of invasion or intrusion into someone's space, with the most negative association being that of rape.

If we use *projecting* as a way to describe empathy, we're well advised, if we want to communicate effectively, that *projecting* is an act of valuing, which can be perceived as an act of caring for another person. With projecting, one enters empathetically into the experience of those he values and loves. The aim is to convey their value and credibility to the one who wishes to empathize. Projecting may also be extended to strangers. In doing so, the empathetic person conveys regard and respect for them, at least, that's the intention of being empathetic.

Those who think of empathy in terms of projecting use words to convey entering someone else's experience, but empathy on the model of *projecting* must stop short of invading, i.e., an aggressive, unlawful, illegitimate or forceful entry. Projecting can be misguided and imperialistic. Those in this camp need to realize how this way of speaking affects others who aren't comfortable using it as a model for empathy. People have to be free to refuse our attempts to project ourselves into their experience. They may not believe that we really understand what they're going through.

Those who use the language of receptivity have a difficulty of similar proportion. They typically use words or models for empathy that imply coming along side another rather than entering into someone's experience. They want to convey getting with rather than getting in. From this perspective, receptivity or *receiving* is perceived as an act of caring that conveys the value of another person. Empathy is engrossed with the other as a way of giving full attention to the experience that's being retold. The receptive person doesn't assume the experience is the same as her own. She comes alongside and attends fully to the experience that's being conveyed. Complete, sustained attention is meant to convey the other's significance and credibility to her.

But, just as with projecting, receiving may be thought of as having a dangerous tendency—in this case a tendency to trap others in attentiveness, of paying too much or too close attention to them.

Empathy as receiving must stop short of entrapment, i.e., aggressively holding onto someone who wants to be released from our gaze. Those who use receptivity must be aware of how this way of speaking affects those who aren't comfortable with it as a model, or are uncomfortable with its intensity. People must be able to escape our attentive gaze if they wish to do so.

In summary, empathy refers to acts in which foreign experience is grasped. In being empathetic, we sense what's presented and what's behind what's presented as someone else's experience. Suppose I wish to be empathetic with the friend referred to earlier, whose brother just died. I offer him a non-anxious presence and attend to his experience of loss. He needs a look from me that isn't a stare, which isn't intrusive. He needs my time. He needs me to suspend my judgments about what he's experiencing, to wait quietly until he's able to let me know what's happening within him, *if he wishes to do so.* He needs to hear my silence or my inquiry as focused on what he's experiencing, not my interpretation of it. Empathy describes rather than prescribes. He needs to be released from my attentiveness when he wishes to be free of it, unless he clearly lets me know that he finds me helpful as he names what he's going through. But the question still begs to be asked: Will I understand his experience?

HUMAN DEVELOPMENT AS GROUNDWORK FOR EMPATHY

As mentioned in an earlier chapter, all action is grounded on theory. When we try to be empathetic, our theories can get in the way. For example, we might think that we can only know what's happening directly to us. We may believe all knowledge is situated so that what happens to others is outside our experience and inaccessible to us. This theory creates a sense of impatience as someone is trying to tell us what's going on. It's hard to be fully attentive if we believe that nothing genuine will come from listening. As we learn to be empathetic, we come to the right way of addressing our own theories as we listen to someone else.

Suppose we see someone hit by a car. We see it and feel *something*, but we don't feel the car hitting our own bodies. We don't sense how the event fits in the injured person's life history. We don't know what the other is experiencing. What does another person need to sense in us to enable him or her to believe we're empathetic? Empathy isn't an activity we accomplish alone. It takes two people. An empathetic act takes place between at least two people and is effective only if both parties want to remain engaged with each other.

How do we learn empathy? What do people already know that's useful as groundwork for learning empathy? How does experience function as we try to be empathetic? We build the basis for successful empathetic encounters by addressing limitations within our own experience. Healthy encounters between parents and infants, as one example, offer a good model for empathy that's neither invasion nor entrapment in the senses used earlier.

In healthy encounters, parents and infants attend to each other and remain able to escape or resist each other's gaze. Recall that in empathy, we are posing a complex question when we ask: *What does the other person need to sense in order to believe that we're relating empathetically with them*? In a fully engaged empathetic act, those who empathize come to sense what the other requires in order to feel understood and they share that feeling to some extent.

Our basic human capacity for empathy shows up if we examine some of the research on infants' ability to engage in interpersonal relationships. This research helps to see how an empathetic relationship works in practice. It also shows how personal experience may prevent us from being empathetic. By using the example of what happens during the experiences of very young children, we can see what might go wrong generally as someone tries to be empathetic.

In the first seven to nine months in an infant's life, there emerges the first deliberate sharing of interpersonal space with those who care for them.[11] Exchanges between the caregiver (in the research it's typically mothers so I use that pronoun) and infant take place through a *shared attention* to a third object. During this time, the child is developing what can be called the subjective self.

This period is also described as a foundation for developing the soul, i.e., the seat of emotion, intuition, receptivity to God, as well as receptivity to other people. The following example explains how shared attention to a third object works.

Suppose an infant's mother turns her head and looks out of the room to gaze at something distressing (Figure #1). Immediately the infant follows her gaze with attentive anxiousness. Neither says anything. The infant can't talk. Pre-linguistic expressions of *shared attention* and *shared feeling* are communicated from infant to mother and back again. In these exchanges, non-verbal intimacy becomes a real possibility: gestures, postures, facial expressions and sounds work together to provide shared meanings as infant and mother gaze at a third object. Infants at this age are capable of initiating an encounter of this kind by gazing at a third object that the mother looks toward as well. Babies are capable of initiating shared attention (gazing with another person at a third object), shared intention (persistently signalling that something is to be understood by the other) and shared affect (shared feelings) even though infants don't have oral language. Affect attunement—the experience of shared attention, shared intention and shared affect—is similar to an empathetic act although if falls short of empathy.

When infant and mother attune themselves to one another with respect to a third object, the mother responds to the infant in a particular way. Affect attunement is the recognition and acknowledgement by the parent of the child's affective state. It's a complex operation involving several important factors:

- An accurate reading of the baby's behaviour by parent or caregiver
- An intimate history of the child's feelings, which gives rise to an ability to participate in those feelings
- The ability to respond with different, non-imitative, but accurate behaviours that signal to the infant that his or her affective states are understood, e.g., "I'm reading you because I'm responding in rhythm, pattern, resonance and synchronicity with your feelings."
- For emotional attunement to occur an infant must be able to read and understand the caregiver's response.[12]

Affect Attunement (Figure #1)

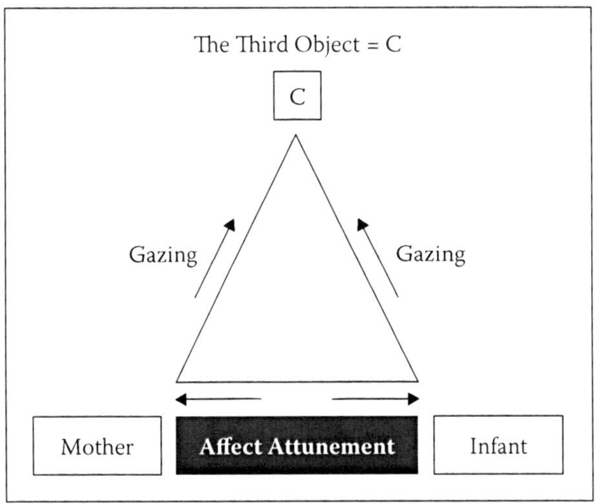

As in Figure #1, a primary way we indicate to children that we're resonating with them, or feeling with them, is through matching the intensity of our responses to the intensity of their actions. Mothers match the beat, rhythm or shape of an infant's gesture or sound but don't imitate it exactly.

Exact imitation is distressing and doesn't contribute to affect attunement. We might remember intensely frustrating experiences when an older sibling repeated our exact words over and over again, trapping us in them. We believed we were being mocked. If mother and child get these encounters right, their attunement builds mutuality. Attunement is a dynamic ongoing process, not a discrete set of episodes or categorical affects. From these rituals emerge pre-verbal, pre-symbolic, proto-symbolic activity (patterns for later use) accomplished without using language.

When it happens, the development of spoken language is a mixed blessing.[13] While spoken language helps us relate to people in a new way, it's a problem for integrating self-experience and self-other experience as it characterized the preverbal affect attunement that infant and mother were good at before spoken language emerged.

The interdependency of the activity of meaning making in preverbal infants is remarkable. Mothers read their infants. Babies inform their mothers of needs and intentions. In constructing meaning together, infants and mothers take turns leading and following to accomplish this essential communicative task. They're highly skilled in sending each other communicative information. When children begin to talk, they narrate their own lives and can change how they perceive themselves. Narrating one's life isn't like other forms of thought. Narrative structure may prove to be a universal phenomenon reflecting the design of the human mind,[14] but what's significant for this investigation, is the problem with using language in an empathetic encounter.

A new level of relatedness is possible when children begin to talk. But, while this shift doesn't eclipse pre-verbal experience, language recasts and transforms inter-subjective experiences. Words and pre-verbal experience lead different lives. There's an ongoing non-verbal as well as a verbalized version of experience. The two versions aren't always in harmony.

Spoken language grabs hold of a piece of the conglomerate of sensing, thinking, feeling, wanting and doing that constitutes non-verbal experience. But words we select never convey the whole of that experience. We have *world knowledge* and *word knowledge* (spoken language). The two don't always match. With spoken language, something's gained and something's lost. The child "gains entrance into a wider cultural membership, but at the risk of losing the force and wholeness of original experience."[15]

A fully empathetic encounter relies upon *world knowledge* and *word knowledge* for its effectiveness. In empathy, we have an opportunity to attend to another person *bodily* in a way that doesn't require spoken language. Although spoken language is useful, it can get in the way of mutual understanding. People may say one thing with words and something quite contradictory with body language. When someone is hurt, we may fail to draw near because we're afraid we may say the wrong thing, so we avoid those who suffer. But empathy doesn't have to speak at all. Of course, it may. If empathy is working effectively, we make use of *world* knowledge (non verbal) and *word* knowledge (spoken language).

A fully participatory act of empathy conveys bountifully that we're understood and safe and that our experience makes sense to at least one other person. Empathy lets us know that we're neither crazy nor alone. Surely, to be understood at this level is a deep longing of the human heart. When we're suffering, or when we overflow with joy, we want others to catch sight of what's going on for and in us.

In terms of the development of a fully empathetic act, young children are able to take another person's perspective and imaginatively put themselves in that person's place. Perspective taking is related to empathy and may provide another way to understand how empathy does and doesn't flourish in the lives of many people. As discussed above, infants are capable of affect attunement with significant people. Johannes van der Ven (1998) provides a useful map for understanding what takes place and what might go wrong as children take another person's perspective, which in turn sheds light on what might go wrong as adults try to be empathetic. He organized his understanding of empathy by outlining levels of demonstrable behaviour in young children in which they were able to catch sight of something from another person's perspective. The following list summarizes his five levels of perspective taking that form the groundwork for empathy, at least potentially.[16]

Perspective Taking And Empathy

Level One: Infants cry when they hear others cry. In mimicry, an infant is able to demonstrate a similar emotion expressed by another person. In this exchange, a child is able to take another's perspective. The activity of putting oneself in someone else's place falls short of empathy and can take two forms. As van der Ven put it, the first form of the exchange is self-focused. Let's say a child, call him Jack, puts himself in another child's place, let's call her Jill, by imagining what it would mean if the situation happening to Jill impinges on him. Suppose Jack hears Jill cry. First he thinks of himself, he's self-focused. The second form of the first level of perspective taking is other-focused. Jack comes to imagine how Jill feels in this situation rather than being concerned about whether what's happening to Jill might happen to him. Even eleven-month-old children are able to function at this level. The first level has some cognitive aspects to it.

Level Two: The second level is explicitly cognitive and consists of two other-focused dimensions. The first dimension of the cognitive aspect of the second level is signalled by Jack's awareness that Jill has internal states that are independent of what Jack is experiencing internally. Jack sees that something is going on inside Jill that's different from what's going on inside him. The second dimension goes further than the immediate presentation of emotion. Jack takes account of Jill's personal history (her story of what's going on), or tries to imagine it.

Level Three: This level is primarily affective. There are two important dimensions. First, Jack realizes that Jill is experiencing and going through her own emotions rather than emotions he might have in a similar situation. The second dimension goes beyond the *here and now* so that Jill's emotions are understood as emerging from her personal history. This empathetic understanding can be found among two to three year olds. Jack focuses on Jill's feeling and has a feeling and a thinking response to her tears. He realizes his feelings are different from hers and imagines what she's feeling. Jack sees her emotion from her perspective rather than his own, to some extent.

Level Four: At this level, perspective taking is transformed into partial sympathy. This happens as Jack experiences compassion for Jill because she suffers from negative feelings such as sadness, grief, worry or hopelessness. Sympathy goes along with his desire to help her. Jack feels sorry for Jill. It's important to note that Jack moved his focus from what might happen to him and is paying attention to what's happening within Jill. van der Ven suggests that it's hard to know how the transformation from perspective taking to sympathy is accomplished and what stimulates it. He suggested that parental modelling of empathy might be central to this possibility in young children.

Level Five: At this level trouble may be introduced into the relation between Jack and Jill because this level involves asking who's to blame for Jill's distress. Three options emerge:

- No one can be found to blame. The absence of someone to blame reinforces the sympathetic distress. Jack feels worse for Jill if no one can be found to blame.
- Someone is identified as causing Jill's distress. This move may lead to anger in Jack as he observes her pain. When someone is found to blame, Jack's feelings may alternate between sympathetic distress and sympathetic anger. Jack may feel anger and sorrow for Jill. Jack may alternate between feeling distressed and feeling angry. This roller coaster may intensify Jack's anxiety.
- If Jill is the one Jack chooses to blame for her distress, sympathy decreases. (It may be that blaming a victim provides this sort of relief for those who make this move.) If someone can be blamed, Jack's anxiety is reduced. The third possibility is that Jack may blame himself for Jill's distress because of something he did or didn't do. Shame and guilt can surface if Jack blames himself. Victim-blaming and self-punitive feelings of shame and guilt (an absence of compassion for oneself and the other) foreclose on empathy.

If he blames himself, Jack may experience genuine regret for having caused Jill's distress. If this is the case, he can resolve the situation by apologizing—which helps both children. An apology provides Jill with justice and releases Jack from guilt. If Jack has harmed Jill, she loses face. If he apologizes, he loses face for a time and a just balance is restored in their relationship. Children must learn to be kind. It isn't automatic.

These five levels offer a model for the groundwork of empathy but they also show how it can run off its rails. Instead of letting empathy relax into compassion, Jack may turn away from Jill, blame her for her own problem, blame himself, and choose to express anger towards her. Jack may turn towards Jill in compassion or turn away in rejection. Many people turn away from someone who's suffering because they have no way to relieve their own anxiety. Perspective taking exposes us to anxiety. The road to empathy is risky. It's not a simple human puzzle; empathy is a complex problem. Even though we have a potential for it, learning empathy requires us to remain focused on the other person and to realize we don't really know what they're going through yet. Empathy is grounded on a capacity we all have, but in learning to be empathetic we also have to learn to relax our grip on our own experience and the theories that arise from it.

Empathy And Proximal Development

The analysis above, based on van der Ven's work, outlined the groundwork for empathy, but he seemed to be working with a learning model based on Jean Piaget's individualistic perspective: empathy is learned on one's own. If we ask how people learn to be empathetic, we can apply a different model, one that allows adults to model the complex skill for children. We learn to be empathetic while we're with empathetic people. From them, we hear/see their reasons for caring about others, we study their ways and sense what it's like to be in their non-anxious presence.

D. Wood (1998) discussed the potential children have 'to learn to think through conversing' by comparing Piaget, Swiss psychologist and epistemologist (1896-1980), and L.S. Vygotsky (1896-1934), a Russian psycholinguist, who published *Thought and Language* in 1934. These men disagreed about the potential children have to converse with adults and with each other as part of a learning process. In part, their disagreement arose because of theories they held about the connection between talking and thinking and what it means to know something.

For Piaget, "genuine intellectual competence amounts to what someone can do unassisted" while Vygotsky understood "a fundamental feature of intelligence to include the capacity to learn through instruction." Vygotsky referred to the capacity to learn with assistance as "the zone of proximal development."[17] In this zone, a child's potential to learn is revealed and realized in interactions with more knowledgeable people. For Vygotsky, "cooperatively achieved success lies at the foundation of learning and development."[18] A zone of proximal development is the ground on which pupil and teacher learn together.[19] The knowledge that passes between them is "embodied in the actions, work, play, technology, literature, art and talk of members of a society."[20]

In contrast, Piaget emphasized the abstract quality of language use. He argued "that language exerts no formative effects on the structure of thinking" but rather, "is a medium, a method of representation, within which thought takes place" because "mental actions and operations, the processes of thought, are derived from action, not talk."[21] Piaget did link talking and thinking. He said that "although language does not create the structure of thinking, it does facilitate its emergence," and suggested that it's "through talking to others, particularly other children, that the child's thinking becomes socialized;" but "although children talk as they play together, they do not, according to Piaget, really *converse*."[22] I suggest it's Piaget's bias toward individualism (learning is what one does on one's own) that led him to dismiss the link between talking with someone and learning to think.

For Vygotsky, childhood speech "is not a personal egocentric affair but the reverse: it is *social* and communicative both in origin and intent."[23] He analyzed the research that led Piaget to make his claim that children don't converse and came away with a different interpretation. To him, speech serves two functions: at first, it serves a regulative, communicative function. Later it serves other functions and transforms the way children learn, think and understand. It becomes an instrument or tool for thought, not only providing a code or system for representing the world, it's the means by which self-regulation comes about.

On his view of language, the initial motivation for gesture and speech is to control the world through the agency of other people and our need for them. Gestures and speech serve this role. To Vygotsky, speech, like any system of movement, is a physical activity, a way of controlling one's body to achieve goals and avoid discomfort. For him, "the overt activity of speaking provides the basis for 'inner speech', that rather mysterious covert activity that often forms the process of thinking."[24] For him, inner speech or thinking has its basis in talking, which implies that physical actions plus the physical activity of speaking become internalized to create the experience of thinking.

Vygotsky considers all forms of thought to be actions. To him, the children's talk that Piaget recorded was "midway between the social and intellectual functions of speech, [because] the child who is talking to himself is regulating and planning his own activities in ways that foreshadow verbal thinking."[25] The process for Vygotsky is recursive. As a particular male toddler discovers how to control the actions of others through speech, his developing knowledge of language acts back on him so that others also regulate his actions through speech.

As the toddler discovers how to gain peoples' attention by speaking and learns how to direct their attention to features of the shared physical world—to solicit specific action and services, inhibit, refuse and so forth—he becomes subject to the same regulative forces through the speech of others. Others begin to control and direct his attention, solicit his services and inhibit his activities. Alongside other-control by verbal means comes verbal self-control-by-others.[26] The toddler begins to control himself as he takes on the controlling speech of others. These are the beginnings of social power, expressed and negotiated between children and adults. Social power operates in the give and take of conversing.

To Vygotsky, speech forms the higher mental processes, including the ability to plan, evaluate, memorize and reason. These processes are culturally formed through social interaction. Looked at this way, talking doesn't simply *reflect* or represent concepts already formed on a non-verbal level. It structures and directs the process of thinking. To him, talk is a product of social experience and evidence for the emergence of intellectual self-control.[27]

As we consider Vygotsky's zone of proximal development, its application to learning empathy becomes apparent. In the presence of empathetic adults, children learn to experience compassion that's directed toward them. They hear and feel the consequences of rules about how to treat other people, and hopefully, why they should treat people with respect and kindness. As she addressed boss culture in her kindergarten classroom, Paley wove stories throughout the conversation to provide an intellectual environment for learning empathy as they practised the rule. These stories created a narrative framework for learning empathy and offered reasons for being kind to other people.

One reason for being empathetic that's built into many children's stories, is a role that injustice and guilt play. To be empathetic, children require a worldview that's larger than their own private experience, one that allows them to interpret their actions and those of others in a way that invites them to be just. Paley worked with worldviews they brought to school to help them interpret others accurately and addressed their hypocrisy when they didn't live up to their own stated values of the best way to treat people. Guilt, shame and misinterpreting other people are obstacles to genuine empathetic encounters, regardless of age.

EMPATHY AND INTERPRETATION

Empathy allows people to reframe their way of thinking about the world. That change comes from within, due to the effects of empathy. Rosenberg, referred to earlier, described the effects of empathy and said that when someone really hears us without passing judgment, when someone listens without trying to take responsibility for us, without trying to alter or mould us, elements of our experience that seemed insoluble become soluble and confusions become clear.[28]

The effects of empathy can be immediate and are always deep. Empathy is healing. But the freedom to be a safe place for others depends upon the condition of our own hearts. Unresolved guilt forecloses on empathy. Guilt, realistic though it may be, traps us within our own personal history and prevents us from hearing the other person.

Empathy isn't simply sharing another person's experience. It requires us to do three things at once: be present to the other, be present to ourselves, and consider yet suspend interpretations that form in our mind as we listen. Being self-aware isn't the same as being trapped in our own perspective. Empathy is not association, imitation, memory or mere flight of fancy.[29] Even though it's an act of imagining—imagining must be truthful in order to be empathetic.

The primary reason empathy differs from these other perceptions is that, in empathy, there's no continuity between the life experiences of the one who's empathetic and the one who receives empathetic attentiveness.

It's difficult to know the truth about experiences that aren't our own. How might our own perspective trap us, especially when empathy requires us to attend to our own hearts? Take, for example, memory. Empathy is different from memory because memory reflects back on something that happened to me at one time in my past. Suppose I recall an embarrassing event, such as the time I was dancing with my husband and suddenly fell down on the dance floor in the middle of the dance. My friends saw me fall. As I recall the event, I now think it's funny. I remember it completely. I remember the sensation of hitting the floor. I feel no pain but recall the shock of finding myself on the floor without knowing how I got there. I remember the event, the surprised looks on the faces of those around me and their words of concern. I can laugh about it now. My experience of remembering isn't the same as the event itself. Memory is different than direct experience. At the time, I didn't laugh, nor did I think it was funny—I was too stunned.

If I see someone else fall on a dance floor, I may have some idea of what's going on, or I may be entirely wrong. Suppose I see a woman fall who has a cruel partner. Suppose she has a weak back. Suppose she fell at another dance and something disastrous followed. If I'm empathetic I set aside my own experience and try to discover what the event means to her. Unlike empathy, in association, imitation, memory or fancy I'm using my own actual experience as a guide for understanding and interpreting what's going on. In empathy, I don't have access to the other person's past, present or future and can't adequately situate an event in the flow of a foreign life story. Empathy attends to the narrative someone tells about his or her experience that holds a place in a life story that I don't know. Empathy requires full attentiveness to the other person without turning away. But how will my personal history and the condition of my own heart influence empathy? How does personal experience influence the way we pay attention?

A Poetry Of Presence

Empathy has rhythm and rhyme. Empathetic encounters have a beauty of gesture and experience that nourish and heal all those it touches. Empathetic experience includes the following aspects in which we:

- Experience events directly—which we call our own experience
- Experience our assumptions, thoughts, feelings and judgments about our own experience
- Observe someone who is going though an event—
- A foreign experience, since it's not happening to us directly, so we
- Have assumptions, thoughts, feelings and judgments about the other's experience.

All four aspects play a part, although more is going on. What part does each aspect play?

In terms of the first and third aspects of experience, our own versus someone else's, one is direct and the other is indirect.[30] Attending to another person empathetically requires that we note the assumptions, thoughts, feelings and judgments that leap to the foreground of our mind, and suspend them all—waiting while the other person guides us through the experience and tells us about it. It's in this sense that we first attend to our own hearts, then release ourselves from being trapped there. The reader may recall that this same process characterizes abduction.

Using language provided by the four aspects of experience, empathy is a direct encounter of indirect experience in which we suspend our interpretation of what's going on until we hear enough about a foreign experience to give us an interpretation that clearly satisfies its owner. In exercising empathy, we give attention to our own theories so that we know what they are and we wait and ask questions, or sometimes we make suggestions that the other can dismiss if they're not accurate. But we can't ask effective questions if we're trapped in our own heart's business.

Empathy is something like reading poetry. The poet conveys in a few dense lines—the essence of something seen, felt or heard—something experienced. As we read the poem, we're not reading about our own experience, we're reading something foreign. With poetry, we realize there's a vast horizon behind the words on the page that informs them. As we read, we're trying to grasp or sense that horizon—a horizon we haven't seen ourselves, though we may have seen one very much like it. Yet reading poetry is a direct experience in itself—it's our own experience of reading that offers insight into what the poet wishes to convey. In plumbing the depths of the poem, we emerge when we sight the horizon that frames the words. To do so, we rely on what we know about patterns of human experience that apply to the poem's horizon, as far as we understand those human patterns.

One obvious difference between relational empathy and poetry reading is that the poet is seldom present as we read. In relational empathy, the other is a text to be read while its author is present. Empathy is no less complicated than reading a poem. Having the author stand before us is an advantage and a disadvantage, depending on how we like to read what's foreign. If all we really want is to get into the poem quickly and get out again without reflecting on own theories, or being conscious of them, if we come with a barrage of words or ideas we wish to impose, having the author present is a nuisance. Authors have a nasty way of disagreeing with our assumptions, thoughts, feelings and interpretations of their work. Poets are particularly annoying if we're in a hurry to stay with our own interpretation.

If, on the other hand, we want to grasp the poem's or person's meaning, we wait patiently until we get enough words or clues to get the poem's context and see its horizon. The metaphor of poetry reminds us that, in empathy, we don't get to read the novel of another person's experience: its past, present and future. We get words, gestures, hints, facial expressions, all of which are condensed signs that require full attention if we want to interpret the meaningful, whole experience.

As I try to be empathetic, I observe the other for shifts that convey whether it's effective. Say the other person gets angry, falls silent or changes the subject? Something's wrong. Empathy has become invasion or entrapment, from the other's point of view. We must stay attentive to the whole person, as we try to be empathetic.

As a Masters student, I had an opportunity to learn about empathy while participating in a research project in public schools. My professor asked me to visit a classroom in which there were twenty-four students: eight who spoke English, eight who spoke a language other than English and eight who spoke English and another language. I chose to observe a grade two child who had little English. As I sat beside her, I asked if I might look at her work. I noticed that sometimes she would speak about her work and sometimes she would fall silent. Then I noticed that if I looked at her work and not at her face (looking at someone's face is my way of signalling that I'm really paying attention) she would speak at length about her drawings. As soon as I looked at her face, she stopped talking. So I carefully avoided looking into her face. We talked for twenty minutes. At the end of the lesson, the classroom teacher approached me and asked how I managed to have such a long conversation with her. I recounted what I'd learned. The teacher said that a twenty-minute conversation was the longest period of time the little girl had spoken all year. Usually, she was completely silent.

If we return to the metaphor of reading poetry, different readers will arrive at different versions of a poem's meaning. Empathy is art and method. Our own experience and self-understanding will influence us as we attend empathetically to foreign experience. We attend to our own hearts first. We wait, acknowledge and then suspend our assumptions, thoughts, feelings and judgments until we have a chance to hear the other. In making meaning together, we work with our own material as well as with the words and gestures of the other person. It's at this point that we recall The Golden Rule: treat others as you want to be treated. It's complex in its application and doesn't guarantee relationships will work out easily. Most religions have a form of it, although I'm not arguing they're all advising exactly the same thing.[31]

We're limited by our own experience as well as informed by it. That's why sometimes we can't understand another person, even though we try, until we get fresh insight. As a seminary professor,

I had opportunity to relate to students in many ways. I led them through life-changing theories and practices, I learned from their thoughts and practice. I listened to them in class, worshipped with them as they led chapel services, sang with them, ate with them, counselled with them, visited their placements, met their families and heard their stories. Seminaries develop a multi-layered teaching/learning community, but sometimes a relationship can go very wrong, as it did with a student I'll call Jane.

Jane was an outgoing, popular student who told me enough of her life story for me to appreciate that her sense of well-being was hard won. We enjoyed each other and occasionally went for coffee. I assumed we had a good teacher/student relationship and still believe we did. But I stepped over a line that led to a breach in the relationship. During coffee, I said something that conveyed to Jane that I disrespected her as person. I can't say exactly what I did, for two reasons: I don't recall what I said, it happened to her not me and she forgave me. Forgiveness has the power to rewrite the past, under certain conditions. The issue for empathy has to do with the conditions in which forgiveness becomes possible and is effective.

The event occurred, something I said—Jane was furious. She expressed her anger in no uncertain terms. Her rage puzzled me. I was extremely uncomfortable but trusted her as a person; though I couldn't grasp the meaning she attributed to what I'd said, I knew it was awful for her. We tried for more than a year to reconcile but couldn't. I wanted to understand what had gone wrong, but no insight came. All my neat professor theories about social interaction were jeopardized if I couldn't resolve the guilt I felt. I also felt angry with Jane. Why did she have to be so angry? Couldn't she just get over it? After all, I said I was sorry. We went to a counsellor together and met several times about it. Nothing helped. While I apologized, it was evident that I didn't understand the significance to Jane of what I'd said. So we held to an uneasy truce.

Then I had my own disastrous experience—which I slowly came to see produced in me rage and humiliation. What was going on? As I was nursing my wounds, I realized what I had to do. I invited Jane to my office and said that the problem between us was 100% my fault. She had done nothing wrong. The fault was entirely mine. Up to that point, I'd been trying to see things essentially from my own perspective. I thought I was being fair by showing how both of us were to blame. It wasn't until I was in a situation that was sufficiently similar to hers (though not the same) that I could make sense of the significance of her rage. Rage follows on the heels of injustice and abuses of power. To make her suffering worse, I had no excuse. I knew better. At least, I made it sound as though I knew better when I taught about these topics in class.

I won't forget the moment in my office when she turned to me and thanked me for confessing. She had begun to forgive me. She could see me without feeling furious, but now, she said, it was as though it had never happened.

I learned from this experience, that, if someone with whom I have a reasonably good relationship suddenly gets very angry, I must take their fury seriously to discover its meaning. If I refuse the opportunity empathy offers, my heart hardens with guilt, shame and unjustified anger. The problem intensifies over time. Unresolved guilt continues to harden the heart. We get so busy building and defending an inner fortress against blame, we can't afford to pause and ask questions that would help us understand what's going on.

THE PROBLEM OF EMPATHY

As we consider the problem, we see that empathy is essentially attentiveness to foreign experience. The fact that another person's experience is foreign to me is helpful and unhelpful in establishing an empathetic encounter.

Let's say that John is going through an experience that calls for attention. He just passed a very difficult exam that's central to his future. He's elated. Judy shares his office and can see that something significant has happened. His powerful experience attracts her attention. She turns to attend to John's experience and gazes at it while John relates what the exam means to him. Judy gives John's joy her full attention without invading or trapping him. At some point in an effective empathetic encounter, John will likely say something that conveys that he knows Judy understands what he's going through or he may simply thank her for listening to him.

But in empathy, things can go wrong and often do, even among very nice people. We must keep in mind that John and Judy have a different relationship to taking difficult exams and it's with respect to these differences that empathy either works or fails. They're on different time schedules: passing the exam is all that matters to John just now.

The differences between John and Judy may lie in the category of common experiences they assign to sitting for exams and to particularities of the exam's meaning in John's life. What are some examples of what might go wrong with empathy as John and Judy gaze at John's experience? Here are a few:

- Judy may partly turn her attention to John but remain mostly inside her own world
- She may interpret his joy as arrogance
- She may claim to be *the* authority on what it's like to pass difficult exams
- She may make assumptions about John's experience she doesn't question or check out
- She may be jealous of John
- She may try to echo John's joy when she doesn't really feel it

John may turn away from the encounter if he thinks Judy is mocking him. She might turn away from him because of envy or pressure from something she's going through. A failure of empathy through turning away is characterized by:

- *Turning away* due to the pressure of the moment
- *Turning away* due to intense feelings in Judy or John
- *Turning away* because of previous experience Judy doesn't tell John but that remains her primary focus, e.g., she just failed an equally important exam
- *Turning away* because of judgments about John's experience

she's unable to suspend

- *Turning away* due to hindering aspects of Judy's personality, e.g., those associated with unresolved guilt or unconquerable anxiety

When I ask myself if I'm empathetic, I'm always asking if I'm attending to someone else's experience, which I realize is foreign to me. I contribute to full empathetic participation in foreign experience if I keep attending to the proper object (the other person's experience) without entrapment (wholly engaged with the other) or invasion (wholly engaged with myself), if I allow the experience to remain foreign (i.e., not mine) and if I don't turn away due to the pressure of the moment or because of my personality. Under these conditions, empathy is full participation in foreign experience if I feel a similar feeling to the inner state of the other—if I experience empathy plus sympathy.

I may be empathetic whether or not I'm in sympathy, but without sympathy relational empathy isn't a fully engaged participatory act. If I can't share the feeling, I remain an observer rather than a participant. Since we can't, and wouldn't want to share all feelings we choose to empathize with, it's essential to understand the difference between gazing upon someone's experience and remaining steadfast in our gaze, without turning away and with actually being able to join in the experience. If we can't remain steadfast, if we turn away, empathy fails. But I'm not obliged to be in sympathy with everyone in every instance of empathy.

A friend of mine is a Federal prison chaplain. At one point, he introduced me to a man who is a notorious sex offender. This man had served his time and was released from prison. He came to our church to find sanctuary from the crowds surrounding his residence that came every week like clockwork. People marched in front of his house to protest his presence in their community.

I remember the day someone in our church showed suspicion toward him. I recollect sensing his pain in the sanctuary. I felt it physically, from across the room. I went to talk with him. He sobbed as soon as he saw me. He told me what happened. We cried together.

He decided that day to return to prison even though his sentence was complete.

He couldn't bear the pressure of censure any longer. He turned to me and said: *What do they want me to do? Lie under a truck and let it run over me?* He spoke quietly. I'll never claim to understand the sorrow he felt. Nor do I understand how anyone could bring himself to do to other people what he'd done—the harm he put his victims though will haunt them for the rest of their lives. I wasn't in sympathy with his feelings (I didn't feel the same feeling) but I could attend to his pain while its tumult rolled over him, so he didn't have to be alone.

Deliberating On Empathy

I want to say more about entrapment and invasion, two ways to mis-direct an empathetic encounter. Each extreme disturbs the balance in empathetic responsiveness.

Deliberating (Figure #2)

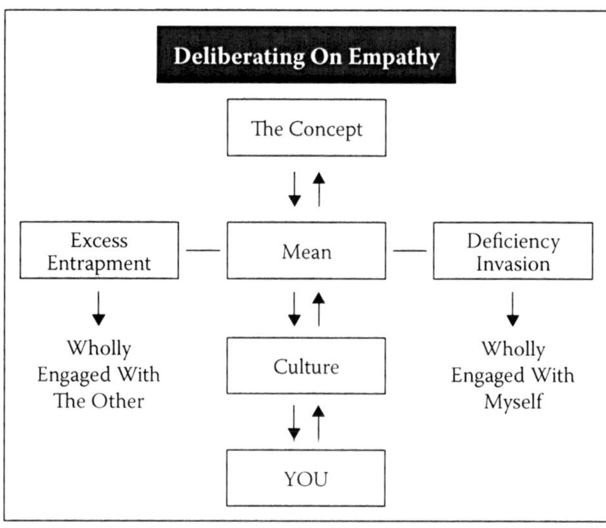

Figure #2 outlines Aristotelian deliberation. If we use his model for thinking about character and consider empathy from the perspective of its excess (entrapment) and its deficiency (invasion) we understand empathy more fully.

In deliberation, we come to see how to draw empathetic responsiveness as a life principle. In terms of this diagram, Aristotle didn't include culture because he thought his culture was the model for every other one. In carrying out deliberation, we research the concept, cultural messages about empathy, our own tendencies with respect to it, an excess of empathy and its deficiency, as well as the mean between the extremes.

The point of deliberating on empathy is to see how to offer our attention to the right person, in the right way, for the right reasons, at the right time and for the right duration of time, so that the encounter is successful. As we deliberate on empathy, a path opens up between excess and deficiency. That path is called the mean. The mean isn't in the middle of the extremes necessarily. The mean of a concept is usually closer to one side than the other. Its position is identified once all the elements are adequately worked out.

If we gather aspects of empathy presented so far, we can say that it's a proactive virtue that enables one person to attend to two worlds of experience—his or her own and another person's. Relational empathy allows other people to feel sure that their experience makes sense to at least on other person so that they can relax and realize they're neither alone nor strange. Empathy is an act of perceiving, an art of imagining, that helps an empathetic person narrate a foreign experience in a way that its owner acknowledges is accurate. Empathy tells the truth but may or may not require us to speak. Empathy relies on sensing our own interpretations but not imprisoned by them. It requires us to reflect on what's in our own mind as we listen to someone else's thinking. Empathy calms anxiety and relieves guilt. With empathy, I learn to be kind to myself and kind to others.

Empathy is a way of perceiving, of seeing the world. It's a gaze that gets its object right. If the object of our gaze is a text, person, our own hearts or a moral act, empathy is essentially attentiveness. It's a focused, informed observation of what's going on that stops short of staring or mimicking the other person (we observe and convey our differences through empathy, so as not to presume that we know exactly what someone else is going through). It's the basis for social literacy, an essential skill in the repertoire of someone who's trying to master that complex skill.

If I wish to deliberate on empathy, I must come to understand what my culture conveys about the idea and its practice and my own pre-dispositions toward it. Does my culture value and demonstrate empathy so that I can learn it? At the outset of this chapter, I noted my own need to understand my current understanding of empathy in order to learn the complex skill. In my case, I had to revise my generalized understanding of women to gain a new understanding of empathy.

METHODS FOR EMPATHY

The role of teachers in learning empathy is profound. Even if empathy is absent from a child's home, empathy at school can show them the way. As teachers, we engage empathy educationally, for example, by using Aristotelian deliberation, by encouraging students to gather cultural material (e.g., magazines, images, songs, stories, movies) that conveys current interpretations of empathy. In addition, we may ask learners to record an experience of conflict and reflect on their reactions after we take them though an Aristotelian exercise. In general, personal reflections should remain private but learners can contribute general insights to classroom discussion that help to illuminate empathy. The process of deliberation situates the concept of empathy in a framework built from cultural and personal perspectives on what empathy is and how it can be exercised.

The mean that's mapped through deliberation is positioned between the extremes of excess and deficiency. In order to assess the extremes, we must decide what empathy essentially is (what sort of attentiveness it is) and that decision is informed by the concept, as we understand it. In this case, empathy is attentiveness to foreign experience. We acknowledge that it's possible to have too much attentiveness so that empathy becomes entrapment, or too little attentiveness so that empathy invades someone else's experience, as a kind of interpersonal imperialism.

As the diagram indicates, empathy's excess is expressed through being wholly engrossed with another person's experience at my own expense. When I'm exercising too much attentiveness toward another person's experience, I lose touch with my needs, feelings, aspirations and goals. I lose myself. Losing myself doesn't help the other person. Generally the other person feels suffocated by excessive concern. Suppose a mother learns that her adult daughter has cancer. The mother loves her daughter and is so entirely focused on her daughter's health that she loses touch with her own well-being. Her daughter may express anger, fall silent or try to slip away from her mother's gaze in some other way. Empathy fails due to excessive attentiveness, due to the mother's refusal to attend to her own life as well as her daughter's life.

In its deficiency, empathy is wholly engrossed with one's own experience at the expense of another person. Suppose a father learns that his teenage son wants to be an artist. The father is sure that an artist's life will lead to poverty and grief. The father loves his son and is so focused on his certainty that the life of an artist is unsustainable that he loses touch with the aspirations of the young man. The son may express anger, fall silent or try to slip away from his father's gaze in some other way. Empathy fails due to a deficiency of attentiveness, due to the father's refusal to attend to the boy's gifts as well as to his own fears.

What's the path empathy takes between its two extremes? The first aspect of appropriate empathy to note is that two worlds of experience must not conflate into one world, as they do in the extremes of excess and deficiency. In excess, the two worlds of a daughter and mother collapse into the daughter's illness. In deficiency, the two worlds of the son and father collapse into the father's certainty that he's right about his son's future. The appropriate path for empathy encourages us to remain calm; anxiety relaxes. For this reason, the mother and father won't locate the mean for empathy in exactly the same spot on the diagram.

Deliberation is personal. The father will become aware that he must lean in the direction of attending to his son's life and therefore in the direction of empathy's excess. The mother will lean towards the deficiency side of the model. She'll lean towards valuing her own life more than she has been doing. In general, we can say empathy has more to do with attending to someone else's experience than being pre-occupied with our own. Therefore, the mean for empathy lies closer to an excess of attentiveness. But how can we become effective at calming the anxiety in our own hearts long enough to allow another person's experience to show up truthfully?

Human frailty leads into conflict if we refuse to learn empathy. Unresolved conflict gets in the way of empathetic listening. We turn away from someone who's expressing negative feelings toward us. Guilt drives us into a cover up operation. Shame closes us down to other people. We want to close our ears to any and all criticism. We can't bear to be in the wrong because it moves us toward feeling worthless and alone. Without empathy, isolation intensifies. In loneliness, we're trapped by troubles in the privacy of our own hearts. This is why unresolved guilt is counter-productive to empathy.

Unresolved guilt keeps us from asking questions because anything we might discover seems too costly to learn. But when we finally muster the courage to ask specific questions, we minimize the cost and lessen the possibility that a critic will reject us completely. In empathy, even if we believe the criticism to be unjustified, we attempt to ask specific questions to find out:

- What our critic means in general
- More information, no matter how hot the topic is for us
- What our critic's words actually mean
- What is the precise accusation
- How our critic is offended and by what
- What you did
- When you did it
- How often you did or said it
- What else the person dislikes about you.

Overall, empathy tries to see the world through another person's eyes. Asking these questions of someone who's hostile toward us usually calms down a situation because the other feels heard. Further, you gain specific information about what it's like to be in your presence.

But empathy doesn't leave us at the mercy of a critic's perspective, even if there is much truth in what we learn when we ask these questions. So we ask ourselves questions after we learn about ourselves from the other person. We ask:

- How do I understand what I'm accused of doing?
- Did I do this wilfully?
- Am I expecting myself to be perfect?
- How do I understand what it means to be human?
- How do I feel about what I did?
- How am I labelling myself now?
- Is the label accurate? Is it fair? Is this label all there is to me?
- What else is true about me?
- Is my regret realistic?
- Is my regret based on a realistic assessment of the negative effects of my action?
- Is the length and intensity of my reaction to myself appropriate to what I did?
- Am I learning from my error and developing a strategy for change?
- Am I being destructive to myself?[32]

These questions often need to be asked in the presence of a witness. Empathy is often expensive. We can't always be the one who offers empathy.

Sometimes we're the ones who need a safe place to find forgiveness. We need someone whose kind and non-anxious presence allows honesty to flourish and who doesn't let us drown in self-punitive negativity. Empathetic people realize they are, at various times, the one harmed and the one who causes harm. Empathy keeps us present to those we've hurt. Empathy helps us not to withdraw from those who have hurt us.

CONCLUSION

The role of empathy in civil society can't be overestimated. It's the heart of self and social awareness and provides the glue that holds institutions and organizations together. It's a complex skill men and women can access—although people may express empathetic concern in different ways, as people in each camp may want to continue doing. And there's an interesting question that emerges if we consider Tom (Dean) and Ted (Associate Dean) from the last chapter. Can Ted be empathetic with Tom? How might that come about? It's hard to imagine Tom being empathetic toward Ted unless he experiences a radical change of heart. Could Ted initiate that change by conveying his discomfort in this work context. After all, a closed state is as harmful to Tom as it is hurtful to Ted, and every other person in the place.

To begin with, Ted has to see his own authenticity and freedom to integrate effectively as part of the work of being there. Unfortunately, for many people in his situation, his boss can keep him working so hard that he comes to believe he has very little time for the luxury of self-reflection, let alone the social reflection that empathy requires. One wonders whether, in some way or other, Tom understands this. In his isolation, neither man would perceive the benefits of self-awareness. But we can at least imagine what would happen at work if Tom went through the empathetic listening process and asked the personal reflection questions after attentively listening to Ted's discomfort. For this to happen, Ted would have to get the courage it would take to rock the boat.

In many of the previous chapters, I've pointed out that learning social literacy depends on having people in our community that already know and practice its skills. The following chapter combines that idea with a description of seven skills of resilience. Courage is one of those skills. Resilience, the capacity to rebound from life's setbacks, develops alongside social literacy on the groundwork of empathy as it's described in this chapter. Empathy plus resilience work together to create and sustain a living environment in which its neighbourhoods, institutions, religious and civic organizations are formed, informed and transformed into centres where all people have a good chance of enjoying a fully human life.

9

LET'S START AT THE VERY BEGINNING

INTRODUCTION

As Gandhi said, "The true measure of any society can be found in how it treats its most vulnerable members." His well known wisdom seems a simple enough concept until one considers the conditions in a society, a community and a family that lead to treating our most vulnerable members well. At that point, we start to deepen our understanding and see how profound a statement it is. At its heart, it's an evaluation of civil society itself.

If we think about children, especially very young children, as an example of a vulnerable population we recognize that many in Western society believe that their care is a parental responsibility. But as we look at what parents need to be effective, we see that their responsibility is nested in community support. How can communities be supportive? Their role is nested in social norms and economic and political realities that shape that support.

A model for considering the interacting levels of support for human growth was identified by Urie Bronfenbrenner[1]. He called it an "ecological model of human development" in which development is influenced by several environmental systems. These systems include the most intimate, the family, (a micro-system) through to the political forces influencing families. One implication of his model is that, in order to look after our most vulnerable people, we need to have children, families and citizens who care about the welfare of others. We also need schools that value relational support in their practices and school cultures. To accomplish such educational aims, we require policies and practices that support its development.

In this chapter, I propose that in order for our communities to prosper, we must look to what's required to support the development of our youngest children and their families. Why do I say this? What happens in the early years literally builds brains and sets the pathways for being able to develop more and more skills. The interactions that parents have, the connections that teachers make at school, all build the architecture of the brain. That architecture includes establishing language and communication skills that impact how children think of themselves, think about what relationships should be like. These interactions build pathways to help the young recognize and manage stress—within them and in other people.

How a child deals with stress has a whole lot to do with how they're able to learn, figure things out, solve problems and be responsible citizens. The issue of early years development isn't just a pleasant idea of getting kids off to the right start. It's about living in a country that can continue to be productive and healthy for a very long time. My purpose in writing is to illustrate some of the social benefits to the country as a whole that result when a society cares for its most vulnerable populations, in this case, young children and their families.

If society intends to support young children, if we want to know how they're doing and how our society is faring with respect to their well-being, we need to monitor their development at the level of the whole population. In Canada we have a tool for monitoring the development of all 5 year olds that is now used in many countries. As researchers have used this instrument, they've observed that almost 1/3 of all Canadian 5 year olds arrive at school without essential skills they need to do well in that educational environment. This instrument, the Early Development Instrument (EDI) reflects what children have learned and experienced before they arrive at school. The distressing reality is that most children who are behind their peers when they arrive don't catch up. They continue to have a multitude of problems with learning and behavior. As a consequence of not having these necessary skills, vulnerable children aren't able to get the most out of the educational opportunities that schools are set up to provide for them.

But this situation could be addressed. The research of Dr Clyde Hertzman[2] at the University of British Columbia indicates that decreasing the overall vulnerability of children by just 1% would increase Canada's Gross Domestic Product (GDP) by 1% over the lifetime of the group. By extension, his work implies that bringing early childhood vulnerability down from 30% to 10% would increase a country's economic growth by 20% over the work lifetime of that group. I propose that Canadians would receive a massive return on their investment in the future if we addressed the source of vulnerabilities picked out by the EDI. Yet what are effective strategies to create change at a societal level, which are clearly needed if 1/3 of our children aren't doing well?

Canada isn't the only country that has vulnerable young children, but not every country sees the issue in the same way. For example, there was sweeping reform in Sweden during the 1980s when gender equity was the rallying cry. While I was in Sweden I noticed that the brain and its development wasn't at the core of this reform. When Swedish people raised the issues of early years development, they talked about gender equity. That's why they have universal preschool. All of the wonderful things I'm going to tell you about brain development were not the prime mover of their reform. Rather, they believe women have as much right to be in the workforce as do men. They also know both moms and dads want their children to be well looked after.

In the United States and Canada the rallying cry is currently focused on building better brains, on school readiness and the impact of early environments on its development. There's also more attention directed to the social and economic conditions that allow early childhood environments to flourish. Nobel winning economists, such as James Heckman[3], after intense scrutiny of these issues, support high quality early childhood programming for socially disadvantaged children as a key factor in economic prosperity. The economic argument for developing a comprehensive approach to early years development is massive. If you want to make a difference in your economy, invest early. If you want to get 17 dollars for every dollar you spend, invest early. In those Canadian neighborhoods, where vulnerability is very high, we know what to do to help children and families so that kids can soar throughout life. President Obama[4], in his December 2014 Washington Summit on Early Child development, stated that:

> "Investing in early child development is one of the greatest investments our country can make."

But these children, their families and their communities require advocacy if environments where young children grow up are to become as healthy as they need to be.

AN UNEQUAL SOCIETY

I dedicate the work I do as an advocate for children and knowledge translator to my dear friend, the late Dr Dan Offord, who worked at McMaster University at the Offord Centre for Child Studies in Hamilton Ontario. Based on his research, he observed that growing up in Canada is like running a race on an uneven playing field. What did he mean? On average, children who suffer the disadvantages of poverty, whose parents didn't finish high school or who experience maltreatment or neglect, do less well. These conditions have a profound effect on a person's life chances. Where you're born, who you are born to, even your postal code can make a difference in how long you're going to live and what kind of job you're going to have. One could think Canadians' health should be good no matter where people reside, because we live in a country that has universal access to healthcare. But this isn't so. One might also think that, because public education is freely available for every child, educational outcomes should reveal that school experience is equitable. This isn't the case.

When data are examined, there are gradients and slopes as one plots income and just about any other outcome, such as education, illness or employment. The poorer you are, the worse your chances:

the fewer your opportunities for good employment, the less schooling you'll get and the more illness you'll suffer. These findings aren't due to poor people being born with lousy genes, or making bad lifestyle choices. It's social conditions that are the determinants of health and have the most impact. That's why Offord dedicated his life to make sure people were thinking about how to ensure every child, no matter where they live, has the opportunity to arrive at the starting line with what they need to soar through schooling and life.

Let's look at one city. Where I come from, Hamilton Ontario, there are kids who are living in poverty. As one example, they don't get to become hockey players because they can't afford the equipment. Even if they get equipment to start with, they can't afford new equipment when their bodies change as they grow up. At school, they can't afford the pizza days other children enjoy unless there's someone on the Parent Council who insists that these days be scheduled on days that are close to the day that their parents' support income checks arrive.

What does it feel like to be the child that can't afford pizza day, when that day is so easy for so many other children? What would it be like—day in and day out—to feel that you don't have as much as other students and be embarrassed about your clothing? We're now able to answer these questions, at least in part. The toxic stress of these environments affects how the brain develops, how well students get along with others, how well they're able to delay gratification, which are all significant features of fitting in at school and feeling that you belong. These conditions affect many characteristics that predict success and failure during a lifetime.

Early Brain Development

Why is it that conditions surrounding childhood have such a long lasting effect? Scientists from many disciplines are coming together to point out how environments in which babies and children exist profoundly affect health, schooling and employment opportunities. The evidence comes from many sources. Longitudinal research, that is, data that were gathered from following the same group of people over a long time and measuring their physical, educational and social development at different points in time, sheds light on what influences health and development long term. In one significant longitudinal study[5], Dr Hertzman looked at results from a British cohort made up of people who were born during one particular week in 1958. In 2014, they're all 56 years of age. Data have been collected on this cohort that covers many factors, for example, smoking during pregnancy, the mother's level of education, occupations in the family of origin, health status and school achievement indicators.

Hertzman focused on specific issues. As one example, he looked at each child's height at age 7 and their math scores, and made a guess at what their health situation would be at 45 years of age. He asked various questions, such as, "Could one predict later health problems such as heart disease or asthma? Could their height at age 7 (relative to their adult height) and math scores be a tell-tale marker of what their first years were like? Could the relationship between the quality of nutrition they received, being read to in the early years and how parents spoke to them be related to later aspects of their lives?" Through his research, he found an association between their childhood results and later health. If they were doing poorly at age 7 on these data they were more likely to have adult diseases like heart disease, lung disease and addictions.

How was it possible for him to propose this connection? The simple answer is that our health isn't based on the quality of our present activities alone. It's also influenced by how our brains and bodies developed early in life. Another study, the Adverse Childhood Experiences study (ACE)[6], made the connection between the number of ACEs one has and adult health. The more ACEs, (e.g., maltreatment, household dysfunction, neglect) the more likely the occurrence of heart disease, depression, suicide and addictions. In an era of ever-increasing worries about health care costs, it seems clear that we're well advised to focus on building better health for someone's future by addressing what happens early in their lives rather than just treating and managing peoples' poor health when they're adults.

THE SOCIAL BRAIN: SERVE AND RETURN

While the health benefits of caring for the young continue to be my concern, the focus in this chapter is on the development of civil personality as an important aspect of the well-being of the young so that their future skills include caring for others. Stress, mentioned earlier, is important in this research. Science researchers look at brain pathways and stress pathways and consider how the immune system gets set up early in life with the hope of discovering how that system might develop so as to last a lifetime. By bringing many fields of study together, implications and connections can be made. In this section, I look at how the environment between a baby and a caregiver initiates a cascade of interactions that have the potential to build civil personality, that is, a child that cares about the welfare of others.

Human beings, as a species, are wired to connect. But the importance of building relationships and connections with our children from infancy isn't always promoted as much as, for example, helping them to develop reading skills. A good friend of mine once described overhearing a lift line conversation between a mother and her adult son at a mountain ski hill. As he was getting off the lift and heading away, the mother asked her son where he was going. He replied he had to go because he was babysitting his kids (her grandchildren). My friend wanted to jump off the lift to tell him he needed to be doing a lot more than babysitting! She wanted to say, "You're the dad. You don't get to babysit unless you pay yourself. Your role as dad is massively important. You are building your kids brains, including how they will feel about themselves and other adults. This isn't just babysitting!"

Children thrive when adults in their lives care deeply about them. The capacity to let people know they're important is one of the things I'll always remember about Dan Offord. When with him, you always felt he was really listening to you, actually attuning to you as you spoke. As his colleague, during our social interaction, I experienced a 'felt sense of connection to him'. I "*felt* felt." I had a felt sense of being heard through his attention to me, just as a child feels with a parent that welcomes her to climb up on his lap so that she's able to completely relax and convey what's on her mind. That sense of connection to significant adults is a requirement for healthy human development. Why? We're a social species. We require human contact and connection, right from the start.

I long to see the day when all children have at least one adult whose eyes light up when they see them. "Connect with me" is a signal little children send out as a frequent request to the adults in their lives. The ability and willingness to respond to them in return is essential to the felt sense of connection that's at the heart of all human relationships. This movement back and forth between adult and child is the serve and return of healthy social interaction. It's a two-way contact that's most important in a child's development. If you can have that back and forth, expressed with delight and awe in the children themselves, they will thrive.

A Child's Temperament And The Role Of Serve And Return

Now what does it take to have one's eyes light up as a child comes near you? Anyone who has more than one child knows that they come into the world with very different ways of interacting because they have different temperaments. Some are easy to figure out. Some are pretty hard. It's easy to have your eyes light up when everything is going smoothly. It's harder if you're deprived of sleep and can't figure out what's making your baby cry so much!

I have five great kids so I know this really well! When we had our first baby we were super anxious, of course, but he was pretty easy to figure out. We could quickly tell what his cries meant. He was very responsive to our back and forth (serve and return) smiling and cooing! He hardly ever cried. We thought we were wonderful parents. Then 18 months later, along came our daughter. First of all, she came out looking like Winston Churchill. The music in the background was the Emperor Concerto. A warning? From birth, parenting her was very different. She was hard to figure out. She cried a lot unless I was holding her. She didn't whimper—it was a 'bring down the walls of Jericho' kind of cry. When she was a baby it took my husband and me a lot of time to help her soothe. But her delight due to these interactions was infectious. She beamed.

People passing by who saw her face would stop and comment on her expression. She felt things in a big way, even as a baby.

But we were exhausted by her high needs. We were sleep deprived, irritable and unsure of what we might be doing wrong. She continued to be intense as a toddler. She delighted in small things and that was wonderful. It was also challenging. She didn't like the feel of things such as the scratchiness of clothing tags, or the stitch lines in her socks, or having her shoes too tight. When she made her mind up about something it was next to impossible to shift her. It was much harder to keep having my eyes light up when we differed, or to have positive back and forth interaction when what I often experienced with her was a battle!

As a little one, she was a challenge to understand and difficult to figure out. To make it more awkward, I was a doctor, a psychiatrist, doing a specialization in child psychiatry. Even with all my training, I'd never heard about temperament. I started reading everything I could find. As one example, I read books with titles such as *Your Difficult Child* or *Your High Needs Child*, all of which helped us understand our girl.

The book *Raising your Spirited Child* by Mary Sheedy Kurchinka[7] really resonated with us. We came to rely on it. It spoke of nine different types of characteristics babies seem to be born with, e.g., intensity of emotional reactions, persistence, sensitivity and reactions to new things. We learned our girl was spirited. She was more intense, persistent and sensitive than was our son. We came to understand that we needed to work on the goodness of fit between us. We came to realize the wonder that she was and stopped wishing she was less intense. We no longer tried to mould her into what we wanted her to be.

My daughter's intensity was good training for a child psychiatrist. She didn't like change. She never took a bottle. She started to walk and then she ran. She started to talk and then talked in sentences. Her developmental path was very different from our first child. Luckily we were well supported. I come from a big family and got all kinds of advice. Some was good. Some was bad. A few people insisted that I just let her cry and that it was okay to let a baby cry it out. They even thought it was good for her lungs. This is one bit of advice I didn't take. Even then, we knew we had to soothe her when she cried and pick her up and that a baby should never be left to cry it out. How are you conveying to a child that you're keeping them safe and love them if you leave them when they need comfort? We knew we couldn't follow those books that said let babies cry. We couldn't justify that reaction in our own hearts. As parents, my husband and I read a lot of books and learned a lot of strategies.

Spirited children can present challenges for parents. It's common for many parents to feel their spirited kids are doing things on purpose—to get them angry or manipulate them. What it came down to with our daughter was a sensitivity issue. She wasn't trying to make us late for a family dinner by having a temper tantrum if she didn't have on the right socks. She was highly sensitive to the feel of things and hadn't yet learned how to manage that sensitivity. It was our job to help her regulate her sensitivity by helping her recognize that the socks made her feel itchy and then help her get a pair of socks that didn't have that impact on her. When we handled the situation that way, it was a relief for everyone. Because of that early experience, in my clinical career, I've recommended Kurchinka's book on the spirited child many, many times.

Why do I emphasize temperament when talking about the early years in connection with a focus on civic personality development? It's because we must think about individual characteristics of each child wherever we work with them, whether at home, school, a sports team, at church, synagogue, temple or the community at large. We need to think of each child as unique with much to offer. In communities, caring about the early years requires addressing how to support each and every child. We need to consider the individual needs of each family. So often children who have high vulnerability also have parents with high vulnerability. To be effective, we ask questions, "What do I know about this behavior? This family? This situation?" Too often we believe it's easier to think we can interpret behavior based on our current understanding and try to manage it from our own perspective, rather than genuinely listening and observing what's going on for and in that child or family.

Having the habit of asking the question 'What do I know about this?' helps when trying to figure out other peoples' behavior. When

I was a resident in medical training, Offord pointed out to me that sometimes educators or doctors have great ideas for how to help children and families but they get confused and frustrated if families don't take advantage of opportunities they set up for them. For example, a teacher might think of having all kinds of fun things for a family to do in school. Then, if families don't turn up, they wonder what's wrong with parents.

What teachers need to ask is "What do I know about this?" If they ask that critically reflective question, they might realize that many parents have no more desire to walk into a school than they have to walk into a dentist's office. These are parents who felt school was awful. For them, it was a place where they felt put down or worse. If teachers want to be effective in helping children and families, it's necessary to ask critically reflective questions at individual and societal levels. This questioning helps to understand complex issues such as temperament. That understanding makes a huge difference in how we work, not just with children, but also with each other.

The Teaching Of The Elders

In terms of our capacity to understand one another, an area I'm learning more about is the wisdom of our First Nations peoples. Several years ago I heard Mohawk Elder Tom Porter speak. The wisdom in his talk was inspiring. He spoke about being raised by his grandmother. He talked about how much he *felt* felt by her, Porter has written down many of the lessons she taught him in a book he titled, *And Grandma Said...Iroquois Teachings.*[8]

What was so remarkable to me was that many of the teachings he described are now supported in scientific literature. His grandmother told him that, when a child is conceived, it's the family who's pregnant. She told him people must look after the whole family that's raising children. Evidence is accumulating on the important role fathers have in the early years of development as well as in the mental health of the children's mother. Porter described his grandmother's advice that a husband should never yell at his wife when she's pregnant. The science of stress shows that high persistent stress in pregnancy is a problem for the developing baby. Children whose mothers experience extreme on-going stress during pregnancy are at increased risk of being premature, smaller than the norm, with smaller heads, that develop more learning difficulties and are more risk of developing Attention Deficit Hyperactivity Disorder (ADHD).

How The Environment Talks To Our Genes: EPIGENETICS

There's another First Nations cultural belief that Canadians would do well to adopt. The belief is that community leaders should consider the next seven generations as they're making decisions. The next seven generations? Why is that? It's the kind of belief Clyde Hertzman was talking about, which was based on his research with children. Essentially, what happens in the early years has a very long reach. The NOVA program (*www.pbs.org/wgbh/nova/genes/*) called *Ghosts in our Genes* tells us that what our grandmother and great grandmother ate has a big influence on whether we'll have diabetes later in life.

How does the process of passing these messages along work? Chemical message tags get placed on top of the Deoxyribonucleic acid (*DNA*). These 'tags' tell the DNA to be active and make proteins, or they tell the DNA to be silent. What's so revolutionary in science is the outlining of how these messenger tags get passed down through the generations. DNA is a molecule that encodes the genetic instructions used in the development and functioning of all known living organisms. A belief that intergenerational transmission of trauma gets passed down through the generations (that first Nations peoples have held for a very long time) has scientific evidence to support it. Their wisdom is something we should have paid attention to a long time ago. The best time to influence a child is 100 years before they're born. From the point of view of the best way to care for children, what happens during one generation affects the following one as well as the generation after that. If we took the needs of children seriously, what would that mean for Canadian social policies and practices?

VULNERABILITIES IN THE EARLY YEARS

The wisdom that Tom Porter grew up hearing was based on a cultural belief that children are the sacred ones in a community. He said that, "They're the heart of the nation. Child rearing is a sacred communal responsibility." Imagine what it would be like if all Canadians actually believed that children are the heart of the community. If children were at the centre of what Canadians care about, what would we focus on in our newspapers? I think it would be very different than what we now see leading the headlines.

In 2007 and 2013, UNICEF Innocenti[9] Reports were made public. These reports addressed the quality of children's lives in developed countries.[10] The research analyzed data on children's well-being in the richest countries of the world and compared the outcomes of that research among those countries. The data included measures for material well-being, education, health and safety, behaviors and risk, housing and environment. In 2007, 21 countries were studied and Canada came 12th out of 21 countries. The more recent report came out in May 2013 and looked at 29 countries. In this report Canadian children's lives ranked 17 out of these 29 countries. Did Canadians hear about their mid-range ranking in the newspapers? No, we didn't. Why was that? When only 45% of 11, 13 and 15 year olds report their parents spend time "just talking to them" compared to the report of children in Hungary at 90%, or where we rank 27/29 in child and youth health and safety indicators, I can't help wondering what our young people think and feel? How can they ever think about civic society if they aren't experiencing parental support in their lives? How about civil personality development?

When we talk about being ranked overall at 17/29, what are we talking about? We're talking about children living in poverty and taking unreasonable risks that negatively impact their life chances. When the report came out, what did hit the paper is that Canadian youth smoke more marijuana than youth in the other 28 countries. That's what hit the newspapers! How is it possible that Canadian children are stuck in the middle of that group of rich nations and it never made the newspapers? Further, the report tells us that we're 27th out of 29 in child obesity and 22nd out of 29 in children's mental health. The research's purpose was provide a platform for the United Nations to persuade rich countries that, if children do well, communities do well and nations do well.

As long as we have high vulnerability in our communities, our children won't flourish. When some of our kids do poorly, it affects everyone. I was listening to a presentation by Ed Rolnick[11] a US economist with the Minnesota Federal Reserve Bank. He observed that people don't even have to like kids to support their needs, but they need to know that children's well-being has an effect on whether there'll be enough dollars around for them to have health care once our country ages and the silver tsunami of Baby Boomers finally hits. Baby Boomers comprise a graying population that will need someone to look after them. Rolnick's point was that the quality of the workforce of tomorrow is based on the well-being of young children today.

There's no question that a lot of money is spent on children and the care of children. Yet it's overwhelmingly spent on physical health care. In terms of health care, about 1500 cases of childhood cancer are diagnosed each year across the country, according to 2014 data from the Childhood Cancer Canada Foundation. Currently, approximately 10,000 children are living with cancer. These health care dollars are much needed and well spent. Most people are aware of the need to act fast with good medicines for children who are affected by cancer.

However, other children suffer conditions that lead to a much higher long-term cost to our health budget, our special education budget and our criminal justice budget. Their plight is largely ignored. As examples, in 2008 there were 85,000 substantiated incidents of child abuse across the country. These investigations were complete. Allegations were found to be provable and substantiated. This number doesn't reflect numerous incidents of abuse in which the children withdraw allegations after family pressure or count cases of neglect where harm is harder to prove. How much are we spending on the well-being of these children and on efforts to prevent childhood maltreatment from happening?

THE BIRTH AND GROWTH OF CIVILITY AND SELF-REGULATION

How do we view children and the influences of childhood on them? Our views of individual and social interaction impacts the way we nurture, educate and support children. Do we want them to grow up to be self-reliant, exploratory, content and able to meet challenges? If we do, how we think of them affects how we interact with them. Do we think, for example, that kids are empty vessels that we mould for success? Do we imagine we can fill them up with information so they're able to get into the right pre-schools, schools and colleges? A young Korean patient of mine called this parenting approach "stuffing the duck."

Adults who rely on this approach may believe childhood behavior and accomplishments should reflect well on them so they can appear to be successful parents. This way of thinking shapes our approach to discipline, education, socialization and skill development. In its extreme, it's an approach that's seriously questioned, for example, in South Korea. Children there report extreme unhappiness and feel suicidal under pressure it creates for them. In another well researched and cited study[12] from the Organization for Economic Co-operation and Development (OECD);[13] South Korea has the highest youth suicide rate in the 34 countries of the OECD;[14] scholastic pressures are a frequently cited cause of their unhappiness.

Could we take another view? Might we see kids as competent, capable and resourceful when they're given the opportunity? Do we see them as able to interact well with others and capable of resolving their problems if they receive appropriate support?

I suggest we reconsider our view of children and childhood. If we think of kids as capable and think of parenting and educating them in terms of supporting them as they use their innate curiosity, love of learning, drive to grow and empathy toward others, we interact differently with them. If we take the second approach, we're able to create an environment in which they learn and where they demonstrate self-regulation. What do I mean by self-regulation? It's an ability to be boss of one's own attention, emotion and behavior at an appropriate level for one's age and culture. It means being able to deal with unexpected changes that you didn't necessarily want, like your classmate taking your favorite toy at school. In a 2 year old, for example, we wouldn't expect a whole lot of self-regulation but by the start of school, at 4 or 5 years old, we expect children to be able to control their attention, emotion and behavior at an appropriate level.

What might self-regulation look like? Suppose a 5 year old, let's call him Jimmy, is playing at school and another child comes up and takes his toy. Jimmy has good impulse control so he doesn't hit out at the other. Instead he regulates his annoyance and calls out to an adult and says to the interloper, "Don't take that. It's mine." A model child might even say, "Why don't we take turns," but that would be your sister-in-law's kid. In contrast, another child who lacks these skills, let's call him Ryan, might hit out at the child who's trying to take away the toy. The simple civil act Jimmy carries out expresses self-regulation. His response uncovers layers of development I want to investigate further. A child who's capable of civility has had positive relationships and likely been well supported and nurtured during his pre-school years.

A third child, let's call him Jerry, may have a similar experience at school, someone takes away his toy, but Jerry has a developmental disorder that interferes with the development of civil skills Jimmy already has. It's essential for teachers to understand Jerry's world but what about Ryan? He not there yet. It's unlikely he's had the benefits of the consistent nurturing parenting Jimmy has experienced, or has never been exposed to children his own age and hasn't developed these skills at this point in his life—which doesn't mean he can't develop them.

Rather than judging Ryan, it's important to ask the question, "What do I know about him?" If he comes from a family or a community where there's high toxic stress all the time, adults may not have been able to spend time with him to help him develop language and self-control over his impulses. If he's living in a situation of neglect, his brain may be constantly on high alert or on guard—constantly warning him that something bad is going to happen. This kind of toxic and constant stress influences how Ryan's brain develops and, consequently, how he acts at school. If a child pushes against him as he enters the classroom, a faster and stronger signal is sent to the threat sensor or fight/flight centre of his brain. Unlike children from non-toxic stress homes, whose 'watch out for danger' centers in the brain haven't been so hyper-acutely tuned, Ryan may interpret the push as an aggressive event that could be harmful. What does he do? He hits back.

Becoming Self-Regulated

Recognizing and managing emotion, stress and learning self-regulation are key to a child's healthy development. I want to say more about self-regulation. Here's one example. When we're sitting attentively focused and listening to someone speak, and taking it in, we're demonstrating self-regulation. The evidence that we're self-regulated is that we're giving our attention to the speaker. We focus intention and behavior on that task. We're not jumping up and down or running around the aisles. In self-regulation, impulsive behavior is inhibited. We're emotionally in control. This is what self-regulation looks like. Now it's easier to be self-regulated if we're interested in the topic and it's harder if the person isn't a good speaker, or the topic is of little interest. Under those conditions, our mind wanders off and we start making grocery lists. We wonder where the woman in the seat ahead of us got the beautiful scarf she's wearing. When we have no interest in the speaker, we're easily distracted. We might begin to feel restless but we inhibit that sense of wanting to leave by shifting around and moving. We look as if we're self-regulated in our posture and perhaps our gaze but in terms of our attention, we're not. In this situation, we're unlikely to take in much new learning.

Even if some people in the audience have terrible personal problems going on, or big life issues that are pressing in on them, with self-regulation they keep their emotions in check. Road rage is an example of the absence of self-regulation. It arises if a driver doesn't recognize his or her emotions or if people don't process them effectively. In road rage, people just react.

In learning to be self-regulated, we first need to be regulated by others. In this way we learn to safely experience our own emotions, recognize these emotions and develop ways of dealing with them. A baby that's routinely soothed when she cries will cry less. Why? Because, as alarming sensations such as *I'm hungry* are repeatedly soothed, the offending stimulus (hunger) fires fewer alarms in her brain cells. The child's brain comes to associate being comforted with her caregiver and to the experience of being soothed. She gradually learns to soothe herself. Her distress at being hungry is extinguished or at least significantly lessened. She also learns that she can have an impact on her environment.

Children and babies can develop strategies for self-regulation very early, although we must acknowledge that some do so more easily than others. Recall that temperament is a factor for many children. As they develop more self-regulation and a sense of security, the easier it is for children to be joyous explorers. When we help children achieve self-regulation, it doesn't mean we're inhibiting them—we're helping them develop pathways for success.

The School Readiness Trap

How do children learn self-regulation? As one might imagine, that learning is many-layered, but for the most part the child learns self-regulation in daily back and forth interactions with the adults in their lives. Initially babies become regulated by being regulated by others and in that way, over time, through relationship, learn to self-regulate. Children also learn to regulate themselves through the community and the cultural expectations of their group. As an example, if a community sees it as rude for children to get food before their elders receive food, children will learn that rule through many interactions in the community over time.

I expect most people in the Western world want children to arrive at school eager and ready to learn and to have already developed some of the rudimentary skills they require to do well in that situation, such as being able to communicate. There's a trap, however, that has developed in the whole school readiness movement. Dan Offord and scientists like him who developed instruments such as the Early Development Instrument (EDI) mentioned earlier, describe and measure all the domains needed for success in school. These domains include the following:

- Physical health and well-being
- Social competence
- Emotional maturity
- Language and cognitive development
- Communication skills and general knowledge

Too frequently people equate school readiness with developing children's text-based literacy and numeracy skills, and, at times, at the expense of social/emotional literacy skills development.

Even if children read and write they will have trouble if they can't get along with others. A better predictor of school success is social and emotional competence and their excitement about learning. These are stronger indicators than a high Intelligence Quotient (IQ) by itself. But do we see parents and educators focusing on opportunities for children to play and explore the world of relationships, even though there's good evidence that this is how they learn best?

Unfortunately teachers and parents are caught in the trap—one that I have coined "the tyranny of cognitive seduction." The trap has us thinking that literacy and numeracy are the most important aspects of early years development and primary markers for success at school. They are important and should be fostered, but not at the expense of play. Children learn through play. Brains are built through play. It's how children acquire knowledge and insight about the world.

In Ontario, where I carry out most of my psychiatric practice, colleagues working in childcare have been getting increased pressure from parents to spend more time preparing kids for school by having them do text-based literacy and numeracy drills, what I tend to think of as drill and kill. Arming themselves with research and support from the Council of Ministers of Education in Canada (CMEC) childcare workers continue to try to persuade parents that having kids learn the problem-solving skills of how to get along with other people is as necessary a set of skills to acquire as is practice in numeracy and text-based literacy.

There are communities across the country where the EDI shows large vulnerability; many children score low numbers on one or more of the five domains bulleted above, as well as in general knowledge. In some wealthier communities vulnerability is evident in children who read and write but have lower scores (are vulnerable) in social competence and emotional maturity. Even though these communities and families are well off, their children can't get along with the others. This is of great concern because it may represent a lack of development in empathy.

It's most likely that the second group has economic and cultural advantages over those in poorer communities and is better able to seize opportunities that come their way later in life. But here's another problem: if their scores on getting along with others are low, how will these children impact the development of civic community when they're involved as adults? If they have little empathy, we're all in trouble. We need to pay attention to developing the whole child in both types of socio-economic settings. Children learn through all five domains: physical, social, emotional, cognitive and communicative. These competencies aren't acquired in isolation from one another; they're acquired together. If love is building brains, the focus is on developing the whole child. The way to address vulnerabilities isn't to single out and pathologize one of the five areas of competence. The way forward is to bring them all up together.

Is Bullying An Absence Of Healthy Relationship?

Like many people, I'm increasingly worried about reports of bullying at school. It seems to start very early and can last and cause damage throughout a lifetime. In Hamilton in 1992, I was part of a research survey that looked at needs and gaps in services with about 3300 children in childcare. Many of the teachers in the survey described children who had aggressive behaviors and noted a need for support in order to deal with them. When we interviewed the teachers, we found it wasn't only physical aggression that caused a problem but also name calling, racial slurs, exclusion and relational aggression—all of which were present in a sizeable number of children. For example, relational aggression in 3 year-olds was alive and well. What that survey told us wasn't that they had to bring in programs to teach children about nice ways to speak, but within the childcare community of parents, they had to build a civic community in which everybody belonged and where everyone had a sense of purpose.

There is a wonderful group of Canadian researchers who study bullying. They have seen that relationships are at the heart of the matter. Their network is named Promoting Relations to Eliminate Violence (Prevnet)[15].

Are we creating a sense of belonging in our childcare centers, play schools, library programs and at home? If a person has a sense of belonging their stress hormone levels go down. Just think about your own experience. Suppose you're working with a team of people and there's someone who's really toxic. Do you feel like going to work? Do more people get sick? Is there more absenteeism? If you sense your contribution isn't valued, how do you feel? How about if you're with someone who makes it clear that your work is appreciated, don't you feel more like participating? Stressful relationships affect the immune system's functioning. We know that if people are in a situation where they feel valued and respected and are given a flu shot, they have less of a reaction to it. If people are in lousy relationships, they have a cold that lasts longer. Immune systems are affected by psychological well-being. As we will see, a sense of belonging has implications for a child's experience of the world.

A Declaration Of Interdependence

A sense of belonging has a major impact on child development. Developing a secure sense of belonging is one of the primary tasks of childhood, but a child can't be successful on her own. Currently, there are kids who are vulnerable to predators on the Internet. This isn't because IT and technology have come in and taken over our kids. It's because society has changed. We haven't kept the family at the heart of what's most important to a young person. Families are now under tremendous pressure to keep up. Work no longer ends when you leave the workplace; there are emails and texts to respond to, even in the middle of the night because we work in a global context.

Young families feel this pressure even more, as evidenced in the work of Dr Paul Kershaw who developed the expression "Generation Squeeze." In his view, we haven't strengthened the interdependence among family members. How many families have or can have family dinners during the week? How many families are able to make sure they have time just to be with their kids? Are parents feeling so much pressure to make sure their kids don't lose out that they busy themselves being chauffeurs to ballet lessons and sports practices? Parents have become managers of their kids' time rather than people that spend face-to-face time with their children. Too often, it looks as if we believe the most important thing is to cram children full of activity and things because they're empty vessels waiting to be filled. They need the skills, we say. We believe that in this competitive world, they need an edge up. But the edge up for children is time spent with family. The edge up is being together building relationships. The edge up is learning to resolve conflict. If we ask ourselves how much time we spend correcting and redirecting our children, and how much we connect with them, I think most of us will find we spend much more time correcting and less connecting. This is a challenge and a problem.

How Are The Children?

If we ask how are children are doing, the reality is, apart from the EDI, we don't have an indicator of how all children are doing. We live in a society that simply doesn't know this. How many kids are in child welfare across the country? The data isn't available. We know how many people have heart attacks. We know how many people are on a particular drug, but don't know how many children are in child welfare across Canada.

What's the percentage of kids who have mental health problems? Dan Offord carried out the Ontario Child Health Survey (OCHS)[16] in 1984. His study showed that in Ontario 1 in 5 kids, aged 4-17 had mental health problems. Has this percentage changed? We don't know. It's taken 30 years to get money to do the study again. It hasn't been a priority. Governments seem to have dollars to bail out big business. But do we have the will to bail out our children? I think part of the reason we don't have the will is that we think childhood is a happy, protected time. We love our kids. We believe that, mostly, they turn out okay.

The unfortunate reality is that in a recent Toronto survey of kids from grades 7 to grade 12, over 60% said they were experiencing overwhelming anxiety. Overwhelming anxiety isn't good for the brain. It isn't good for problem solving. Our kids are the canary in the mineshaft in a society that's not paying enough attention to what makes civil life possible for them. At its core, civil life is about learning how to care about other people and yourself in relationship to them and realizing how to demonstrate interdependence with them.

Why do people who care about civil interdependence worry when they hear about bullying? One of the reasons is that it gives us a picture of whether kids are learning to be empathetic. Are they learning to care about others? Thankfully, in Ontario, we're now talking about student well-being strategies and educational engagement through the lens of their well-being rather than bullying prevention. Our youth justice system is talking about relational custody and using strengths-based counseling.[17] Why? Because what we've been doing for so long hasn't improved the life chances of children and youth. According to much of the research, as in the Toronto example, the situation is getting worse. What's the mechanism behind some of these changes? Changes in approach are based on brain research.

THE MAGNIFICENT PLASTIC BRAIN: NATURE OR NURTURE?

I've been saying that what happens in the early years lasts a lifetime. How is it that events in infancy and childhood get under the skin and affect development for life? To answer the question as simply as possible--it has everything to do with the brain. Researchers who study the early years care about the brain because "we are our brain." It's the master organ, responsible for who we are, how we think and feel. The brain develops during a lifetime as its formed and changed through individual experience.

As one example, I'm a Canadian citizen and have lived in this country for almost 50 years. Yet, I have a Scottish accent. Why is that? It's due to my early life experiences and their impact on my brain. I spent my first 11 years in Scotland. While I was there, my brain cells, called neurons, got fired up in the hearing and speaking centers of the brain. They were wired up together pretty solidly. All of the neurons that got wired up together cause me to speak with a Scottish accent. If I'd been born in Canada, the firing of neurons would have taken place in a pattern that sounded Canadian; if I grew up in France, I would sound French. At birth, my brain was ready to learn any language, even multiple languages. It was my experience—this exposure to a Scottish accent – that sculpted my brain cells and gave me my accent. Neurons that get wired up together so that a person can speak with a Canadian accent didn't get used as I was learning language. They weren't used and hence they got pruned away.

As a consequence, I can only speak with a Scottish accent. My two younger brothers speak with a Canadian accent. My older brothers and sister speak with a Scottish accent. My children are bilingual. They speak with a Canadian accent, but do a great imitation of my Scottish accent. Now what about your experience? What about your brain? If you were to hear my Scottish accent, some of your brain's neurons would fire up and perhaps would ask you to think about some Scottish comedians. Perhaps you would think of some Scottish actor's roles like Mrs. Doubtfire. So you hear that sound and you think, "Oh there is a Scottish accent." And what about Star Trek? Who remembers Scotty? "Och, captain she'll never hold." You hear my Scottish accent and think of your experience with hearing a Scottish accent. As I speak with a Scottish accent, I kindle those neurons, those brain cells and mostly it's funny—if you're remembering Scotty or a comedian. So I have lit up the areas of your brain that got wired up earlier to hear my accent and now you think, "Oh isn't that nice." On the other hand, if you have a mother-in-law who's Scottish and is difficult to be around, who you think doesn't like you, a completely different area of your brain will fire up as I'm speaking.

Brains are built by personal experience. What you love, what you hate, what you laugh at—all of it is built up over time through experience. Here's an example of what I mean based on a story that I heard from the Chief Justice of Ontario. She talked about a book she'd read that was written by a young man who said he was 10 years old when liberated from a concentration camp during WWII. After the war, he went to Switzerland. One day, his Swiss teacher asked him to come to the front of the class, look at a picture of William Tell and tell the class what he saw in that picture.

Who was William Tell? He lived in the area we call Switzerland as it was trying to become independent. An Austrian magistrate didn't want the country to be independent. This magistrate tried to exert his influence over people and so he put his hat on a pole in the town square. All the people were supposed to bow as they passed by the hat. William Tell refused to bow. Because he wouldn't submit to bowing, the magistrate told William that he and his son would be executed unless he shot an arrow and knocked an apple off his son's head. The picture given to the boy who had been in the concentration camp depicted William Tell with a crossbow and arrow in his hands. The image showed him stretching his bowstring and preparing to shoot an arrow in the direction of his son as the boy stood in front of tree with an apple perched on his head.

The boy stood at the front of the class with William Tell's picture in his hands. He said nothing. He froze. He couldn't talk. The teacher said, "Tell me what you see." He couldn't talk. Finally he was able to say that it didn't make sense to him. "What do you mean?" asked the teacher. He replied, "They never used ammunition on children. They only gassed them." His brain was constructed by experience. As he looked at the picture, his neurons wired up a primitive, fearful, on-guard, frozen area of his brain. When Swiss kids looked at the picture, they saw one of their heroes and filled in the whole story. They knew William Tell loved his son and would never want to hurt him. Because of experience with this nationally important story, when they looked at it, different areas of their brains released dopamine, a pleasure neurotransmitter.

Let's look at the brain from another perspective. I have a degree in music. That was my first degree. Every time I tell this story I hear the William Tell music in my head, which some of us remember from childhood. It was the Lone Ranger theme on television. I listened to that music while I was doing my philosophy and music degree. My brain is constructed by my experience of the story and the music. My brain lights up the dopamine when I think about it or hear it.

If you're thinking of children whose life experiences have been destructive to them, there's some good news. Those who do research in the areas of psychology and psychiatry used to think it was genes that were responsible for different behaviors associated with the example of William Tell. Then we thought it was environment that built up these responses to an event. We'd argue about nature versus nurture. Is it our genes or is it the environment that shapes us? We may have had fun in these discussions but it was a waste of time. We now know that it's genes interacting with the environment that builds the person that we become. It's nature and how it's affected by nurture that influences development. The early years are the greatest opportunity to affect how a brain is moulded and constructed by experience.

Brain Plasticity

Plasticity refers to how the brain changes because of experience. That's why we have to pay a lot of attention during the early years. Parent/baby or caregiver/baby interactions literally turn on brain cells and cause those cells to make connections with other brain cells. The more stimuli and experience that comes in, the stronger these signals and pathways become. If children hear lots of words and explanations during the day and are picked up when they're distressed those related areas in the brain get linked up together. There's good research to show that we can rewire brains by creating new experiences if a child hasn't benefitted from good connections due to early childhood experiences, but just like building a house, reparation isn't easy or simple. It's harder to reconstruct and renovate a house and a brain; repair takes a lot more energy and effort after the early years have passed.

Can a child who experienced neglect early ever make up that lost time and development? The data are very mixed. Some evidence from Romanian orphanage studies show that children who were removed early and placed in high quality foster care improved significantly compared to their peers who remained in these institutions. Getting it right in the early years matters a great deal. Those who have children under 6 years old, as they read this information, may wonder how soon they can put the book down to go and hug their kids. Those who have kids over 6 years may think they've already blown it. But here's the other big part of this story. Brains don't stop growing. Early years are the greatest period of plasticity but opportunities for change don't stop there.

Another magnificent time for renovation is during adolescence as brains are again under construction. Often parents think that the disruption during teenage years is due to hormones, but it isn't. It's the brain. Research on adolescent brain development has expanded as technology has developed ways to look at the brain in action—this research is relatively new, over the past decade or so. Researchers have learned there's a significant change going on in the brain of a young person. Again, experience is what builds the brain. The activities and experiences that young people engage in sculpt the brain. Suppose it's guitar or drama lessons, those areas of the brain develop. If it's social isolation and/or violent video games those experiences profoundly affect brain growth. Whatever gets used is what wires up brain cells; what doesn't get used is snipped away or pruned.

During adolescence, as the brain is sculpted and changed, it's busy making connections. What's not used over and over again is getting snipped away. As an example, the emotional part of the brain is undergoing significant change. This change is different from earlier development in which instructions and patterns began to form, such as: Stop, Plan, Think, Organize, and which characterized brain development up to adolescence. What a young person is doing or saying is under construction.

What do I mean by saying the brain is under construction? And how long is this construction going on? Significant change in the brain lasts until someone is about 25 years of age.

THE BRAIN'S CAPACITY FOR CHANGE OVER A LIFESPAN

There's a huge part of brain research that's important for me as a child psychiatrist in my work with families. The brain is capable of change throughout life—absolutely throughout life. I've a mantra in parenting: *Progress not perfection.* Another mantra I use in clinical work is, *Never give up on a child.* I have story after story of the power one person can have to change a child's or young person's life.

As examples, when I work in rural communities, I've seen that the person who can provide the right conditions to change a young person's life may be the school janitor. For another young person that I know, it was a school principal that noticed this young man could only spend half of his time in school and then would need to de-compress. That principal also noticed the young man loved talking about senior citizens. So she organized his schedule to let him spend half his day at school and the other half of the day playing bingo, helping clean up and doing other odd jobs at the seniors residence next door to the school.

That principal used her insight into a strength-based counseling approach and into her observation of skill-based preferences to help a young person benefit from schooling. She didn't simply think about the pathology of a boy who wouldn't come to school. She asked herself what she knew about him and focused on what she could learn about him through careful observation.

The reason to shift from believing our current assumptions about children so that we begin to ask what we actually know about them is based on understanding that brains can change throughout life.

The good news is that if you're working with people who believe they can't change, now you know they can. But people have to want to change. The question is, how to help people want to change.

It Starts At The Very Beginning

The brain is responsible for what we think. But when does thinking begin? It starts with the infant's development *in utero*. There's good research to show that if parents read to their baby *in utero*, after they're born babies recognize books that parents first read to them. They also recognize mom's voice and dad's voice. That's the positive side. But for babies whose moms are exposed to intense, persistent stress during pregnancy, there are signs they will have more problems later on, partly because stress affects a person's body chemistry. For example, levels of Cortisol increase in mothers that experience intense, persistent stress during pregnancy. Cortisol is a body hormone that's secreted by the adrenal gland. As Cortisol increases due to high stress *in utero* it affects the developing brain.

Human babies are born extremely dependant on their caregivers. Their brains weigh only about 1/3 to 1/4 of what they'll weigh by the time a child is 6 years old. That level of brain prematurity isn't seen in any other species. At birth, an infant brain is nine months premature. Researchers believe that human brain prematurity is related to ancestral experiences as earlier generations developed new skills, such as using tools and walking upright. An enlarging brain, built by this new experience, couldn't be delivered through the narrow and shallow pelvis of its mother. So the infant is delivered prematurely in terms of its brain. Despite this prematurity, a human baby is well designed to make sure there are systems set in place to have caregivers who are crazy about them and want to look after them.

What does that mean for the first year of life? During that year, babies should be treated as if they were in what we might call an external womb. As a consequence, the Canadian federal policy of 12-month parental leave should support the reality every infant finds itself in.

At birth all the billions of brain cells are in place and they have been since about the 20 weeks gestation period, but they haven't made significant connections or networks with other neurons. Many crucial developmental windows, or sensitive periods, are most open and responsive in the first 5 years of life. Research into brain development identifies the experiences children have in their earliest years as the source for making these essential connections among neurons in the brain.

Some actions aimed at paying attention to brain development in the early years are becoming common practice. As an example, at doctors' visits in the first two years of life a baby's head is measured. Why do doctors do this? Measuring the brain helps establish that new brain wiring is happening as it should. Babies who are extremely neglected show a failure to thrive, which is observable based on the size of their heads and their bodies, which don't grow at the right pace. It's experience during these early years that builds connections among all those brain cells. Development results from all the connections that happen in the brain. Given the profound vulnerability of babies in their first year, we must ensure that we have social policies to support young families so they can stay home or find loving caregivers, get the resources they need and have the general social support they require. We must support young mothers who develop depression or anxiety *post-partum* because this condition can interfere significantly with their ability to carry out the serve and return that babies require in order for early experiences to establish secure brain development.

At birth, everything is in place. But what happens during pregnancy to start the brain development ball rolling? The 'brain' starts to develop as a neural tube within a few days of conception and continues to develop throughout pregnancy and after birth. Brain cells migrate to their appropriate geographic location in the brain during the first 20 weeks of pregnancy, if no toxins interfere with this movement. Alcohol is a known toxin that not only affects facial features in the developing foetus and other physical features as well; it can also affect brain development throughout pregnancy.

In particular, alcohol affects where brain cells go, how they grow and how they communicate with one another.

Early in the first trimester of pregnancy the baby's face is developing. If high levels of alcohol are in the mother's blood during this time it can affect developing face cells so that they grow in a way that produces the identifiable features of Foetal Alcohol Effect (FAE). However, at any time during pregnancy alcohol can negatively affect the brain. The majority of people who have the foetal alcohol spectrum of disorders don't have the identifiable facial features. They may have a normal IQ but the brain is affected nonetheless. They may have issues that impede their progress, such as attention problems, self-regulation issues, learning difficulties and other developmental challenges. At no point during pregnancy is it safe for mothers to drink alcohol.

During brain development, the first cells to develop essential connections among the neurons are sensory. What do I mean? From the start, a baby's brain cells are in place in various areas of the brain and are set up to expect stimulating experiences to occur. The brain is ready and programmed to receive stimulation. As stimulating experiences occur and enter the brain, they come in first through the senses, as an example, through sound. Signals such as a mother's voice are picked up and sent through fingerlike branches called dendrites. Stimulation enters the brain and turns on chemicals that initiate a signal. As a signal gets stronger it reaches a critical threshold and causes the release of other signals to fire off a neurotransmitter, or cell messenger. These cell messengers cause the next brain cell, or neuron, to get into the action and start the firing process too. As stimuli come in over and over again, the signal gets stronger and stronger. As this happens, neurons fire these signals and connect with other neurons.

Cells communicate by sending out neurotransmitters into the space between neurons—an activity called synapses. It's the new synapses and dendrites (connections) that actually cause the increased brain size doctors measure in the first 2 years of life. As parents or caregivers read to babies over and over again, the process of creating synapses takes place. Connections between and among brain cells are re-enforced. If stimuli come in over and over again, they build a huge highway in the brain. It's built of all these connections that occur in cells that get used over and over again as stimulation enters the brain. If there is a little bypass that didn't get used very much it shrivels up and goes away; brain cells that fire up together are the ones that wire up together.

What's behind the drive to create these brain highways? The work of Dr Andrew Meltzoff was some of the earliest work that looked at a baby's drive to connect and imitate what was coming in through his or her experience. In a now famous paper[20], written in 1977, he included a picture of an adult and a very young baby. In the picture, the baby is clearly imitating the mouth gestures of the adult. I said earlier that a baby has an ability to ask for the environment that helps it survive. What does that look like? What's the purpose of the imitation captured in Meltzoff's picture? What does serve and return, the back and forth between adult and infant, accomplish in the early years?

Meltzoff's picture tells us about a human baby and the brain. His image demonstrates the powerful drive to connect that helps a baby learn it can have an effect on another person so that something happens. This capacity to connect creates a bond that has an adult fall crazily in love with the baby. In this way, babies learn they can make a difference. The baby experiences, "Wow, I do something and something happens back." It was a significant revelation that babies have this capacity.

With this revelation, people wanted to improve baby brain development. When scientists first started reporting that enriched environments stimulate brain growth in rats, people got very excited. If rats in enriched environments had better memories and bigger brains, wouldn't it be great to create enriched environments for human babies. People jumped on the bandwagon. Products flooded the market, such as Baby Einstein, flash cards and many others. But what if what works with rats doesn't fit human experience?

What babies need to grow great brains isn't fancy programs. They need daily back and forth, serve and return, that's possible during face-to-face interaction with loving, responsive, caring adults. Babies are intensely curious about their environments. They're like little scientists that pick up cues from all around them. As an example, some of the brain research describes babies in India that are able to observe adults precisely. As a result, they shake their heads in a particular way. These infants also note the particular way adults raise their eyebrows. As other examples, little babies can tell if someone they see on a screen is speaking their own language or a different language, even if the sound is turned off. As these little scientists notice clues from their surroundings, they learn about the environment and start learning communication strategies so that later on they can learn language.

A tiny infant has a remarkable capacity to engage adults so that this learning is possible. When I'm presenting to audiences I play a video to reinforce this point. The video captures the experience of a 7-day old child named Jordan interacting with his grandfather. As his grandfather puckers his lips, the baby does the same. The infant even reaches out to touch his grandfather. We see Jordan smile in delight in return to his grandfather's smile. When my youngest son was born in 1994 we wouldn't have recognized the social interaction pattern so clearly conveyed through the video between Jordan and his grandfather in our own little infant. We wouldn't have understood because we didn't expect this level of social interaction from a 7-day old infant. We thought it would come much later. In 1994, smiling, puckering, reaching toward an adult face was attributed to gas! We had no idea babies were that competent and capable from birth. What does the video tell us? It tells us that we need environments in which people fall madly in love with their kids through the serve and return of social interaction.

We also need to do more research on the importance of dads in babies' lives. We have all kinds of research on the impact of moms and babies and their inter-personal interaction, but we don't have nearly as much on the influence of fathers. What we do know is that when moms pick up their babies or interact with them, they use a baby voice. They say things such as, "Oh, you're so cute." When a dad comes in, he's more likely to say something like, "Hey, how're ya' doing kid." When babies are in their car seats, a mom will come in and snuggle up close. Dads come into the car and do this bump, bump thing on the baby's tummy to make the infant laugh. Dads interact differently with their babies. It's important to infant development that they do. As an example, how often have you seen a mom toss her baby in the air and catch it? Dads do that frequently. It's fantastic for babies.

The experience of being tossed in the air and caught fires different neurons than those that fire when an infant is cuddled. But when my kids were little, I didn't know it was good for them, neither did my husband. If dad threw his baby in the air, others would get nervous and say, "Oh no, don't do that. That's not good for the baby." We didn't have research to tell us it was good. It's important for a baby to have experiences of excitement and high energy and recognize that there are different ways people like to interact. The brain is a social organ. But there's something we need to keep in mind. It's a social organ that's affected by how much stimulation comes in.

The Power Of Words

Brains are built by experience. If it's good experience, the architecture that's formed is solid. If it's negative experience, that also builds the brain. Brain plasticity has a dark side. A baby can't discern whether an experience is beneficial or not. It's simply changed by experiences it has. Take for example, language development. In an important study, carried out by American psychologists Betty Hart and Todd Risley[21], they gathered data on the number and significance of spoken language in the early years. Hart and Risley devised a method for sampling the actual number of words that young children heard. They studied a group of 42 families over several years and counted up the number of words the children heard during that period of time. They also looked at the children's vocabulary development. These families were grouped in welfare, working-class and professional home categories.

What they found was that the number of words kids heard was very different based on whether they were living in a poorer family or in a well-to-do family. They observed that, on average, kids living in poorer families heard about 13 million words in the first 3 years of life. 13 million sounds like a lot. When you consider 13 million words, imagine those dendrites and neurons that are taking in information and sending out signals. The more often the stimulation comes in, and comes in over and over again, the bigger the brain's pathways. But with 13 million words coming in, how big is the highway compared to kids in well-off families who heard, on average, 43 million words in the early years? How big will brain pathways be if a child has heard 43 million words in the first 3 years of life? Right from the start, in those children there's already a 30 million-word gap between the two groups.

That gap is more than twice the number of words poorer children experienced in the first 3 years. Children in professionals' homes were exposed to an average of more than fifteen hundred more words per hour than children in welfare homes. Over one year, that amounted to a difference of nearly 8 million words, which, by age 4, amounted to a total gap of 32 million words. They also found a substantial gap in tone and complexity of the words used. As they crunched the numbers, they discovered a direct correlation between the intensity of these early verbal experiences and later achievement.[22]

Does the number of words a child hears really make a difference? When researchers looked at kids in the study to see how many words they had, they couldn't be certain of any differences at 16 months of age because language is just developing at that point. Differences showed up at 24 months. Children who heard more words had more language. By the time they start school (in Ontario kids start school at three years eight months) some kids have 500 words and others have 1200, 1300 or 1500 words.

What difference does it make if children access more words when they arrive at school? These children have more options. Suppose a child approaches another who has access to 500 words only. If a conflict arises, such as an argument over a toy, the child with 500 words will have fewer weapons of choice as he or she reacts to the first child. Generally, it will be the fists. If children have 1200 or 1300 words, they have access, not only to more words; they've had all kinds of experiences to help integrate signals in the brain. It's important to note in the Hart/Risley research that it wasn't just being poor that left children with fewer words. Some of the kids from a poorer family had 1200, 1500, even 1600 words. Why? These kids had moms and dads who talked to them, read to them and listened to them so that the back and forth movement between adults and children was maintained. Some of the kids with rich parents had only 500 words. Why? Both parents worked. They hired caregivers who weren't speaking to these children in their own language, or perhaps, in any language at all.

Another study was carried out to replicate the Hart & Risley study. These researchers looked at 19-month old children in poorer families in certain areas of the United States. During a 10-hour period, they put a little microphone on each child and listened to the spoken language these children experienced. They didn't count TV watching. Nor do videogames count in terms of holding the brain's attention for language. They counted face-to-face language experience. What they recorded in those 10-hour periods was a massive variation in the number of words a child heard. When they calculated the number of words per hour, some heard 67 words in a 60-minute period, which is a language experience that includes fewer words than someone will hear in a 30-second television commercial. Other children in the research heard 1200 words in that one-hour period.

The number of words children hear isn't a poverty issue. There are fantastic parents who rear kids in their own bedrooms while living in poverty yet parent better than some wealthy families who think they know it all and have it all. Positive language experience is about parenting; it's motivated by a concern for the well-being of children in the present and the future. But I'm not just talking about talking. Good language experience that builds healthy brain pathways throughout the early years is about talking to your baby and listening to what your baby says in return. It's about picking up a baby's cues and having the back and forth interaction, the serve and return that builds those big highways in the brain.

When Do We First See Empathy?

In addition to developing big brain highways based on a rich experiences of words, the empathy that a child develops through the back and forth experiences of good parenting helps a child learn the important social skills at the core of civil character—of becoming someone who cares about other people. If parents want their children to learn empathy, they spend time watching, listening and becoming co-researchers with them in the world when they are still very young.

Empathy is learned in relationship. Yet we're living in a society in which there's more parental isolation than we've had in the past. We're losing our parenting DNA. Adults aren't passing down ordinary practices that happened in a village or extended family. What does that mean for all of us during this present moment? I was recently in a meeting and was told about young parents who are desperate for information. They're talking and talking to their babies, but aren't listening to them. The children's treatment centre where I work developed a video called *Heads up and Ready to Roll.* The video teaches parents that it's good to put a baby on their tummy so the baby can have his or her head up as they learn to roll over. In my experience, this practice was common in the past. Parents didn't need a video. They'd seen aunts and uncles teach their babies how to roll over.

What does empathy look like? To depict it, I frequently show a video clip of research that was carried out by Felix Warneken and Michael Tomasello[23] in their research on altruistic behaviour in the early years. In one section of the video, a toddler who's about 15-18 months old is standing beside his mother who's seated in a chair in the corner of a room. She's watching the behavior of a stranger, an adult male. The man is standing in front of a closed cabinet, trying to put a few toys into it. He attempts to put them into the cabinet by softly banging them against its closed door. He carries out the action twice. The mother remains seated in the chair and watches the man who can't put away his toys. After a moment of observing the man's action, the toddler leaves his mother's side and goes over to open the cabinet for the man. He then looks up at the stranger and moves out of his way so he can put the toys away.

This brief clip eloquently captures the child's social nature. The small boy 'read the mind' of a stranger. The toddler hadn't been in the room before and hadn't viewed that particular dilemma before yet understood what the man was trying to do. He put himself in the mind of the other. We call this empathy. The researcher didn't cue the little boy or ask anyone for help. His mother didn't instruct him. He just knew what the man wanted to accomplish. He also looked up at the stranger to let him know that he could try again to put away his toys.

How did the toddler learn to do that? Was it a fancy program called Empathy-r-Us? No. The key is that the toddler already knew how to do it. He didn't learn empathy through a program. He learned it through thousands of interactions with loving adults that predictably responded to his needs. During these social experiences, they conveyed to him that it was all right to have these encounters and they would help him if he got stuck. The little boy appears well attached to his mother and seems to feel safe enough to venture away from her side to assist another person. Babies learn to read social cues by having their own cues read and responded to by those who care for them.

The power of serve and return is massive. We learn empathy though humane caring. A child can learn to care for others in high-quality programs for moms and tots but the most important ethos is in daily interactions each child has with people in his or her most intimate environment. As a result, we have to think of how to help families provide support for children during the early years? In addition, how can we encourage intergenerational connections among families so that healthy parenting practices are passed on? It still takes a village to raise a child. Village conditions impact all children within the sphere of their social influence.

THE IMPACT OF STRESS ON THE BRAIN

A final key concept in realizing the importance of early years experiences on serve and return is the impact of stress on the developing brain. When speaking about the early years, I frequently use a video clip produced by psychologist Ed Tronick that he calls the *Still Face Experiment.*[24] In the video, a mother faces her little one and plays with the baby. At one moment, the mother turns away and then faces the baby again with a still face (completely unresponsive). She shows no signs of engagement no matter what her baby does. At first, the baby tries to engage her mom. She points, smiles, gestures and then starts to protest until she's screeching. Because the mom doesn't respond, the baby becomes more and more distressed. She looks away, cries and even loses body posture by flopping forward in her highchair. The mother returns to interacting with the baby. All is well.

Imagine if children experienced a Still Face every day. What would happen? They would try and try but stress hormones would constantly, chronically be turned on. Eventually they would stop trying, but their stress levels would remain very high.

In the experiment, the baby experienced intense but passing stress. Based on much research, we now know what causes a human stress system to be activated by involving several systems in the brain. The Harvard Centre on the Developing Child has wonderful resources on the topic of stress in children's lives. In their work, they've demonstrated different levels and types of stress. First of all, there's positive stress. Not all stress is bad. Some stress motivates people to get things done. There's also tolerable stress, for example, if someone who's close becomes ill or dies. Illness and death are difficult to deal but nurturing, supportive relationships help people manage them. In contrast, toxic stress is worrisome and damaging. Toxic stress exists in a human system itself. It's systemic stress that's experienced repeatedly and unbuffered by healthy human relationships. Toxic stress is what children living in neglect and maltreatment experience every day.

In the video the little baby falls apart behaviorally. The child can't hold herself together bodily. The experiment lasts two minutes. During that time, mom doesn't respond in the usual way. Imagine the impact on the brain if toxic stress is continuous. The areas of the brain that are particularly vulnerable to high levels of stress hormones are those responsible for new memory and learning. Toxic stress affects areas of the brain that help with problem solving, thinking through to the consequences of actions, remembering and managing emotion. In other words, toxic stress impacts the very areas of the brain that allow a child to develop empathy and civility.

Do we know enough about the relationship between stress, the brain and the human stress system? Sonia Lupien and Robert

Sapolsky write about the complicated stress system in a way that makes it accessible. Sapolsky wrote a book called *Why Zebras Don't Get Ulcers*.[25] They don't get ulcers because, as they eat their food, the process of munching is stress relieving. The only time a zebra gets stressed is if a lion is around chasing or ripping a zebra apart. Human beings however are wonderfully creative. We can get stressed just by thinking about things. Lupien[26] looked at reasons people experience stress and situations that turn on stress system hormones. To explain the human stress system, she uses the acronym NUTS to stand for Novel, Unpredictable, Threat to the ego and Sense of loss of control.

If we look at her model and consider what makes us feel stress, we can apply it to many experiences. Suppose we say it's time pressure that stresses us out. But what is it about too little time or a looming deadline that's stressful? What is it that makes time feel stressful? Do we feel stressed, even if we're doing something difficult, if we've done it many times before? Again, if we're feeling stressed, we can ask ourselves, "Is it novel? Is it unpredictable? Is it a threat to the ego? Does thinking about it create the sense we may lose control?" I was teaching a class of 400 medical students and asked them to imagine they would be graduating June 30, 2016. I asked them to imagine July 1, 2016. The day before they were medical students. Now it's July 1, 2016. They're doctors in an emergency room. Is it NUTS? You betcha!

The stress system is an ancient system built to keep us alive and help us perceive and discern a threat and act on it. All mammals have a stress system. Deep inside the brain is a group of neurons, called the Amygdala and the Hippocampus. These areas of the brain form 2 parts of the body's stress system. They're part of a complex, marvelous system that keeps us safe. How does it work?

To put it simply, if we see a snake we need to have a system that's fast enough to allow us to react so we're ready to run or remain on guard. When we see the snake, a superfast signal is sent to our Amygdala—our fight, flight or freeze centre in the brain. We require input from other areas of the brain to help us discern whether it's a snake or a stick. Otherwise we would be jumping in fear every time we saw a linear object on the ground. We need a survival safety system. Otherwise we might say, "Oh, what's that interesting slithering thing?

Is that a rattling sound I hear?" We'd never survive as a species without a stress initiated survival system.

Stimuli turn on the Amygdala deep in the brain. The Amygdala sparks a series of signals that pass through several structures and reach the adrenals on top of the kidneys. Adrenalin is released. We're ready to run. We breathe faster and sweat. Our digestion slows as we prepare for disaster. Again, what happens if you skid on ice while driving your car? All the sensations you experience come from your adrenals in action. The experience of skidding sends a signal for the adrenals to release Cortisol—a stress hormone noted earlier.

Normally, Cortisol goes up in the morning and down at night. If we have a persistent stressor, the adrenals increase the release of Cortisol, which in turn converts into energy. As a result, if you're running, you can keep running. We need Cortisol in stress situations but also need the system to turn off the stress chemical tap. If the tap is always on with no way to shut down the signal our body is overwhelmed by these chemicals. High persistent levels of Cortisol are bad for brain and body.

In ordinary circumstances we have another part of the system to regulate the release of Cortisol, the Hippocampus. It's the cluster of neurons responsible for, among other things, new learning and memory. For example, because London cab drivers need to know so many different routes in and around London, they have huge Hippocampi.

The Hippocampus is part of learning. It's part of the stress system, both for memory as well as for regulating Cortisol levels. It has receptors on it that monitor how much Cortisol there is around and sends a negative feedback message to stop its release. There's a balancing act in the body: the Amygdala fires adrenaline and Cortisol; the hippocampus figures out what's going on and says, enough Cortisol and turns it off. However, the system can get primed to act too quickly and intensely. This is what happens in anxiety disorders and if kids experience toxic stress. The sad reality is that when a child's brain is forming in the earliest years it's the most vulnerable to the damages of toxic stress.

Children that experience toxic stress because they live in neglect or intense poverty or experience maltreatment will have exaggerated

Cortisol responses. Their Amygdalae seem to be easily triggered. They perceive threat and aggression in situations that may not be intended as such, but their brain energy is consumed by vigilance—for very good reasons. They're thinking, "Watch out! What's going on? Is this safe?" If the brain is absorbed with these messages and busy with them, the Hippocampus isn't free to learn about multiplication tables or how to get along with others. Let's take an ordinary example. Suppose a door slams shut very suddenly. For most of us it would be a surprise or shock. Our adrenaline would go up. But then we would say, Oh yes it's really windy. That's what happened. But for those who experience toxic, persistent stress, every time a door had slammed in the past they knew mom was coming in to beat them. What would their brains do? The thermometer for stress responses—how it gets turned on and how fast it goes up and stays up—is rigged in early childhood.

We know that high persistent levels of Cortisol can damage the brain, cause fibromyalgia and many other medical conditions. It also damages the learning system. It affects how the immune system is going to respond to stress later on. High persistent levels wire the brain and the immune system.

As a child psychiatrist working with children, I try and find ways to explain how the brain works to help the young understand the process so that they can become agents in their well-being and recovery.

I try to make things simple. I explain to them that when I heard about the stress system, the Amygdala made me think of a porcupine. I have a wonderful porcupine puppet to show them. When a porcupine senses danger it prickles up to protect itself. In the brain, the porcupine Amygdala starts a cascade of signals leading to a release of adrenaline and Cortisol. The porcupine sends a signal down through stress system pathways: Release adrenaline; release Cortisol; it's not safe here!

Now the Amygdala has a friend called the Hippocampus. I have a hippopotamus puppet. The Hippocampus is all about working with the porcupine and tries to tie together knowledge from earlier experience, connecting it to the present. Problems start if the porcupine is firing over and over again. If the porcupine isn't receiving messages from the hippocampus, it continues to bombard the hippopotamus as well as the brain. What happens under these conditions is that the hippo gets overwhelmed, tired and worn out and goes to sleep. What we know at the cellular level is that high Cortisol causes cell damage.

CONCLUSION

Why do the first five years last forever? The quality of a child's environment builds the infant, toddler and adolescent brain. It's the quality of adult/child relationships during the serve and return, back and forth of social interaction in everyday experience that sculpt its architecture so that, under favorable conditions, it provides a strong solid foundation for learning, particularly, learning to care about other people.

But the dark reality of brain plasticity is that poor environments create weak foundations. Toxic stress damages that foundation as much as does poor nutrition. The work of creating civil society is to address conditions that prevent families from being able to create healthy conditions for their children. Yet it's too easy to blame parents. We must wholeheartedly address barriers that are in the way of adults being the parent he or she longs to be. The willingness and ability to create a healthy relational environment is a responsibility of civic personality.

In this chapter, I've emphasized the role of at home, ordinary social interaction as the centerpiece of healthy brain development but I also want to acknowledge work Mary Gordon developed as a school-based program called *Roots of Empathy* that was referenced in an earlier chapter. She told this story to the Dalai Lama during a Seeds of Compassion Conference[27].

I love to repeat the story because it's a profound example of brain plasticity and hope. In her book, *Roots of Empathy*[28], she tells the story of a visit made to a school by a baby and its parents. It was an Elementary classroom. The baby and parents came to the class once a month for a school year. The kids watched the baby grow. They predicted what the baby might be doing at the next visit and learned lots of relevant material about a child's life. This is Mary's story.

> There was this one boy in the class who was 14 years old even though the other kids were 12 years old. Life hadn't been very good to him. He had seen his mom murdered when he was 4. He'd been in all kinds of foster homes. He'd likely had all of the diagnoses that I know how to give. The mom was talking this day about temperament as she interacted with her own baby in the class. She said, you know, we wanted a snuggly baby, but you get the baby that gets sent to you and you love him as he is. Our baby loves to interact with the world. So we had to get this snuggly pack. We put him in the snuggly pack and he kicks his legs and he interacts. She then asked if anyone would like to try the snuggly pack? Well didn't this boy say that he would like to. So up he came and the mom handed him the baby and the baby snuggled right in. And then during the rest of the class he sat in a rocking chair, rocking back and forth and the baby snuggled right in with that boy. At the end of the class he brought the baby back and handed him to its mom. Then he turned to the *Roots of Empathy* facilitator and said, "Do you think that someone who's never been loved can learn to be a dad?" That baby, that program changed that boy's life. He felt the power of connection.

I've touched in the chapter on neurons, synapses, temperament, non-verbal communication, empathy and the power of relationship. At the core of everything I want to convey is the power that one person can have on another person. The power conveyed through serve and return—of listening as much as we talk to our infants, toddlers, older children and adolescents. That's what we need to be taking into the work we do with our own kids and the kids in our communities. Can you imagine what would happen if we pooled the power of serve and return and brought its impact to our motivation to build an ecological model of human development that was introduced at the beginning of this chapter? What an enormous difference we could make for all the kids in our communities, our schools as well as in our cities.

10

THE RESILIENT CITY

INTRODUCTION

In the previous chapter, Jean proposed that the well-being of our country is linked to the well-being of our children. Their freedom to flourish arises from care they receive when they're very young. In her view, civility is built from a capacity to care for others that arises from being well cared for ourselves. It's motivated by social concern. Social literacy is its educational outcome. A willingness to be civil grows through learning the complex skills embodied in social literacy.

Jean also unpacked an ecological model of human development that's typified by a social order made up of concentric circles of caregivers who concern themselves with the welfare of others and offer relational support people need to survive and thrive, first in the family, then in the schools and communities they experience. An ecological development model relies on the policies and practices that enable people to be free to flourish. These policies and practices have roots in the principle of inclusion explored in the thought experiment outlined in chapter one, based on Paley's kindergarten experiences—a principle of inclusion that allows all children to enjoy the freedom to flourish at school.

At present, however, for many North Americans, living in a free country isn't the same as being free. This dissonance isn't what we expect in countries that enjoy abundance to an extent that's evident in

Canada and the United States. A lack of freedom hinders the growth of social literacy, which relies on a just distribution of relational resources that permit people to live fully human lives. Jean's concentric circles of human development work together best if the social order provides stability. Social literacy is a complex skill we learn by working towards stable complexity in human relationships. Its aim is to be authentic and well integrated with others so that we jointly maintain a relational habitat with the commitment, skill and energy many people expend to protect the earth's ecological environment.

In this chapter, I explore the city as a site for learning social literacy. My purpose is to say that the city is a meaningful living space if it provides a healthy environment. Cities aren't neutral spaces. They shape identity. We are who we are in part due to stories that circulate through cities, accumulating along public and private pathways, to coalesce in an image of what's possible and desirable in public life. The stories we choose, or fail to notice we use, shape expectations for city life. They have potential to support civility by inspiring our collective imagination. Urban research demonstrates that broad economic benefits result if we look after cities. Social literacy implies that we reward ourselves handsomely as we contribute to the well-being of interlocking streets and neighbourhoods that make up our fragment of civil life. If we choose to be civil, we're paid back in full because citizens enjoy more security, freedom and opportunity within a well-functioning city.

To affirm these points about cities, I first describe resilience, then situate the potential for learning social literacy in the myths, leaders and work that shape urban life. The meaning of cities is carried through myths that convey the way the world is, or could be. In addition, social literacy flourishes with a certain type of leadership. If leaders are bad and citizens are self-absorbed, cities flounder or capitulate to the highest bidder. In contrast, human needs theories call for the kind of neighbourliness that makes life bearable for all. To create ways that sustain the relational habitat of the city, good leaders know how to be good neighbours.

Meaningful work is also a component of healthy city life. In addressing work, I compare two cities, one built on efficiency and another on development, to demonstrate how resilience creates a civil society that knows how to treat people well and learns to rebound from societal setbacks. The word development is ambiguous in this chapter, as I hope will become evident. My purpose throughout is to position the resilient city at the heart of a socially literate, civil society.

RESILIENCE AND RECOVERY

For individuals or groups, resilience is neither fortress-like toughness nor unreflective accommodation. These strategies may allow someone to survive; resilience is an opportunity to thrive. It's a way of thinking that's characterized by accuracy and flexibility. It supports stable complexity. Resilience is a human capacity to adapt and thrive. It's a state of mind, a manner of thinking, a set of inner strengths and skills that focus on building healthy character. Some people seem to be born resilient. Others show us that resilience is a complex set of strategies that can become an acquired strength.

At this point, common definitions for resilience include the ideas that it's a pattern of positive adaptation in the face of past or present adversity, a set of inner resources, competencies and strategies that permit individuals to survive, recover and thrive after stressful events, so that people learn from these experiences how to function better in the future. It's a thinking style that enables people to rebound from life's setbacks.

From my own perspective, resilience includes complex emotional and social skills, resources and strategies that are organized around seven components. These components are connection, courage, mindfulness, empathy, work/life satisfaction, emotional literacy and social literacy. I developed these competencies in the approach designed for the not-for-profit youth agency in Edmonton Alberta Canada called iHuman that's mentioned in the Preface. The program is called *Building for Resilience* (BFR). Its seven components are described as follows:

- **Connection** is a felt sense and process of reaching out to people and opportunities to join with them so that those links are secure, dependable and interdependent. With a healthy sense of felt connection, we're as comfortable and quick to reach out to get help, as we are to reach out to give it. The opposite of connection is isolation.

- **Courage** is a way of thinking and acting that takes account of fear, doesn't turn away or shrink back, but grasps opportunities with bravery and boldness. It's neither cowardice nor rashness but involves people in loving, forgiving (releasing) and saying ouch when someone hurts them. Courage is similar to Dr Martin Brokenleg's four part (on-line) model for courage that includes belonging, independence, mastery and generosity. To fit with the overall BFR program, I substitute the term agency for his term independence.
- **Mindfulness** involves emotional and mental awareness. Emotional awareness is an ability to identify personal feelings before, during and after an encounter and to recognize emotions in other people. It's a set of skills, strategies and knowledge that allows people to recognize and account for emotions that arise within them and within other people. Mental awareness refers to what a mind can do—its capabilities—which are the mind's capacity to focus attention so that learning occurs, to expend energy to pay attention, to see what's going on, to understand, reason, make decisions and put them into play, to make new decisions and to be conscious of past and present experience at the same time. A primary skill for mental awareness is critical thinking, which focuses attention on the assumptions (memes) that people rely on in the life stories or myths they live by.
- **Empathy** is the ability to describe and convey what someone else is going through in a way the other acknowledges is accurate, often referred to as empathetic responsiveness. Some of the important ideas in empathy include a need to be empathetic with ourselves *and* with others; empathy may/may not include feeling sympathy for/with someone else; empathy helps us resist being obsessed by or consumed with ourselves or other people.
- **Life/work Satisfaction** is a hopeful sense of personal happiness built on the fulfillment of basic needs, self-care, connection with others, compassion, creativity, persistence and fair play. BFR asks

people to reflect on what they believe about happiness. Specific time and relational management strategies help people consider the nature of their work/life balance. Two primary questions shape a person's understanding of life/work satisfaction: What do I bring to the table? What's it like for other people to work with me?

- **Emotional Literacy** is the ability to read emotions and keep behaviour aligned with important personal core values. The goal of emotional literacy is authenticity. A model for authenticity is found in Socrates' *Apology,* a speech he gave at his trial to explain his understanding of what makes life good. Emotional literacy is an underlying emphasis for building resilience; authenticity is at the heart of the self-assessments that are outlined at the end of chapter two of this book, all of which form part of the BFR program.
- **Social Literacy** is the ability to read what's going on during a social interaction and enhance or repair that encounter while people are still in it. The goal of social literacy is integration, which isn't simply conceptual understanding but involves learning complex practical social skills. These skills are supported and enhanced by the self-assessments that comprise the program and through the guided interactions among people that engage in the program throughout the time they spend together.

All components of *Building for Resilience* circulate around a pivot point—transformative learning. Transformation comes about as people become aware of how they think and act and ask themselves whether these are ways they want to continue to think and act. Learning of this kind requires us to remove our lenses, like taking off eye glasses, to have a look at how we use these lenses to see the world. When we put them back on, we're aware of how they influence what we see. We become critically aware of our own thinking and acting, not simply to abandon it, but to become conscious and intentional about the ways we think and act.

Emotional literacy (authenticity) and social literacy (integration) are learned together during BFR and create a counterpoint to strengthen each other. These two terms provide a framework for helping people to know how to be themselves when they're with others, whether it's people that matter a great deal, or work mates, acquaintances or even strangers. An enhanced social literacy is an outcome of the BFR program.

The heart of these components of resilience is a strong felt sense of connection made possible by our ordinary human capacity to be in relationship with others. A felt sense of connection is more than an awareness, it's a reliable assurance that gives permission to trust and depend on others to provide fundamental human needs, i.e., the relational resources people need to live a fully human life. A secure sense of felt connection is conveyed by a willingness and ability to reach out to people and opportunities, to join with them, so that those links are reliable.

Connection is at the heart of BFR, but is also the heart of civility. The opposite of connection is isolation. People that are isolated live inside a worldview they organized from childhood that is based on the meaning they've made out of life events. If people are isolated, their own story of how the world works is the only one they hear. They have a hard time believing there are other ways to experience life. They tend to think and act alone and aren't self-aware. If they're leaders in the workplace, like Tom, they perpetuate isolation that keeps others inside individualistic silos of experience. For Tom, collaboration is too costly. Isolation is a social virus but comes to feel as if it's the only safe way to experience the world in a workplace that's led by people like Tom.

Isolation is a serious social problem that forecloses on our ability to be resilient and on our willingness and ability to be civil. Isolated people may appear strong, but their strength is brittle, easily shattered, perhaps as an outcome of brokenness itself. These people barricade themselves and explode under pressure. They're difficult if not impossible to connect with; ultimately, at times, they may be dangerous to be around. They live in a world that's on the edge of collapse. If people want to be socially literate, they must perceive the effects of isolation and redress damage it creates during social interaction. Isolation flourishes if a context conveys a particular sort of myth about social life.

MYTH AND THE MEANING OF CITIES

Isolation leads to collapse but contains another serious error as well. It misleads us about social life. The presence of other people is a social fact—regardless of how we think about or feel toward them, and regardless of whether they meet our most pressing needs effectively, or fail to do so. Isolation isn't only uncivil; it forecloses on resilience because it's an attempt to convey that other people don't matter. Given the existential quality of social life, this is a delusion—one that fails to acknowledge how others are involved in our own survival. Due to its inaccuracy about social life, isolation breeds social instability.

Resilience flourishes in communities typified by stable complexity. With stable complexity, we have a habit of paying attention to stories we live by and asking whether they meet fundamental human needs. We choose and support good leaders. We work hard to create and sustain meaningful work. If we lived in a perfect world, we wouldn't need to be resilient. Like justice, resilience tells us what to do if relational needs aren't met or when unavoidable life circumstances create hardship and trauma. Resilience is about making repairs to the relational habitat rather than longing for a perfect city. It's a telltale sign of social literacy.

Jean and I agree that social literacy depends on a healthy environment. This chapter is about cities because they're big enough, but not too big, to focus creative energy on common problems facing human development. Ecological wisdom encourages people to be human and humane by thinking globally (humanity as a whole) and acting locally (addressing particular needs).[1] If we look after cities, we create and perpetuate memes that undergird equality, promote humanizing images of all citizens, offer learning opportunities for all forms of literacy, create support for leaders who know how to foster neighborliness and engage in every effort to make work meaningful and satisfying.

As we'll see, cities operate as model and opportunity for serving aims and functions of social literacy. City life is accessible. The possibilities it offers to those who are socially literate are boundless. Whether it's because we keep the streets in our neighbourhood free of trash, vote thoughtfully after considering candidates carefully, tend a beautiful front yard, volunteer at a local not-for-profit or elementary school's reading program, donate to causes that help the poor or greet people with a smile as we pass them on the street, social literacy enhances city life. Those who are socially literate express a fundamental freedom to make the world a better place and carry out relational habitat maintenance to benefit everyone who lives within the city limits.

Every city is a system. The structures of a given city produce the behaviour we see in it—for better or worse.[2] Canadian urban theorist Jane Jacobs argues that the energy that originated in city life was a sustained, creative interdependent city economy that made possible other new kinds of work, including agriculture.[3] She argued that cities, not rural agrarian areas, were the genesis of economies that spurred the development of human culture, which was the main driver of its evolutionary surge, "outrunning environmental and physical constraints."[4] Human beings can't live without their cultures,[5] which are rich systems of experience, fact and myth.

Another urban theorist, Lewis Mumford, noted research that explores the origin of cities and pointed out that it relies on evidence wrapped in myth.[6] Pre-history is full of stories that tell about what we think happened when we've no written record. It's important to keep in mind that we're reading myth as we encounter that research, which isn't the same as saying it's untrue. For example, Mumford identified a formative invention of Neolithic technology, not in weapons and tools, but in the making of containers. Tools and weapons support the movement and muscle that are essential to nomadic existence. Once cities develop, people depend on inventions to enable settlers to shift from large-scale hunting to farming and from gathering to gardening so that they can remain in one place and sustain themselves.

Evidence suggested to Mumford that containerizing produce in clay and other materials was essential to forming city life. Or, perhaps, it was cities that made their invention necessary. He extended his metaphor to say that a city is a special kind of container, a "receptacle for storing and transmitting messages."[7] The image of cities as centralized messaging spaces connects to the meme concept developed in the chapter on cultural learning. Memes are messages that cities preserve and publicize. Civic-minded people raise questions about what the memes in their cities limit and allow. The image of a city as a central messaging space is crucial for seeing its potential to harm or help the growth of social literacy.

In Mumford's view, this messaging capacity has potential to make a city into a symbiotic site or a predatory space. From a different perspective, but to make a similar point, Foucault said that a city must be a coercive system—everyone's freedom is strictly curtailed—or it must be a site with punitive institutions to incarcerate people who refuse to use urban freedoms wisely. He offered a choice between two negative outcomes: a coercive infrastructure applied to everyone versus imprisoning institutions applied to a few. Implicitly, incarcerating institutions are preferred, at least by those who manage to remain outside of them.

Mumford thought civic liberty might be possible but was hard to achieve. In the tension between freedom for no one and incarceration for a few there lives a longing for a quality of city life that strongly influences civic imagination. In the trajectory of urban discourse, there's an underlying, persistent longing for a perfect city. Historically, civic perfection was held up against the image of evil city life. Myths of a perfect city dogged the heels of thinkers, from Christian theologians such as Augustine and John Knox, secular theorists such as Jean-Jacques Rousseau and Karl Marx, to city developers[8] such as Le Corbusier (1887-1965).[9] Their theories shaped the stories we tell about civic life. In paying attention to them, we become freer to think about the stories we want to perpetuate as a way to shape our own city life.

Augustine's book *The City of God* portrayed peace as its primary driving force and the essence of civic perfection. Peace, he believed, was possible only with eternal life that came after this earthly life.[10] John Calvin (1509-1564), a founder of Protestantism, saw Geneva as a site for radical reform to unite spiritual, moral and civic life to achieve the creation of a theocracy—a city ruled by God's Providence. He wanted Geneva to be that perfect city. John Knox, a leader of Presbyterianism, saw Geneva as 'the perfect school of Christ'. Although most people in Geneva supported Protestantism, the degree of religious control over civic life was contentious.

At the time, there was a strong reaction against the evils of another dominant city, Paris in France—a tension that tended to go along with idealizing Geneva. Rousseau (1724-1776), a modern French reformer, romanticized country life by writing the novel *Emile* in which he described rearing the boy in rural quietness, peace and solitariness—outside Paris. Emile was Rousseau's version a new Adam, a modern individual. His romantic love-hate ambivalence toward cities is embedded in myths we continue to tell. Whether due to religious zeal or a desire for architectural purity, modern cities contend with a perfectionism that drove some of the horrors of eighteenth, nineteenth and twentieth century injustice. Modern city development is multi-layered; its texture is felt in the tension among cities characterized by dynamic complexity and cities that form around one dominating system of myth, leadership and work. The search for the perfect city is at the core of that tension.

Searching for perfection also fueled a modern secular thrust that became the tragedy of development. Many modern city developers relentlessly constructed then erased civic spaces in their search for the perfect city—projects they carried forward simply because they could, despite the human cost.[11] Before addressing an urban theorist who didn't prize perfection, and who constructs a city myth that supports social literacy, I pick out relationships between religion and humanity to say more about myth's role in understanding cities. My purpose is to help civic minded people reflect on myths that circulate through city life so that they can ask themselves whether these are stories they want to continue to live by.

Myth Matters

What is myth? From Neanderthals onward, as one example, it's evident that humanity had a belief in a future life similar to life lived on earth. As a consequence, people told stories to explain life after death, although they couldn't see it for themselves. Myths offer meaning. We're meaning-seeking beings and easily fall into despair without myths to hold this world and the next in a relationship that makes sense, whether our stories suggest there is life after death, in which humanity continues in some form, or there isn't a next life—life on earth is all there is. In either case, with myth, we can't be certain. We take myths on faith. As a consequence of not knowing for sure, we use stories—or accept stories revealed to us—to communicate the meaning and value that life on earth holds for us. Rituals surrounding death are a clear sign of the presence of myths that explain and require these rituals and give them significance.

Human beings have ideas that go beyond everyday experience. A sense of what's beyond the present moment is nourished by the imagination, which is the faculty that links religion and myth. Myths aren't necessarily true or false; they're meaningful. Reason may tell us what's true; imagination tells us what's real. Myth tells us about extreme, one time only experiences and about invisible, ultimate realities. Early in human history, myth wasn't theology in a modern sense. It was about experience. Myths aren't escapist. They force people to face up to the realities of life and death.[12] Myth is about transcendence—a capacity hard-wired into being human. It's a capacity to go beyond the ordinary, to be moved by someone or something beyond what's experienced through the five senses. It's a capacity to feel ecstasy and imagine what life could be like even if it isn't good at present. Transcendence is scientifically verifiable as a human capacity. It allows us to connect with others, the world and what's beyond visible reality.

In moments of transcendence we rely on stories about what the world beyond our senses is really like and what to expect from this life. It's not a question of whether people use myth to make sense of life—it's about which myths they use. Myths are stories we live by. Everyone has them. As one example, Freud invented his un-neighborliness myth to counter and eradicate, if possible, certain other myths.

The need for myth to offer meaning is as great as our need for food, clothing and shelter. Myths nurture and protect us. They arise culturally, although people may not be conscious of their content. Myths are somewhat automatically relied upon, especially if things go wrong. If someone were to ask us, we might not be able to tell that person about our myths, or we might feel too shy to do so. Myths, especially religious ones, tell us what leaders, citizens, cities and work are about. Just as genes are recipes for how to make a human body, myths are meme environments that tell us how to make human life bearable. At their core, they tell us how to treat ourselves and other people. They function by forming and informing citizens, by conveying the significance of everything and everyone.

In their role as central messaging spaces, cities contain myths and convey them to those who live there. These myths have power to humanize or dehumanize a city's populace. Myths may also be captured in visual images, for example, that prize and promote gender equality or advertize women's subservience to men's sexual preferences. They may focus attention on accumulating wealth as the sole indicator of social value or they may support a society in which healthy family life and the well-being of the young are what make a city great.

Myths have a particular function. Cities were initially sites of religious worship but over time the gods seemed increasingly distant. As American theologian Karen Armstrong outlines their development, by 800 B.C.E., the emergence of religious and secular myth-rich systems as we know them took place. From 800 to 200 B.C.E., the *Axial Period*, traditions arose including Confucianism and Taoism in China, Buddhism and Hinduism in India, monotheism in the Middle East and Greek Rationalism in Europe. They were associated with Hebrew prophets of the eighth to sixth centuries (B.C.E.), the sages of the *Upanishads*, the Buddha (c.563-483) in India, Confucius (551-479), the author of the *Dao De Jing* in China and fifth century Greek philosophers, e.g., Socrates (469-399), Plato (c. 427-347) and Aristotle (384-322) B.C.E.[13]

These traditions gave myth an interior and ethical interpretation. Myths are moral stories. While these traditions aren't identical, they were acutely conscious of suffering and stressed the need for more spiritual, less external ritual practices. They insisted that worshippers should treat fellow-creatures with respect, recoiled at violence and preached compassion. They taught people to look for truth in themselves, not only to rely on priests and religious experts. They taught that old values should be questioned and subjected to critical scrutiny. While they proposed that myths could be recast, they insisted that myth itself was a human necessity. To lose touch with our stories is to lose an aspect of our humanity.

The Post-Axial Period (200 B.C.E.-1500 C.E.) saw the rise of three monotheistic religions that claimed to be historical as well as mythical. Jews, Christians and Muslims believe that God is active in history and in actual events in this world.[14] They maintain a commitment to myths that tell us how to treat others and ourselves; they're moral as well as religious systems. Religious myth places limits on how we treat each other because everyone is accountable to God. Secular myths set rational limits on moral action by appealing to humanity and often base that obligation on Greek Rationality or the myth of a Social Contract, as did Rousseau in the 1700s.

With the rise of modernity, after 1500 C.E., there was constant moral tension between modern developers and ethical systems embedded in religious and secular myths. The perfect city plays a role in that tension. It's as essential to read secular myths that inform city life, as it is to understand religious ones. In reading myth reflectively, and discerning its impact on habits of heart, mind and body, we can consider the possibility of city life without wishing for perfection. But we're well advised to pay attention to humanity's need for myth. Social literacy won't flourish without the moral core communicated by both religious and secular myths as outlined above. The wisdom of these traditions places how we treat one another at the centre of what it means to live a good life—which is not to say a perfect one.

CITY LEADERSHIP

Jane Jacobs refused to search for the perfect city. As a widely referenced urban theorist, she pointed to a city's potential to create and sustain stable complexity so that diversity stimulates more diversity and keeps a city healthy. To her, civility is a balance of interdependence and privacy,[15] like the rhythm of social literacy that supports authenticity and integration and the dynamic capacity our genes possess to be assertive and integrated within a living human being.

For Jacobs, cities need all kinds of diversity, intricately mingled in mutual support so that city life operates decently and constructively and citizens sustain and advance their society and civilization as a whole.[16] I rely on her theories to carry forward Mumford's central messaging role for the city, but first pick out leadership patterns written across human history that impact whether stable complexity will thrive in cities—that is, the emergence of their leaders.

A leader is someone who has followers. One who's capable of generating civic structures that enhance stable complexity is someone who asks good questions about the myths that shape city life, reflects on what it means to lead a particular group of people so they flourish as citizens and continues to learn while leading. Leadership raises issues that must be understood; especially about the stories leaders tell themselves about privilege.

Leadership myths go back a long way. The first Greek historian, Herodotus, tells the story of twelve warriors (equals) that wanted to establish a settlement so they chose one of their members to be king. The king chosen built his rule on one condition. None of the eleven were to visit him at home without telling him they were coming. Now that he was king, they needed an appointment. He gave them reasons that protected his privacy and set him apart; e.g., he might be with his wife and wouldn't wish to be disturbed.

One of the eleven refused to conform to his rule and visited the king unannounced. The new king killed him. The pattern of kings kept to this route. Once a man was set above others to govern, he came to see himself, and be seen by others, as a different sort of person with distinct privileges. Regardless of their ordinary humanity, kings stand above others. This was Foucault's point in describing sovereign power. Kings have opportunity to separate themselves from other citizens. In that separation—in their position, prestige and power—they mete out retribution and take in tribute. As a result, they might build kingship on what social theorist Jared Diamond referred to as 'kleptocracy'.[17] In contrast to egalitarian leaders, kings of this sort use separation to gather an excess of goods and wealth.

The bargain of kingship runs something like this: kings provide essential, useful services to everyone by receiving tribute and assessing taxes. They have a positional advantage to take and keep payment for these services. Given their access to tribute, taxes, soldiers and property, they may take to a limitless extent and impoverish people they were chosen to lead. Opportunity to take is built into a king's double value.[18] The myth of superiority gives kings permission to take resources as they wish and to do so capriciously.

But being a leader is not synonymous with being a bad king. Diamond analyzed practices of many leaders and noted that, while some unabashedly transfer net wealth from commoners to upper classes, the difference between a kleptocrat and a wise statesmen, between a robber baron and a public benefactor, is one of degree: the issue is the amount of what's kept by the king and handed out to privileged people versus the degree of redistribution to ordinary citizens.[19] He noted that President Mobutu of Zaire is a kleptocrat because "he keeps too much tribute (the equivalent of billions of dollars) and redistributes too little tribute (no functioning telephone system in Zaire)" compared with George Washington who spent taxes on widely admired public programs and didn't enrich himself as the first President of the United States of America.[20]

The distance between leaders and followers is not the essential conflict when someone becomes a kleptocrat. Distance is part of good leadership. It's there for a reason. In observing the dance of civil life, a good leader goes up to the balcony, so to speak, and observes the people, patterns, practices and purposes of those who move around the dance floor. Leaders must live in enough solitude to allow them to lead with integrity.

Tension Paley felt as she discussed the rule 'you can't say you can't play' is remarkable for its insight. She felt pressure from a desire to conform to social hierarchies children brought to kindergarten. She felt a pull from her own experiences of exclusion and recognized that there's something compellingly attractive about being on side with winners: beautiful, wealthy people that make us feel good about ourselves if they turn attention to us. That lure has social power. Yet it's distance that keeps leaders just and fair. If they use distance wisely, it's a wellspring of moral courage.

One difference between cities that flourish and those that flounder is found in their leadership's refusal to be greedy and use distant from ordinary people to stockpile goods for themselves. Leaders are similar to and different from citizens. In working out tension between being near and different, they rule justly or take too much for themselves. The myths they live by inform and justify their behaviour. Contemporary political ideologies that leaders use to support their rule won't promote justice unless these myths are committed to the equal worth of everyone at some level.[21]

In an earlier chapter, I outlined Freud's distain for the masses. Myths of privilege spread widely in the last century among participatory democrats of the New Left, even though they professed to be egalitarian. At the end of the 1960s, a prime example was Herbert Marcuse's book *One Dimensional Man*, a paradigm among left-thinking social democrats. According to him, Freud and Marx were obsolete but their offensive attitude toward ordinary people didn't disappear. Marcuse wrote that:

> the masses have no egos, no ids, their souls are devoid of inner tension or dynamism: their ideas, their needs, even their dreams, are 'not their own'; their inner lives are 'totally administered,' programmed to produce exactly those desires that the social system can satisfy, and no more...[and they] recognize themselves in their commodities; they find their soul in their automobiles, hi-fi sets, split-level homes and kitchen equipment.[22]

Despite its protestation to dismiss him, Marcuse's sentiments echo the derogatory myth Freud perpetuated about humanity as a whole.

Bad leaders use distance to disdain ordinariness as a way to justify their privileged access to excess. Cynicism about humanity is endemic to the corrupt rule of kings. Even modern kings think of ordinary people as machines.[23] Dawkins's idea that genes are replicators and the human body is its machinery is a cynical, reductionist view of humanity as a whole. Myths that leaders tell about humanity give permission to use and abuse people.

Goleman summarized leadership by pointing out that good leaders are great listeners, encourage people, communicate effectively, are courageous, have a good sense of humor (not in a mocking tone), show empathy, are decisive, take responsibility, are humble and share authority. Having a bad boss is like talking to a blank wall. Bad leaders are driven by doubt, are secretive, intimidating, have bad tempers, are self-centered, indecisive, arrogant, mistrustful, and blame others when things go wrong.[24] Because they have a positional advantage, if leaders act without mercy or justice, they engender conditions of servitude in people that work for them. If you recall Beck and Cowan's analysis, they present a closed model for leadership, one that prevents people from realizing their full potential.

Cities And Inequality

Inequality is an outcome of bad leadership. I want to explore the idea that cities structure behaviour and open up or close down the possibility of a fully human life for many citizens. American journalist Barbara Ehrenreich took on three roles in a life experiment to answer the question of whether the lowest rung of working class people in the United States could afford housing. She became a waitress, a cleaner and a Wal-Mart salesperson to study relationships between minimum wages and housing.[25] She noted that every one of the six jobs she took on required concentration and the mastery of new tools and skills. Though she's highly educated, each job involved a steep learning curve and was a self-contained social world with its own personality, hierarchy, customs and standards. Each job made her sort out these systems from the bottom, a talent that was necessary for her survival.

At the end of her research, she concluded that salaries were too low and rents were too high for an average healthy person in the United States to maintain herself by the sweat of her brow. Her summary pointed out that, since wealth has been steadily increasing globally (for the past 150 years), low wage earners have fallen behind that trend. Falling behind creates and sustains a dependent, available class of workers to fulfill the least desirable jobs in a capitalist economy. Her observations of the least advantaged were consistent with brain-body research on effects of social oppression. At the start, she wondered why low-wages earners didn't just apply for other positions, especially since she saw they were treated without respect. She summarized their behavior and saw it as endemic to their economic position. Why didn't they protest? She offered several reasons for their silence.

In the first place, they didn't know about their options and worked such long hours they couldn't find time to see a doctor when necessary, let alone search for other jobs. They followed an unwritten rule she referred to as 'the money taboo'. Workers don't talk about wanting more money without risking retaliation. No one wants to reveal they're underpaid in a society that celebrates wealth. While we openly compare the price we pay for things, no one wants to compare the price they're paid, unless the salary is six-figures (and in Canada is reported in the newspaper).

Another aspect of silence among low-wage earners is related to the deference they give to unreasonable, cruel bosses. Deference amounts to a loss of self-respect if one is at the same time dismissed even when reasonable requests arise from significant beliefs or family needs. Goleman analyzed harmful effects of an oppressive organization[26] to say silence encourages a bad king's exploits. Deference itself acts back on workers to imprison them further in a harmful setting. While deference might offer workers a chance to feel close to a powerful, wealthier person, so it has a tiny, temporary payback, it's part of the social system created by poor wages.

Showing obvious and persistent deference to a boss fulfills his or her unjust expectations. As with all kleptocrats, bad bosses expect workers to express effusive esteem, to signal that employment is a favor they extend rather than a contractual agreement both sides control and shape through democratic processes of request and complaint. The excess attention bad bosses expect is a demand they can enforce by withholding a worker's civil rights. Ehrenreich was warned as she became a waitress that her purse could be searched at any time. Drug tests, rules about talking, warnings about 'time theft', unreasonable work schedules—all were used to keep workers silent. Those who stepped out of line faced unexplained punishments, had schedules and assignments unilaterally changed, experienced direct confrontation and threats of job loss, or were fired without cause.

She concluded that "if low-wage workers do not always behave in an economically rational way, that is, as free agents within a capitalist democracy, it is because they dwell in a place that is neither free nor in any way democratic,"[27] and that violates the social contract that holds a society together. Social literacy doesn't survive if people are treated like machines and social contracts are violated. It may be a sign of abuse if workers are "preposterously deferential and uncritical" of their leaders.[28]

Once again, deference shown to leaders isn't inherently harmful. Deference allows for distance between leaders and followers, mentioned earlier, and permits leaders to act in a manner that's fair to everyone. Attention is like money—it measures human worth. A reasonable amount expresses human value. If desire turns to obsession, social life is threatened. As with kleptocrats who take too much money and withhold social goods, attention addicts build fortresses around themselves that are typical of narcissism. Those afflicted with a desire for excess attention are socially and emotionally unavailable when ordinary human needs arise. Bad kings barricade themselves behind the demand for unreasonable amounts of attention and turn a work setting into an abusive context.

Bad bosses create abusive contexts but one person alone can't generate all the effects abuse initiates. Most workers are actively or passively complicit with abuse or the boss couldn't be successful at sustaining it. While bad bosses aren't solely responsible for systemic abuse, they're in the best position to improve a work environment. But they may mistakenly feel justified in receiving excessive deference because of myths they tell themselves about what to expect from life. As a result, the system operates at the level of the lowest common dominator.

WHAT'S TO BE DONE?

How would social literacy impact institutional abuse? In being authentic and integrated, socially literate people are well aware of what's going on. To begin with, they realize they have several options. Firstly, they may affirm an abusive work culture, which implies full, uncritical participation and absorption in it. Secondly, they may negate it, which implies unending criticism that allows cynicism to fester. Thirdly, they may withdraw into apathy, turn away and refuse to take responsibility for the situation. Fourthly, they may drown in social warfare that wears them out and marginalizes them as well.

While it's important to acknowledge these options and consider their impact, social literacy supports none of these reactions but tries to pick its way toward healthy democratic participation. These four futile reactions to institutional abuse—absorption, cynicism, apathy and exhaustion—get in the way of social literacy. Absorption and exhaustion suffocate attempts to bring about change because people are enmeshed in an unjust context. Cynicism and apathy encourage emotional distance and fail to engender concern for maintaining the relational habitat of a workplace. Socially literate people initiate change, realizing that it's "not...revolution which should give meaning to life; one must first love life in order...to become a revolutionary."[29]

Social literacy produces change by relying on developed capacities to speak the truth while remaining concerned for and connected to those who are different, but also knows that "trust is feasible only where honesty is usual."[30] Speaking truth requires support from others. Karl Marx understood that fact when he urged workers of the world to unite.[31] It's costly to speak the truth except in communities that support equality and promote important public goods. A public good is "an institution or attribute of society from which no one is excluded. Clean air is an example, as are stable property rights that make market exchange possible, or good non-tolled roads and national defense.[32]

Speaking the truth may be dangerous but it's also the first step to freedom. Social literacy is an activity of learning how to be near and different from others—how to be in relationships without getting lost in them—how to integrate with others and remain authentically able to exercise voice.[33] The idea of voice implies it's possible and not too costly to speak openly if we're being hurt by a given context. Voice refers to the freedom to say that certain conditions are objectionable. It doesn't develop if people have no safe exit from a context that's causing pain. Exercising voice is integral to becoming socially literate.

Voice is absent in abusive settings and extreme poverty. Extreme poverty is a trap characterized by disease, isolation, climate stress and environmental degradation so that families are chronically hungry, unable to secure health care, have no access to safe drinking water, sanitation, education for all their children and many lack rudimentary shelter, or essential clothing, such as shoes.[34] These conditions exist in Canada and the United States. Civic responsibility implies addressing them if they're found inside one's own city limits. The four reactions—absorption, cynicism, apathy or exhaustion—do nothing to alleviate suffering at home or around the globe and don't teach people how to exercise voice. Resisting these reactions is hard intellectual, emotional and cultural work that relies on social intelligence informed by our best understanding of universal human needs.

What Does Everyone Need?

I've been saying that human beings have relational needs, basic to their capacity to survive and thrive. How does addressing human need build social literacy and contribute to a thriving city? Collaborating with social theorist Amartya Sen, whose work at the United Nations has impacted human rights globally, as well as with women in Africa and India, American philosopher Martha Nussbaum analyzed human needs that would support social literacy because they imply a fundamental human need for relational resources so that all people may live a truly human life.[35] To her, as with Pierre Bourdieu, human needs are first met at home. Social literacy is grounded on material/relational support parents give children through their caring concern. A primary parental gift is emotional availability, which requires their needs to be adequately met.

Nussbaum created a comprehensive list of needs based on her perspectival *capabilities approach* in which she invites people to see neighbors in a new way. Her list takes nothing for granted. It's built on experiences she had among women who are poor and marginalized, living in India and Africa without the most basic rights of a fully human life. Nussbaum used her experience to reveal conditions that are worse than those of the low wage earners that

Ehrenreich studied. But this isn't to say conditions in America are acceptable.

Poverty (above all, enduring poverty) limits individual capacity for autonomy and self-esteem[36] and violates basic requirements of a civil society. Even if the poor in America today are better off than the poor were 100 years ago, or, as are poor women elsewhere (as some might argue), poverty is relative. The city is shaped by the position of the majority. For those left out, the effects are corrosive.[37] Suppose a man hasn't the resources to own a car. Cities are built around car travel. His ability to lead a full life is restricted by his lack of access to transportation, unless public transportation is entirely effective for him. If the majority of people drive their own cars, the need for effective public transportation has little influence on policy and practice. His job prospects are thereby limited by the way the majority of city dwellers are able to live.

Inequality endangers society.[38] People hate living alongside extravagance if they don't have enough to eat. Even if they're isolated from the wealthy, they see extreme wealth on TV or in the street. Images of wealth are inescapable. Equality theorists know opportunity and merit aren't built on what people can do on their own. Bill Gates Sr. said it clearly about the U.S.:

> Success is a product of having been born in this country, a place where education and research are subsidized, where there is an orderly market, where the private sector reaps enormous benefits from public investment. For people to assert that they've grown wealthy in America without the benefit of substantial public investment is pure hubris.[39]

Gates's myth about the masses is very different from Marcuse's story in *One Dimensional Man.* Myths about poverty shape civil life, as do attitudes toward development itself.

To Nussbaum, successful social environments are measured by whether everyone in a given society has social, relational and material support to live up to their capabilities if they so choose. She's arguing for capability not for actual functioning. She believes citizens have these capabilities whatever else they may have or pursue. Her point is to describe environments in which full human functioning is available. In good enough cities, the political goal isn't mere human survival; it's a focus on a livability that isn't violated by hunger, fear, or the absence of opportunity. Resilient cities, as central messaging spaces, contain memes that make it possible for all people to imagine themselves as those who can attain a fully human life.

The momentum of history moves against imagining that possibility. To Bourdieu, we're historical subjects. The social world is an accumulated history that takes time to amass; it persists in its being as a form of social energy, inscribed in the objectivity of things, as a result of which everything isn't equally possible for everyone.[40] He observed that if the social world weren't an accumulated history, banked in human being, life could be seen as a game of perfect equality of opportunity, like a game of Roulette, in which every moment is completely independent of each previous one, so that at each moment anyone could become anything.[41] But memes that dominate a city constrain our options—especially for some people.

As an example, Nussbaum argued that we can't expect women living in communities where they've never experienced equality, mutual respect or a fair assessment of their merit, and have never even seen a woman treated as though she had equal value, to hope to be so treated.[42] Yet human needs are built on that hope. Her list includes the following:

- **Life.** Being able to live to the end of a human life of normal length; not dying prematurely, or before one's life is so reduced as to be not worth living.
- **Bodily Health.** Being able to have good health, including reproductive health, which implies that every sex act is free of coercion and infection, every pregnancy should be intended and every birth should be healthy;[43] to be adequately nourished; to have adequate shelter.
- **Bodily Integrity.** Being able to move freely from place to place; having one's bodily boundaries treated as sovereign, i.e., being able to be secure against assault, including sexual assault, child

sexual abuse and domestic violence; having opportunities for sexual satisfaction and for choice in matters of reproduction.

- **Senses, Imagination, and Thought.** Being able to use the senses, to imagine, think and reason—and to do these things in 'a truly human way', a way informed and cultivated by an adequate education, including but by no means limited to, literacy and basic mathematical and scientific training. Being able to use imagination and thought in connection with experiencing and producing self-expressive works and events of one's own choice—religious, literary, musical and so forth. Being able to use one's mind in ways protected by guarantees of freedom of religious exercise. Being able to search for the ultimate meaning of life in one's own way. Being able to have pleasurable experiences and avoid non-necessary pain.
- **Emotions.** Being able to have attachments to things and people outside ourselves; to love those who love and care for us, to grieve at their absence; in general, to love, to grieve, to experience longing, gratitude and justified anger. Not having one's emotional development blighted by overwhelming fear and anxiety, or by traumatic events of abuse or neglect. (Supporting this capability means supporting forms of human association that can be shown to be crucial in their development.)
- **Practical Reason.** Being able to form a conception of the good and engage in critical reflection about the planning of one's life. (This entails protection for the liberty of conscience.)
- **Affiliation.** A. Being able to live with and toward others, to recognize and show concern for other human beings, to engage in various forms of social interaction; to be able to imagine the situation of another and to have compassion for that situation; to have the capability for both justice and friendship. (Protecting this capability means protecting institutions that constitute and nourish such forms of affiliation and also protecting the freedom of assembly and political speech.) B. Having the social bases of self-respect and non-humiliation; being able to be treated as a dignified being whose worth is equal to that of others. This entails, at minimum, protections against discrimination on the basis of

race, sex, sexual orientation, religion, caste, ethnicity or national origin. In work, being able to work as a human being, exercising practical reason and entering into meaningful relationships of mutual recognition with other workers.

- **Other Species.** Being able to live with concern for and in relation to animals, plants and the world of nature.
- **Play.** Being able to laugh, play and enjoy recreational activities.
- **Control over One's Environment.** A. Political. Being able to participate effectively in political choices that govern one's life; having the right of political participation, protections of free speech and association. B. Material. Being able to hold property (both land and movable goods), not just formally but in terms of real opportunity; and having property rights on an equal basis with others; having the right to seek employment on an equal basis with others; having the freedom from unwarranted search and seizure. (These provisions with regard to property rights do not assume that having more and more is best since property is a tool of human functioning and not an end in itself.)[44]

Ehrenreich's research showed that these human needs were unmet, in her view, due to economic oppression—even though the people in her research live in a wealthy country.

Yet Nussbaum didn't base her approach on the actual realization in everyone of these capabilities. Rather she asked, what can we require of a social environment, in this case, a city, through the development of policies and practices, so that everyone can realize these capabilities if they so choose? She analyzed the difficulty of realizing them in an environment that aims to thoroughly discourage some people. Her measure of success isn't whether people live up to their own capabilities. Someone may rationally choose not to live up to one or more of them.

I recall a Vietnamese student, an excellent young man, who had an opportunity to attend a school to provide him with education that would extend his already evident skills. He refused the opportunity. He remained with his aging parents who would have been alone in the city if he chose to go to this school in a city nearby, the only one of its type, even though his city offered him the financial means to pursue the opportunity. I sensed he made a rational choice. He loved his parents. They loved him. They were poor now but his father had been a respected chef in Vietnam. While visiting them, I felt sure his decision was personal, conscious and rational. It was directed by his view of what constitutes a good life. I sensed that his worldview enabled him to flourish as a fully human person and I believed that the city he lived in would offer him other opportunities that didn't require him to leave his parents.

Nussbaum's point is that a life that lacks any of these capabilities because the social environment withholds them, no matter what else that life includes, will fall short of a fully human life. Her focus is on creating social settings that spend resources on primary needs. The aim of public planning is to secure everyone's capability to perform these important functions. She asks whether people in a city are put in a position of mere subsistence. A human capabilities approach asserts that there's a moral claim on cities to bring their livability in line with "the right educational and material support, [so that people] can become fully capable of the major human functions"[45] outlined in her list. These needs exert a claim on human community. It's only right that they impact meme environments and messaging roles that are a central aspect of city life.

MEANINGFUL WORK

A third environmental aspect of a resilient city is the quality and kind of work available within it. Social theorist Marshall Berman analyzed modern development by examining what he called the 'tragedy of development' as exemplified in Goethe's Faust.[46] Berman argued for the primacy of communication and dialogue in cities, and acknowledged their message–making role, because he observed that modern development, as a romance with machines, was matched by its remoteness from people.[47] He based his motivation to prize the city by agreeing that "the free development of each [person] is the condition of the free development of all,"[48] a sentiment consistent with Ehrenreich and Nussbaum. To Berman, modern folk assert their dignity in the present, even a wretched and oppressive present and their right to control their future by striving to make a place for themselves in the world, a place where they feel at home.[49]

To Berman, what makes us modern is the desire that earth should feel like home, which is interesting to compare with earlier myths. To him, an impulse to make the world feel like home runs deep. Freedom to feel at home needs the support of relational resources. A strong pull that cancels out that feeling was an equally urgent modern tendency—a city developer's desire for development, which is a desire that prevents cities from feeling like home because these great achievements turn out to exact great human costs.[50] Many modern developers were driven by a compulsion to use "every part of [themselves], and of everybody else, to push [themselves] and others as far as [it's possible to] go;"[51] it was a romantic quest for self-development[52] and city development. The motivation of the literary figure of Faust as paradigm for modern developers is captured in a story Faust tells himself about one of his projects:

> Standing on an artificial hill created by human labor, he overlooks the whole new world that he has brought into being, and it looks good. He knows that he has made people suffer ('Human sacrifices bled, / Tortured screams would pierce the night'...). But he is convinced that it is the common people, the mass of workers and sufferers, who will benefit most from his great works. He has replaced a barren, sterile economy with a dynamic new one that will 'open up space for millions / To live, not securely, but free for action....' It is a physical and natural space, but one that has been created through social organization and action.[53]

The space Faust opened up forced masses of people to act on his whim and take no rest.

For developers who function like Faust and bargain with the devil to secure their own interests, people are in the way. Berman noted a typically modern style of evil that's "indirect, impersonal [and] mediated by complex organizations and institutional roles"[54] making the urge to develop relentlessly necessary. If masses of people are caught in a developer's social schemes they adopt passivity and utility as a mean of survival. They become silent and useful for Faustian purposes and don't realize their freedom to live a truly human life.

Exploring this human trap in detail, Ehrenreich and Nussbaum showed that women in North America, India and Africa demonstrate passive acceptance of unreasonable work and family demands. But they live in a double bind. They're in the way but they're also the means by which development advances. Nussbaum's *capability approach* addresses that double bind. Her list is grounded on two questions: If we're going to acknowledge that a given life is human, what do we believe must be included in that life?[55] If we take biology as relatively constant in human experience, what's necessary to include in the public environment as support for developing the functional capabilities of every person?

In city life, there is often tension between those who demand equality and those who love plenty. The latter might not feel safe as they build high walls around piles of personal wealth. If one walks around a wealthy neighborhood, devices to protect private property proliferate. Those who have more, perceive their wealth as a target for other people's envy: kleptocracy is anxiety producing. To redress a leader's tendency toward kleptocracy, Nussbaum made it clear that each item on her list is separate. She noted that we can't "satisfy the need for one of [the items on the list] by giving a larger amount of another one."[56] We can't suppose an absence of political liberty is evened out by tremendous economic growth.[57] A large GNP says nothing about the resilience of cities or the well-being of every citizen.

Two Models For Work In City Life

To describe resilient city life, I distinguish two urban types that serve to clarify that possibility. Jacobs described two cities to convey how dynamic complexity might work. She refers to them as efficient versus developing cities. She contrasted Manchester and Birmingham (later also London) as models for the modern city during the mid-1800s in Britain. A developing city (in her sense, it's a positive description) offers the best environment for dynamic complexity (and therefore social literacy), while an efficient city may all but extinguish their potential.

Manchester stood as an example of the perfect city, praised by many, including Karl Marx and Frederick Engels. It was a center for the textile industry. All aspects of life within its limits were drawn to maintain the manufacture of cloth. Its systemic focus was efficiency, even though many observers, including Marx, were appalled by "sordid living conditions and terrible death rates [in] Manchester" and saw an "immense and ominous" social gulf between mill owners and a poor, hopeless mass of workers. Yet even Marx believed the "efficiency of Manchester was a portent of the cities of the future—if not all cities, at least capitalist" ones.[58]

Manchester's economy was easy to see and understand. It was clear how everything conspired to promote a huge industry at the centre of an economic vitality that benefited some people. Jacobs noted that Marx based much of his analysis of capitalism and class struggle on that city and, even if he saw its alarming side, appeared to have thought of it as rather grand, as did others, such as Disraeli. The appalling force of its internal logic was perceived as faceless productivity, so much so that Marx's analysis of power relations took on a quality and tension that pitted productive labour against unproductive labour,[59] a distinction that dis-privileges reproductive labour, i.e., work that takes care of children, the elderly and the household.[60]

To get a sense of what an efficient city feels like from inside, think of a mining town in which all those who live within its borders work at the mine. The mine owner is rich. Workers are dependent upon his provision of food, clothing and shelter through the company store where he sets prices as he pleases in the absence of irritating competition. Innovation among workers at any level is cut off because it threatens the status quo, a system maintained rigorously as a total economy in which each of its aspects is seen as essential to a continuation of the whole. Since he owns everything and has freedom of access to everyone, the mine owner eradicates competition as it arises. The town is an economy that produces goods and services. Human beings are at the mercy of productivity. Efficient owners obliterate resistance in a smooth running unity they're able to oversee and manipulate. For a visual, visceral view of an efficient city, see Charlie Chaplin's movie *Modern Times*. Nazi Germany is a well known instance[61] of appalling efficiency. Other examples of efficiency were found on cotton plantations in the United States.[62]

In an efficient city, opposition, criticism and critique are snuffed out. The power of the owner, or in Foucault's terms the sovereign power of the king, invests every human body in the city so that a worker's only freedom is to comply with or stay out of a king's presence. The worker's body is preserved through absolute obedience. Workers watch how the boss operates to avoid his wrath. The reduction of human value in an efficient city has lasting social effects. Workers are enslaved to the boss. In his analysis of social trust, Putnam saw a pattern of low social capital in areas in the United States he believes is only explained by overlaying the historic regions where slavery was strongly invested. He constructed a geographical equation between low levels of social trust now and high levels of slavery in the past.[63]

In an efficient city, everything flows toward an end carved out by those in charge and this end is synonymous with the industry itself as well as the owner himself. Since efficiency "is the ratio of work accomplished to energy supplied," there are two relevant factors to measure: input of energy and the quantity/quality of work accomplished.[64] A system is increasingly efficient if the input of energy accomplishes more and more work. When the idea of efficiency is adopted by a city, what matters is that work should increase productivity. Workers' lives aren't relevant to productivity since other workers can usually be got somehow.[65] Human capital is secondary to monetary capital accumulation, which an owner enjoys.[66] If he ever has an uneasy conscience, he reminds himself that, after all, he provides work for a mass of people.

Efficiency in the sense outlined by Jacobs didn't arise with Manchester,[67] though it was a good example. A historical lesson from efficient cities is that they collapse from the sheer weight of the circulating harm stimulated by the stupidity, cruelty and injustice that flow freely within them, moved by unlimited greed in the heart of their leaders. Productivity driven by efficiency is vulnerable to collapse. Jared Diamond saw that productivity fuelled by efficiency collapses in on itself, as demonstrated by Manchester and the famous case of Easter Island, because these social environments eat away at their own roots. At the time of her writing Jacobs identified "only two cities in all of Britain [that] remain economically vigorous and prosperous. One is London. The second is Birmingham.[68]

She pointed out that Marx was incorrect to identify the basic conflict in economic life between workers and owners. That conflict is important but secondary to one she noted among people "whose interests are with already well-established economic activities, and those whose interests are with the emergence of new economic activities."[69] Conflicts among well established v. emerging economies is never put to rest except by stagnation, since well established activities are typically advantaged and easily win that contest. A cycle continues: innovations of today are entrenched practices of tomorrow. Efficiency eradicates opposition and generates stagnation. Recognition and reward go to workers whose passivity and docility assure their continuity with the status quo. In efficient cities, resistance *isn't* futile but it's *believed to be so.*

Marx identified correctly that resistance must have support from human solidarity—workers must unite to establish internal connections if efficiency is to be held accountable for its de-humanization. But for all his invective against bourgeois economy, he enthusiastically embraced the personality this economics produced.[70]

Is social literacy opposed to capitalism? No. Part of learning social literacy is the realization that capitalism doesn't have efficiency as its only model. Efficiency collapses in on itself because it's a de-humanizing, predatory consumption of the very materials that sustain its existence. A second model (the developing city) is a healthy basis for resilience and stops short of judging capitalism, growth, productivity and social power to be inherently harmful.

It was the messiness of Birmingham that bothered theorists who preferred Manchester. What was going on in Birmingham could be described neither precisely nor concisely. In the mid-1800s this city had a few relatively large industries but nothing to match Manchester. Its internal logic was constituted by small organizations employing no more than a dozen or so men; many had fewer. Independence, failure and good fortune operated within its city limits. Small businesses weren't rationally or efficiently consolidated. Able workers broke away from existing businesses to set up a piece of the business on their own based on their innovation and invention. Jacobs interpreted the pattern in both cities and thought Birmingham had a fairly high level of development work while Manchester had a relatively low level. It's the nature of work itself, to some extent, which distinguishes the two cities.[71]

In order to understand how to have a resilient city, let's consider the nature of work. If efficiency, when allowed total control in a city, eats away its own roots, development work is nourished by the fruit of its labour. Creators of new work must have insight and combine an idea or observation with a suggestion from the work they're currently doing in order to make a new departure.[72] Innovation relies on an industry already in play for its departure from it. Old work nurtures new work in a healthy environment. Rather than eating at its own roots, innovation and change are nourished by curiosity that arises as an aspect of the work shows potential to generate a new product. Of course, in economic terms, inventions may eradicate the need for old work but under the best conditions, old work and new work mesh. As one dies, the other sets off a generation that sees value in the new work. Yet development is risky business.

If development is risky, recall that growth in a city modelled on efficiency has stagnation as its primary outcome—stagnation and collapse. If cities are grounded on development, old skills and goods are conserved by combining old and new work in a way that respects the past but adapts to the present.[73] To Jacobs, new work doesn't come into being due to consumer demand. New work and innovation emerge from ideas suggested by materials or skills involved already in old work and by specific problems in carrying out that work.[74] For example, the original 3M Company made sand for construction work. Someone decided to make sandpaper. It wasn't any good because the sand wouldn't stick to the paper. During the process of trying to fix problems, they got interested in adhesives.

What are myths about capitalism that thrive in a resilient city? In David Harvey's and Mumford's terms, a city is a meaning-generating, message-sending site. But some forms of capitalism build and rebuild the geography of a city in its own image. The logic of capital accumulation produces a space which is a distinctive geographical landscape of transport, communication, infrastructures and territorial organizations. Given a Faustian approach to development, a habitat will facilitate "capital accumulation during one phase of its history only to have to be torn down and reconfigured to make way for further accumulation at a later stage."[75] It's capital investment that contains the seeds of its own surcease. But city spaces are places where crimes caused by efficient capital accumulation can be resisted. Harvey cites Baltimore, which houses a city-wide movement for a living wage that relies on alliances between institutions, communities and especially churches to create what he calls a "social unionism at work within the politics of place,"[76] as one such example.

Why should we focus on a resilient city in economic terms? Why think about Marx, for example? In part, it's because his *Communist Manifesto* is astonishingly descriptive of current circumstances. There's growing interest in its anti-capitalist urge among those who worry about the well-being of the globe. Cities caught in global currents are habitats for humanity under siege. We can't separate universal concerns from particular conditions. Violence done to a human body in one city impacts how human bodies are treated elsewhere. The force of Marx's argument was built on revealing what was happening to specific workers. It's still true that what can happen to the globe is implicated by what's done to a particular worker.

But a Marxist argument such as Harvey's tends to draw the conflict between a free play of efficient capitalism and its only plausible opponent, i.e., anti-capitalism (though he argues for bringing together particular interests to ground a general interest as a core task to be addressed, as does Jacobs,[77] and he uses ecology as a metaphor for its accomplishment).[78] He's right to say capitalism is not a physical thing; it's a social relation.[79] It survives by occupying space and producing space[80] and by producing workers that keep that space open for unjust practices that perpetually dehumanize them. But if capitalism is a social relation then there's space available daily to resist injustice and create a refuge from its dehumanizing effects. It's precisely its nature as a social relation that opens up the opportunity to educate people about being socially literate. Social literacy provides social and emotional skills to keep a city open for maintaining its relational habitat.

While a competitive impulse in capitalism could drive owners to fix spaces so they can feed and breed, to use a natural analogy, the fitness of organizations must be moved by another set of impulses. In order for an organism to feed and breed it must preserve its environment. It's economically rational to care for the city if one wishes to succeed. Work that preserves a habitat produces and sustains those who are eventually productive in it. This relation is the root of all forms of capital accumulation and are necessary to it.[81] If we want to preserve our relational habitat, we resist injustice with social love as we cooperate with city folk who also want to live under conditions of equality and fairness. If capitalists meet resistance and understand how it supports their own interests as well, they might respond positively to messages resistance offers them. But the movement toward efficiency must be challenged because its momentum is sparked and sustained by greed.

RECOVERY AND RESILIENCE

What would a developing city feel like from inside? Jacobs imagined a future in which cities are like mining towns in quite a different sense than cited earlier.[82] In a developing city, problems such as garbage and waste are addressed with ingenuity and resourcefulness, as is beginning in some cities, with their green bins. In Hamilton Ontario, the city composts Christmas trees and offers the resulting soil freely to those who pick it up. The mining operations in a developing city generate work that replenishes the city's roots. Through innovation and invention city problems create development work. A city isn't a space to parade wealth; it's a place to create it.

A resilient city has an ecologically motivated concern that every person should live in spaces of hope. Maintaining a city's relational habitat is a primary way to offer that hope. Jacobs describes habitat preserving traits in values and behaviours that sustain relational resources that are implicit in Nussbaum's list of human needs.

These human traits are aesthetic appreciation, fear of retribution, awe expressed as veneration, persuasiveness and corrective tinkering and contriving.[83] As she put it, these traits "seem to have been components of [humanity's] makeup since time immemorial....[and] are what we have" to work with[84] as we maintain a habitat, whether it's the earth's resources or human relationships.

These saving traits establish and maintain social trust and motivate social love—two attitudes extinguished by efficiency but consistent with resilience in its resolute acceptance of reality, its sense that life is meaningful and its exceptional ability to improvise.[85] Using an analogy from nature, Jacobs showed that successful predators, large or small, are symbiotic with their habitats,[86] rather than destructive of them, a contrary point to Dawkins's selfishness principle.

But the option to maintain the environment isn't the only possibility for a city's future. As noted earlier, a tendency for people to isolate themselves can lead to personal collapse. Jacobs identified several tendencies that lead toward cultural collapse. If we understand its patterns, we realize how important civility and civic action are in preventing collapse. When a society collapses, Jacobs described its ethos as a Dark Age.

She identified a Dark Age as a period in which a dead end has led to the complete loss of cultural knowledge and the skills required to correct and re-stabilize a group's existence. Easter Island, mentioned earlier, is an example of a Dark Age.[87] The people died out. The island is uninhabited. When I was in Bolivia in 1998, I saw the remains of Bolivia's Altiplano, an area that once supported fruit trees and agriculture more productive than Canadian farmers will ever experience, given our way of farming. Now the Altiplano is a barren, treeless desert. It's empty.

While its agricultural barrenness is painful to see, the loss of memory is the most troubling aspect of collapse. While we were there, we heard of a Canadian researcher who took aerial pictures of the area and discovered rectangular forms in the earth that turned out to be remains of a unique farming method that produced that earlier abundance of fruit and vegetables—a farming method long forgotten by local people. Regaining memory, meme-based ways of doing things, can bring people back from the edge of a Dark Age to recover their socio-economic vitality.

Jared Diamond outlined ecological processes that lead to collapse: deforestation, habitat destruction, soil problems of erosion, salinization and infertility; water management problems; overhunting, overfishing, negative effects of introduced species on native species; increased per-capita impact of people on human-caused climate change, build-up of toxic chemicals in the environment, energy shortages and the full usage of earth's photosynthetic capacity.[88] As these conditions begin to apply to a region, it may appear wealthy and productive for a period. But eventually, processes that support excessive productivity undermine the long-term livelihood of the region, a point that's consistent with the harm inherent in efficient city economies.[89]

A thought experiment may suffice to capture the essence of collapse. In the overfishing dynamics of Eastern Canada, several features of the industry undermined its longevity. Certainly the behavior of countries that refused to respect Canadian boundaries was an issue. What was less obvious was the process of production itself that included building large ships to catch fish. The cost and upkeep of the ships and the hauls to justify their size eventually led to overfishing a resource Canadians thought was inexhaustible. In collapse theories, processes that undermine an area are consistent. Sometimes they speed up due to war or disease but often, as with Easter Island, the practices of people themselves have deeply imbedded harm built into them so that it might be said that they bring collapse on themselves.

But collapse isn't inevitable. If people are paying attention, if they're mindful, there are self-correcting resources available that depend on saving traits that show up in human culture. Jacobs identified traits bestowed through evolution that cut across cultures over long spans of time and aren't at odds with competitive success. To her, looking after the environment isn't at odds with competitive success, e.g., in contrast to Dawkins's gene theory. As mentioned, saving traits are gifts of consciousness, which include aesthetic appreciation, art and its practice, fear of retribution, a capacity to feel awe, an ability to use language, an inborn capacity to tinker and contrive and a sense of responsibility for how people treat each other.[90]

We can think of Shakespeare's influence on the development of the individual as an example of saving traits that enhance cultural insight and increase the likelihood of adaptation and growth. Self-correcting strategies resist collapse and include processes Jacobs explained in detail. The four processes she described are bifurcations, positive feedback loops, negative feedback controls and emergency adaptations.[91] To explore their role in recovery, let's continue with our imaginary city linked to the overfishing crisis in Eastern Canada and apply these self-correcting resources to our thought experiment.

As we do that, note how Jacobs spoke about city problems. She thought they were problems of organized complexity. The term is related to distinctions in scientific thought that explain differences between problems of simplicity, problems of disorganized complexity and problems of organized complexity. To her, the city is organized complexity (stable complexity) because its problems show an essential feature of organization; they have a sizable number of factors, as does disorganized complexity (simplicity implies two factor relationships), but the factors are interrelated into an organic whole. Variables in city problems shift simultaneously in subtly interconnected ways.[92] (I prefer to apply abduction to understand organized complexity; Jacobs relies on induction.)[93] The point is that city problems aren't to be treated deductively only, e.g., to allow Faustian planners to apply self-serving solutions from generalizations they foist on cities.

If we apply the first self-correcting process to our imaginary city, bifurcation refers to a decision point or fork in the road. A bifurcation is an abrupt discontinuity that isn't the cause of trouble; it's a response to the build up of instabilities and stresses.[94] A bifurcation forks off, it's discontinuous with what has gone immediately before. Since cities need ample, volatile trade with other cities, and if we discover the looming depletion of codfish stocks, our city faces a bifurcation. With a bifurcation, it's no longer business as usual. Fisheries can't go on functioning according to practices that arose when the dominant pattern was to build large fishing ships and discourage small fishing boats. In terms of collapse, if the fishing industry comes to a halt, it won't be long before people forget how to fish.

The second process, a positive feedback loop, refers to systemic reporting and responding within a city's organized complexity. In general, feedback controls register that a correction is necessary and at the same time trigger an appropriate correction. When cod stocks fail, large boats can't catch enough fish to support themselves, while small boats that are more sensitive to the availability of fish stocks can monitor quantities, support themselves on smaller catches and conserve the supply overall. A resilient system is one that gets and acts on appropriate feedback, just as a resilient person is one who gets and acts on appropriate responses from other people—instead of ignoring or silencing those people. For a system to be resilient, corrective strategies aren't affected by vicious circles that amount to the dead end of a Dark Age. Dead ends don't correct an instability reported by the system, they intensify it.[95]

Suppose large boat crews disrupt small fishers, lobby government for protection, making it impossible for small fishers to fish. A vicious circle arises: large boats continue fishing, which threatens everyone's prospects. Vicious circles do damage and are self-terminating[96]—fish stocks will disappear. If the city relies entirely on the fishing industry, it can reach a dead end. In social interactions, the addictive cycles of a kleptocrat and narcissist are vicious circles that end in collapse if no bifurcation disrupts them—if no fork in the road presents itself and persuades them to turn down a different path and if no one reports to them that a correction is necessary.

The third process, negative feedback controls, provides a balance between predators and prey. In eco-systems for example, negative feedback controls bring addictive behaviour to a halt from within a system. As an example, a thermostat registers a rise in heat and then cuts back the temperature in a room. But feedback in general is only as good as the accuracy of its reporting.[97] This is why excess deference shown to a bad boss is self-defeating for the whole relational system in the workplace. Negative feedback controls are useful if data are accurate and if purposes and corrective responses employed are functionally integrated.[98] E.g., if large or small-scale fishers lie about cod stocks, that feedback won't fuel an appropriate response.

The fourth process, emergency adaptations, responds to temporary imbalances.[99] This self-correcting strategy works with instabilities that are short lived but devastating. For example, the government could place a moratorium on cod fishing in the waters near our imaginary city. Adaptation is temporary because the city is dependent on fishing. A longer-term solution needs to be found. But the point for social literacy has to do with insights that come from the city's troubles. The city must find new work arising from the fishing industry to produce something people know how to do or can learn to do. They're in a healthier position if the city economy was already characterized by development in Jacobs's sense because they would be experienced in creating new work out of old work through innovation and invention. If the city were resilient the crisis would be ameliorated by new work that had already built up, but which perhaps hadn't yet been given the attention it needs in order to thrive.

Effectively using the four self-correcting processes allows organized complexity to become stable, i.e., to be experienced as stable complexity. In terms of learning social literacy, the possibilities for applying self-correcting processes to city problems is utterly dependent on the social and emotional skills that are characteristic of resilience and its seven components listed earlier. Without the social and emotional skills to negotiate the relational landscape, it's less likely that people will have resources to maintain their relational habitat. It's the quality of social trust that emerges from the effective use of these skills that allows economic growth to follow.

CONCLUSION

In public life, democracy supports stable complexity. Civic-minded citizens give feedback to leaders through protest and the vote.[100] Equality at work provides people with life satisfaction. A city needs a healthy environment in which citizens can find food, work and have families, in a way that allows them to compete with other cities and hope for a good future. Resilient cities attend to the memes that structure the environment so that respect is granted to every person so that everyone has access to an environment in which essential needs are met. Further, a resilient person is a good neighbour who respects other people's humanity in all they do and prizes what citizens hold in common.[101] Rethinking civic myths is another way to affect change and open opportunities for finding and creating meaningful work.

If we learn social literacy, we do the hard work of providing relational resources to others at the same time that we access them ourselves. *If we learn it*—here's the issue. Lessons of social literacy begin in kindergarten with teachers who understand, as did Paley, that children are capable of great good but need guidance through the rules, maxims and principles that impact public life. Social literacy isn't learned through force, humiliation or punishment. Without a social literacy curriculum, we treat people the way we have been or fear we might be treated, rather than how we want to be treated ourselves. Learning the lessons of social literacy may be a lot of work but learning social literacy is what keeps us human and what makes public life good.

END NOTES

CHAPTER 1

[1] I use the expressions a felt sense of connection and a sense of felt connection interchangeably.

[2] Dan Goleman, *Social Intelligence* (New York: Bantam Books, 2006), 84.

[3] *Social Intelligence*, 97.

[4] Anthony Giddens and Patrick Diamond, (Eds.), *The New Egalitarianism* (Cambridge: Polity Press, 2005), 40.

[5] Martha Nussbaum, *Women and Human Development*, (Cambridge: Cambridge University Press, 2000), 72.

[6] Mary Gregor, (Trans., Editor), *Immanuel Kant, The Metaphysics of Morals,* Cambridge: Cambridge University Press, 1996).

[7] *Women and Human Development*, 73.

[8] *Social Intelligence*, 5.

[9] Charles Derber, *The Pursuit of Attention* (New York: Oxford University Press, 2000).

[10] Even among young children, the tendency to exert social power by telling others who can and can't play with the group is established by the time they come to kindergarten. See V. Gussin Paley, *You Can't Say You Can't Play* (Cambridge, Massachusetts: Harvard University Press, 1992).

[11] Anthony Giddens & Patrick Diamond, *The New Egalitarianism* (Malden, MA: Polity Press, 2005), p.44.

[12] Pierre Bourdieu "The Forms of Capital," in J.G. Richardson, (Ed.)

Handbook of Theory and Research for the Sociology of Education (New York: Green, 1983), 248-250.

[13] Robert Putnam, *Bowling Alone* (New York: Simon and Schuster, 2000), 93-99.

[14] Robert Putnam, *Making Democracy Work* (Princeton, New Jersey: Princeton University Press, 1993), 124-125.

[15] *Making Democracy Work,* 126-130.

[16] Jane Jacobs, *The Death and Life of Great American Cities* (New York: Vintage, 1992), 112. First published in 1961.

[17] *Bowling Alone,* 25.

[18] *Making Democracy Work*, 115.

[19] Pierre Bourdieu, *Practical Reason: On the Theory of Action* Randal Johnson (Trans.) (Redwood City, CA: Stanford University Press, 1998), 40.

[20] *Practical Reason*, 43.

[21] *Practical Reason*, 60.

[21] *Practical Reason*, 61.

[22] *Practical Reason*, 98.

[23] *Practical Reason*, 84.

[24] *Practical Reason,* 86.

[25] *You Can't Say*, 3.

[26] *You Can't Say*, 63.

[27] *You Can't Say*, 21.

[28] *You Can't Say*, 20.

[29] *You Can't Say*, 15.

[30] *You Can't Say*, 33-34.

[31] *You Can't Say*, 100.

[32] *You Can't Say*, 16.

[33] *You Can't Say*, 21.

[34] *You Can't Say*, 48.

[35] *You Can't Say*, 122.

[36] *You Can't Say*, 115

[37] *You Can't Say*, 99.

[38] *You Can't Say*, 87.

[39] *You Can't Say*, 15.

[40] *You Can't Say*, 45.

[41] *You Can't Say*, 45.

[42] Jerome Kagan, *Galen's Prophecy: temperament in human nature* (NY: Basic Books, 1994).

[43] Patrick Lencioni, *The Five Dysfunctions of a Team* (San Francisco: Jossey-Bass, 2002), 95.

[44] The right to education was established in the Universal Declaration of Human Rights. This Declaration was adopted by the General Assembly of the United Nations on 10 December 1948 by a vote of 48 in favor, 0 against, with 8 abstentions. Wikipedia, [July 10,13]. The Universal Declaration of Human Rights, Article 26 states that: (1) Everyone has the right to education. Education shall be free, at least in the elementary and fundamental stages. Elementary education shall be compulsory. Technical and professional education shall be made generally available and higher education shall be equally accessible to all on the basis of merit. (2) Education shall be directed to the full development of the human personality and to the strengthening of respect for human rights and fundamental freedoms. It shall promote understanding, tolerance and friendship among all nations, racial or religious groups, and shall further the activities of the United Nations for the maintenance of peace. (3) Parents have a prior right to choose the kind of education that shall be given to their children. In addition to the UDHR, documents that pertain to children's rights include the following: The Geneva Declaration of the Rights of the Child (1924), the Declaration of the Rights of the Child (1959), The International Covenant on Civil and Political Right, Articles 23-24 (1959), and The International Covenant on Economic, Social and Cultural Rights, Article 10 (1966).

[45] I'm indebted to Andrew Trevoy at the Ogilvie Law Firm in Edmonton for this point about courts of law and courts of equity.

[46] See a discussion of the *Famous Five*, who were 5 Alberta women who won the persons case in Canada in 1929.

[47] I'm indebted to Daniel Watson for the insight and wording of this thought.

[48] Wesley Newcomb Hohfeld, *Fundamental legal conceptions as applied in judicial reasoning: [sic] and other legal essays*. Walter Wheeler Cook (Ed.) New Haven, Yale University Press, 1919. Reprinted by Legal Treatises, 1800-1926, Yale University Press, p. 64.

[49] A careful reading of Hohfeld's essays reveals he under-analyzed the term disability from our current perspective of it at least. In this discussion, it must be kept in mind that it refers to no-ability to alter a legal relation, for others, or for oneself.

[50] This is an interesting point that Hohfeld makes. Liability refers generally to responsibility. He uses the example of those (e.g., African Americans) who weren't required to form juries. It's contestable whether people want their responsibility limited by race and gender, as was the case in the United States in Hohfeld's day.

[51] *Legal conceptions*, 50. Hohfeld pointed out that the terms he used are so basic to our language that definition is difficult. In this case, he defined disability *vis a vis* the map itself. Since power is ability, it's opposite is dis-ability or the absence of ability. Power as ability refers to human agency or agency relations. Disability in this sense refers to a person who has no ability or agency with respect to a particular legal dispute. Mental and physical abilities aren't the issue here but may provide what Hohfeld refers to as the operative facts of the case.

[52] I acknowledge that this statement in the syllogism raises the question of whether all social experiences constitute access to education. At this point, we're discussing one child's impact on another child at school. My point is that children have no-right to make a decision that impacts another child's access to social experiences at school. I don't intend to limit a teacher's duty to remove or prevent children from entering social experiences at school due to a specified need or requirement that schools make clear in advance.

[53] *Fundamental legal conceptions*, p. 14.

[54] I'm indebted to Edmonton Kindergarten teacher, Karen Bellous, for these insights about the legal aspects of IPPs and Report Cards.

[55] This point relies on the having school material that's well calibrated to a child's ability.

[56] Anita Farber-Robertson, *Learning While Leading* (Alban Institute, 2000). Foreward by Chris Argyris.

[57] *Learning While Leading*, 13-14.

[58] Wilder Penfield, The Mystery of the Mind, (Princeton, NJ: Princeton University Press, 1975), 83-90. Penfield, a Canadian Neurosurgeon, gave the medical community a map of the brain/body mechanism (the homunculus) that's still in use. His research is fundamental to the development of brain research. In this book, he asked the question: What does the mind do? Through his research, he posited that the mind: focuses attention; is aware of what's going on; decides what's to be learned and recorded; reasons; makes new decisions; understands; acts as if with an energy of its own; makes decisions and puts those decisions into effect by calling on various brain mechanisms, by an expenditure of energy (electricity); programs the automatic sensory-motor mechanism (depicted by the homunculus).

CHAPTER 2

[1] *Interpersonal Rejection*, 5.

[2] Kipling D. Williams, et al, Eds. *The Social Outcast* (New York: Psychology Press, 2005), 166.

[3] Josephine Klein, *Our Need for Others and its Roots in Infancy* (London: Tavistock), xv.

[4] Kate Distin, *The Selfish Meme* (Cambridge: Cambridge University Press, 2005), 119)

[5] *Selfish Meme*, 39-47.

[6] *Selfish Meme*, 42.

[7] Mary Douglas, *Natural Symbols* (New York: Pantheon, 1982).

[8] Thomas J. Oord, *Science of Love* (London: Templeton Foundation Press, 2004), 9.

[9] *Science of Love,* 43.

[10] *Science of Love*, 42.

[11] Daniel Goleman, *Social Intelligence: The new science of human relationships.* (New York: Bantam Books, 2006).

[12] *Social Intelligence*, 331.

[13] *Social Intelligence*, 11.

[14] *Social Intelligence*, 11-12.

[15] *Social Intelligence*, 11.

[16] *Social Intelligence*, 12.

[17] *Social Intelligence*, 235.

[18] *Social Intelligence*, 223-237.

[19] *Social Intelligence*, 12.

[20] *Social Intelligence*, 80.

[22] *Social Intelligence*, 16.

[22] *Social intelligence*, 60.

[23] *Social intelligence*, 60.

[24] *Social Intelligence* , 96.

[25] *Social Intelligence*, 15-17; 70.

[26] *Social Intelligence*, 83.

[27] *Social Intelligence*, 83.

[28] *Social Intelligence*, 85.

[29] *Social Intelligence,* 152.

[30] *The Selfish Meme,* 123.

[31] *Social Intelligence,* 164.

[32] *Social Intelligence,* 84.

[33] *Social Intelligence,* 84.

[34] *Social Intelligence,* 84.

[35] *Social Intelligence,* 84.

[36] *Social Intelligence,* 85.

[37] *Social Intelligence,* 95.

[38] This story is found in Anette Ejsing, *Theology of Anticipation: A constructive study of C.S. Peirce* (Eugene, OR: Pickwick Publications, 2006), 3.

[39] *Theology of Anticipation,* 3.

[40] I'm not suggesting these were Peirce's actual thoughts as he discovered the thief, only that they may be some of the ways to think as we try to catch a thief. Abduction requires a quick mind—one that has conscious access to its theories about people and the world as well as self-discipline enough to suspend judgement in order to receive data from people and the world without foreclosing on them due to our pre-judgments of these data.

[41] Malcolm Gladwell, *Blink* (New York: Little, Brown and Company, 2005), 23.

[42] *Blink,* 33.

[43] *Blink,* 33.

[44] *Blink,* 43.

[45] *Blink,* 43.

[46] Gladwell outlined John Gottman's research in which he used thin-slicing to investigate the quality of marriage. Through his observation, Gottman noted that "having someone you love express contempt toward you is so stressful that it begins to affect the functioning of your immune system." *Blink,* 33. Through observing video tapes of couple interaction, Gottman predicted with remarkable accuracy marriages that would remain for another 15 years and those that would break up in the same period of time. *Blink,* 33. Tone of voice is indicative of contempt, which means that someone who hears tone of voice will be able to realize a relationship is in trouble, since respect and its absence are most clearly communicated through tone of voice. *Blink,* 43. The role of contempt is like that of disgust which has the effect of total rejection and exclusion from community. Tone of voice is caught in an instant and resides in every utterance, so a marriage counsellor, for example, can hear it and would use its presence

or absence to identify the patterns of engagement in marriage through an abductive approach to gathering information.

[47] *Theology of Anticipation*, 3-14.

[48] Hubert L. Dreyfus, *On the Internet* (New York: Routledge, 2001), especially 32-49.

[49] Most of the following analysis of habit has its basis in Sang Hyun Lee, *The Philosophical Theology of Jonathan Edwards* (Princeton: Princeton University Press, 1988), 15-46.

[50] It's unlikely Aristotle and Aquinas were concerned about trying to describe women's experience.

[51] Howard Gardner, *Multiple Intelligences* (New York: Basic Books, 1993), 236.

[52] *The Selfish Meme*, 20.

[53] *The Selfish Meme*, 22.

[54] Kathy Kolbe, *The Conative Connection* (New York: Addison-Wesley, 1990); *Powered by Instinct* (Phoenix, AZ: Monumentus Press, 2004).

[55] *Conative Connection*, xiv.

[56] *Conative Connection*, 27.

[57] *Conative Connection*, 107.

[58] See an extensive exploration of Bowlby/Ainsworth in *Developmental Psychology* (1992), 28, 759-775.

[59] Mary Gordon, *Roots of Empathy* (Toronto: Thomas Allen Publishers, 2005), 85ff,

[60] Howard Gardner, *Frames of Mind* (New York: Basic Books, 1983); *Multiple Intelligences* (New York: Basic Books, 1993).

[61] *Frames of Mind*, x.

CHAPTER 3

[1] See for example, Gabor Maté *In the Realm of Hungry Ghosts* (Toronto: Vintage, 2008).

[2] Richard Sennett, *Respect in a World of Inequality* (New York. W.W. Norton & Company, 2003). [page number?]

[3] Nel Noddings, *Happiness and Education* (Cambridge: Cambridge University Press, 2003).

[4] Mary Gordon, *Roots of Empathy* (Toronto: Thomas Allen Publishers, 2005), 71.

[5] *Roots of Empathy*, 71.

[6] *Roots of Empathy*, 117.

[7] Dr Ota is now an independent consultant in Brighton.

[8] Josephine Klein, *Our need for others and its Roots in Infancy* London: Tavistock, 1987), 247.

[9] *Our need for others*, 248.

[10] Resources used included the following: Leslie A. Pal, *Beyond Policy Analysis* Ontario, Canada: Nelson Thomson Learning, 2001. Robert D. Putnam, *Making Democracy Work: Civic Traditions in Modern Italy* (Princeton, New Jersey: Princeton University Press, 1993). Robert D. Putnam, *Bowling Alone: The collapse and revival of American Community* (New York: Simon and Schuster, 2000). Barbara A Misztal, *Trust in Modern Societies* Cambridge: Polity Press (Blackwell), 1996. Stephen Baron, et al. Eds. *Social Capital: Critical Perspectives* (Oxford: Oxford University Press, 2000). Partha Dasgupta, *Social Capital: A Multifaceted Perspective* (Washington, The World Bank, 1999). Peter.A. Hall, July 1999, Social Capital in Britain, *British Journal of Political Science.* Alan J. Roxburgh, *The Missionary Congregation, Leadership, & Liminality* (Harrisburg, Pennsylvania: Trinity Press International, 1997; Miroslav Volf, *Exclusion and Embrace: A Theological Exploration of Identity, Otherness and Reconciliation* (Nashville, Tennessee: Abingdon Press, 1996); John Ralston Saul, *On Equilibrium* (Harmondsworth, Middlesex, England: Penguin, 2001); Sherri Torjman, *Social Capital and the 'Our Millennium' National Project,* 2001; Nan Lin et al., *Social Capital: theory and research,* 2001; Don Cohen, *In Good Company: How social capital makes organizations work,* 2001; Gabriel Almond and Sidney Verba, *The Civic Culture: Political Attitudes and Democracy in Five Nations* (Princeton, NJ: Princeton University Press, 1963); James Coleman, *Foundations of Social Theory* (Cambridge, Mass.: Harvard University Press, 1990); Pierre Bourdieu, "The Forms of Capital," in John G. Richardson, ed., Handbook of Theory and Research for the Sociology of Education, Ed. JG. Richardson, New York: Green, 1983.

[11] Robert Putnam, *Making Democracy Work*, (Princeton: Princeton University Press, 1993).

[12] Thomas J. Oord, *The Science of Love* (Philadelphia: Templeton Foundation Press, 2004), 9; 43; 42.

[13] *Making Democracy Work*, 163.

[14] Robert Putnam, *Bowling Alone* (New York: Touchstone, 2000), 293.

[15] *Bowling Alone*, 294.

[16] *Bowling Alone*, 95.

[17] Peter D. Kramer, *Against Depression* (New York: Penguin, 2006).

[18] *Bowling Alone*, 261-265.

[19] *Social Intelligence*, 164.

[20] *Social Intelligence*, 173.

[21] What follows is a summary of Joyce E. Bellous, *Educating Faith*, Clements 2006, 19-37.

[22] Eugene Gendlin, *Experiencing and the Creation of Meaning* (New York: The Free Press of Glencoe, 1962), 1.

[23] *Experiencing*, 3.

[24] *Experiencing*, 11.

[25] *Experiencing*, 14.

[26] *Experiencing*, 15.

[27] *Experiencing*, 39.

[28] *Experiencing*, 53.

[29] *Experiencing*, 138.

[30] *Experiencing*, 167.

[31] *Our Need for Others*, 76.

[32] *Our Need for Others*, 77.

[33] *Educating Faith.*

[34] *Our Need for Others*, 64.

[35] *Our Need for Others,* 130.

[36] *Our Need for Others*, 131.

[37] *Our Need for Others*, 65.

[38] *Our need for others*, 65

[39] *Our need for others*, 86.

[40] *Our need for others*, 87.

[41] Daniel N. Stern, *The Interpersonal World of Infants* (New York: Basic Books, 1985).

[42] Pierre Bourdieu, *Outline of a Theory of Practice* (Cambridge: Cambridge University Press, 1977), 10-15.

[43] Pierre Bourdieu, *In Other Words: Essays towards a reflexive sociology* Matthew Adamson trans., (Cambridge, England: Polity Press, 1990), 22.

[44] J.L. Austin, *How to Do Things with Words* Cambridge, Massachusetts: Harvard University Press, 1962.

[45] Pierre Bourdieu, *Language and Symbolic Power* J. Thompson (Ed.) G. Raymond and M. Adamson (Trans.) Harvard University Press, 1993), 8.

[46] *Frames of Mind*, xvi-xvii.

[47] Thinking and feeling are inter-related in cognition. See Renate Nummela Caine and Geoffrey Caine, *Making Connections: Teaching and the Human Brain* (New York; Addison-Wesley, 1991), 90.

[48] See the discussion of bracketing in Irena R. Makaryk, (ed) *Encyclopedia of Contemporary Literary Terms: Approaches, Scholars, Terms* (Toronto: Toronto University Press, 1995), 511-514.

[49] *Language and Symbolic Power,*17.

[50] Craig Calhoun, Edward Li Puma and Moishe Postone, (eds) *Bourdieu, Critical Perspectives* (Great Britain: Polity Press, 1993), 3.

[51] *Our need for others*, 6.

[52] I want to distinguish empathy from sympathy and support. In sympathy, I am able to feel what D feels. In support, I am able to agree with and encourage D in the direction D is moving. In empathy, I am able to articulate D's position in a way that D would agree accurately portrays its meaning, but I may neither sympathize with nor support what D is doing.

CHAPTER 4

[1] Richard Sennett, *Respect in a World of Inequality* (New York: W.W. Norton & Company, 2003), 58.

[2] *Respect*, 59.

[3] *Social Intelligence*, 4-5.

[4] *Social Intelligence*, 6.

[5] *Social Intelligence*, 6.

[6] I don't intend to cast aspersions on the word context in general. I define it as I do in this chapter to set it apart clearly from the process of becoming community that I want to emphasize.

[7] *The Selfish Meme*, 2.

[8] Karen Armstrong, *A Short History of Myth* (Edinburgh: Canongate, 2005), 90.

[9] Jan Sokol, "An Address from Elsewhere: "The message of Levinas in the Czech dissident milieu," Caroline Bayard & Joyce E. Bellous, (Eds.), in *Philosophy Today* Vol.43, No.2/4, (Summer), 1999:143-150.

[10] *Social Intelligence*, 223-237.

[11] *Social Intelligence*, 230.

[12] This analysis is based on Mary Douglas's *Natural Symbols*. Her work is

based on Basil Bernstein's research from the 1970s in which he analyzed the speech codes among boys in the London school system.

[13] Short History of Myth.

[14] The city is spelled Catal Huyuk in Jacobs's and Armstrong's work. Its ruins remain in Turkey. Çatalhöyük was a very large Neolithic and Chalcolithic proto-city settlement in southern Anatolia, which existed from approximately 7500 BC to 5700 BC and flourished around 7000 BC. It's the largest and best-preserved Neolithic site found to date. Wikipedia.

[15] *Collapse*, 6-7.

[16] Jane Jacobs, *The Nature of Economies* (New York: Vintage Books, 2000), 96

[17] Jane Jacobs, *Dark Age Ahead* (New York: Vintage, 2005).

[18] See the Guatemalan example in, Rigoberta Menchu, *I Rigoberta...*

[19] *Nature of Economies*, 126-131.

[20] *Nature of Economies*, 130.

[21] Joyce E. Bellous, *The Obligations of a Global Neighbour...*

[22] Zygmunt Bauman's *Liquid Love* (Cambridge, UK: Polity Press, 2003), 99.

[23] The word liquid is a reference to Bauman's *Liquid Love.*

[24] *Liquid Love*, xi.

[25] *Liquid Love*, 69.

[26] *Liquid Love*, 75.

[27] *Social Intelligence*, 311.

[28] David Berlinski, *The Devil's Delusion* (New York: Crown Forum, 2008), 10.

[29] *Pursuit of Attention*, p. xxiv.

[30] *Pursuit of Attention*, p. xxv.

[31] The 10 ways of speaking, acting and thinking outlined here are adapted from David Burns, *Feeling Good: The new mood therapy* (New York: Avon Books, 1992), 135.

[32] Pierre Bourdieu, quoted in *Respect*, 55.

CHAPTER 5

[1] G.A. Hillery, *Communal Organizations* Chicago: Chicago University Press, 1972.

[2] *Communal Organizations*, 9.

[3] *Communal Organizations*, 8.

[4] *Communal Organizations*, 147.

[5] *Educating Faith*, 309-344.

[6] *Educating Faith*, 329-365.

[7] *Educating Faith*, 334-336.

[8] Kwame Anthony Appiah, *Cosmopolitanism: Ethics in a world of strangers* (New York: W.W. Norton & Company, 2006), xv.

[9] Mary Gregor, Ed. Kant: *Metaphysics of Morals* (Cambridge: Cambridge University Press, 1996), 50.

[10] *Cosmopolitanism*, xiii.

[11] *Cosmopolitanism*, xvi.

[12] Charles Taylor, "The Logic of Recognition" in *Multiculturalism and the Logic of Recognition* Amy Gutman, ed., (Princeton, NJ: Princeton University Press, 1992), 25-75.

[13] See Michel Foucault, "Governmentality," in *Ideology and Consciousness*, Vol.6, 1979: 5-21.

[14] See Peter Drucker, The End of Economic Man. New York: John Daly, 1939.

[15] *The Logic of Recognition*, 35.

[16] Mary Douglas, *Natural Symbols* (New York: Pantheon Books, 1982).

[17] A short history of myth, and Peter Nguyen's thesis.

[18] J.A.K. Tomson, (Trans.). Aristotle: Ethics. Harmondsworth, Middlesex, England: Penguin Books, 1976.

[19] Peter Brown, *The Body and Society* (New York: Columbia University Press, 1988).

[20] M.A. Strauss. "A Sociological Perspective on the Causes of Family Violence," in M.R. Green, Ed., Violence and the Family. Boulder: Westview Press, 1980.

[21] Peter Tuyen Nguyen, *A Theological and Cultural Foundation for Veneration of Ancestors Among Vietnamese Catholics and Its Liturgical Implications*. Hamilton, Ontario: McMaster University, unpublished thesis, 2007.

[22] *The Logic of Recognition*, 47.

[23] *The Logic of Recognition*, 48.

[24] Pierre Bourdieu, *Acts of Resistance* (New York: The New Press, 1998), 8-9.

[25] Will Kymlicka, *Liberalism, Community, Culture* (1989), 9-20.

[26] There are various ways that autonomy was constructed during modernity. A key question to ask has to do with where the rules come from and whether one is able to concoct one's own.

[27] Joyce E. Bellous, "A Postmodern Critique of Educative Church Experience as Voluntary," in *A Believers Church: A Voluntary Church* William H. Brackney, Ed., (Kitchener: Pandora Press, 1998), 149-177.

[28] "A Postmodern Critique."

[29] See Vera Brittain, *A Testament of Youth* (New York: Macmillan, 1933).

[30] See Colin Morris, *The Discovery of the Individual*:1050-1200 (New York: Harper and Row, 1972).

[31] Rousseau perpetuated a dependent role for individual women by establishing economic dependence between Emile and Sophy in this novel, Emile, and by maintaining this dependence as essential to the romantic ideal he envisioned for their marriage. While they were romantic partners, Sophy's economic dependence created a safety margin for him; she had to remain with him, even if he was difficult to live with, or abusive. Rousseau saw dependence as essential to the household's viability. In his view, women should have a domestic identity as wives and mothers; men should have a public identity as citizens of the state. Wollstonecraft encouraged the public life of women, while retaining a powerful emphasis on the roles of wife and mother. Wollstonecraft was less influential than Rousseau, and individualism came to describe male experience in a way that it didn't for women. In Canada, women became persons (and able to run for political office) in 1929, through the efforts of The Famous Five.

[32] John Rawls, *A Theory of Justice* (Cambridge, Mass: Harvard University Press, 1971), 3-4.

[33] *A Theory of Justice*, 136-142.

[34] See Frantz Fanon, *The Wretched of the Earth* (New York: Grover Press, Inc., 1968).

[35] See I Rigoberto Menchu.

[36] *Our Need for others*, xv.

[37] Robert Kegan, *The Evolving Self* (Cambridge Mass: Harvard University Press, 1982), 28-45; 222.

[38] *The Evolving Self*, 19.

[39] Robert Kegan, *In Over Our Heads* (Cambridge, Mass: Harvard University Press, 1997), 267.

[40] *Over Our Heads*, 266.

[41] *Over Our Heads*, 278.

[42] *Over Our Heads*, 270.

[43] As part of our investigation, we may abandon the formal aspects of our own family religion. We may stop being Christian, Jewish or Muslim, as our family was and may still be. Kegan's point is that, *contra* Freud, growing up doesn't require us to walk away—but does require us to have a good look at what we were when we were young.

[44] *Over Our Heads*, 266-270.

[45] *The Evolving Self*, 7.

[46] *The Evolving Self*, 7.

[47] *The Evolving Self*, 11.

[48] *The Evolving Self*, 12.

[49] Corinne Ware, *Learning While Leading* (USA: Alban Institute, 2000), 19.

[50] *Learning While Leading*, 13.

CHAPTER 6

[1] The Canadian Broadcasting Company.

[2] Margaret Atwood, *Payback: Debt and the shadow side of wealth* (Toronto: Anansi Press, 2008), 16-17.

[3] *Payback*, 17.

[4] *Payback*, 20.

[5] *Payback*, 21.

[6] Pierre Bourdieu, *In other Words: Essays towards a reflexive sociology* Translated by Matthew Adamson (Cambridge, England: Polity Press, 1990), 23.

[7] *Social Intelligence*, 54.

[9] Alan Fogel, *Developing Through Relationships: Origins of Communication, Self and Culture* (Chicago: University of Chicago Press, 1993), 48.

[10] Eric Hobsbawm, *On the Edge of the New Century* (New York: The New Press, 2000), 31-40.

[11] *Developing Through Relationships*, 29-36.

[12] *Social Intelligence*, 228.

[13] *Social Intelligence*, 228.

[14] *Dictionary of Philosophical Terms*, 325.

[15] *Dictionary of Philosophical Terms*, 325.

[17] In the literature that supports social literacy, psychologists that investigate social interaction present this argument that they have to face when they present their data and theories to psychologists who operate from an individualistic methodology.

[18] In order not to fall into the trap of false gender neutrality, I use the gender exclusive term to accurately reflect the privilege afforded men during modernity that continues in those individuals who maintain a modern frame of mind.

[19] See for example, J. M. Schwartz and S. Begley, *The Mind and the Brain* (New York: Regan Books, 2002).

[20] Immanuel Kant, "An answer to the question: What is Enlightenment?" in *Kant: Political Writings* ed. Hans Reiss, (Cambridge: Cambridge University Press, 1991), 54-60.

[21] Michel Foucault, "What is Enlightenment? In *The Foucault Reader,* Paul Rabinow (Ed.). (New York: Pantheon Books, 1984), 32-50.

[22] *What is Enlightenment*, 33.

[23] *What is Enlightenment*, 50.

[25] *Metaphysics of Morals*, 182.

[26] [A short History of Progress, Wright, 72]

[27] Sigmund Freud, *Totem and Taboo* (New York: Vintage, 1946. First published in 1918.

[28] Michel Foucault, *Discipline and Punish* (New York: Vintage, 1979).

[29] Joyce E. Bellous, "Children, Sex and Sacredness," in *International Journal of Children's Spirituality*, Vol. 7, No. 1, 2002, 73-91.

[30] Steven Watts, *The People's Tycoon: Henry Ford and the American century.* (New York: Vintage Books, 2006), especially pp. 200-224.

[31] Anthony M Coniaris, *Philokalia: the Bible of Orthodox Spirituality* (Minneapolis, MN: Light and Life Publishing Company, 1998), 34-35.

[32] The People's Tycoon, 152ff.

[33] Discipline and Punish, 85.

[34] While Ford clearly aimed to improve working conditions, his drive for productivity on the assembly line eventually required that workers need not think for themselves. In addition, the space his power created allowed others to use violence, threat and aggression to sustain the remarkable productivity of his Ford plants. See *The People's Tycoon*, 200-224.

[35] Margaret Atwood, *Cat's Eye*. See, for example, pages 55, 57, 65 and 67—but the entire novel provides a context for these pages.

CHAPTER 7

[1] *Theology of Anticipation*, 3-14.

[2] Not her real name, this scenario combines the real life experiences of several people that experienced social learning as a way to improve how they interact with others.

[3] *The Selfish Meme*, 2.

[4] Richard Dawkins, *The Selfish Gene* (Oxford: Oxford University Press, 1976).

[5] *Selfish Gene*, 36.

[6] *Selfish Meme*, 8.

[7] See for example, Robert Putnam, *Bowling Alone* (New York: Touchstone, 2000).

[8] Jane Jacobs, *The Nature of Economies* (Toronto: Vintage Canada, 2000), 121-125.

[9] *Social Intelligence*, 333.

[10] See Hebrews 11:3, particularly in the NIV (2011). Also see the *Selfish Meme*, 116.

[11] *Selfish Meme*, 2.

[12] *Selfish Meme*, 2.

[13] *Selfish Meme*, 5.

[14] *Selfish Meme*, 14.

[15] *Selfish Meme*, 8.

[16] *Selfish Meme*, 10.

[17] *Selfish Meme*, 20.

[18] *Selfish Meme*, 148.

[19] *Selfish Meme*, 22.

[20] *Selfish Meme*, 42.

[21] *Selfish Meme*, 59-60.

[22] She notes that the similarity between genes and memes is not at all exact, particularly at this point.

[23] *Selfish Meme*, 61.

[24] *Selfish Meme*, 60.

[25] *Selfish Meme*, 93.

[26] *Selfish Meme*, 123.

[27] *Selfish Meme*, 126.

[28] *Selfish Meme*, 137.

[29] *Selfish Meme*, 115.

[30] *Selfish Meme*, 149.

[31] *Selfish Meme*, 150.

[32] *Selfish Meme*, 154.

[33] For example, the *Scientific American* magazine May 2009 contains two references to the emergence of farming, one on page 56 and one on page 48. The two dates show up in the issue without comparative comment.

[34] *Selfish Gene*, x-xiii.

[35] Stephen Shennan, *Genes, Memes and Human History* (London: Thames & Hudson, 2002), 38.

[36] Robert Putnam, *Making Democracy Work*, (Princeton: Princeton University Press, 1993), 124.

[37] *Making Democracy Work*, 142.

[38] Robert Putnam, *Bowling Alone* (New York: A Touchstone Book, 2000), 19.

[39] Mary Gregor, (Ed.), *Kant: The Metaphysics of Morals* (Cambridge: Cambridge University Press, 1996), 202.

[40] Metaphysics of Morals, 223.

[41] Sigmund Freud, *Civilization and its Discontents*, London: The Hogarth Press, 1969), 46.

[42] *Civilization and its Discontents, 46.*

[43] *Civilization and its Discontents, 51.*

[44] *Civilization and its Discontents, 47.*

[45] Pronounced 'chick sent *me* high'.

[46] Quoted in D.E. Beck and C.C. Cowan's *Spiral Dynamics: Mastering values, leadership and change*, Oxford: Blackwell Publishing, 2006), 30.

[47] *Spiral Dynamics*, 6.

[48] *Spiral Dynamics*, 71-103.

[49] For a thorough analysis of the tact as I am thinking of it here, see Hans-Georg Gadamer, *Truth and Method* (New York: Crossroads, 1991).

[50] *Spiral Dynamics*, 79.

[51] While Beck and Cowan are remarkably insightful as one tries to understand change, there seems to be a somewhat deterministic tone in the language they use to described closed individuals. I suggest one alternative to remaining closed is available through Action Science, which refers to designed blindness rather than psychological blindness.

[52] The summary of the term culture and the components of culture outlined

here are taken from the nearly exhaustive analysis of the concept found in A.L. Kroeber and Clyde Kluckhorn, et al., *Culture: A Critical Review of Concepts and Definitions.* Papers of the Peabody Museum of American Archaeology and Ethnology, Harvard University, Vol. XLVII—No.1, 1952: 145-158.

[53] *Culture: A Critical Review, 147.*

[54] *Culture: A Critical Review, 145.*

[55] *Women and Human Development,* 111-119.

[56] Clifford Geertz, *Interpretation of Cultures* (New York: Basic Books, 1973).

[57] *Interpretation of Cultures*, 49.

[58] *Culture: A Critical Review.*

[59] *Culture: A Critical Review*, 182.

[60] Allen Wood and George di Giovanni, eds., *Kant: Religion Within the Boundaries of Mere Reason* (Cambridge: Cambridge University Press, 1998), 3-14.

[61] Reinhold Niebuhr, *The Irony of American History* (1952) quoted in Harold Innis, *Changing Concepts of Time* in the Introduction, James W. Carey (Oxford: Rowman & Littlefield Publishers, Inc. 2004), vii.

[62] *Science of Love*, 43.

CHAPTER 8

[1] Robert Rosenthal, et al. The PONS test manual: profile of non-verbal sensitivity (New York: Irving, 1979).

[2] Marshall B. Rosenberg, *Non-violent Communication* (Encinitas, CA: Puddledancer Press, 2000).

[3] *Non-violent Communication,* 144.

[4] *Oxford English Dictionary.*

[5] *Canadian Oxford Dictionary.*

[6] Nel Noddings, *Caring: A Feminine Approach to Ethics and Moral Education* (Berkeley, California: University of California Press, 1984), 30-32.

[7] David Burns, *Feeling Good: The new mood therapy* (New York: Avon Books, 1992), 135.

[8] Edith Stein, *On the Problem of Empathy* Waltraut Stein (Trans.), (The Netherlands: Martinus Nijhoff, The Hague, 1964).

[9] *Feeling Good*, 135-137.

[10] Woodruff Smith, *The Circle of Acquaintance: Perception, Consciousness and Empathy* (Boston: Kluwer Academic Publishers, 1989), 155.

[11] Daniel N. Stern, *The Interpersonal World of Infants* (New York: Basic Books, 1985).

[12] *Interpersonal World*, 36.

[13] *Interpersonal World*, 174-182.

[14] *Interpersonal World*, 174.

[15] *Interpersonal World*, 177.

[16] Johannes A. van der Ven, *Formation of the Moral Self* (Grand Rapids, Michigan: Eerdmans, 1998), 313-315.

[17] David Wood, *How Children think and Learn* Second Edition (Oxford: Blackwell, 1998), 26.

[18] *How Children Think*, 27.

[19] Joyce E. Bellous. "Spiritual and Ethical Orality in Children, Educating an Oral Self," in the *International Journal of Children's Spirituality* Vol. 5, No. 1, 2000, 9-26.

[20] *How Children Think*, 27.

[21] *How Children Think*, 28.

[22] *How Children Think*, 28 (italics mine).

[23] *How Children Think*, 29.

[24] *How Children Think*, 29.

[25] *How Children Think*, 29-30.

[26] *How Children Think*, 30.

[27] *How Children Think*, 31.

[28] *Non-Violent Communication*, 119.

[29] *Problem of Empathy*, 14.

[30] Edith Stein refers to the first and third aspects of experience as primordial and non-primordial. Direct or primordial experience refers to experience in which the object of perception is present before me here and now.

[31] Margaret Atwood, *Payback* (Anansi, 2008), 1-40.

[32] *Feeling Good*, 137ff.

CHAPTER 9

[1] Urie Bronfenbrenner, "Ecology of the family as a context for human development: Research perspectives". *Developmental Psychology*, Vol. 22, Issue 6, 1986, 12-1649.

[2] Clyde Hertzman, "The economic costs of early vulnerability in Canada",

Canadian Journal of Public Health, 2010.

[3] James Heckman and Alan Krueger, *Inequality in America: What Role for Human Capital Policies?* Alvin Hansen Symposium Series on Public Policy, (MIT Press, 2004).

[4] https://www.whitehouse.gov/blog/2014/12/10/invest-us-president-obama-convenes-white-house-summit-early-education.

[5] Clyde Hertzman, "From Kindergarten readiness to fourth-grade assessment: Longitudinal analysis with linked population data", *Social Science and Medicine*, Volume 68, Issue 1, January 2009, 111-123.

[6] http://www.cdc.gov/violenceprevention/acestudy/index.html

[7] Mary Sheedy Kurchinka. *Raising Your Spirited Child: A Guide for Parents Whose Child is More Intense, Sensitive, Perceptive, Persistent, and Energetic*, (William Morrow, 2006).

[8] Tom Porter. *And Grandma Said... Iroquois Teachings*, (Self published: Xlibris, 2008).

[9] The **United Nations Children's Fund** (**UNICEF**) is a United Nations Program headquartered in New York City that provides long-term humanitarian and developmental assistance to children and mothers in developing countries. It is one of the members of the United Nations Development Group and its Executive Committee. UNICEF was created by the United Nations General Assembly on December 11, 1946, to provide emergency food and healthcare to children in countries that had been devastated by World War II. In 1953, UNICEF became a permanent part of the United Nations System and its name was shortened from the original **United Nations International Children's Emergency Fund** but it has continued to be known by the popular acronym based on this previous title.

[10] In keeping with UNICEF's mandate to advocate for children in every country, the Centre's Report Card series focuses on the well-being of children in industrialized countries. Each Report Card includes a league table ranking the countries of the OECD according to their record on the subject under discussion. The Report Cards are designed to appeal to a wide audience while maintaining academic rigour.

[11] http://www.minnpost.com/driving-change/2012/04/making-case-early-ed-art-rolnick-has-had-enormous-impact

[12] *OECD Economic Surveys: Korea 2014*, (OECD, June 2014).

[13] **OECD** is an international economic organization made up of 34 countries founded in 1961 to stimulate economic progress and world trade. It is a forum of countries committed to democracy and the market economy, providing a platform

to compare policy experiences, seek answers to common problems, identify good practices and coordinate domestic and international policies of its members.

[14] **OECD**

[15] www.prevnet.ca.

[16] http://ontariochildhealthstudy.ca/ochs/about/1983-ochs/.

[17] See for example, Michael Unger's work on strengths based counseling.

[18] Andrew N. Meltzoff and N. Keith Moore, "Imitation of Manual and Facial Gestures by Human Neonates", *Science*, New Series, Volume 198, October 7, 1977, 75-78.

[19] Betty Hart and Todd Risley, *Meaningful Differences in the Everyday life of American Children* (Baltimore, MD: Brookes Publishing, 1995).

[20] Felix Warneken and Michael Tomaselo, "Altruistic Helping in Human Infants and Young Chimpanzees", *Science*, Vol 311, no 5765, March 2006, 1301-1303.

[21] http://www.thedoctorsvideos.com/video/5740/Still-Face-Experiment-Dr-Edward-Tronick

[22] Robert Sapolsky, *Why Zebras Don't Get Ulcers, Third Edition*. (Holt Paperbacks, 2004).

[23] Sonia Lupien, "Effects of stress throughout the lifespan on the brain, behaviour and cognition", *National Review of Neuroscience*, Volume: 10, Issue: 6, 2009, 434-445.

[24] http://dalailamacenter.org/programs/speakers-series/mary-gordon

[25] Mary Gordon, *Roots of Empathy: Changing the World Child by Child* (Toronto: Thomas Allen, 2005).

CHAPTER 10

[1] Zygmunt Bauman, *Liquid Love*, 99.

[2] Peter M. Senge, *The Fifth Discipline: The art & practice of the learning organization.* (New York: Doubleday, 1990), 68-92.

[3] Jane Jacobs, *Economy of Cities*, (New York: Vintage, 1969), 32-36.

[4] *Short Hisory of Progress*, 16.

[5] *Short History of Progress*, 27.

[6] *City in History*, 24.

[7] *City in History*, 99.

[8] In this chapter, the idea of development is complex. It's presented positively in the second city model but it's also presented negatively earlier in

the chapter to capture some of its impact on the last 200 years of civic history.

[9] Marshall Berman, *All That is Solid Melts into Air* (London: Penguin Books, 1988), 7.

[10] Augustine of Hippo, *Selected Writings: The Classics of Western Spirituality* (Mahweh, NJ: Paulist Press, 1984), 433-478.

[11] *All that is solid*, 40.

[12] Karen Armstrong, *A Short History of Myth* (New York: Canongate 2005), 46.

[13] *Short History of Myth*, 79-80.

[14] *Short History of Myth*, 105.

[15] Jane Jacobs, *The Death and Life of Great American Cities* New York: Vintage Books, 1961), 59ff.

[16] *Death and Life*, 241.

[17] Jared Diamond, *Guns, Germs, and Steel* (London: W.W. Norton & Company, 1999), 267-268.

[18] *Short History of Progress*, 72.

[19] *Guns, Germs and Steel*, 276.

[20] *Guns, Germs and Steel*, 276.

[21] Anthony Giddens and Patrick Diamond, *The New Egalitarianism* (Cambridge: Polity, 2005), 42.

[22] *All That is Solid*, 28.

[23] *All that is Solid*, 29.

[24] *Social Intelligence*, 227.

[25] Barbara Ehrenreich, *Nickel and Dimed* (New York: A Metropolitan/Owl Book, 2001).

[26] *Social Intelligence*, 223-237.

[27] *Nickel and Dimed*, 210.

[28] Stephen Lewis, *Race Against Time* (Toronto: Anansi, 2005), 79.

[29] Sylvie Courtine-Denamy, *Three Women in Dark Times: Edith Stein, Hannah Arendt, Simone Weil* translated by G.M. Goshgarian (Ithaca: Cornell University Press, 2000), 85.

[30] Jane Jacobs, *Systems of Survival* (New York: Vintage Books, 1992), 35.

[31] Karl Marx, *The Communist Manifesto* (New York: Washington Square Press, 1964). First published in 1848.

[32] *New Egalitarianism*, 44.

[33] Hirschman, Albert O. *Exit, Voice and Loyalty.* Cambridge, Massachusetts:

Harvard University Press, 1970.

[34] For a full explanation of the extreme poverty of the kind I observed in Liberia, see Jeffrey D. Sachs, *The End of Poverty* (London: Penguin, 2006), 19-20.

[35] Martha Nussbaum, *Women and Human Development* (Cambridge: Cambridge University Press, 2000); Martha Nussbaum, *Sex and Social Justice* (Oxford: Oxford University Press, 1999).

[36] *New Egalitarianism*, 109.

[37] *New Egalitarianism*, 45.

[38] *New Egalitarianism*, 109.

[39] *New Egalitarianism*, 44.

[40] Pierre Bourdieu "The Forms of Capital," in J.G. Richardson, (ed.) *Handbook of Theory and Research for the Sociology of Education* (New York: Green, 1983), 242-243.

[41] "Forms of Capital," 242.

[42] *Women and Human Development*, 112-113.

[43] These assertions about reproductive health are taken from the 1994 International Conference on Population and Development. See Amy O. Tsui, Judith N. Wasserheit, and John G. Haaga, eds., Reproductive Health in Developing Countries (Washington,D.C.: National Academy Press, 1997), 13-14. This approach to reproductive health, like all the needs that Nussbaum outlines, is intended to undergird government policy and practice. That is, governments could be held accountable to eradicate practices that violate reproductive freedom. For example, when I was in Bolivia in 1998, we visited an agency that worked with children born to women prisoners. These children were born due to drunkenness and rape. In that country, men and women are held in separate prisons. But these women got pregnant when male prisoners were shipped in bus loads and allowed into the women's prison during Mardi Gras celebrations once a year. The men would be provided with alcohol and access to them and there was no way for the women to protect themselves. Since Bolivian prisons house but do not feed prisoners, the women not only suffered from rape and exposure to harm but they had to feed more mouths than they brought to prison with them.

[44] *Women and Human Development*, 78-80.

[45] *Women and Human Development*, 43.

[46] Marshall Berman, *All that is solid melts into air: the experience of modernity* (London: Penguin Books, 1988).

[47] *All that is solid*, 26.

[48] *All that is solid*, 10.

[49] *All that is solid*, 11.

[50] *All that is solid*, 40.

[51] *All that is solid*, 50.

[52] *All that is solid*, 62.

[53] *All that is solid*, 65.

[54] *All that is solid*, 67.

[55] *Women and Human Development*, 40.

[56] *Women and Human Development*, 81.

[57] *Women and Human Development*, 81.

[58] *Economy of Cities*, 87.

[59] *Three Women*, 67.

[60] See Pierre Bourdieu's analysis of the importance of reproductive labour for every other form of capital accumulation in "Forms of Capital."

[61] Inge Scholl, *The White Rose* Arthur R Schultz trans. (Middletown, Connecticut: Wesleyan University Press, 1983).

[62] Harriet Beecher Stowe, *Uncle Tom's Cabin* (Boston: John P. Jewett & Company), 1852.

[63] Robert Putnam, *Bowling Alone*, 293-294.

[64] *Economy of Cities*, 89.

[65] Bernstein describes efficiency from a different perspective than I'm following in Jacobs. I don't say efficiency is inherently evil. I'm not opposed to what Bernstein's asserts about it necessarily. Rather, when a city (institution) is totalized by efficiency, human life is reduced to a zero value. For his view of efficiency, see W.J. Bernstein, *The Birth of Plenty* (New York: McGraw-Hill, 2004), 41- 44.

[66] If the number of workers decreases and the need for their labour is constant or increasing, their value goes up.

[67] An efficiency and collapse pattern can be found in medieval cities and even earlier, as far back as 2500 years. See Jacobs 1969, 92-93. For an expansive treatment of the social collapse in addition to Jacobs's work, see Jared Diamond *Guns, Germs, and Steel* (London: W.W. Norton & Company, 1999); and Jared Diamond, *Collapse* (New York: Penguin, 2006).

[68] *The Economy of Cities*, 89.

[69] Jane Jacobs, The *Death and Life of Great American Cities*, (New York: Vintage, 1992), 249. First published, 1961.

[70] *All that is solid*, 96.

[71] *The Economy of Cities*, 86-94.

[72] *The Economy of Cities*, 60.

[73] *The Economy of Cities*, 68-70.

[74] *The Economy of Cities*, 59, 63.

[75] David Harvey, *Spaces of Hope* (Berkeley, California: University of California Press, 2000), 54.

[76] *Spaces of Hope*, 50.

[77] *Spaces of Hope*, 72.

[78] *Spaces of Hope*, 71.

[79] *Spaces of Hope*, 28.

[80] *Spaces of Hope*, 31.

[81] *Forms of Capital.*

[82] *The Economy of Cities*, 107-117.

[83] *Nature of Economies*, 130.

[84] *Nature of Economies*, 130.

[85] Jill Dann and Derek Dann, *The Emotional Intelligence Workbook*, (London: Hodder, 2012), 149.

[86] *Nature of Economies*, 121.

[87] *Dark Age Ahead.*

[88] *Collapse*, 6-7.

[89] *Collapse*, 11.

[90] *Nature of Economies*, 126-131.

[91] *Fifth Discipline*, e.g., 68-92.

[92] *Death and Life*, 428-448.

[93] *Death and Life*, 440.

[94] Jane Jacobs, *Cities and the Wealth of Nations* (New York: Vintage Books, 1984), 208.

[95] *Nature of Economies*, 96.

[96] *Nature of Economies*, 99.

[97] *Nature of Economies*, 108.

[98] *Nature of Economies*, 109.

[99] *Nature of Economies*, 84-118.

[100] Jane Jacobs, *Dark Age Ahead* (New York: Vintage, 2005), 21.

[101] The discovery of the complete genome, the set of human genes

packaged in twenty-three separate pairs of chromosomes, was publicized in 2000. The human genome is the set of instructions for how to build and run a human body and tells us something about the history of our ancestors since the dawn of time. See Matt Ridley, *Genome* (New York: Perennial, 2000), 2.

INDEX

A

B

O

P

R

T

U

V

W

CPSIA information can be obtained
at www.ICGtesting.com
Printed in the USA
LVOW10s0345091216
516531LV00001B/1/P

9 780981 014937